HEINRICH HIMMLER

HEINRICH HIMMLER

A PHOTO HISTORY OF THE REICHSFÜHRER-SS

MAX WILLIAMS

FONTHILL

Fonthill Media Limited
Fonthill Media LLC
www.fonthill.media
office@fonthillmedia.com

First published in the United Kingdom and the United States of America 2014.
Reprinted 2016 and 2020.

British Library Cataloguing in Publication Data:
A catalogue record for this book is available from the British Library

ISBN 978-1-78155-405-0

Typeset in Sabon 10.5/14
Printed and bound in England

Contents

Acknowledgements

I extend sincere thanks to all who contributed to the finished work and in particular:

Stephen Tyas, a fastidious researcher and author, for his help and advice throughout this project. Without his assistance, the finished article would not and could not have been completed.

Michael D. Miller, friend and author. Always helpful and willing to share information, Mike is a valued friend in the world of SS biographical research. An author in his own right, his books are fast becoming a mainstay in the study of the men who made the Third Reich tick.

The same applies to Andreas Schulz and Dieter Zinke who have produced a series of biographies in the German language on SS and Police Generals second to none.

Michal Sika, an avid collector of images, who provided numerous opportunities for your author to obtain important photographs.

Tony Rojas, for providing several important images. His valuable contribution cannot be underestimated.

Katrin Himmler, great niece of Heinrich Himmler and author of the acclaimed book 'The Himmler Brothers,' for her willingness to help where she could.

The late Stuart Russell, a good friend and expert on Wewelsburg, his death has left a gaping hole in the research of Heinrich Himmler and his SS organisation.

The late James Townsend, another friend who provided valuable assistance before his untimely death.

Joe Wotka, Jim Toncar, Martin Bogaert, Tilman Taube, Kurt Gamer, Peter Etherington, Andrey Bespalov, Andreas Seeger, Ole Korsemann, Tom Pooler+.

Several contributors who provided valuable assistance, but preferred to remain anonymous and to anyone who contributed, but whose name has been omitted. Thank you.

Preface

Adolf Hitler, idolised by millions and none more so than Heinrich Himmler, was just twenty-nine years of age when 'the war to end all wars' finally finished and catapulted him into the volatile post-war arena of politics. The road to Hitler's political evolution and his formation of the Nationalsozialistische Deutsche Arbeiterpartei (NSDAP) is well trodden in historical studies and the extremist nature of his policies does not require further expansion. Suffice to say that whenever he expressed his views in open forum, they inspired vigorous debate, sometimes degenerating into violent reaction. It soon became clear to Hitler that if he wished to continue to spread the NSDAP gospel in public, he would need protection. In addition, differences between some cliques within the Party encouraged internal squabbling and promoted vigorous opposition to some of Hitler's views. Hitler's close associate and sometimes chauffeur, Julius Schreck, doubled as his bodyguard and in March 1923, he formed a dedicated protection squad from the ranks of the 'old fighters.' This became known as the Stabswache and its brief was to provide physical protection for Hitler at public and Party meetings.

In May 1923, the Stabswache changed its name to the Stosstrupp Hitler and it was placed under the command of Josef Berchtold, a man whose talents were more akin to the needs of such a unit. Berchtold and his men participated in the failed Munich Beer Hall Putsch of November 1923, playing a major role in the abortive assault on the police headquarters in Ettstrasse. Members of the Stosstrupp took part in the march on the Reichswehr Ministry and were also present at the Bürgerbräukeller. They were also in attendance when the marchers were fired upon at the Feldherrnhalle. Berchtold escaped unhurt across the border to Austria and with the Party in disarray and its leader subsequently imprisoned, the Stosstrupp Hitler could no longer operate effectively.

During his incarceration in the fortress at Landsberg, Hitler ordered Ernst Röhm to take charge of the Sturmabteilung (SA.) With Hitler's release from custody in December 1924, the Party was re-formed and Hitler, now active again, once more required protection. Hitler directed Julius Schreck to form a bodyguard detachment in April 1925 and Schreck christened the new formation, consisting of eight men, Schutzstaffel (SS.) Nearly all were original members of the Stosstrupp Hitler who met regularly at the Torbräu beer hall in Munich. They wore the Party brown shirt, but with a black tie to distinguish them from the SA. Later their uniform also consisted of black 'coffee can' hats and black trousers.

By December 1925, the SS numbered approximately two hundred genuine members. In April 1926, Berchtold returned from exile and took command of the infant, but expanding, SS. In addition to its role as protector, the SS was also tasked with distribution of advertising leaflets for the Party newspaper, the *Völkischer Beobachter*. At the second Party convention in Weimar on 4 July 1926, Hitler referred to the SS as his elite force and entrusted it with the care of the sacred Blood Flag.

On 27 July 1926, Hitler appointed Captain Pfeffer von Salomon as Reich SA Leader and on 1 November 1926, Hitler ordered that von Salomon be known by the title Supreme SA Leader. At the same time von Salomon was given superiority over the SS, with Berchtold being authorized to use the title Reichsführer-SS.

Berchtold felt his position under threat and fears that the SS would be swallowed up by the much larger SA were intensified by his differences with some senior officials within the NSDAP. In March 1927, Berchtold resigned and was replaced as Reichsführer-SS by his deputy, Erhard Heiden.

Heiden managed the SS with strict rules, even impressing opponents, but his tenure as Reichsführer-SS was not without problems. The internal struggle with his superior, von Salomon, did not dissipate with the exit of Berchtold. Hitler had referred to the SS as an elite organization and SS men regarded themselves as a cut above the rest, especially the undisciplined SA. It irritated the SS cadre to acknowledge that it was subordinate to the SA and its cause was not helped by a scandal involving the Reichsführer-SS himself.

SS member Franz Rottenberger ran a firm which supplied clothing to the SS and in which Heiden also had some control. Another firm, in Kaiserstrasse, Munich, supplied Rottenberger and Heiden with the black trousers which formed an integral part of the SS uniform. At the end of 1928, it transpired that this firm was owned by a Jew. Rottenberger and Heiden were alleged to have made large profits from the purchase and subsequent sales to the SS. Heiden heard rumours of the scandal breaking and approached Hitler on 1 December 1928 with his intention to resign as Reichsführer-SS. This materialised on 6 January 1929 with his written resignation. The scandal broke on 16 January 1929 with a newspaper article headlined 'Jews as Hitler Suppliers!' Heiden was subsequently suspended from SS duties, culminating in his resignation from the SS on 22 January 1929. Rottenberger also resigned from the SS, declaring complete innocence. The ensuing hearings within the Party lasted for many months.

Hitler announced on 20 January that he had appointed Heiden's deputy as Reichsführer-SS with effect from 6 January 1929. The new Reichsführer-SS had extremely defined ideas about the SS. 'The SA is the infantry of the line, the SS the Guards. There has always been a guard; the Persians had one, the Greeks, Caesar and Napoleon, Frederick the Great, right up to the world war. The SS will be the imperial guard of the new Germany.' So spoke the man who was determined to fulfil Hitler's description of an elite organization and who would guide the SS through the next sixteen years; that man was Heinrich Himmler.

Introduction

Of all the personalities of history demonized by post-war writers, Heinrich Himmler ranks among the most reviled. His legacy is one of hatred, violence and cold blooded murder on a vast scale. A Jekyll and Hyde character, variously described by his contemporaries and those who followed as charming, loyal, polite, a pedant, an eccentric, an organizational genius, a fool, a desk killer and a loving father. Himmler was certainly all of those to varying degrees and his complex persona has provided numerous writers and historians with an abundance of material. Himmler biographers have cogitated over the available references and have delivered countless interpretations of his core character, but it is not the intention of this study to join their numbers.

In the early pre-war days there is little doubt that Himmler was highly respected by his SS men and the German populace who knew him from newsreels and newspapers. As the war progressed, even his faithful SS subordinates grew to distrust his judgment. This is borne out by a conversation between two men who knew him well, secretly recorded without their knowledge in an interrogation centre of the 15 Army Group on 22 May 1945. At the time, they were totally unaware that Himmler was already in Allied hands and was about to take his own life.

SS-Obergruppenführer Karl Wolff had been Himmler's close associate from the early 1930s as first his adjutant and then chief of his personal staff. He had accompanied Himmler everywhere on duty and was also included in Himmler's social circle. The Reichsführer had selected Wolff to be his eyes and ears at Hitler's headquarters as his liaison officer when war broke out and had subsequently appointed him as the highest SS authority in northern Italy when the soft underbelly of the Reich became vulnerable following the capitulation of Italy in 1943. SS-Standartenführer Eugen Dollmann was fluent in Italian and had served as both Himmler's and Hitler's official interpreter with Mussolini and his foreign minister Count Ciano.

The revealing conversation went as follows:

...Wolff:

Yes, [*Frau Goebbels was*] attractive and intelligent. Frau Himmler was nice, too.

Dollmann:

But so common and vulgar. ... Wherever 'Dame Marga' [*Frau Himmler*] appeared, something untoward happened.

Wolff:

And 'Puppi' [*Gudrun Himmler*] was an abominable child, but you could never say anything to her father about her; that was dangerous.

Dollmann:

What happened to the adopted child? [*Gerhard von de Ahe*]

Wolff:

I only know that it was given most unkind treatment. ...

Wolff:

The Reichsführer is of course more to blame than anyone. It was his task not to lose his influence over the people working with him. It's only because of his half measures that the whole of the German nation is today guilty of bloodshed. The Reichsführer never made a single unequivocal decision. His great mistake was that he didn't get rid of all the irresolute men in good time.

The Reichsführer saw the whole gigantic war guilt and catastrophe inevitably coming towards us. But he didn't have the courage to say so. On the contrary, he even added to it. Oh hell! If someone has gone mad and is leading the whole nation to utter destruction; surely the Reichsführer had a higher duty to perform. He should have made use of his power and eliminated the Fuhrer.

Dollmann:

Then at least he would have performed a truly historic deed. Where is it really that the fault lies in the Reichsführer? Surely in his lack of humanity. There's certainly a lack of personality. Because at one time he definitely had great ideas.

Wolff:

But even the ideas he had pilfered. He is a very intelligent man with a very keenly developed sense for picking out the right things, but there is nothing human about him. All his friendships went to pieces, every single one. He shamelessly exploited everybody; he stole everybody's best ideas and plans. He took some of Rosenberg's ideas for instance; he picked the best out of everybody's work and then very cleverly put it together again. In the early days he led us with consummate skill; he preached beautiful, good and noble ideals. Throughout the years when we fought for power, and the following years when he was still dependent on his men, he threw his whole heart and soul into it. And for that reason the hearts and the whole mental and physical strength [the willingness to fight] of his men belonged to him. Later on that was too much trouble for him. He became too powerful, and just as he aped the Führer in more or less everything, he then began to use force and take advantage of his power. From that moment on he was responsible for the most fantastic injustices and instances of ingratitude. While I was still there I somehow managed to smooth things over. But then, when he broke even with me, it was all over. I told him, or rather I had him told by a third person, that even if we won the war, the Reichsführer would find himself completely isolated, or at least only surrounded by a few desperadoes. Everybody who had an ounce of character preferred to break stones for the rest of his life rather than remain with him.

During the twelve years that I stood beside the Reichsführer I tried never to let a shadow fall over the things we undertook to do. I tried to remain honest and not to go the same way as all the others, but while I was having all sorts of difficulties with my family he made things as awkward as he could. I was in the Reichsführer's headquarters one day. My wife was with the children at a place on the Baltic Coast near Königsberg. I wanted to go to my wife, but Himmler told me that I would have to stay at headquarters. I told him that from where my family was staying I could reach him in an hour and a half if he needed me.

That immediately made him angry. On the next day I decided to tackle him on the subject once and for all. The Reichsführer said: 'You don't seem to understand the position you're in; you don't appreciate the situation in which you find yourself?' I replied: 'Oh yes, Reichsführer, I know the situation I'm in even better than you do.' Then I went up close to him and looked him straight in the eyes. He was sitting behind his writing desk. 'I have to admit that I don't quite understand you,' I said. 'Even if you personally have changed your attitude towards me, don't you think that it might be unwise to undermine my authority so intentionally and publicly in front of everybody, when one day you may stand in bitter need of it?' I looked straight at him! He changed his tune immediately, 'Very well, what I said wasn't meant like that at all. I've done what I've done for perfectly definite reasons, please try to appreciate that.' I said: 'I don't expect any favours from you, but I do expect to be treated honourably. After all, I too played my part in the creation of the SS.'

All those people who were always talking about honour and trying to educate us have let us down and now it is we who have to pay, we have to submit to bad treatment by the Jews. And why? Because everything was always done half-heartedly.

It was perfectly clear to the Reichsführer what he ought to do—he was to jump from a plane and disappear for ever. I pray God that he may have found the courage for that last act. I shall always protect his family and the families of the others too, but if he still shows cowardice now, then I can't be held responsible if decent people

> have to go to Palestine and Syria to work in sulphur mines—all because certain gentlemen want to save their skins.
>
> No, if the Reichsführer's alive now, there's only one possibility left for him: not to sham death now, but to step before the people and say that the SD and the police, especially in Russia, were carrying out orders which he had given.

Dollmann:

> He should have stepped forward and said 'These men are guilty and these performed such and such acts by my orders.' It's absolutely contemptible and rotten that he has just disappeared.

Wolff:

> He should have fallen in the fighting. Even a suicide would have been a manly way out, although it carries an admission of guilt. The question is whether he will give himself up or whether Dönitz will hand him over.

As history records, Himmler did not offer himself up in acceptance of responsibility for the crimes commited by his SS legions. He left the world stage in a small ground floor room of a house in Lüneburg with British army officers frantically trying to resuscitate him from the effects of a vial of potassium cyanide he crushed in his jaws. Behind him he left the unanswered question of who claimed the ultimate responsibility for the orders to attempt to physically destroy the European Jews and other ethnic groups looked upon by the Nazis as racial enemies. The only other viable and more likely candidate had also voluntarily withdrawn from the arena three weeks previously in an underground bunker in Berlin. The debate continues.

A large part of the biographical narrative that follows is taken from the surviving copy of Himmler's personal pocket diary for 1939 and his desk diaries for the war years 1940 to March 1945. Himmler's 1939 diary was owned by the late James Townsend, an old friend of this author and a hoarder of Third Reich ephemera who had acquired the diary from the then avid Himmler collector, Tom Pooler. The photographic copy of Himmler's diary for 1940 was used for this study, the original being held by the Bundesarchiv in Koblenz. His 1940 diary quoted here is his private diary and not his service schedule as used for 1941–1942. Consequently, the latter records with whom he held meetings, mainly in the SS organisation, plus the general subject matter. The entries in Himmler's service diaries were not only in his handwriting, but also exhibit the handwriting of others such as Adjutant Werner Grothmann and Himmler's secretary Erika Lorenz.

Himmler's service diaries for 1941–1942 have been published and are therefore easily accessible. His diaries for 1943 and the first half of 1944 exist in their original handwritten format and it was photocopies of the copies held by the Imperial War Museum in London that Himmler's movements and appointments for this period that were utilised for this project. There are missing sections, such as over the Christmas period 1943, and Himmler's jagged scrawl in his own hand is not the easiest handwriting to read. Added to the poor quality of the photocopies for these years, his movements, meetings and appointments, outside the scope of well documented events, have been put together as far as is possible within the parameters allowed by deciphering what is recorded and from unpublished notes provided by British historian and author Stephan Tyas. No diary after mid-March 1945 apparently exists, or at least has not yet been discovered and much of the information regarding Himmler's day-to-day movements for the last weeks of his life is due in no small part to the diligent research of Stephen Tyas and German historian and author Peter Witte, who together researched all manner of sources to compile a workable sequential chronicle of events for 1945. Marga Himmler's diaries for the period 1937–1945 were transcribed by the historian David Irving from *Werkstatt Geschichte 25* from a draft copy held by the USHMM Washington DC and selected extracts with minor corrections are used for this study. Additional information has been inserted where necessary in order to put the daily life led by the Reichsführer-SS into perspective.

The decision to include his movements as recorded in his diaries on an almost day-to-day basis, particularly for the war years, was taken in order to illustrate his responsibilities and the character of his daily routine. Himmler was a 'hands on' individual who liked to see things for himself. He was one of the most active members of the Third Reich hierarchy, regularly filling his schedule with meetings and personal inspections. His mobility provided him with direct access to his commanders and his troops and gave the impression that he dealt personally with all matters. He made full use of transport links by air and rail and was rarely at his Berlin headquarters in Prinz Albrecht Strasse during the war.

Himmler's military adjutant during the latter war years was SS-Obersturmbannführer Werner Grothmann. During the Doctors' Trial at Nuremberg, he provided a testimony of Himmler's relationship with Professor Dr Karl Gebhardt who was subsequently convicted and hanged. It gives a good insight into how Himmler conducted his numerous meetings at his Feldkommandostellen [*field headquarters*:]

> I, Werner GROTHMANN, born on 23 August 1915 at Frankfurt a.M., last SS-Obersturmbannführer in the Waffen-SS and Chief Adjutant to Reichsführer-SS HIMMLER, interned in the British Civilian Internment Camp at Fallingbostel, at present in the military prison at Nuremberg, have been warned that I render myself liable to punishment if I submit a false affidavit. I declare under oath that my statement is true and was made for the purpose of being submitted as evidence to the Military Court No. 1 at the Palace of Justice, Nuremberg, Germany.
>
> On the subject: From 1940 to 1945, I was Adjutant to Reichsführer of the SS

HIMMLER; since 1942 as Adjutant I was entrusted with the handling of military matters in HIMMLER's staff. As such, I am in the position to testify about the general organization of the Field-Headquarters [*HIMMLER's Headquarters*]. Reports of a military character were submitted to HIMMLER through me, matters concerning police affairs were submitted through Lt. Col. of the Police SUCHANEK; the handling of incoming and outgoing mail for HIMMLER was exclusively in the charge of Dr. Rudolf BRANDT, HIMMLER's personal advisor. HIMMLER himself ordered persons to attend conferences with him; he always conducted those conferences alone with the person concerned, i.e. without BRANDT, SUCHANEK or myself being present. Information regarding the subject of the conference was usually not given by HIMMLER.

At my time, the physicians on HIMMLER's staff were the Finnish chiropractor, Dr. GERSTEN [*sic*], who, during his presence at headquarters, treated HIMMLER daily; furthermore, a so-called 'permanent escort physician' who attended trips to the front and who was also responsible for the medical care of the personnel of the Field-Headquarters, from 1941 to 1942, Dr. WITTMANN was escorting physician from 1942 to autumn of 1944 it was Dr. STUMPFEGGER, and from the autumn of 1944 up to the armistice it was Dr. Müller.

During my assignment as Adjutant to HIMMLER, Prof. GEBHARDT held the position of consulting surgeon of the Waffen-SS. In this capacity he frequently visited the front units of the Waffen-SS where he also performed operations. Furthermore, Prof. GEBHARDT was also Chief Physician at Hohenlychen at that time; HIMMLER visit Hohenlychen approximately two or three times a year. He used the opportunity especially around Christmas to visit the wounded and also see his two children, who lived at Hohenlychen, later in the vicinity. Dr. GEBHARDT's visits to HIMMLER's headquarters during my period of office as adjutant [*from 1940–1945*] usually lasted only a few days; the announcement of his visit mostly came through me, without giving any reasons. I have never attended any conferences between HIMMLER and GEBHARDT. As far as I remember, only HIMMLER and GEBHARDT were present at those conferences, following HIMMLER's custom. Neither HIMMLER nor GEBHARDT informed me even afterwards about the subject of those discussions.

In respect of his collaborators, too, HIMMLER obeyed the Führer's command concerning Secrecy, which permitted information to be given only to the extent necessary for the execution of certain duties by the person concerned. In conversations in the presence of several people, as for example discussions at the table, only those matters were discussed which were not subject to secrecy.

In addition to the above mentioned *tête-à-tête* conferences between HIMMLER and GEBHARDT, I only remember one conference at which besides Professor GEBHARDT also Professor GRAWITZ was ordered to appear. The subject of this conference, too, remained unknown to me. Frequent conferences at regular intervals between HIMMLER and several SS physicians together never took place in my time.

In addition to activities as already mentioned, Professor Dr. GEBHARDT, since August 1944 to my knowledge was Heersgruppenarzt with the Army Group Oberrhein, since January 1945, Heersgruppenarzt with the Army Group Weichsel.

Nuremberg, 27 January 1947

Signed: Werner GROTHMANN

The availability of Himmler's diaries for certain periods and the lack of it for others introduced an inherent problem of providing a large amount of source material over some periods and others having little or no information. Where possible the gaps have been filled with known historical facts or information gained from other reliable sources. There has been no effort to give opinions and where this has unavoidably occurred, there is no intention by the author to influence the reader one way or another.

The man who took a relatively small group of political soldiers and created a vast organization which even now stimulates emotions nearly seventy years after it ceased to exist, was one of the most photographed men at the pinnacle of the Third German Reich hierarchy. A selection of the resultant images, frozen in time, is the rationale of this work, but a brief historical synopsis of the subject matter is also provided for reference purposes. The photographs are a cross-section of private snaps, family photos, official photos and press photos. They are not presented in any strict chronological order as many are undated, although effort has been made to show them roughly in sequence with the events in Himmler's life.

Max Williams
London, 2014

ONE

Heinrich Luitpold Himmler—The Early Years

Himmler could never be described as an archetypal SS man. He was of medium height and build; in later life he developed a small 'pot belly.' His hair was on the dark side of fair and his eyesight was poor, resulting in his having to wear spectacles all his life. From his teenage years he grew a small moustache, a common fashion of the time, but possibly to distract attention away from his undersized slightly receding chin. He possessed a strange gait, his feet splaying outward as he stepped, an idiosyncrasy accentuated and more noticeable by his wearing of high leather boots and riding breeches. He had a high bridge to his nose, not enough to warrant a description of crooked, but sufficient to notice on the cast of his death mask. Himmler would certainly not have passed the strict appearance guidelines laid down for all prospective SS candidates in the early days and which Himmler himself administered stringently, checking photographs of all applicants with a magnifying glass at his desk.

His constitution was weak and he suffered from ill health from a small child. His nervous stomach cramps are well documented and one wonders what a modern examination and diagnosis would have revealed. By chance, he made the acquaintance of a Swedish private practitioner who promoted the use of massage to ease discomfort. Felix Kersten's methods had successful, *albeit* temporary, results with Himmler's abdominal complaints and he became indispensible for the Reichsführer-SS.

Himmler's pedantic opinions, expressed so ardently as a boy and adolescent, remained a trait of his character throughout his life and certainly had an effect on the administration of his SS organization. Although extremely defined in his attitudes on all subjects, Himmler was apparently an excellent listener, absorbing all information and reasoning before coming to a decision.

He displayed a sensitive nature, maintaining a loving relationship with his daughter and showing a caring attitude towards his wife, even after the marriage failed and they became estranged. The couple remained married to the end despite Himmler falling deeply in love with his private secretary and producing two children with her.

Himmler's own upbringing was disciplined; his schoolmaster father (Josef Gebhard Himmler, born 17 May 1865 in Lindau) did not leave his authoritarianism in the classroom, meticulously monitoring his three sons' development and progress. The family was firmly catholic and the mother ensured that the boys were indoctrinated in and practised the faith. However, the family was a close-knit unit; the boys respected and loved their parents without reservation and the parents gladly returned their sentiments.

It was into such an embryonic family atmosphere that the future Reichsführer-SS entered this world, drawing his first breath on 7 October 1900 at 2 Hildegardstrasse, Munich. The joyous parents already had one son, Gebhard, born 29 July 1898. The new infant weighed in at a healthy 7 lb 3 oz and his father, Gebhard Himmler senior, proudly announced his birth in a letter to his former pupil, Prince Heinrich of Wittelsbach, asking permission to name the child after his royal patron and requesting that the prince be his Godfather. The Prince duly obliged and Heinrich Luitpold Himmler was christened in the catholic faith. A third son, Ernst, was a later welcome addition to the Himmlers, arriving on 23 December 1905. Mother Himmler, Anna Maria Auguste (born Heyder, 19 January 1866 in Munich) was assisted in the family home by a nanny, Thilde, whom the boys all came to love.

The family moved around as a consequence of Gebhard senior changing his teaching job. In the summer of 1902, they moved to Passau and thence back to Munich in early 1904. Heinrich attended the Cathedral School in Munich from 4 September 1906 until July 1908. From September 1908 until July 1910, he attended the Amalien School in Munich. He moved to the Kaiser Wilhelm High School in Munich from September 1910 until July 1913 and from September 1913 until June 1917, Heinrich attended the High School in Landshut. Also at this school, where his father was director, Heinrich's older brother Gebhard befriended a classmate, Karl Gebhardt, the later SS-Gruppenführer and head surgeon of the SS. The Himmler family lived in an imposing house on Dreifaltigkeitsplatz in Landshut.

In 1915, as soon as he was old enough, Heinrich attended military training in the youth army cadets. In November 1916, the family was devastated to hear that Heinrich's Godfather and namesake, Prince Heinrich, had been killed in action in Romania. The enormity of his demise was not lost on the sixteen year old youth with ambitions to join the prince's regiment as an officer cadet. On 7 June 1917, Gebhard senior wrote to the prince's mother, Princess Arnulf and requested help for Heinrich to join either the 1st[r] or 2nd Bavarian Infantry Regiment as an officer cadet. Upon being told that there were no vacancies for officer cadets, Heinrich applied to the Imperial Navy as an officer cadet, but this was also unsuccessful, his poor eyesight letting him down badly in the entrance medical requirements.

Desperate to fight and severely disappointed by his rejections, Heinrich opted to leave school prematurely and on 6 October 1917, he registered with the War Welfare Service Office in Landshut in order to carry out emergency war service work. When all seemed lost, he received notification on 23 December 1917 that there was a vacancy for an officer cadet in the Royal Bavarian 11th Infantry Regiment number 9 'von der Tann.' He was ordered to report on 1 January 1918 in Regensburg for six months basic training.

From 15 June 1918 until 15 September 1918, Heinrich attended an officer cadet course at the Fähnrich School in Freising and gained a certificate of maturity to be an officer. The school commander, Oberstleutnant von Braun, described him as '... a very successful student ... excellent, active, energetic young man with faultless manners, free from objections and fit to be an officer.' This was immediately followed by a two-week course with the 17th Machine Gun Company in Bamberg and on 1 October 1918, he began a period of home leave in Landshut. He returned to his unit to continue his training and when the armistice was signed in November, Heinrich had not seen active service. Once again bitterly disappointed, he was ordered on home leave. At the end of November he returned to Regensburg to assist with the disarmament of his regiment and on 17 December 1918 he was demobilized and left the army.

He returned to his family home in Landshut where he joined the Bavarian People's Party (BVP.) A special course for young men who had been forced to cut short their education for reasons of war was introduced and Heinrich attended such a course at his father's school in Landshut from January until June 1919. Fervently nationalist and frustrated by his inability to fight in the war, he recognized that the various Freikorps units could provide him with an opportunity to defend the Fatherland and satisfy his lust for bravery. In April 1919, he joined the Freikorps Landshut and the Reserve Company of the Freikorps Oberland, serving in the latter during May 1919 as adjutant of the commander of the Reserve Company.

Gebhard senior expressed his concerns over the effect that Heinrich's military service was interfering with his education and on 15 July 1919, Heinrich at last graduated. From 1 August until 15 September 1919, Heinrich attended a practical course in agriculture in Oberhaunstadt near Ingolstadt, but this was cut short when he fell ill on 2 September with paratyphus. He was admitted to the hospital in Ingolstadt on 4 September and he remained as an in-patient for three weeks. Once recovered, his doctor, Dr Quenstedt, advised his parents on 18 October that Heinrich should rest from practical work for a year and so his course was postponed.

He enrolled at the agricultural faculty of the Technical High School in Munich and the University of Munich where, from 28 October 1919 until August 1920, he studied agriculture, specializing in chicken breeding. At first he lodged with his brother Gebhard at Schellingstrasse 5, but soon found his own lodgings nearer the university at Amalienstrasse 28/4. The Himmler brothers took their meals at the home of Frau Loritz who offered board and lodgings at Jägerstrasse 8.

Heinrich's passionate desire to wear military uniform had not receded and on 4 November 1919 he joined the 14 Alarm Company of the 21st *Schützenbrigade* in Munich. His elder brother was also a member along with a close friend and cousin, Ludwig Zahler. Heinrich wrote in his diary on 1 December 1919, *'Today I wear uniform again. For me it is always the most precious clothing one can wear.'*

In January 1920, Heinrich participated in a mass demonstration in Munich against the death sentence of Anton Graf von Arco-Valley, the assassin of socialist leader Kurt Eisner and during this year his anti-Semite beliefs were heavily influenced and developed through the writings of authors such as Arthur Dinter. Heinrich also joined the Apollo student fraternity, but his attempts to acquire the trademark duelling scars as recognition of his honour did not materialize as he would have hoped. Added to his lack of a facial badge of honour was his failure to participate in the other fraternal occupation, that of consuming large quantities of beer. Heinrich's delicate constitution forbad him the opportunity to join in with his fraternity brethren, but he did attend the meetings in the local *Kneipe*. Eventually, he was able to satisfy one of his desires by picking up a nick on his face during a fraternity sabre fight, but the wound was so minor that it was almost impossible to see the resultant small scar in later years.

The Himmler brothers and their cousin 'Lu' Zahler participated in military patrols with the Alarm Company during what became known as the Kapp Putsch and Heinrich's experiences kept his military interest alive, but promoted his fears of anti-nationalist politics. His military ardour was, however, cut short by the insistence of the Allies to disband all the *Schützenbrigade*, including Heinrich's beloved 14 Alarm Company. He responded by immediately joining the *Einwohnerwehr*, yet another device to avoid disarming, and the *Schützengesellschaft Freiweg*, an organisation formed by ex-soldiers in order to continue military training in preparation for the day when their services would again be required.

To fulfil his education, Heinrich was required to complete his university course, including a year *Praktikum*, within three years. A relative of the Loritz family operated a 120 acre farm in Fridolfing near the Himmler family's summer holiday location of Tittmoning and he offered Heinrich a place for his *Praktikum*. Heinrich visited the Rehrls and immediately took to the farmer, Herr Alois Rehrl, taking up the offered position of farmhand on 1 September 1920. For mobility and not wishing to be cut off in the countryside, Heinrich purchased a motorcycle.

Heinrich worked hard on the farm, operating machinery, digging irrigation ditches, sacking and hauling bags of flour and working in the fields. The farm buildings consisted of the farmhouse, agricultural buildings, a mill and a small power station. The original buildings were torn down in 1958 and replaced with the existing structures.

Much to everyone's surprise, Heinrich loved the work and his first impression of the likeable Herr Rehrl, ten years his senior, was confirmed. In return, the Rehrls treated Heinrich as a member of the family, Frau Rehrl doing his washing and cleaning. Herr Rehrl took Heinrich with him to exhibitions, meetings of the local historical society and even to the church choir which Heinrich joined. During his stay on the Rehrl farm, Heinrich attended a course of instruction at the Fridolfing machine factory of Epple and Buxbaum. Much of what Heinrich learned about agriculture was from Herr Rehrl whom Heinrich described as 'extremely well informed ... on all subjects. ...' The two spent hours discussing farm management, history and current affairs. They walked, hunted and fished together and his time with Herr Rehrl obviously influenced Heinrich's views on peasant customs and traditions. The two men remained lifelong friends, with Alois Rehrl joining Heinrich's SS in 1936. In May 1942, Heinrich made sure that Frau Rehrl was included in a list of ladies to receive a gift of coffee. In October/November 1942, SS-Obersturmführer Rehrl visited the field headquarters of the Reichsführer-SS, regularly dined with his former farm labourer in the company of senior SS officers and also accompanied him on an inspection visit to the Crimea. During the afternoon of 30 October, Heinrich and Rehrl visited the grave of SS-Untersturmführer Rehrl who one can only assume was the young son of Herr Rehrl. Heinrich followed this up with a visit to the Rehrl farm in Fridolfing in the afternoon of 21 November 1942. The following year, prisoners from the concentration camp at Dachau were allocated to work on the Rehrl farm. Rehrl eventually reached the rank of SS-Sturmbannführer, attached to SS-Standarte 31 in Landshut and also held Waffen-SS rank of SS-Sturmbannführer der Reserve on the Personal Staff RFSS. As a mentor and important influential guide to Heinrich's early life, farmer Alois Rehrl is often overlooked.

Heinrich completed his year long *Praktikum* at the end of August 1921, but he did not return to the Technical High School in Munich until November. Around this time he was toying with the idea of leaving Germany and travelling the world. His parents arranged for him to work for two months at the United Factory of Agricultural Machinery in Ingolstadt. The company were extremely pleased with his work and were sorry that he had to leave them. In the meantime, in preparation for his return to his studies, he found lodgings with a Frau Wolff in Briennerstrasse, quite close to the university in Munich. Upon his return, he found that many of his previous acquaintances had left Munich and he was now expected to take on more responsibilities in the running of his own life. His brother Gebhard was working in Ingolstadt and his closest friend, Lu Zahler, was occupied with trying to earn money to enable him to marry his fiancée, Käthe Loritz. His other close boyhood friend, Falk Zipperer, had left the city. This enabled Heinrich to throw himself into his circle of acquaintances around his military career and politics, always with the intention of furthering his own ambitions.

Twice he visited Princess Arnulf and they discussed the 'good old days' and the unfortunate fast disappearing values of previous years. Heinrich, now a senior in the Bund Apollo, was considered somewhat of a 'dinosaur' in his attitude to modern trends and he began to rapidly lose interest in the fraternity, whilst still attempting to attend its meetings. His relationship with the opposite sex was strongly influenced by his upbringing in which his family values of a strict prohibition on pre-marital sex held sway. He experienced all the normal urges of a young man in his early twenties, but his powerful prudish beliefs prevented him from exercising what his body was telling him. He remained ignorant of the delights of sexual release.

Heinrich's attitude towards homosexuality was one of a lack of morality displayed by the degenerative elements abundant in post-war Germany. In short, he found homosexuality disturbing. It was around this time, in early 1922, that he encountered Captain Ernst Röhm in the Arzberger Beer Cellar. Röhm's views on the dangers of Bolshevism struck a chord with the young Heinrich and he fell under the captain's influence, soon joining the *Reichsflagge* at Röhm's suggestion.

In spring 1922, Professor Gebhard Himmler was appointed as Rektor of the Wittelsbach Gymnasium in Munich and in May, he left the rest of the family in Ingolstadt and moved to Munich alone. He took temporary lodgings and during the summer he was able to meet Heinrich for dinner on numerous occasions. They discussed Heinrich's future and the costs involved in maintaining both Gebhard Junior and Heinrich during another year of schooling. In late May, Heinrich applied for admission to the Political Science Department of the Munich University under a scholarship scheme and a month later he was notified that his application for both had been successful.

On 5 August 1922, Heinrich gained his diploma in agriculture from the Technical High School, but still faced the problem of how to find living expenses for the coming academic year. The outlook was doom and gloom. However, the old policy of utilising past acquaintances paid off again. On 15 August 1922, Heinrich received an offer of employment with a nitrogen fertilizer company in Schleissheim. It originated with an old teacher, Professor Huolezeck, whose brother was an official with the company, Sticksoff-Land GmbH. The offer was for the position of technical assistant at a salary of 4000 marks per month and was available immediately. Although galloping inflation was eroding the quoted salary whilst Heinrich contemplated the position, he decided that negotiations to adjust it could be made after he was in post. His family had by now moved back to Munich and Schleissheim was only a few miles away which would enable him to keep in close contact with family, friends and political acquaintances. Heinrich readily accepted the position and on 1 September became the latest recruit to the company. Viewing this relocation as a temporary arrangement, Heinrich was unaware that within a year the move would enable him to not only achieve his desire of joining the

Reichswehr, but would also provide the springboard to his joining the NSDAP.

Heinrich's responsibility with his new employer was in research on manure and although he again proved himself to be a conscientious, competent, hard working employee, the idea of a life in manure as a prospect did not unsurprisingly 'tick all the boxes' with the future Reichsführer-SS. In addition, spiralling inflation did not help the rather meagre pay with which he was rewarded. The political atmosphere was at boiling point and various paramilitary based organizations were springing up everywhere. Bavaria was no exception and Heinrich's options were many. In 1923, he left the Bavarian People's Party and aligned himself to the right-wing nationalist Captain Röhm. Röhm had close links with the NSDAP and the young Himmler followed suit and joined Hitler's party on 1 August 1923. His allocated NSDAP membership number was 42 404.

The political situation was not helped by the Bavarian Government being at odds with the Berlin Government over comments made in the Bavarian press, plus a shift to the left by the Thuringia Government. Bavaria was fearful of yet another communist threat and moved towards mobilization. Still dreaming of a military career, Himmler seized the opportunity and, after leaving his job on 1 September 1923, he joined the 4 Company (Company Werner) 1st Battalion 19th Infantry Regiment (Munich) on 15 September. At last he was in the Reichswehr.

Röhm became embroiled in a struggle for control of the *Reichsflagge* and as a consequence formed a brand new organization known as the *Reichskriegsflagge*. Himmler dutifully resigned from the *Reichsflagge* and immediately joined the *Reichskriegsflagge* on 17 October 1923.

The two main protagonists in the political battle, Bavaria and Berlin, appeared to be settling their differences and as a concession, Bavaria agreed to disband the numerous paramilitary units, including the Company Werner. On 8 November, Himmler's longed for military career came to an abrupt end after only several weeks. However, events were fast overtaking Himmler's original military career plans and he had already chosen the road to revolution behind Röhm and Hitler. What transpired became colloquially known as 'the Beer Hall Putsch' and Himmler's life would never be the same again.

Captain Röhm and his *Reichskriegsflagge* supporters were in the Augustiner Beer Hall awaiting orders on 8 November 1923. Their number totalled around four hundred men, including Heinrich Himmler, his brother Gebhard and several of Himmler's friends from Schleissheim. Röhm received word from Hitler at the Bürgerbräukeller and the jubilant group set off across Munich towards the War Ministry on Leopoldstrasse. At the head of the group, carrying the imperial war ensign, was Heinrich Himmler. On arrival, Röhm was refused entry and his response was to erect a barbed wire barricade around the entrance to the building. The following morning, 9 November, his men were in turn surrounded by police units in a confused stand-off. Hitler's attempt to relieve Röhm ended in the debacle at the Feldherrnhalle and Röhm was forced to surrender. The *Reichskriegsflagge* leaders were arrested and the columns of followers were forced to hand over their weapons and go home after identifying themselves to the police.

In the weeks that followed, Himmler was in a kind of limbo. All the organizations to which he belonged, including the NSDAP, were banned. Many *Reichskriegsflagge* members went into hiding for fear of being arrested and Himmler organized letter drops for those in hiding so that they could keep in touch. The main leaders of the Putsch were imprisoned in Landsberg and Stadelheim Prisons. On 15 February 1924, Himmler visited Röhm in Stadelheim and discussed the political situation with him. Many *völkisch* organizations sprang up to fill the void left by the illegal groups and Himmler began to study and work hard for the *völkisch* cause. He toured small towns in northern Bavaria on his motorcycle making speeches and he wrote articles for the rural press. None of these activities provided him with an income and now living again with his parents, he became desperate to find suitable employment.

Himmler went to extraordinary lengths in his quest for paid work. He had maintained a correspondence with a Turkish student and investigated working in Turkey. He also contacted the Russian embassy, suggesting that he might find work in the Ukraine. In June 1924, he applied for the position of secretary to Gregor Strasser, a pharmacist from Landshut and the local leader of the *Nationalsozialistische Freiheitsbewegung*. His application accepted in early July, Himmler left Munich for Landshut and embarked on a new career away from farming.

In addition to his secretarial duties, Himmler became Strasser's deputy in all matters. By 1925, he had joined the *Bund Artam* and was deputy leader of *Frontbann* in Lower Bavaria. During this period, Himmler also became interested in the 'blood and soil' ideology and his racial beliefs became intrinsically fundamental to his way of thinking. His anti-Semitism intensified and he became more outspoken. On 2 August 1925, Himmler rejoined the regenerated NSDAP with the new party membership number 14 303. The same day he joined the SS and was allocated SS membership number 168.

At last Himmler's star was in the ascendancy; his titles included national speaker for the NSDAP, party propaganda leader for Lower Bavaria, NSDAP Gau Secretary for Lower Bavaria and in 1926, Deputy NSDAP Gauleiter and Managing Director for Gau Niederbayern-Oberfalz, followed by Deputy NSDAP Gauleiter for Oberbayern-Schwaben. 1926 also saw Himmler appointed as Gau-SS-Führer for Niederbayern, based in Landshut. On 12 September 1926, Himmler transferred to Munich on his appointment as Deputy to the Reich Propaganda Leader. In March 1927, Hitler appointed Erhard Heiden as Reichsführer-SS and Heinrich Himmler was seen as an ideal deputy. On 1 March, Himmler became Deputy Reichsführer-SS. The die had been cast.

The SS was subordinate to the much larger SA, but his new elevated position placed Himmler on the staff of the Supreme SA Leadership. He was for all intents and purposes the Reich NSDAP leader for propaganda and officially took on that responsibility on 2 January 1928, a post he was to retain until replaced by Dr Josef Goebbels.

Himmler's life was going through several upheavals around this time. During a sudden downpour of snow in Bad Reichenhall in December 1926, Himmler had taken shelter from the weather in a hotel foyer. Almost colliding with a woman and showering her with snow from his quickly removed hat, they struck up a conversation. Her name was Margarete Boden and at thirty-four years of age she was eight years his senior. She was the daughter of a German landowner from Goncerzewo in West Prussia, was a qualified nurse and had been divorced following a short disastrous marriage to a man named Siegroth. 'Marga' Boden now ran a small clinic in Berlin which she had opened with her father's money. According to Gebhard Himmler, it was her hair that had attracted his brother to her. In some photographs a serious horizontal scar is evident on her left cheek and it is plainly evident that she was conscious of the disfigurement as most photographs favour her right profile. The cause of this injury remains a mystery. Whatever it was, their relationship developed and Himmler experienced sex for the first time, apparently instigated by her. They continued their relationship mainly by correspondence and by 3 July 1928 when the couple married in Berlin-Schöneberg, contrary to the wishes of Himmler's parents, Marga had agreed to sell her clinic and set up home in Bavaria where Himmler had found the couple a small house with pens for chickens in Waldtrudering near Munich. On 8 August 1929, Marga gave birth to a baby girl whom the couple named Gudrun.

Reichsführer-SS Erhard Heiden relied upon his deputy for the everyday running of the SS and Himmler introduced strict guidelines for uniform and conduct within the SS. SS Order no. 4 on 17 January 1928 decreed that all practical duties of the SS would be administered by Party Member Himmler and that all orders would be signed by either Heiden or Himmler. Many pedantic rules bore the trademark of the fastidious Deputy Reichsführer-SS and Himmler would certainly not have approved of the scandal which was about to break in December 1928, causing the resignation of Heiden on 6 January 1929. Apparently, Heiden had profited from the purchases of black SS trousers from a Jewish tailoring firm. Hitler announced on 20 January 1929 in Weimar that he had appointed Heinrich Himmler as the new Reichsführer-SS, with effect from 6 January 1929. Himmler's destiny was sealed.

TWO

Reichsführer-SS

Heinrich Himmler was the fourth man to hold the title of Reichsführer-SS. He had been preceded by Julius Schreck, Josef Berchtold and Erhard Heiden and he was not the last incumbent, being succeeded in the final days of the war by Karl Hanke. However, it is the name of Himmler which is synonymous with the role. Himmler immediately set about putting his ideas into action whilst accepting that the SS remained subordinate to the much larger and more powerful SA under Captain Pfeffer von Salomon.

On 14 September 1930, Himmler was elected as NSDAP representative of Wahlkreis 24 (Oberbayern-Schwaben) in the Reichstag elections. Hitler issued an order on 7 November 1930 that confirmed the subordinate position of the SS to the Stabschef of the SA [*by this time Röhm*] and also re-established his own authority over the SS as Oberste Führer der Schutzstaffel, whilst at the same time recognizing the independent status of the SS. The SS was also authorized to wear a black uniform in order to distinguish it from the brown SA uniform. In a single move, Himmler became leader of a Party organization independent of, but junior to, the SA. This status quo would remain for another four years. On 25 February 1931, Himmler was given control of the security service for the protection of Hitler and the NSDAP hierarchy.

By May 1931, Himmler had introduced strict criteria for the acceptance of new recruits to the SS. Not only did the applicant have to meet certain racial characteristics in appearance, but also had to have excellent dental history and be able to prove Aryan descent. A good portrait photograph was required to accompany each application and Himmler himself examined the appearance of each candidate. All SS men were told that they could only marry with the authority of the Reichsführer-SS. It was under these strict conditions of entry that an application form and photograph landed on Himmler's desk in June 1931. The aspiring candidate was new NSDAP member number 544 916, an ex-naval officer whose application was accompanied by a recommendation from a senior SS and

SA officer, Friedrich Karl Freiherr von Eberstein. Himmler pored over the form and examined the photograph. What he saw impressed the Reichsführer-SS. The man was not only of Nordic appearance and an ex-officer, but also had experience in intelligence work; a more than suitable recruit to organize a planned brand new SS intelligence service. Himmler, apparently somewhat confused between intelligence officer and communications officer, agreed to meet the applicant in person and a meeting was arranged for 16 June. Himmler was impressed and asked the interviewee to quickly sketch an outline plan for an intelligence service. The submission convinced Himmler and Reinhard Heydrich was immediately appointed as his intelligence chief, officially joining the SS in Hamburg on 14 July 1931. The two men's paths were inexorably linked for the future.

On 25 January 1932, Himmler was appointed head of security for the Brown House in Munich. From April to June 1932, there was a government prohibition on the wearing of uniforms for both the SA and the SS. Himmler was elected as Reichstag representative for Thuringia on 31 July 1932 and by order of the Führer on 15 December 1932, Himmler was authorized to wear the rank insignia of an Obergruppenführer, effective 1 January 1933. He accompanied Hitler and Hess to a meeting, arranged by economics wizard Wilhelm Keppler, with Franz von Papen in the house of the financier Kurt von Schröder on 4 January 1933 where the role of the NSDAP in a future government was thrashed out. This was a major step towards Hitler being accepted and appointed by von Hindenburg as Reich Chancellor on 30 January 1933.

Keppler and von Schröder were important members of an economic group which became known as the Keppler Circle. Wilhelm Keppler joined the NSDAP in 1927 and in the spring of 1932, at the instigation of Hitler, formed a loose circle of friends to study economic issues. The group's secretary was Fritz Kranefuss, an early associate of Keppler. Some historians believe that the basis of future NSDAP economic policy can be sourced to the initiatives of the Keppler Circle. Keppler eventually became a SS-Obergruppenführer on the staff of the RFSS and a State Secretary in the Foreign Ministry, with von Schröder attaining the SS rank of Brigadeführer. Other members included:

Hjalmar Schacht
Albert Vögler
Friedrich Reinhart
Ewald Hecker
August Rosterg
Emil Heinrich Meyer (Dresdner Bank)
Franz Heinrich Witthoefft
Emil Helfferich
Leopold Plaichinger (associate of Wilhelm Keppler from Odin-Werken)

Max Otto Luyken
Gottfried Graf von Bismarck-Schönhausen
Otto Steinbrinck (private secretary of Friedrich Flick)

After Hitler seized power in January 1933, Himmler exploited the opportunity to use the Keppler Circle for the benefit of the SS and transformed the group into the Freundeskreis Reichsführer-SS (Circle of Friends of the RFSS.) The members donated annually approximately 1 million Reichsmarks to the Reichsführer-SS from 1935 to 1944. For this purpose the 'special account S' at the J. H. Stein Bank in Cologne was established on 25 February 1936 by Otto Steinbrinck and Kurt Freiherr von Schröder in a letter to Emil Heinrich Meyer, a member of the board of directors of the Dresdner Bank. Kurt Freiherr von Schröder was appointed as administrator of the account.

Wilhelm Keppler was interrogated on the framework of the group for the Nuremberg trials. From memory, he named a number of members who at least temporarily belonged to the circle of friends and who had active participation on the basis of the donations and other documentation. Kurt von Schröder wrote to Himmler on 21 September 1943 including a list of contributions in the total amount of 1,100,000 RM for the year 1943. [*This letter is listed as exhibit US-322 / EC-453 for the Nuremberg trials.*]

The known members of the Circle of Friends of the Reichsführer-SS are as follows, listed alphabetically with their functions not being exhaustive:

Hermann Behrends, Dr. jur., SS-Gruppenführer und Generalleutnant der Polizei und SS-Sturmbannführer der Reserve der Waffen-SS, Higher SS and Police Leader in Serbia and Montenegro, Staff Officer of Volksdeutschen Mittelstelle;
Rudolf Bingel, Siemens-Halske;
Gottfried Graf von Bismarck-Schönhausen, Regional President in Stettin and later in Potsdam;
Karl Blessing, Unilever, later Bundesbank Chief;
Wilhelm Börger, Ministry of Labour;
Heinrich Bütefisch, I. G. Farben;
Kurt Dellmann, SS-Obersturmführer;
Friedrich Karl Dermietzel, Deputy of Reich Doctor of the SS and Polizei, SS-Brigadeführer;
Hans Fischböck, Reichskommissar for the Four Year Plan;
Friedrich Flick, Mitteldeutsche Steelworks;
Rudolph Firle, Norddeutscher Lloyd;
Herbert Ludwig Wilhelm Göring, Ministry of Economic Affairs, cousin of Hermann Göring;
Karl Ritter von Halt, Deutsche Bank;

Franz Hayler, State Secretary in the Ministry of Economic Affairs;
Ewald Hecker, Ironworks of Ilseder Hütte;
Emil Helfferich, Chairman of Hapag, Director of DAPG;
Otto Heuer, Director General of Schütte AG;
Erich Hilgenfeldt, Head of National Socialist People's Welfare;
Richard Kaselowsky, Dr August Oetker KG, Bielefeld;
Hans Kehrl, SS-Oberführer;
Wilhelm Keppler, after 1938 State Secretary in the Foreign Ministry;
Fritz Kiehn, paper manufacturer and SS-Obersturmbannführer;
Wilhelm Kleinmann, State Secretary in the Reich Transport Ministry;
Fritz Kranefuss, Braunekohle-Benzin AG, Himmler's representative, SS-Brigadeführer;
Carl Vincent Krogmann, First Bürgermeister of Hamburg;
Karl Lindemann, Director of the Dresdner Bank, Deutsche Reichsbank, DAPG, Norddeutscher Lloyd, Melchers & Co., Bremen;
Freiherr von Lüdinghausen;
Emil Heinrich Meyer, Chairman of the Dresdner Bank;
Werner Naumann, State Secretary in the Propaganda Ministry;
Otto Ohlendorf, State Secretary in the Ministry of Economic Affairs, SS-Gruppenführer;
Alfred Olscher, Reichs-Kredit-Gesellschaft AG;
Oswald Pohl, Chief of the SS Central Office for Economic Administration;
Karl Rasche, Board of Directors of the Dresdner Bank;
Herbert Reichenberger, SS-Untersturmführer;
Friedrich Reinhart, Chairman of Commerzbank;
Hellmut Röhnert, Rheinmetall-Borsig;
Erwin Rösener, SS-Obergruppenführer und General der Waffen-SS, Higher SS and Police Leader Alpenland;
August Rosterg, Kali-Konzern Wintershall AG;
Hjalmar Schacht, President of the Reichsbank;
Ernst Schäfer, SS-Standartenführer, SS-Ahnenerbe Office;
Walter Schieber, Head of Armaments Delivery Office in the War Ministry;
Heinrich Schmidt, Wintershall Kali-Konzern;
Kurt Schmitt, former Minister of Economic Affairs, CEO Allianz AG;
Kurt Freiherr von Schröder, Banker, J. H. Stein Bank;
Wolfram Sievers, Chief of SS-Ahnenerbe Office;
Otto Steinbrinck, Gewerkschaft Preußen;
Albert Vögler, Vereinigte Stahlwerke AG;
Wilhelm Voss, Hermann-Göring-Werke;
Hermann Waldhecker, Director of the Reichsbank;
Hans Walz, Boschwerke;
Franz Heinrich Witthoefft, Chairman of the Supervisory Board of Commerz and Private Bank;

Karl Wolff, Personal Adjutant and Chief of the Personal Staff Reichsführer-SS, SS-Obergruppenführer und General der Polizei und Waffen-SS;
Walther Wüst, Professor of Indo-European Linguistics and Departmental Chief SS Research and Education in SS-Ahnenerbe.

In February 1933, Himmler and Marga sold their small house in Waldtrudering and moved with their daughter to the city centre. Initially, Himmler did not receive any major government job in the new regime. On 10 March, he was appointed as Police Director in Munich and five days later became Political Advisor for police questions in Bavaria in the State Interior Ministry. On 22 March 1933, Himmler opened the concentration camp in Dachau for 5,000 inmates who were considered as a political threat to the State. On 26 March he became Police President of Nuremberg and by 1 April he had been appointed as the Political Police Commander in Bavaria. On 10 April Adolf Wagner made Himmler responsible for all 'protective custody' matters, a euphemism for incarceration in a concentration camp.

Also in April 1933, Himmler's predecessor Erhard Heiden was arrested on Heydrich's orders in the Café Orlando in Munich. Whether he knew something about Himmler from their time together in the late 1920s will never be known because he was murdered soon after. Himmler displayed no mercy to his former boss, an old fighter from the Stosstrupp Hitler.

On 10 July 1933, Himmler was selected as a Prussian State Councillor. Throughout the remainder of 1933 and into early 1934, he took control of numerous state political police organizations including Lübeck, Hamburg, Württemberg, Baden, Anhalt, Hessen-Darmstadt, Weimar, Thuringia, Bremen, Saxony, Oldenburg and Brunswick. The Himmler-Heydrich partnership eventually controlled all the political police authorities in the Reich, but not Prussia which was retained by Prussian Minister President Hermann Göring. On 20 April 1934, Prussia also fell to Himmler when he was created Inspector of the Prussian Secret State Police (Gestapo.) Himmler was now in an unassailable position, but he still wanted total control of the Reich Police which was the responsibility of the Reich Interior Minister, Wilhelm Frick.

1933 was also the year that the Reichsführer-SS had been introduced to Karl Maria Wiligut-Weisthor via one of his SS officers and was immediately impressed with Wiligut's knowledge of German mythology and tradition. In September 1933, Wiligut joined the SS under the name Weisthor and was placed in charge of Germanic history within the Race & Resettlement Department. One of Wiligut-Weisthor's first contributions to the SS was the design and introduction of the SS-Totenkopf Ring [*death's head ring.*] This ring was to become something akin to a marriage ring, symbolising eternal loyalty between members of the SS. The ring, manufactured by the Gahr jewellery company, bore Himmler's engraved signature on the inner edge and was accompanied by a citation signed in ink by the Reichsführer-SS.

Himmler now looked for ways to release his SS from its subordinate position under SA-Stabschef Röhm. His opportunity arrived when Hitler's ear was being bent by the Wehrmacht Generals over the strength and ambitions of Röhm and his SA. The events of 30 June 1934 and the following day are well documented as the 'Night of Long Knives' or the 'Röhm Putsch.' Himmler joined the vultures circling their quarry and added names to the list of intended victims. Röhm was gunned down in his Stadelheim prison cell and many fell prey to the shooting squads the length and breadth of Germany as old scores were finally settled. On 20 July 1934, Hitler thanked the SS for their special services on the 30 June and ordered that the SS was henceforth an independent organization in the NSDAP, no longer subordinate to the SA-Stabschef. Himmler was affirmed as Reichsführer-SS, only answerable to the Supreme SS-Führer, Adolf Hitler himself. He was also created a Reichsleiter of the NSDAP.

Another page opened in Himmler's life when on 27 July 1934 he declared that he had identified Wewelsburg Castle in Westphalia as the spiritual home of the SS. The triangular three turreted building stood atop a hill overlooking the valley below. Himmler ordered renovations to the existing building and fantastic plans were drawn up to redevelop the whole area as a centre for the SS. The village of Wewelsburg was surrounded by ancient diggings of pagan sites and on Himmler's instigation local archaeological sites were developed within the SS framework. The unusual rock formation nearby, known as the Externsteine, had been identified as an exceptionally interesting site because of the pagan altar and carvings.

At the Wewelsburg Castle Himmler installed a Burghauptmann and created a SS school. In the north tower a room for special meetings of his SS-Gruppenführer and SS-Obergruppenführer was commissioned, with a crypt below where twelve of his closest Gruppenführer and Obergruppenführer would be buried in a circle around an altar. A guestroom for Hitler was also prepared, but it was never used by him. In support of Himmler's beliefs and interest in ancestry, he founded the Ahnenerbe Society on 1 July 1935. Himmler was at an advantage with his agricultural and farming background when dealing with the NSDAP doctrine of 'blood and soil.' Richard Walther Darré was chief of the SS-Race and Settlement Central Office and was also the Reich Farmers' Leader, subsequently being appointed by Hitler as Reich Minister for Food and Agriculture. Darré has often been referred to as the original 'Green' campaigner with ideals far in advance of his time.

[*Himmler's movements from 1935 onwards are mostly taken from available diaries and are therefore more comprehensively recorded in more detail where the information is available.*]

Over Christmas 1934 and the New Year 1935, the Himmlers played hosts to the Darré couple at Gmund where they were joined on 1 January 1935 by Johannes Johst and on 2 January by the Lorenz family. Himmler made a visit to the Berghof on 3 January for a 4 p.m. meeting with Hitler. By 12 January, Himmler was back in Berlin and he found time on 13 January to visit his young brother, Ernst, for a midday meal. Back into his routine at Prinz Albrecht Strasse, Himmler held a meeting with Admiral Canaris on 14 January. He attended a wedding in Rosenheim on 26 January and travelled on to Garmisch to attend the SS skiing tournament. On 29 January, he was in Berlin, but was feeling ill and did not attend his office until 4 February. He carried out an inspection tour on 9 February in Weissenfels and then spent the evening with Heydrich.

Himmler's usual round of office work, meetings and inspection tours are reflected in his 1935 diary. Mainly staying in Berlin during February and March, he paid visits to various towns and SS facilities including Sachsenburg concentration camp on 16 February and Wewelsburg and the Externsteine on 8 March. He returned to Gmund on the last day of March where he received visits from Oswald Pohl, Gebhard Himmler and his parents on 5 April. Himmler attended the wedding of Arthur Greiser in Berlin on 9 April and the lavish wedding of Hermann and Emmy Göring at the Berliner Dom on 10 April 1935. That evening he flew to Munich and drove on to Gmund. On 12 April there was a Gauleiter conference in Munich followed by a Reichsleiter conference which demanded his attendance. The majority of time during this period, Himmler remained at Gmund and enjoyed some hunting when not receiving and entertaining guests.

On 29 April 1935, Himmler attended the marriage of Hans Adolf Prützmann to Christa von Boddien in Leissienen before visiting the Greisers in Danzig. He returned to Berlin the following day. On 1 May the first May Festival was celebrated and he had a long meeting with Hitler at the Reich Chancellery. Himmler was unwell for the next few days and received the treatment of a head massage daily at his office. He visited Wewelsburg and the Externsteine again from 12 to 13 May. On 17 May, he returned to Gmund, but first visited his parents' apartment in Munich to celebrate his father's 70th birthday. The next day his parents came to Gmund. Back in Berlin on 21 May, Himmler called on Therese Wendler, the mother of Richard Wendler, the later SS-Gruppenführer and Governor of Krakow and the brother of Gebhard Himmler's wife Mathilde. After leaving, he headed for the Reichstag where Hitler delivered a speech. Himmler hosted an evening meal at his home on 22 May attended by Admiral Canaris and Reinhard Heydrich, two old naval colleagues and now intelligence service rivals. He took Marga to Wewelsburg on 25 May for a rare visit by her and they stayed overnight in his suite at the castle.

In June Himmler returned to Gmund where he received Sepp Dietrich, Fritz Weitzel and Kurt Daluege on the 12th. The Reichsführer attended a SS leaders' meeting in Lötzen on 15 and 16 June and slept at Schloss Finkenstein, the eighteenth-century castle used by Emperor Napoleon Bonaparte as a love nest in 1807 for his liaison with Maria Walewska.

Himmler attended an inauguration in Verden on 21 June and then visited Heydrich on 22 June 1935 for the Summer Solstice and topping out ceremony on Heydrich's newly built summer home near Burg on the Baltic island of Fehmarn. He returned to Berlin on 24 June and the next day he was appointed as a State Councillor. On 29 June, Himmler carried out an inspection at the Braunschweig SS officer cadet school before travelling once more to Wewelsburg where he attended a double SS wedding on 1 July as guest of honour.

July 1935 passed without notable incident, Himmler attending to his duties as normal and commuting between Berlin and Gmund. In the middle of the month he spent several days at Apfeldorf. He visited the SS officer cadet school at Bad Tölz on 29 July. There are no entries in Himmler's diary for the first seventeen days of August 1935, but he was at Gmund on 18 August and interestingly his diary notes his efforts for the Reich Sports Badge on 22 August, followed by a pack march on 24 August. Once again, no entries appear for the period 25 August—2 October. This period witnessed the introduction of the Nuremberg Race Laws at the Reichsparteitage from 10 September—16 September 1935.

THREE

The Spectre of Racial Purity

The Laws for the Protection of German Blood and German Honour (5 September 1935.)

Moved by the understanding that the purity of German blood is essential to the further existence of the German people, and inspired by the uncompromising determination to safeguard the future of the German nation, the Reichstag has unanimously resolved upon the following law, which is promulgated herewith:

Section 1
Marriages between Jews and citizens (German: Staatsangehörige) of German or kindred blood are forbidden. Marriages concluded in defiance of this law are void, even if, for the purpose of evading this law, they were concluded abroad.

1. Proceedings for annulment may be initiated only by the Public Prosecutor.

Section 2
Extramarital sexual intercourse between Jews and subjects of the state of Germany or related blood is forbidden. [*This was termed race defilement.*]

Section 3
Jews will not be permitted to employ female citizens under the age of 35, of German or kindred blood, as domestic workers.

Section 4
Jews are forbidden to display the Reich and national flag or the national colours.
1. On the other hand they are permitted to display the Jewish colours. The exercise of this right is protected by the State.

Section 5
1. A person who acts contrary to the prohibition of Section 1 will be punished with hard labour.
2. A person who acts contrary to the prohibition of Section 2 will be punished with imprisonment or with hard labour.
3. A person who acts contrary to the provisions of Sections 3 or 4 will be punished with imprisonment up to a year and with a fine, or with one of these penalties.

Section 6
The Reich Minister of the Interior in agreement with the Deputy Führer and the Reich Minister of Justice will issue the legal and administrative regulations required for the enforcement and supplementing of this law.

Section 7
The law will become effective on the day after its promulgation; Section 3, however, not until 1 January 1936.

October 1935 was a mobile month for the Reichsführer-SS and he was able to take part in a number of hunting sessions. Hunting was an important method of relaxation for Himmler and he carried on with this hobby throughout his term as Reichsführer-SS and even into the war years. Hunting was a way of life to most rural Bavarians and Himmler was no exception. He gained a great deal of relaxation and pleasure from the sport and subsequently had his own hunting lodge at Valepp, south-east of Tegernsee, which he used during the war and often entertained guests there. On 12 October 1935, Himmler went hunting with Herbert Backe, Hermann Reischle and Wilhelm Meinberg, all from the SS Race Central Office. Himmler had earlier held a meeting between Walther Darré, Karl Wolff and Karl Maria Wiligut-Weisthor on 9 October in Berlin and the hunting expedition may have been an opportunity to discuss racial issues. On 30 October Himmler was Göring's guest at Schorfheide, the area north of Berlin requisitioned by the Reichsmarschall for his hunting pleasure. Wiligut was Himmler's expert advisor in the occult and pagan customs and Himmler was extremely interested in his field of expertise around this time.

On 12 December 1935, Himmler founded Lebensborn and ordered that all SS men must contribute financially. He believed in procreation and in fact ordered his SS men to reproduce for the good of the Aryan race. The Lebensborn homes were introduced with the intention of raising the birth rate of Aryan children from extramarital relations of racially pure and healthy parents on the basis of Nazi racial hygiene and health ideology.

Himmler attended the Beer Hall Putsch celebrations in Munich in November 1935 after another hunting excursion in Braunschweig and a visit to the barracks of SS-Regiment 'Deutschland' in Dachau on 7 November. He held a special meeting for all SS-Gruppenführer in Munich on 8 November and then travelled to Berlin where he stayed for a week. Back at Wewelsburg from 17 November to 19 November, he entertained Bormann, Buch, Darré, Reischle, Backe and Meinberg at his Westphalian castle retreat.

Himmler's diary records that he was ill in Berlin on 10 December and that he was confined to his house until 12 December. On 13 December 1935, he attended the wedding of his personal advisor Dr Rudolf Brandt and the next day he returned to Gmund where he stayed for the remainder of the year 1935.

The new year of 1936 began as a relatively quiet period for Himmler. His SS waged a political war against the Church and freemasonry, both seen as threats to the new Germany. Heydrich's SD led the way and was even tasked with investigating witchcraft. On 7 March Hitler re-occupied the demilitarised Rhineland in breach of the Versailles Treaty of 1919. 1936 was also the year of the XI Olympiad held in Berlin, a propaganda coup for the Nazi regime and the year marked the start of the Spanish civil war which Hitler used as a testing ground for some of his rebuilt Wehrmacht, particularly Göring's Luftwaffe .

On 17 June 1936, Himmler was appointed Reichsführer-SS and Chief of the German Police as State Secretary in the Reich Ministry of the Interior. By gaining command of the German police, he achieved the steps necessary to implement his master plan of a 'police state.' He also introduced the Julleuchter, a ceramic candle lamp of an ancient Germanic design that had been brought to Himmler's attention by Professor Hermann Wirth. This Julleuchter was manufactured at the new SS-Allach Porcelain Factory and was classified as an award. Similar to the SS-Totenkopfring and the SS Honour Sword, the Julleuchter was accompanied with a citation. In a speech to SS-Gruppenführer on 8 November 1936, the Reichsführer-SS made it clear that the primary requirement for bestowal of the Julleuchter was that the recipient must be married. He intended that the Julleuchter itself would be utilised by the SS family during certain festivities.

2 July 1936 marked the one thousandth anniversary of the death by cerebral stroke of the Germanic King Heinrich I in AD 936. King Heinrich, popularly known as Henry the Fowler, was looked upon by National Socialists as a founding father of the modern German nation and the original pioneer of Lebensraum in the east. A popular myth of today is that Himmler saw himself as the reincarnation of King Heinrich. Himmler held a ritual torch lit anniversary celebration at the tomb of the Saxon King in the Church of St Servatii in Quedlinburg accompanied by the chief of Anenherbe, Wolfram Sievers, plus several high ranking SS officers and the local Gauleiter, Rudolf Jordan. Himmler placed a wreath on the vacant tombs of King Heinrich and his wife Mathilde before addressing the dignitaries gathered in the church crypt. Nordland Verlag produced a printed illustrated pamphlet of Himmler's speech to mark the occasion. Himmler commissioned extensive archaeology work at the church and ordered that a thorough search be

conducted for the true remains of the dead king which had been removed from the tomb, but they were never found. Church literature of today simply states that the SS misused the church building.

Himmler's beliefs in pagan rituals encouraged him to leave the Catholic Church on 9 October 1936, henceforth declaring himself a 'God believer.' By 1936 the idea of a new religious order was becoming firmly entrenched within the SS and many SS members were withdrawing from the established church. Himmler was sensible enough to realise that the process would need to be a slow evolution and that many of the older generation would never change their religious convictions. That said, it would certainly appear from the number of Himmler's most senior leaders that withdrew from the church throughout 1936 and 1937, that pressure must have been applied within this group.

On 29 October 1936, Gebhard Himmler senior died of pancreatic cancer in Munich. His funeral two days later was attended by a phalanx of senior SS officers and NSDAP officials. Himmler's ever increasing responsibilities meant that his visits home became fewer and a great strain was placed on his marriage. The Himmler couple had purchased a house, 'Lindenfycht' near Gmund, on the shores of the Tegernsee and Marga and Gudrun lived here for most of the time. The Himmlers had added a young boy, Gerhard, the son of deceased SS-Scharführer Kurt von der Ahe to their family by the adoption process, but he developed into a rather unruly boy whose school performance left a lot to be desired. Apparently he joined the SS as a young recruit in 1945, but Himmler mainly ignored him and he became estranged from the family. Himmler remained a loving father to Gudrun, but his relationship with Marga grew distant and although they remained polite and friendly, their marriage was at an end in all but the law.

There were strong, but unconfirmed rumours that Himmler had a passionate affair with the Munich concert singer, Karoline Diehl. She later married Dr Sigmund Rascher, a Luftwaffe medical doctor who worked for a period at the Dachau Concentration Camp and who is infamous for his high altitude and low temperature medical experiments on inmates.

Hedwig Potthast was born in Cologne on 6 February 1912, the daughter of a merchant. She attended school in Trier and subsequently studied at the Economic Institute for Interpreters in Mannheim where she graduated in 1933. She found employment as a government clerk in Koblenz and worked there until the autumn of 1935 when she applied for a transfer to another post where she could use her knowledge of English. She took a position in the media office at the Secret State Police building in Prinz-Albrecht-Strasse in Berlin. Still unable to use her language skills, she requested another transfer or termination of her employment, but she was told that she would not be given permission to resign and in January 1936 was offered a position as one of Himmler's secretaries. She accepted and soon became his principal private secretary.

Hedwig was twelve years younger than Himmler; slim, attractive and possessing an unassuming but very amenable personality. Everyone liked her and she became known by her pet name of 'Häschen' around the office and among the close circle of the Reichsführer. When interrogated post-war, she maintained that she supervised Himmler's Personal Chancellery and was in no way concerned with his SS activities. Himmler and Hedwig formed a close attachment which grew into a deep love affair. Although Himmler refused to divorce Marga, Hedwig left her job in 1941 in order to set up home as his kept, but devoted mistress. He provided her with an apartment in Berlin-Steglitz at Bismarckstrasse 47c and he also obtained a cash advance from Bormann to build a house near the Königsee in Bavaria, Haus Schneewinkellehen. Hedwig bore Himmler two children: Helge, on 5 February 1942 and Nanette Dorothea on 3 June 1944. After the war, Hedwig shunned publicity and died in 1997.

From 27 February 1937 until 9 March 1937, German criminal police officials carried out a mass round up on Himmler's orders of around 2,000 convicted criminals and incarcerated them in concentration camps. This was the first time that non-political prisoners were sent to concentration camps in large numbers. On 15 July 1937, the concentration camp at Buchenwald was opened near Weimar.

On 13 November 1937, Himmler created the role of Higher SS and Police Leader (HSSPF) based upon existing military districts [*Wehrkreise*.] With direct responsibility to the Reichsführer-SS, this move consolidated his power over each police district and he further increased his powers by a decree issued on 14 December 1937 suppressing criminal activities. The directive gave wide sweeping powers to police for the round up of habitual criminals, persons gaining a living from crime and those guilty of behaviour deemed as 'asocial.' No specific crime had to be identified and Gypsies were included in this category.

As RFSS and Chief of the German Police, Himmler was now in a position to represent Germany at high level international conferences. Along with Kurt Daluege, Reinhard Heydrich and Karl Wolff he travelled to Rome in October 1937 to attend the 12th anniversary celebrations for the founding of the Italian Police Corps and on 18 October he was received by Benito Mussolini who may have invited Himmler and his wife for a holiday, as the pair began a sightseeing trip in Rome on 14 November 1937, having travelled there by train. They moved on to Naples on 17 November and Marga noted in her diary that she was suffering from an upset stomach. Sufficiently recovered, she joined Heinrich the following day on a visit to both Pompeii and Herculaneum. On 19 November, Marga joined Eugen Dollmann who was acting as their interpreter to visit the Villa La Floridiana and the old town of Naples before being joined by her husband for a climb to the summit of Mount Versuvius. In the afternoon, the party drove to Cosenza, arriving late at night.

The next day they drove to Giovanni and Himmler's car suffered a mechanical fault *en route* which had to be repaired. Their journey continued on 20 November and they crossed by ferry to Sicily, finally arriving in Taormina where they were to stay for several days. They relaxed swimming, playing tennis, sightseeing and playing cards (doppelkopf.) The party was joined by Dr Rudolf Brandt on 27 November and it appears that the weather was not kind to them. They left Taormina on 2 December and flew to Libya on 4 December after visits to Palermo, Catania and Malta. Their trip included a visit to a desert oasis at Sadance. On 7 December, the Himmlers saw a mosque and the Jewish quarters which Marga noted as '... *horrendously dirty and which stink. The Arabs are much, much cleaner. ...*'

The couple returned to Rome via Naples and both Heinrich and Marga suffered from an apparent bout of food poisoning, Marga confined to the train salon for a whole day with stomach cramps and vomiting. They returned to Berlin on 14 December and then headed for Munich by train on 17 December to spend Christmas 1937 at Gmund. Marga notes in her diary for 31 December 1937:

> Now the year has ended. How much grief and worries it had brought, but for H. [*Heinrich*] also a lot of recognition, advancement and honours. Our beautiful trip was an outstanding event. We want to spend New Years night with the Oswalds. All five of them were here. The boys left, but Herr and Frau Oswald stayed until Monday morning.

On 5 January 1938, the Himmlers entertained the von Tschammer und Osten couple, the von Ebersteins and von Reichenaus at Haus Lindenfycht. Himmler also paid a visit to the Berghof. By 10 January, they were back at their house in Berlin where renovation work was being carried out. Marga mentions that in January 1938 her husband was very busy, often working late into the small hours and that he had many worries. She wrote on 26 January:

> ... H. has many worries and even more work. Poor Blomberg. I feel sorry for him.

Marga's note referred to the Blomberg affair. The Minister for War, Generalfeldmarschall Werner von Blomberg, was a widower with five children when on 12 January 1938 he married a typist, Erna Gruhn, with both Hitler and Göring acting as witnesses at the wedding. Shortly after, some obscene pornographic photo postcards were handed to Kurt Müller, head of the Kripo Identification Bureau and after some digging in the files, he discovered that the woman in the photographs was none other than the War Minister's new wife. She was photographed in erotic positions with a man who was discovered to be a Jew. Müller reported his findings to the head of the Reich Criminal Police, Arthur Nebe. On being given the news, Nebe exclaimed, 'Good God Müller, this woman has kissed the Führer's hand!' The information was passed to Wolf-Heinrich Graf von Helldorf, the Police President of Berlin, who in turn informed General Keitel and it eventually reached the ears of Göring who desired the post of Reich Minister for War and saw this as an opportunity to oust his rival. He advised Hitler and erroneously told him that Erna von Blomberg was a prostitute. When informed of the crisis, the unsuspecting von Blomberg refused to leave his wife or even criticise her and as a result, on 27 January 1938, he was forced to resign as Reich Minister for War.

The young Gerhard von der Ahe was already proving to be a problem child and Himmler was not happy with his behaviour. On 30 January, Marga notes:

> ... Püppi [*Gudrun*] tries very hard and studies a lot. Gerhard behaves very badly; he lies, steals and plays truant from school. I don't know what to say. H. is very unhappy about this. We told his mother when she was here. Gerhard was not nice to her.

At the beginning of February, Marga noticed her husband was very nervous. Himmler had been heavily implicated in the failed plot to discredit the head of the army, Generaloberst von Fritsch when accusations of his homosexuality were revealed to be false and contrived. For a while, Himmler's position was extremely tenuous, but he survived Hitler's reshuffle which appointed von Ribbentrop as Foreign Minister and Hitler himself as supreme commander of the Wehrmacht. The post of War Minister, so coveted by Göring, was abolished.

March 1938 saw Hitler seize control of Austria and Himmler and Heydrich arrived in Vienna on 13 March ahead of their Führer. Marga had packed her husband's field grey uniform and after this date, he was less often seen in his black Allgemeine-SS uniform, abandoning it totally after the outbreak of war. The Austrian police chiefs soon witnessed what the SS partnership meant for them. Those considered unreliable were quickly replaced with loyal SS men and those deemed complicit in the arrest and execution of the SS men responsible for the murder of Chancellor Dollfuss in July 1934 were imprisoned and executed.

Himmler was kept busy by events and his family life suffered. He was away for many days at a time and Marga was left to entertain, manage the household staff and bring up the two children. Gudrun appears to have been a model child, but Gerhard continued to prove a disappointment, stealing and lying. His mother stated she did not want him back, but that she still wanted to benefit from the financial arrangement with the Himmlers. Marga constantly complains in her diary that she was dissatisfied with the house servants, regularly changing them.

On 3 May 1938, the new concentration camp at Flossenbürg, north-east of Nuremberg, was opened by the camp inspectorate.

The Himmlers were once again in Rome for the visit of Hitler to Mussolini in early May 1938. Marga became quite friendly with Annelise von Ribbentrop and the women went sightseeing while their husbands carried out official duties. On their return to Berlin, Marga was again unwell and called on the services of the Himmler family doctor, Dr Michael Setzkorn.

Marga's diary indicates that her husband was at Wewelsburg on 19 May 1938 and that she was visited by her sisters-in-law Hilde and Paula Himmler on 24 May. She also mentions a visit to Dachau in the entry for 5 June before returning to Gmund where building work on the house was almost complete. Marga also alludes to her husband being at home and going hunting in the evenings. By 26 June, she was complaining that Himmler was never at home and did not treat her feelings with any importance. She stated on 3 July 1938:

> I have been married for ten years today. H. is not here, but called. In spite of my happiness I have had to deprive myself of much. H. is almost never home and is interested only in his work. ...

Yet another concentration camp opened its gates on 8 August 1938 at Mauthausen near Linz in Austria. This was the first camp opened outside the pre-Anschluss borders and was sited at a granite quarry works. The material from here would benefit the business enterprise of the SS.

On 17 August 1938, Hitler formally recognized the role of the SS-Verfügungstruppe in a decree which stated that the SS-VT was a '... standby troop in war and peace ... for special political tasks of the Reichsführer-SS and Chief of the German Police and which I reserve the right to deploy for each individual case, or for mobile deployment in the context of the framework of the mobilized army.' This decree was the birth of what became known as the Waffen-SS.

Adolf Eichmann was a specialist in Jewish affairs in Department IVB of the SS-Sicherheitsdienst (SD.) He was tasked by Heydrich to organise the emigration of Jews from Austria and on 20 August 1938, Eichmann was posted to the newly opened the Central Office for Jewish Emigration in Vienna. The local Gauleiter, Josef Bürckel, announced:

> To all offices of the Party and State in Austria
>
> Undesirable interruptions and delays have occurred in the emigration of Jews; in addition, the question of Jewish emigration has been dealt with inefficiently by certain offices.
>
> To assist and expedite arrangements for the emigration of Jews from Austria a Central Office for Jewish Emigration has therefore been set up in Vienna IV, at Prinz Eugen Strasse 22.
>
> The Central Office will be responsible for dealing with the following matters, in cooperation with the Government Offices concerned:
>
> 1. The creation of opportunities for emigration through negotiations for entry permits with the competent German and other emigration organizations.

2. Obtaining the foreign currency required for emigration.
3. Establishment and supervision of professional re-training centres.
4. Cooperation with travel agencies and shipping companies to ensure the technical arrangements for emigration.
5. Supervision of Jewish political and other emigration associations with regard to their attitude concerning emigration.
6. The issuing of guidelines and continuous contacts with all offices connected with the emigration of Jews from Austria. ...

All Party offices and other authorities are instructed to pass on all applications for emigration to the Central Office for Jewish Emigration immediately and without taking action of their own for the time being, and to send all Jews anxious to emigrate to the above office. Jews who wish to emigrate are in future to apply only to the Central Office for Jewish Emigration. This office will control further procedures and, in particular, obtain the permits required for emigration from the competent office, and supervise the final emigration.

The Regulation applies, for the time being, to the Gau Vienna and Lower Danube. The procedures in other areas are regulated by the Central Office for Jewish Emigration in consultation with the local Gauleiters.

A central office for Jewish Planning in conjunction with the Central Office for Jewish Emigration is definitely still under consideration.

I entrust the general direction of these Central Offices to the SD-Führer of the SS-Section Upper Danube and Inspector of the Security Police, SS-Standartenführer Governmental Director Dr Stahlecker. He is herewith invested with the necessary powers to carry out his commission. In particular, he is entitled to order the transfer of officials of the Authorities concerned with emigration to the Central Office for Jewish Emigration.

Events on the world stage began to gain momentum and British Prime Minister Neville Chamberlain attended a meeting with Hitler in Bad Godesberg on 22 September 1938 where Hitler demanded the annexation of the German Sudetenland from Czechoslovakia. A further meeting was held in the Führerbau in Munich between Germany, France, Great Britain and Italy. Czechoslovakia was not invited. Agreement was reached in the early hours of 30 September 1938 and German troops crossed the frontier and occupied the Sudeten territory on 1 October. Hitler annexed the Sudetenland after the Munich Agreement and immediately toured his new province accompanied by Himmler. The German speaking population greeted Hitler with rapturous cheering and flag waving.

At the end of October 1938, Himmler visited Italy and Marga joined him in Verona on 28 October. Unknown to the Himmlers, a major event was about to unfold in Germany, triggered by the actions of a young Jew in Paris.

In August 1938, the German government announced that all resident permits for foreign visitors would be revoked and new applications were necessary. With Himmler's agreement, no foreign Jews would be given new permits and the Polish authorities declared that it would not recognise Jews of Polish origin after 31 October 1938. On 26 October, Himmler ordered the Gestapo to arrest all Jews of Polish origin and to expel them immediately to beat the Polish deadline. Thousands of Polish Jews were herded onto trains and dumped at the border. Among them were the parents of Herschel Grynszpan, a young Jew living in Paris. When the Polish authorities refused to accept the Jews, they were left stranded with no belongings and nowhere to go. Young Grynszpan was angry and on the morning of 7 November he entered the German embassy in Paris with a revolver and with the intention of shooting the German ambassador. He was shown into the office of the unfortunate twenty-nine years old Third Secretary, Ernst vom Rath, whom he shot without warning, screaming that he represented 12,000 persecuted Jews. Grynszpan was immediately arrested and vom Rath died of his wounds two days later.

This event was used as a platform for anti-Semite violent actions throughout Germany, triggered by a speech by Dr Goebbels at the Munich Putsch celebrations. Untold damage was carried out at Jewish owned business premises and synagogues with glass littering the walkways from broken shop windows. The progrom became known as Krystallnacht [*night of broken glass.*] Hundreds of Jews were arrested and detained without charge and many lost their lives.

Himmler accompanied his wife to Salzburg on or about 9 November after the Putsch celebrations in Munich. He was officially on vacation and he wanted to do something different every day, so he included visits to the Grossglockner Mountain, the Rehrl farm in Fridolfing and even did some hunting on the Krepps Estate.

Marga noted in her diary that Himmler's constant absence from home was having a detrimental effect on their daughter. By mid-December, Marga was wistfully dreaming of her recent days with her husband in Nuremberg on 7 December and a visit to Quedlinburg on 8 December.

The oft forgotten element of what later became known as 'the holocaust' was the SS policy towards the Gypsy and Sinti people. On 8 December 1938, Himmler issued a decree for combating the Gypsy problem, declaring the Gypsies as an inferior race and tasking the criminal police with opening a database and identifying every Gypsy residing in the Greater Reich. This was the first step towards eradicating Romany travellers in the German sphere of influence.

FOUR

Expansionist Policies

Himmler spent Christmas 1938 and saw in the New Year 1939 at Gmund. He took time out on 2 January to build a snowman with his daughter in the grounds of Haus Lindenfycht after a quick visit by Oswald Pohl. The following day he received Fritz Kranefuss in the morning and then paid a visit on the von Schirachs. The tenth anniversary of Himmler's appointment as Reichsführer-SS was celebrated on 6 January and he drove to the Berghof to receive the congratulations of Hitler.

Himmler returned to Berlin on 8 January. The following few days were marked by visits and meetings with von Ribbentrop, SS-Obergruppenführer August Heissmeyer and SS-Gruppenführer Walter Schmitt. Himmler also called on Göring on 12 January to express his best wishes for the New Year.

On 14 January, Himmler visited Braunschweig [*Brunswick*] and stayed overnight making two speeches, first to police officers and then to SS officers. Leaving Braunschweig, Himmler motored to Wewelsburg where he stayed the next four days in the company of Reich Minister Walther Darré, State Secretary Herbert Backe and Gauleiter Josef Terboven. Himmler flew to Munich on 19 January to visit his mother on her birthday and then flew on to Berlin. He held a Gruppenführer conference in Berlin from 23 to 25 January, spending the evening of 24 January as the special guest of the SS-Leibstandarte 'Adolf Hitler.'

On the occasion of the 'Day of German Police' on 28 January 1939, Himmler made an uncharacteristic public comment concerning the concentration camp system. His motive was to counter the unfavourable stories that had been circulating and he declared that the withdrawal of freedom was a strict and sharp measure. The treatment was strict, but fair and provided inmates with the opportunity to exercise formal hygiene guidelines with a healthy meal regime whilst providing tuition in new skills and craftwork. The atmosphere sounded ideal, but was far from the truth. At the Reichstag meeting on 30 January, Hitler made his famous speech referring to his prophetic warning to the Jews.

Marga Himmler was an in-patient at the Hohenlychen clinic from 31 January

1939 being treated by Professor Dr Gebhardt. Frau Annelise von Ribbentrop was also a patient at the time and underwent a frontal lobotomy procedure. Marga records in her diary that she was able to look through Frau von Ribbentrop's medical notes which astonished her. On 2 February, Himmler came down with a bout of influenza and was confined to his bed for three days, receiving a visit from Dr Brustmann on 3 February. Marga states that Gudrun was also ill. Himmler felt well enough to visit Marga at Hohenlychen on 5 February and returned to his office in Prinz Albrecht Strasse on 7 February. He was soon on the move again, visiting Weimar, Breslau, Dresden and staying with SS-Obergruppenführer Josias Erbprinz zu Waldeck und Pyrmont at Schloss Arolsen where he was able to hunt. On 14 February, the Reichsführer attended the launch of the battleship *Bismarck* in Hamburg.

On 17 February 1939, Himmler flew to Warsaw as a guest of the Polish police. He stayed for several days and included an extended hunting trip at Bialowicze. The visit went well and provided excellent opportunities for both police forces to exchange ideas. There was no hint of the coming disaster.

Himmler returned to Berlin on 22 February, but flew to Munich the following day in time for the celebrations to mark the founding of the NSDAP. From Munich he flew to Stuttgart on 26 February and then drove on to Wiesbaden, staying overnight before a flight back to Berlin on 27 February. On 1 March, he attended a diplomatic reception at the Reich Chancellery and was a guest of Heydrich for the evening of 6 March to celebrate his thirty-fifth birthday the next day.

In March 1939, Hitler occupied the remainder of Czechoslovakia and once again visited his conquered territory. Himmler and Heydrich accompanied him to Prague, but the welcome was rather more subdued than the reception in the Sudetenland. This was the first German occupation of a territory populated with a non-German majority. Himmler was suffering from catarrh at the time. He was in the newly created Protectorate of Bohemia-Moravia from 15 March to 17 March, before travelling to Vienna and staying at the Hotel Imperial. On 18 March, Himmler visited the concentration camp at Mauthausen near Linz. His duties kept him away from Gmund throughout March and again Marga complained bitterly of his continual absence.

Himmler was at the launch of the battleship *Tirpitz* in Wilhelmshaven on 1 April 1939 and he was able to visit Gmund on 2 April where he stayed until 17 April, playing tennis, cards and visiting friends, family and colleagues. During this period, he also had numerous visits from Felix Kersten, indicating that he was suffering from his abdominal cramps. In the evening of 19 April, he joined Hitler at the Reich Chancellery to celebrate the inauguration of new SS-Untersturmführer to mark Hitler's fiftieth birthday the following day. Himmler was present next to Hitler in the Wilhelmstrasse on 20 April to take the salute from the SS and other troops marking the birthday with a march past.

On 23 April 1939, he flew to Munich and held a meeting with Professor Walter Wüst and on 25 April he visited Dachau with senior Wehrmacht officers and then visited the SS-Standarte 'Deutschland.' He flew to Berlin on 26 April and stayed there until a visit to Dessau on 5 May. This period was busy with diplomatic functions and Marga notes that her husband was suffering from toothache. She continuously complained of staff problems and also recorded that Gudrun was suffering from worms. One of her close friends around this period was the wife of SS-Brigadeführer Wilhelm Graf von Wedel, the Police President of Potsdam. Von Wedel's health had not been good of late and Himmler, who liked the count, was concerned. The lonely Marga often spent time with the count's wife and the families socialised. Graf von Wedel finally succumbed to his lengthy illness and died on 19 October 1939 in Potsdam.

On 6 May 1939, Himmler visited his old schoolfriend Falk Zipperer in Bad Godesberg and stayed overnight. He visited the NSDAP political education facility at Vogelsang before taking a flight to Kassel on 8 May. From Kassel he drove to Wewelsburg where he stayed until returning to Berlin on 10 May by road. Two days later, he was in Salzburg having flown there to carry out an inspection of the police units. At midday on 13 May, Himmler was aboard Hitler's special train when it departed from Munich for an inspection tour of the west wall defences, he returned to Berlin via Munsterlager on 20 May. During his absence, the concentration camp inspectorate opened a camp for women at Ravensbrück on 15 May.

Himmler participated in foreign diplomacy by lunching with von Ribbentrop and Count Ciano in Berlin on 21 May before spending the evening at the Reich Chancellery. The following day, he took lunch with the Italian ambassador before a meeting with von Ribbentrop that evening.

On 23 May 1939, Himmler attended the state funeral of General of Cavalry Friedrich Graf von der Schulenburg in Potsdam. Schulenberg was a SS-Gruppenführer and was posthumously promoted to SS-Obergruppenführer by Hitler. Himmler also attended the private family burial the next day in Tressow Mecklenburg. On 25 May, SS-Obergruppenführer Kurt Daluege held a naming ceremony in Berlin-Steglitz for his baby son and Himmler was invited. Himmler was in Sabow [*now Zabowo Poland*] from 27 to 30 May visiting his sick father-in-law.

Himmler attended the Reichskriegertag (National War Veterans' Day) in Kassel on 4 June, but immediately flew back to Berlin for the state visit of Prince Paul Prince Regent of Yugoslavia. Himmler was a guest of Göring at Schloss Charlottenburg in the evening. He also attended the parade of the Legion Condor through Berlin on 6 June [*Marga mistakenly records this event as 7 June.*]

On 9 June, Himmler flew to Munich where the next day he held a conference for SS leaders in the main hall of the Deutsches Museum. He was in Nuremberg on 11 June and held another SS leaders' conference at the barracks before visiting the estate of SS-Gruppenführer Wilhelm Freiherr von Holzschuher at Artelshofen near

Nuremberg. Holzschuher had recently been in a power struggle with Gauleiter Fritz Wächtler when allegations of irregularities in the administration of Regensburg were levelled against the Gruppenführer. Himmler did not abandon his man, but he received no further promotions in the SS and his son later testified that his father had participated in the anti-Hitler conspiracy and was in fact arrested by the Gestapo. Von Holzschuher died in 1965.

Himmler next proceeded upon a whistle stop motor tour of the Protectorate from 12 to 14 June 1939 and by 15 June he was a guest of the Görings at Karinhall. On 16 June, he attended a meeting of 'old fighters' in Gelsenkirchen and then appeared briefly in Wewelsburg on 17 June before a ceremony at the war memorial in Essen the same day. He flew from Essen to Quedlinburg on 18 June and visited the Church of Saint Servatii which he records as 'Heinrichsdom,' prior to his return to Berlin. He attended upon Hitler in Munich on 25 June and returned to Berlin that evening by air, totally unaware of an impending problem which would manifest itself the following day.

Marga Himmler was good friends with the wife of SS-Brigadeführer Hermann Freiherr von Schade and she promised her friend that she would speak to Himmler about the possibility of von Schade becoming Police President of Munich. This post was already occupied by SS-Obergruppenführer Karl Freiherr von Eberstein, an old party member and a favourite of Hitler. Himmler and von Eberstein had often had their differences and Himmler decided to replace him on grounds of ill health with von Schade, despite von Eberstein being in excellent health. Himmler told von Eberstein of his plans at the conference in Munich on 9 June. Von Eberstein was incensed, privately telling close colleagues that the police presidency was not within the gift of the Reichsführer-SS, but was a matter for the Reichsminister of the Interior [*Wilhelm Frick*.]

On 26 June, Hitler held a military procession in the Königsplatz in Munich in honour of his Italian allies. He stood on the steps of the Führerbau and watched the parade for which von Schade had been given responsibility. Nearby stood a healthy looking von Eberstein. The parade did not go well and at the conclusion von Schade strolled over to Hitler, gave an awkward salute, turned and walked away. Hitler was furious and demanded to know why such an inept officer had been given a task obviously above his capabilities. When informed of the circumstances, Hitler overruled Himmler and even appointed von Eberstein as a Ministerialdirektor. Von Schade did not get the post and received no further promotions in the SS.

Himmler stayed in Berlin for the remainder of June 1939. On 1 July, he attended the night ceremony in Quedlinburg marking the death of King Heinrich I on 2 July 936. In Hamburg on 2 July, Himmler was present at the state funeral of General Knochenhauer who had died on 28 June. After the funeral, Himmler drove to Kühlungsborn on the Baltic to be with Marga and Gudrun who were holidaying there. He drove back to Berlin on 5 July and was there until 12th July, leaving the city briefly on 11 July to view a new aircraft prototype with Hitler at Jüterbog airfield.

Himmler arrived in Gmund on 12 July and immediately took the opportunity to hunt. He attended the Munich Art Festival from 14 to16 July, but was in Gmund again on 17 July, spending his time hunting at Valepp, playing tennis, cards and swimming. He had two days in Innsbruck on 23 and 24 July and returned to Gmund via Garmisch where he paid a visit to the von Wedels. He remained at Gmund for the first two weeks of August 1939 and this period was a time of relaxation. Gudrun was being tutored at home by Fräulein Görlitzer, a daughter of the Deputy Gauleiter of Berlin. Marga noted at this time that young Gerhard's behaviour had also improved. The Himmlers received a return visit in Gmund by their friends, the von Wedels.

In the background during this period of apparent idyll, Hitler was planning to invade Poland ostensibly in order to recover Danzig and the Danzig Corridor. Himmler paid quick visits to von Ribbentrop's castle retreat at Fuschl on 7 and 9 August. Himmler's diary has no entries from 12 to17 August 1939, but we know from Marga's diary that her husband was away on a special mission for the Führer on 13 August and that her father died on 15 August. Himmler was in attendance for a special secret meeting at the Berghof on 16 August which also involved Heydrich, Müller and Wolff at which Hitler divulged his plans to attack Poland within days.

Marga also noted in her diary on 17 August that the propaganda cry of *'ein Volk! ein Reich! ein Führer!'* was heard for the first time and she records that it was Himmler who had first thought of the phrase. On 19 August, Himmler attended the funeral of his father-in-law in Stargard. In Berlin the following day, he accompanied Marga to the railway station to board her train to Munich. She was headed for Gmund.

On 21 August, Himmler flew south to visit Hitler again at the Berghof and his diary logs that he flew back to Berlin the same day and remained there until the first week of September. However, there is some confusion around this as Karl Wolff testified at Nuremberg after the war that he was present with Himmler at the Berghof on 22 August 1939 when Hitler made his famous speech to his Wehrmacht commanders. Did he confuse this meeting with the meeting at the Berghof on 16 August? Civilian attire was ordered by Hitler for both meetings to maintain an air of secrecy.

That Hitler desired war against Poland is borne out by his despatch of von Ribbentrop to Moscow to sign a non-aggression pact with Molotov, thus securing freedom of movement against Poland without any intervention from Moscow. The wording of his speech at the Berghof also confirms his intentions:

I have called you together to give you a picture of the political situation, in order that you may have some insight into the individual factors on which I have based my decision to act and in order to strengthen your confidence.

After this we shall discuss military details.

It was clear to me that a conflict with Poland had to come sooner or later. I had already made this decision in the spring, but I thought that I would first turn against the West in a few years, and only after that against the East. But the sequence of these things cannot be fixed. Nor should one close one's eyes to threatening situations. I wanted first of all to establish a tolerable relationship with Poland in order to fight first against the West, but this plan, which appealed to me, could not be executed as fundamental points had changed. It became clear to me that, in the event of a conflict with the West, Poland would attack us. Poland is striving for access to the sea. The further development appeared after the occupation of the Memel Territory and it became clear to me that in certain circumstances a conflict with Poland might come at an inopportune moment. I give as reasons for this conclusion:

First of all two personal factors:

My own personality and that of Mussolini.

Essentially all depends on me, on my existence, because of my political talents. Furthermore, the fact that probably no one will ever again have the trust of the whole German people as I have. There will probably never again in the future be a man with more authority than I have. My existence is therefore a factor of great value, but I can be eliminated at any time by a criminal or a lunatic.

The second personal factor is the Duce. His existence is also decisive. If anything happens to him, Italy's loyalty to the alliance will no longer be certain. The Italian Court is fundamentally opposed to the Duce. Above all, the Court regards the expansion of the empire as an encumbrance. The Duce is the man with the strongest nerves in Italy.

The third personal factor in our favor is Franco. We can ask only for benevolent neutrality from Spain. But this depends on Franco's personality. He guarantees a certain uniformity and stability in the present system in Spain. We must accept the fact that Spain does not as yet have a Fascist party with our internal unity.

The other side presents a negative picture as far as authoritative persons are concerned. There is no outstanding personality in England and France.

It is easy for us to make decisions. We have nothing to lose; we have everything to gain. Because of our restrictions [*Einschränkungen*] our economic situation is such that we can only hold out for a few more years. Göring can confirm this. We have no other choice, we must act. Our opponents will be risking a great deal and can gain only a little. Britain's stake in a war is inconceivably great. Our enemies have leaders who are below the average. No personalities. No masters, no men of action.

Besides the personal factors, the political situation is favorable for us: In the Mediterranean, rivalry between Italy, France and England; in the Far East, tension between Japan and England; in the Middle East, tension which causes alarm in the Mohammedan world.

The English Empire did not emerge stronger from the last war. Nothing was achieved from the maritime point of view. Strife between England and Ireland. The Union of South Africa has become more independent. Concessions have had to be made to India. England is in the utmost peril. Unhealthy industrialization. A British statesman can only view the future with concern.

France's position has also deteriorated, above all in the Mediterranean.

Further factors in our favour are these:

Since Albania, there has been a balance of power in the Balkans. Yugoslavia is infected with the fatal germ of decay because of her internal situation.

Romania has not grown stronger. She is open to attack and vulnerable. She is threatened by Hungary and Bulgaria. Since Kemal's death, Turkey has been ruled by petty minds, unsteady, weak men.

All these favorable circumstances will no longer prevail in two or three years' time. No one knows how much longer I shall live. Therefore, better a conflict now.

The creation of Greater Germany was a great achievement politically, but militarily it was doubtful, since it was achieved by bluff on the part of the political leaders. It is necessary to test the military. If at all possible, not in a general reckoning, but by the accomplishment of individual tasks.

The relationship with Poland has become unbearable. My Polish policy hitherto was contrary to the views of the people. My proposals to Poland [Danzig and the Corridor] were frustrated by England's intervention. Poland changed her tone towards us. A permanent state of tension is intolerable. The power of initiative cannot be allowed to pass to others. The present moment is more favourable than in two or three years' time. An attempt on my life or Mussolini's could change the situation to our disadvantage. One cannot for ever face one another with rifles cocked. One compromise solution suggested to us was that we should change our convictions and make gestures. They talked to us again in the language of Versailles. There was a danger of losing prestige. Now there still is a great probability that the West will not intervene. We must take the risk with ruthless determination. The politician must take a risk just as much as the general. We are faced with the harsh alternatives of striking or of certain annihilation sooner or later. ...

... The following special reasons confirm my view. England and France have undertaken obligations which neither is in a position to fulfil. There is no real rearmament in England, but only propaganda. A great deal of harm was done by many Germans, who were not in agreement with me, saying and writing to English people after the solution of the Czech question: 'The Führer succeeded because you lost your nerve, because you capitulated too soon.' This explains the present propaganda war. The

English speak of a war of nerves. One factor in this war of nerves is to boost the increase of armaments. But what are the real facts about British rearmament? The naval construction program for 1938 has not yet been completed. Only the reserve fleet has been mobilized. Purchase of trawlers. No substantial strengthening of the Navy before 1941 or 1942.

Little has been done on land. England will be able to send at most three divisions to the Continent. A little has been done for the Air Force, but it is only a beginning. Anti-aircraft defence is in its initial stages. At the moment England has only 150 anti-aircraft guns. The new anti-aircraft gun has been produced. There is a shortage of predictors. England is still vulnerable from the air. This can change in two or three years. At the moment the English Air Force has only 130,000 men, France 72,000, Poland 15,000. England does not want the conflict to break out for two or three years.

The following is typical of England. Poland wanted a loan from England for her rearmament. England, however, only granted credits in order to make sure that Poland buys in England, although England cannot make deliveries. This suggests that England does not really want to support Poland. She is not risking eight million pounds in Poland, although she poured five hundred million into China. England's position in the world is very precarious. She will not take any risks.

France is short of men caused by a decline in the birth rate. Little has been done for rearmament. The artillery is obsolete. France did not want to embark on this adventure. The West has only two possibilities for fighting against us:

1. Blockade: It will not be effective because of our autarky and because we have sources of supply in Eastern Europe.
2. Attack in the West from the Maginot line: I consider this impossible.

Another possibility would be the violation of Dutch, Belgian and Swiss neutrality. I have no doubt that all these States, as well as Scandinavia, will defend their neutrality with all available means. England and France will not violate the neutrality of these countries. Thus, in actual fact England cannot help Poland. There still remains an attack on Italy. Military intervention is out of the question. No one is counting on a long war. If Herr von Brauchitsch had told me that I would have replied: 'Then it cannot be done.' It is nonsense to say that England wants to wage a long war.

We will hold our position in the West until we have conquered Poland. We must bear in mind our great production capacity. It is much greater than in 1914–1918.

The enemy had another hope that Russia would become our enemy after the conquest of Poland. The enemy did not reckon with my great strength of purpose. Our enemies are small fry. I saw them in Munich.

I was convinced that Stalin would never accept the English offer. Russia has no interest in preserving Poland, and Stalin knows that it would mean the end of his régime, no matter whether his soldiers emerged from a war victorious or vanquished. Litvinov's replacement was decisive. I brought about the change towards Russia gradually. In connection with the commercial treaty we got into political conversations. Proposal for a non-aggression pact. Then came a comprehensive proposal from Russia. Four days ago I took a special step, which led to Russia replying yesterday that she is prepared to sign. Personal contact with Stalin is established. The day after tomorrow von Ribbentrop will conclude the treaty. Now Poland is in the position in which I wanted her.

We need not be afraid of a blockade. The East will supply us with grain, cattle, coal, lead and zinc. It is a mighty aim, which demands great efforts. I am only afraid that at the last moment some swine or other will yet submit to me a plan for mediation.

The political objective goes further. A start has been made on the destruction of England's hegemony. The way will be open for the soldiers after I have made the political preparations.

Today's announcement of the non-aggression pact with Russia came as a bombshell. [*The pact was not signed until the following day.*] The consequences cannot be foreseen. Stalin also said that this course will benefit both countries. The effect on Poland will be tremendous.

[*Source of English translation: Speech by the Führer to the Commanders in Chief on August 22, 1939, in United States Department of State, Documents on German Foreign Policy: From the Archives of the German Foreign Ministry. Washington, DC: United States Government Printing Office, 1957–1964. Series D (1937–1945), The Last Days of Peace, Volume 7: August 9–September 3, 1939. Document 192, pp. 200–04.*]

[*Source of original German text: Ansprache Hitlers an die Oberbefehlshaber am 22. August 1939 über seine Absicht, Krieg zu führen und seine politischen Vorbereitungen dazu, sowie Voraussagungen über die Haltung anderer europäischer Staaten und den wahrscheinlichen Kriegsverlauf (Beweisstück US-29), in Der Prozess gegen die Hauptkriegsverbrecher vor dem Internationalen Militärgerichtshof. Nürnberg 14. November 1945–1. Oktober 1946. Volume XXVI, Amtlicher Text—Deutsche Ausgabe, Urkunden und anderes Beweismaterial. Nuremberg 1947. Reprint: Munich, Delphin Verlag, 1989. Document 798-PS, pp. 338-44.*]

Molotov and von Ribbentrop signed the non-aggression pact on 23 August 1939 and the die was cast. War was inevitable.

FIVE

Into the Abyss

As history records, Hitler's onslaught against Poland commenced in the early hours of 1 September 1939. As an excuse to open hostilities, Himmler's SS had provided the means and the tools to carry it out. Reinhard Heydrich's SD cohorts faked border incidents, the most successful and well known being at the radio station at Gleiwitz where SS troops disguised as Polish soldiers stormed the radio station, fired shots and transmitted a radio message on local radio in Polish. Before departing, they left at the scene the lifeless body of Franz Honiok, an ethnic German suitably disguised in Polish military dress. Gestapo chief Heinrich Müller had arranged to provide the 'canned goods' as the unfortunate victim was called. Honiok was known to have Polish sympathies and was picked up by the Gestapo in Hohenlieben [*today Lubie, Poland*] on 30 August. Kept in custody until needed, he was drugged and taken to the radio station, laid semi-conscious inside the door of the transmitter building and shot. Hitler made suitable protests and released the swarm of German troops on Poland.

Himmler spent the final days of peace in Berlin, spending much of each day with Hitler and playing his usual game of tennis. There was a flurry of activity at Prinz-Albrecht-Strasse during the night of 31 August 1939 with Himmler remaining in his office all night. The next day Hitler announced the war against Poland to the world in his speech to a rapturous Reichstag meeting in the Kroll Opera House and Himmler was there to hear it. By 3 September it had developed into a European theatre war and with dominions stretching across the globe on every continent, almost the entire world was participating in the conflict.

In the early days of confrontation Himmler was attached to the Army Group North of Generaloberst Fedor von Bock. On 3 September, Himmler left Berlin aboard Sonderzug 'Heinrich' and from the HQ of von Bock, Himmler issued an order via telex to his security troops operating behind the front line in occupied territory, to immediately execute armed Polish insurgents without trial. From this single action it soon became clear to the regular army that Himmler's security troops had been given a 'special task' in the campaign. They were the Einsatzgruppen (Special Action Groups) of the Police and Security Service and their role was clarified on 11 September by the commanding officer of the army, Generaloberst Walther von Brauchitsch, to his Chief of the General Staff, General Franz Halder.

Himmler himself was extremely mobile as a war commander during the first days of the conflict, setting a pattern for his style of leadership. Using Grossborn as a base, he toured the areas of the front through which the German war machine had swept, sometimes accompanying Hitler and some independantly. After several days he was in Ilnau near Oppeln, often using a Fieseler Storch light aircraft for increased mobility. Moving on from Ilnau to Gogolin by air, he also toured Lodz on 13 September and then stayed near Hitler at Karlshorst until 17 September when he was visited by Kurt Daluege and August Heissmeyer. Himmler was soon on the move again, first to Lauenburg, then to Danzig on 19 September and on to Zoppot before returning to Danzig. He returned home to Berlin on 26 September, the Poles already defeated.

Under the umbrella authority of the Reichsführer-SS at a meeting in Berlin Reinhard Heydrich issued orders on 21 September 1939 that Polish Jews must be concentrated in major cities with rail links, all Reich Jews must be transferred to Poland along with all remaining Gypsies and that freight cars were to be used for the purpose. Six days later, Himmler established the Central Office for Reich Security under SS-Gruppenführer Reinhard Heydrich. Known as the Reichssicherheitshauptamt (RSHA) it fused together the security police (Sipo or Gestapo,) the criminal police (Kripo) and the SD. This would be the SS department tasked with the future annihilation of the European Jews and the Gypsies.

On 12 September 1939, Himmler was named as the permanent deputy and representative of Wilhelm Frick in matters of Reich administration and on 7 October he was appointed as Reich Commissioner for the Strengthening of German Nationality (RKF.) The month of October 1939 also saw him take on the role of Reich Commissioner for Resettlement. From 24 October to 28 October, Himmler toured the occupied areas of Poland with Friedrich-Wilhelm Krüger, Karl Wolff and Hanns Johst. Himmler used his position as RKF to order the deportation of Poles and Jews to the territory of the General Government on 30 October, a mass enforced movement of nearly one million people.

Meanwhile Marga Himmler was working with the German Red Cross as a nurse. Gudrun had been packed off to the relative safety of Gmund. Himmler stayed in Berlin for the first ten days of October, only flying briefly to Warsaw on 5 October for the military victory parade. He embarked on an official visit to northern Italy via Innsbruck on 10 October. Back in Berlin on 14 October, he was suffering badly from stomach cramps. He left Berlin on 20 October, bound for Bromberg and Danzig, but he was back in the capital on 22 October and attended the funeral of his family friend Graf Wedel on 23 October. In Bromberg on 20 October, Himmler witnessed the execution of twenty Poles. Apparently it had a profound effect on the Reichsführer-SS, his adjutant Joachim Peiper reporting that it left Himmler almost speechless for days.

The following day, Himmler flew to Posen and began a quick tour of inspection of conquered Polish towns—Lodz, Gnesen, Kalisch, Warsaw, Lublin, Radom, Kielce and finally Krakow, before returning to the Reich capital. From Berlin, Himmler flew to Prague on 30 October and at Beroun he inspected the SS-Verfügungstruppe Division. This was the first of several inspections of SS and Police Divisions he conducted around this time—SS-Polizei Division on 2 November in Wandern, SS-Totenkopf Division on 4 November in Dachau. Felix Kersten attended to his patient in Berlin on 5, 6 and 7 November and travelled with him to Munich on 8 November for the Putsch anniversary celebrations. Himmler was present in the Bürgerbräukeller for Hitler's speech in the evening and also left ahead of schedule when Hitler decided to depart earlier than usual.

Himmler was in Nuremberg *en route* to Berlin when he received the news at 1 a.m. on 9 November that an attempt had been made on the life of the Führer. A solitary carpenter, Georg Elser, acting on his own initiative, had secreted a timed improvised explosive device in the pillar behind the rostrum in the Bürgerbräukeller. He had set the ignition for when Hitler usually wound up his speech, but the device exploded after Hitler had unexpectedly left early, killing eight people, injuring sixty-three and seriously damaging the hall. Elser was subsequently arrested soon after by pure chance, but at a meeting with Himmler in the Reich Chancellery during the evening of 9 November, Hitler was adamant that it had been the work of the British secret service. He ordered Himmler to take necessary steps to find the culprits. Himmler set up a special investigatory commission and two British agents, Sigismund Payne Best and Richard Henry Stevens, were seized during an illegal incident at Venlo in neutral Holland by Heydrich's secret intelligence service, led by Walter Schellenberg. By 15 November, Himmler and Heydrich were able to report personally to Hitler at the Reich Chancellery that all the culprits had been apprehended.

Himmler was omni-present in Berlin for the remainder of November 1939, only leaving for quick inspection tours on 20 November (SS-Totenkopf in Dachau) and 28 November (SS-Polizei in Zielenzig.) December 1939 began largely as November had ended, in Berlin, working at his office in Prinz-Albrecht-Strasse and visiting Hitler at the Reich Chancellery. Himmler flew to Posen and Lodz on 12 and 13 December and was in Berlin in the evening of 13 December for a meeting of the Circle of Friends of the Reichsführer-SS. He was in Rome with Mussolini on 20 and 21 December and returned via Munich, Wiesbaden and Bad Ems where he accompanied Hitler on 23 December at a Christmas dinner provided by the SS-Leibstandarte 'Adolf Hitler.' That evening Himmler returned to Wiesbaden and stayed at the Hotel Nassauer Hof. He also found time to call on the family of SS-Brigadeführer Max Thomas. Himmler was in his Berlin office by 5 p.m. on 24 December and spent Christmas and the New Year at Dohnenstieg 10 in Berlin-Dahlem, the large imposing house he shared in the capital with Marga and Gudrun.

Himmler conducted an inspection of Ravensbrück concentration camp on 3 January 1940. He visited Lübeck and Hamburg on 6 January, taking in a quick visit to Neuengamme concentration camp and an inspection of the SS-Germania Regiment at the Langenhorn barracks, north of Hamburg, before returning to Berlin where he remained until a flight to Lodz on 15 January for an overnight stay. He was in Munich on 18 January, but back in Berlin by air on 19 January. Himmler stayed at his office for several days until leaving by train headed for Krakow on 25 January. He diverted to Przemysl on 26 January before going to Zakopane via Krakow on 27 January. From Zakopane on 28 January he drove to Kattowitz, again via Krakow, and was in Kattowitz and Königshütte on 29 January, returning to Berlin on 30 January.

Himmler left Berlin by car on 6 February and motored to Wewelsburg via Magdeburg, Hanover and Bielefeld arriving at 9 p.m. He visited the Externsteine again on 8 February and entertained SS-Obergruppenführer Fritz Weitzel at the castle on 9 February. From Wewelsburg, Himmler wrote a love note to his beloved Hedwig. The next day he drove to the airfield at Paderborn and took a flight to Berlin where he returned to his office at Prinz-Albrecht-Strasse.

On 12 February, Himmler was a guest of Göring at Karinhall, but left early at 4.30 p.m. He had a meal with the Circle of Friends of the Reichsführer-SS on 14 February and worked at his office for several days, interspersed with visits to Hitler at the Reich Chancellery. He joined Hitler on his special train to Munich on 23 February, visited Reichsleiter Franz Xaver Schwarz on 24 February and flew back to Berlin at 3 p.m. on 25 February.

Himmler took a flight to Göppingen at 1 p.m. on 4 March 1940 and began a four days inspection tour in the Black Forest region, taking in Schwäbish Gmünd, Lorch, Münsingen, Freudenstadt, Freiburg, Radolfzell and Lake Constance, before flying back to Berlin on 7 March. Marga Himmler records in her diary on 7 March 1940 that she was in Poland and she made remarks on the Jews living in filthy conditions in Posen, Lodz and Warsaw, the blame for which she attributed to 'their dirty habits.' [*Himmler's diary has an entry on 15 March 1940, noting that Marga was in Posen and Bromberg.*] Himmler visited Gauleiter Alfred Meyer in Münster on 11 March and moved on to Koblenz by air on 13 March, paying a visit to the Napola facility at Oranienstein on 14 March *en route* to Wiesbaden. He was back at his desk in Prinz-Albrecht-Strasse later that day and he did not leave Berlin again until flying to Paderborn on 17 March for another stay at Wewelsburg accompanied by several SS generals including Sepp Dietrich, Fritz

Weitzel and Theodor Eicke. Himmler flew back to Berlin on 20 March in time for an evening with Hitler. Himmler watched a film in his office on the evening of 21 March and was with Hitler again at midday on 22 March.

Marga and Gudrun had by now joined Himmler in the family house at Berlin-Dahlem, but he was once again on the move on 27 March, this time to Essen via Werl to visit Gauleiter Josef Terboven. Himmler was back at Wewelsburg on 28 March where he stayed until his return to Berlin on 30 March. He visited Weimar on 4 April and diverted to Kranichfeld on 5 April prior to flying to Essen from Weimar for another call on Gauleiter Terboven. From there he flew to Eger [*now Cheb in the Czech Republic*] on 6 April and carried out an inspection visit at Flossenbürg concentration camp. He flew to Berlin from Karlsbad [*now Karlovy Vary*] on 7 April.

Himmler was in Prinz-Albrecht-Strasse on 9 April 1940 when German forces invaded Denmark and Norway, ostensibly to protect Norway from British occupation. This was a busy time for him and he was constantly flitting back and forth between his office and the Reich Chancellery. The dual invasions were almost unopposed and the occupation of both countries was completed with incredible rapidity. King Christian X in Denmark surrendered almost immediately, but the Norwegians were not so ready to accept defeat, continuing resistance with the help of British forces until forced to concede by circumstances elsewhere.

Hitler had now successfully carried out three campaigns of invasion and occupation, boosting confidence for the inevitable major showdown to come. Himmler once again celebrated the success by playing tennis on a daily basis. At a meeting with Hitler on 19 April the appointment of the SS and Police Leader for Norway was discussed and the SS General selected by both Hitler and Himmler was SS-Obergruppenführer Fritz Weitzel, currently commanding the area of Düsseldorf. Gauleiter Josef Terboven was Hitler's choice as Reich Governor.

Before leaving his office for Ansbach at 6 p.m. on 24 April, Himmler received the report of their initial findings in Norway from Terboven and Weitzel. From Ansbach, Himmler travelled on to Munich where he stayed overnight before an inspection of Dachau concentration camp on 25 April. Leaving Dachau, he visited his mother in Munich before going to Gmund and Prien. He flew back to Berlin on 26 April.

He left Berlin on 4 May by air to Lodz [*German Litzmannstadt*] before an onward journey the next day to Lublin where he was greeted by the SSPF [*SS-und Polizei Führer -- SS and Police Leader*] SS-Brigadeführer Odilo Globocnik, the ex-Gauleiter of Vienna. Himmler stayed overnight at Globocnik's villa and drove on to Chelm on 6 May before flying back to Berlin from Lublin airfield. He dined in the capital with von Ribbentrop and the Italian diplomat Bernardo Attolico on 9 May.

SIX

War in the West

On 10 May 1940, Himmler notes in his diary the words 'beginning of the offensive.' Hitler's armies commenced their offensive in the west by sweeping through the Low Countries, by-passing the defensive French Maginot Line and instigating a 'Blitzkrieg,' or 'lightning war,' taking everyone by surprise. Himmler left Berlin on 11 May on his special train, Sonderzug 'Heinrich,' accompanied by von Ribbentrop and Reich Minister Hans Heinrich Lammers. His special train was to become a second home to the Reichsführer-SS, not only using it as his method of transport, but as accommodation and mobile field headquarters [*Feldkommandostelle.*]

It consisted of a salon car where Himmler dined, slept and held small conferences in addition to bathing and toilet facilities. There were additional sleeping compartments for guests to sleep and sit and accommodation for staff in other coaches, a dining car and a radio communications carriage. The train was protected from air attack by anti-aircraft guns at the front and rear of the train and when at a standstill in sidings for any length of time, it was also protected by camouflage netting. When stationary, the train was guarded by Himmler's special train protection escort group named after whichever train he was using; at first Sonderzug 'Heinrich' and later superseded by Sonderzug 'Steiermark' from 1 February 1943. In addition to the escort group [*Begleitkommando*] and RSD close protection officers, the train had the RFSS headquarters staff from Himmler's personal staff, seconded to the train when in use. For a short period in 1944, Himmler's train was designated 'Transport 44.'

Many of the top officials in the Third Reich government and Wehrmacht utilised the rail network throughout Europe and consequently several had their own personal trains, including Hitler whose train was codenamed 'Amerika.' Himmler used several linked carriages which had been upgraded to salon car status and were propelled by steam engines. The salon cars were built by Wegmann & Company of Kassel to an extremely high Pullman standard and Himmler's personal carriage was modernised from the original on three occasions. The train had the added advantage of mobility and Himmler made regular use of it, especially during campaigns. Sonderzug 'Heinrich' and Sonderzug 'Steiermark' also had their own Feldpost number: 35 360. Himmler utilised his special trains as his field headquarters more than any other Third Reich leader.

Karl Wolff joined his train on 13 May and Himmler paid his first visit to Hitler's field headquarters, codename 'Felsennest,' in Rodert, south-east of Bad Münstereifel, on 14 May 1940. The next day Himmler transmitted a reply to a postcard from Heydrich who was seeing active service on the western front with the Luftwaffe. In it, he wished him luck and sent greetings from Wölffschen (Karl Wolff,) Rudi Brandt and Häs'chen (Hedwig Potthast) which indicates that all three were present on Sonderzug 'Heinrich.' He kept his train close to Hitler's HQ for the next few days before leaving by car for Aachen, Maastricht and Hasselt on 16 May. For much of the journey, Himmler preferred to take the wheel himself. From the Hotel Warson in Hasselt his route took him to Eindhoven, Tilburg, Breda, Antwerp and Brussels before returning to Felsennest via Malmedy on 19 May.

A new concentration camp was established by the camp inspectorate on 20 May 1940 in a former Polish army barracks outside the Silesian town of Oswiecim. It is better known by its German name of Auschwitz.

The ensuing days saw Himmler remain on his train, receiving visits from various SS leaders and entertaining the two Reichsminister, von Ribbentrop and Lammers. On 24 May, it appears that Himmler played host at a lunchtime gathering which included Wilhelm Frick, Wilhelm Stuckart, Hans Lammers and his own brother Gebhard. [*The latter may have been Prof. Karl Gebhardt, but the entry in Himmler's diary omits the letter 't.'*] The following day he attended a meeting at the Felsennest with Hitler and Arthur Seyss-Inquart. Hitler had previously agreed to Himmler's suggestion that Seyss-Inquart be appointed as Reichskommissar in the Netherlands, the appointment taking effect on 18 May 1940.

Himmler was on the move again by the end of the month and was in Phillipeville on 31 May, moving towards the front at Dunkirk via Cambrai, Arras and Bailleu. He arrived in Den Haag on 2 June for a meeting with Meinoud Rost van Tonningen, the radical Dutch Nazi. His comprehensive excursion behind the front lines was probably by road as his diary does not mention flights or his train until Sonderzug 'Heinrich' is noted again on 4 June. This inspection tour was geared to be a morale booster for the troops in addition to Himmler satisfying his own urge to be a front line soldier. From 1 June 1940, Himmler's many titles included that of the Chief of the Waffen-SS Kommando.

From 4 June, the Sachsenhausen satellite camp of Neuengamme outside Hamburg became autonomous as a camp in its own right. The main business of the camp was the production of bricks.

By 5 June, Himmler was back at Felsennest with Hitler and the SS journalist Gunter d'Alquen and the next day Hitler moved his field headquarters to

Brûly-de-Pesche with the new codename 'Wolfsschlucht.' Himmler paid his first visit to Wolfsschlucht on 8 June 1940. Italy finally threw its hat in the ring and declared war on France and Britain on 10 June 1940. Himmler spent the following week touring behind the lines and visiting various conquered towns, culminating in his arrival in Paris where he encamped in the Ritz Hotel on 16 June. He embarked upon a quick tour of the city the next day, also taking in the Château de Malmaison and the vast palace at Versailles.

He was once again on board Sonderzug 'Heinrich' on 18 June. During the night of 19–20 June, Himmler received the bad news that his HSSPF in Norway, SS-Obergruppenführer Fritz Weitzel, had been killed by bomb shrapnel during an air raid on his hometown of Düsseldorf where he had been paying a visit. Weitzel had been warned of the dangers of driving through the streets during a raid, but he ignored the advice and paid the ultimate price. Himmler's diary entry for 20 June is blank. Weitzel was buried in the main city cemetery and his grave is still there today, having been moved twice.

The month of June 1940 was not kind to Himmler as he also lost his personal driver, Hans Bastian, who apparently killed himself in a freak accident whilst 'toying' with his MP38 machine pistol.

Himmler drove to Wolfsschlucht on 21 June and then went to the site of the signing of the armistice in 1918 at Compiègne, where Hitler had decided the French should sign their surrender the next day. Himmler returned to Wolfsschlucht that same evening and then on to his train where he held meetings on armistice day, first with Richard Hildebrandt and Jakob Sporrenberg and then in the evening with Philipp Bouhler and Leonardo Conti. At 1.35 a.m. on 25 June 1940, the French surrender came into effect. Britain and her dominions now stood alone.

Himmler spent several days travelling around aboard his train and joined Hitler on 29 June at his field headquarters codenamed Tannenberg at Kniebis in the Black Forest, also accompanying him on an inspection of the troops quartered in the vicinity the next day. Himmler remained quartered on Sonderzug 'Heinrich' until returning to Berlin on 6 July.

He stayed in Berlin until flying to Munich on 9 July 1940 where he called in on his mother and then journeyed on by road to Gmund where he stayed for two nights, taking a flight back to Berlin from Munich on 11 July. Himmler flew from Berlin to Freiburg and drove to Belfort, crossing the French frontier on foot on 13 July. He spent that night at the Grand Hotel Belfort before moving on to Dijon on 14 July, staying overnight. On 15 July he drove on to Besançon and spent the night in the town before flying to Berlin on 16 July.

There followed several days where he worked at his office in Prinz-Albrecht-Strasse, but he dined with the Italian diplomats Alfieri and Ciano on 20 July and regularly called in at the Reich Chancellery. When Hitler decided to go south to the Berghof, Himmler was not far behind. On 28 July he left for Gmund arriving at

1.30 a.m. on the morning of 29 July. He did not stay long and flew back to Berlin the same day. On 31 July, he flew to Emden and drove to Den Haag via Groningen, arriving at 10.30 p.m. He visited Leiden and Amsterdam on 1 August, but only for a quick visit as he was back in Den Haag the same night. He drove to Arnhem and on to Cologne the following day, boarding his aircraft for a flight to Berlin-Staaken.

Himmler's diary reveals he then worked daily in his office, but most days he found time to play an afternoon game of tennis in the warm Berlin summer. It also discloses that he was worried about his health around this time as entries of his weight began to appear each day from 6 August, written in green pencil, starting at 150 pounds. He stayed in Berlin, at his desk every day and held several high level meetings with members of Hitler's government, with diplomats and relaxing on the tennis court. At 4 p.m. on 17 August, Himmler flew to Munich and then motored on to Gmund, rounding off the evening with a game of bridge. On 18 August, he worked at his desk from 11 a.m. until heading over to the hunting lodge at Valepp. He played tennis in Bad Tölz on 19 August. He was able to stay on at Haus Lindenfycht for several days, but this was a time of war and so he did not venture far from his desk. In connection with his role as a military leader, he was Chief of the SS-Führungshauptamt from 15 August 1940. He did find time to play tennis and went hunting, but Himmler could not risk being away from Hitler for too long and was back at his side on the Obersalzberg on 23 August, spending the whole afternoon and evening with his Führer.

Himmler received professional visits from Felix Kersten on 25 and 26 August, but was still playing tennis daily. He flew to Berlin on 28 August after a visit to his mother in Munich. On 30 August 1940, he conducted an inspection of Sachsenhausen concentration camp in Oranienburg.

September opened with Himmler at his office desk in Berlin. On 6 September there is a single word entry 'Metz' and it appears he stayed for two nights before hotfooting it back to Gmund on 8 September and flying to Berlin the following day. Whilst in Metz, he was the guest of Sepp Dietrich's Leibstandarte-SS 'Adolf Hitler' and he presented the unit with its new unique Deutschland Erwache standard. His daily routine was much the same over the next weeks, working in Prinz-Albrecht-Strasse, playing tennis, receiving the odd visit for treatment from Kersten, dining with various dignitaries and calling in on Hitler at the new Reich Chancellery in Voss Strasse. He called Haus Lindenfycht by telephone regularly, maintaining contact with Marga and especially Gudrun.

On 26 September 1940, Himmler took a flight to Cologne and drove to Düsseldorf where he visited the grave of the recently deceased SS-Obergruppenführer Weitzel. At 5 p.m. he flew back to Berlin and the following day held meetings with Count Ciano and von Ribbentrop. Himmler had further meetings with Ciano and the Spanish diplomat Serrano Suner on 29 September and with the Reich Press Chief Dr. Otto Dietrich on 1 October.

After working at his office in Prinz-Albrecht-Strasse and the customary telephone call to Haus Lindenfycht on 2 October, Himmler boarded his aircraft bound for Breslau [*today Wroclaw, Poland.*] Upon landing, he travelled by car to Neisse [*today Nysa, Poland*] and onward to Busau [*today Bouzov, Czech Republic.*] He was accompanied by Karl Wolff, Rudolf Brandt, Oswald Pohl and Otto Hoffman [*sic, correct Hofmann.*] The next day the party travelled on to Partschendorf [*today Bartošovice, Czech Republic*] and then to Freudenthal [*today Bruntál, Czech Republic*] before returning to Busau where they stayed until flying back to Berlin from Olmütz [*today Olomouc, Czech Republic*] on 5 October.

The morning of Himmler's fortieth birthday on 7 October 1940, found him in the German capital where he received birthday greetings from his mother in Munich and Marga and Gudrun in Gmund by telephone. He took a flight to Munich later that day and was in Gmund by 8 p.m. where he took a call from Hitler who was at the Berghof. He was then able to relax and open his birthday gifts. He stayed at Gmund until a flight to Berlin on 9 October, going straight to Hitler at the Reich Chancellery after a quick call into the office at Prinz-Albrecht-Strasse. He joined Karl Hermann Frank in a meeting with Hitler on 11 October and the next couple of days were spent in his usual office routine, interspersed with the odd game of tennis.

Hans Frank had issued orders establishing a ghetto in the Polish capital, Warsaw and these directions began to be implemented on 16 October 1940. The ghetto was sealed on 15 November 1940, creating the largest ghetto in terms of both area and population.

On 14 October, Himmler flew from Berlin to Oppeln [*today Opole, Poland.*] He visited the Annaberg, a Nazi site commemorating the 1921 Battle of Annaberg, and spent the night at Schloss Weichsel before flying to Berlin from Kattowitz on 15 October. After another day at his desk and a game of tennis, he took a flight to Paris at 10 a.m. on 17 October. He did not stay long, flying on to Bordeaux the same day and then motoring down to Dax where he stayed overnight.

Himmler crossed the frontier into neutral Spain at Irun on 19 October and drove on to San Sebastian and Burgos where he was greeted by General Franco and then continued his onward journey to Madrid by train. On 20 October, Himmler had meetings with Spanish diplomats including Franco and Suner in the Spanish capital. Himmler remained in Madrid, touring local sights and meeting dignitaries, fêted by the Spanish as a very special guest, before leaving for Barcelona by air on 23 October. He spent his last night in Spain in the capital of Catalonia and flew to Marseilles on 24 October. He paid lightning visits to Lyon, Besançon, Freiburg and Nuremberg before landing in Berlin that evening.

Spending the next day in his office, Himmler flew to Krakow on 26 October. The following day he drove to Tschenstochau [*today Częstochowa*] and after spending the night there, he moved on to Sosnowice-Dombrova [*today Sosnowiec-Dabrowa*] and thence to Kattowitz [*today Katowice*.] He flew to Breslau and drove to Striegan, visiting Gross-Rosen concentration camp on 28 October 1940 before returning to Berlin where he remained until going to Gmund on 6 November in time for the Putsch anniversary celebrations in Munich on 8 and 9 November. He was back at his desk in Berlin on 11 November and remained in the capital until visiting the SS barracks at Hillersleben on 16 November, staying overnight. Back in Berlin on 17 November, he was to stay put until leaving for Florence via Munich on 20 November.

Mussolini received Himmler in Rome on 21 November and the chief of the German police attended a number of conferences with high profile Italian diplomats and members of the Duce's Fascist Party. Himmler left Rome for Munich on 23 November after a successful diplomatic mission and by the next morning he had returned to Berlin where he reported to both von Ribbentrop and Hitler.

His usual Berlin daily routine recommenced keeping him in the capital and away from his wife and daughter. By now Marga was regularly alone at the marital home in Berlin-Dahlem, having left Gudrun in the safety of the shores of the Tegernsee at Gmund, away from possible air attacks. Marga's diary complains of her loneliness and the cost of the regular telephone calls to Gmund. Her work with the German Red Cross kept her occupied, but it was scant compensation for her separation from her family. The marriage no longer held the same attraction for her husband who was by now becoming intensely involved with his personal private secretary, Fräulein Hedwig Potthast, a relationship that would soon develop into deep love, had it not done so already.

From 7 to 9 December 1940, Himmler conducted an inspection tour of Konigsberg, Friedrichsberg and Krasne [*today Krasnyy, Russia*] sleeping overnight in the latter location. On 9 December he visited Reichsmarschall Hermann Göring in Rominten [*Turbaza, Russia*] and then travelled to Insterburg [*today Chernyakhovsk, Russia*.] By 10 December he was back at his Prinz-Albrecht-Strasse desk.

On 12 December Himmler went to the SS-Junkerschule Braunschweig [*SS officer cadet school Brunswick*] where at 6.30 p.m. he was guest of honour at a passing out parade. The following day Himmler was in Apeldoorn addressing the SS-Division 'Deutschland' and that night he left for Wewelsburg where he was to stay until 16 December when he flew from Paderborn to Berlin. Whilst at Wewelsburg, Himmler visited the nearby Gut Böddeken, a former monastery, on 15 December.

Himmler stayed in Berlin until 23 December when he again flew to Munich and visited his mother before heading for Gmund for the Christmas holidays. For him it was a working holiday, never straying too far from his desk or telephone. His 1940 diary ends on 31 December with him working at his desk in Haus Lindenfycht and with a weight reduction to just over 145 pounds.

On 2 January 1941, the Himmler couple took lunch with their guests at Lindenfycht, Rost van Tonningen and his wife. The next day, Himmler ventured into Munich and visited his mother and Reichsleiter Schwarz before consulting Dr Fahrenkamp. He left Gmund for Berlin on 5 January and attended the funeral of von Ribbentrop's father on 6 January. There is an entry on 7 January which records a morning appointment with his optician and a handwritten entry by Grothmann on 8 January which states that the Reichsführer was not in Berlin.

Himmler's round of meetings at Prinz-Albrecht-Strasse continued until he visited Ravensbrück concentration camp on 14 January 1941 for a full inspection tour. He had previously tasked Dr Ernst-Robert Grawitz to research a cure for gonorrhoea using inmates at the camp. During his visit it became clear to Himmler that no work had been carried out and that the camp doctor knew nothing of the project. This resulted in terse correspondence with the chief SS physician.

The Reichsführer was back in Munich on 19 January 1941, not returning to Berlin until 23 January. On 20 January Himmler, Heissmeyer and Pohl escorted Anton Mussert, the Dutch National Socialist, around Dachau concentration camp of which they were inordinately proud. The camp visit was extensive and Mussert was able to see most facilities at close hand. Himmler also showed Mussert around some NSDAP sites in Munich and introduced him to several high profile party members.

The Reichsführer visited Göring on 24 January. At 5 p.m. on 25 January, Himmler had a meeting with Ludolf von Alvensleben at which he relieved von Alvensleben from his duty as chief adjutant of the Reichsführer-SS and appointed him as SS-Führer on the Personal Staff RFSS. Himmler discussed with Heydrich on 26 or 27 January 1941, the future role of the Einsatzgruppen in the coming war against the Soviet Union.

On 28 January 1941, Himmler travelled to Norway where, over the next few days, he met Josef Terboven, Generaloberst von Falkenhorst and Wilhelm Rediess, the unfortunate Weitzel's replacement as the new HSSPF. Himmler remained in Norway for the first two weeks of February, returning to his office on the 16th. This period in Marga's life was very difficult. She noted in her diary again how lonely and alone she felt with her husband constantly away, her separation from her daughter, domestic staffing problems and to add to her woes, by now she knew of Himmler's serious relationship with Hedwig Potthast.

Himmler's next few weeks were occupied with meetings and mundane office work as noted in his service diary. There is even an entry on 19 February for a haircut. Himmler also found time for visits to Munich and a three day rest at his home on the shores of the Tegernsee.

On 1 March 1941, Himmler flew to Gleiwitz and met Gauleiter Bracht before driving to the camp at Auschwitz where he conducted an inspection of the facilities and the local area. He was accompanied by Gauleiter Bracht, Karl Wolff, Eric von dem Bach, Richard Glücks, the local NSDAP leader Walter Springorum, Rudolf Höss and representatives of the management staff of I. G. Farben Industries. That same day, Himmler ordered Höss to expand the camp to hold up to 30,000 inmates, to drain local swamps, construct a synthetic rubber factory for I. G. Farben and to create a new camp facility at Birkenau capable of receiving 100,000 prisoners. This would all be in preparation for the coming war in the east.

Himmler's service diary indicates his involvement in numerous schemes, including hospital administration, the use of wind motors and quarrying to name but a few, as well as military and political situations in the occupied territories and also his personal sessions with Felix Kersten and the barber, Werner. His workdays consisted mainly of various meetings with his staff and senior officials in the SS. To describe him as 'having a finger in many pies' would be an accurate reflection of how he administered his responsibilities as head of the SS and Police. By 13 March 1941, a draft had been issued for the direction of special areas of Case Barbarossa and Himmler was designated to carry out special tasks as representative of the Führer in questions of political administration. His actions, however, were to remain subordinate to the overall military operations and were not to interfere with their implementation.

At 11 a.m. on 20 March 1941, Himmler attended the exposition in Berlin on the planning and reconstruction of settlements in the east. Other notable attendees recorded in the diary were Rudolf Hess, Fritz Todt, Philipp Bouhler, Martin Bormann, Reinhard Heydrich, Kurt Daluege, Hermann Behrends, Hans Jüttner, Gottlob Berger and Otto Hofmann. By 12.30 p.m., Himmler was back at his office receiving treatment from Kersten. It is obvious that Himmler was suffering badly from stomach cramps around this time as Kersten returned the following day for further treatment and was subsequently a regular visitor over the following weeks, sometimes on a daily basis.

Himmler's physical condition was not the only health problem in the Himmler family around this time. During the weekend of 22–23 March, Gudrun Himmler became ill with stomach pains and vomiting. Himmler rushed to Gmund and Dr Fahrenkamp and a Dr Dingeldey were consulted. On 24 March, Gudrun was diagnosed with appendicitis and underwent an emergency operation to remove her appendix. Himmler was relieved enough to return to Berlin on 25 March.

Himmler created what amounted to a private armed force for the RFSS when, on 7 April 1941, the Einsatzstab RFSS came into being. It was formed out of elements of the 1st and 2nd SS Infantry Brigades and the SS Cavalry Brigade, with Kurt Knoblauch as its commander. It was renamed the Kommandostab RFSS soon after inception and gradually grew to a strength of about 25,000 men.

On 8 April 1941, Himmler and Daluege discussed plans for Operation Barbarossa and the following day, discussions continued on the subject with Oswald Pohl and Hans Prützmann. Much planning was afoot as Himmler held conferences with several of his senior SS men over their roles in the coming conflict. Among these were Ernst Schmauser, Eric von dem Bach and Jakob Sporrenberg. By 11 April, Himmler was in Carinthia where he conducted tours of inspection before moving to Maribor on 17 April. He returned to Carinthia and remained there until heading back to Berlin on 27 April.

The sub-camp at Gross-Rosen was established as an autonomous concentration camp on 1 May 1941.

In early May 1941, Marga noted in her diary that her husband and von Ribbentrop's relationship had taken a turn for the worst, the reason being unclear. Himmler visited the Leibstandarte-SS 'Adolf Hitler' in Greece from 6 to 10 May and passed on his congratulations for their successes in the Balkans campaign. He took leave in Gmund for a week from 11 to 18 May, but still attended upon Hitler at the Berghof and was present at a meeting there of Reichsleiter and Gauleiter on 13 May. He was in Berlin again on 18 May.

It was during this period that Rudolf Hess made his flight from Augsburg to Scotland in the forlorn hope of discussing peace terms with Britain before the start of Operation Barbarossa. On 10 May 1941, Hess took off in a Messerschmitt Bf110 and eventually parachuted into captivity, his mission a total failure. Whether Hitler or Himmler knew of Hess' plans in advance remains a matter of conjecture.

Himmler returned to Norway on 21 May and was present when the newly formed Norwegian SS swore an oath of allegiance to Hitler and Quisling. A directive issued with the agreement of the High Command of the Wehrmacht in Himmler's name and dated 21 May 1941, lays out the instructions for the role of the Higher SS and Police Commanders (HSSPF) appointed to carry out the special orders of the Reichsführer-SS in the occupied territories. This included the special duties entrusted to the Einsatzgruppen and Einsatzkommandos of the Security Police.

Himmler met with Professors Grawitz and Clauberg on 27 May 1941 to discuss the use of human sterilization and Clauberg delivered a presentation with regard to possible sterilization of persons with 'tainted' blood. It appears that Himmler gave his tacit approval to Clauberg's project and authorised further investigations into sterilization. Clauberg gained subsequent notoriety for his ruthless x-ray sterilization experiments with Dr Horst Schumann in Block 11 at Auschwitz I.

Mauthausen concentration camp was the first camp opened outside the frontiers of the old Reich. Himmler conducted an inspection of the camp and quarry in April 1941, accompanied by Oswald Pohl, Dr Ernst Kaltenbrunner and the local Gauleiter, August Eigruber, who wore black Allgemeine-SS uniform on this occasion. There is no record of this visit in Himmler's service diary, but he was certainly in Austria between 11 and 27 April. On 31 May 1941, Himmler returned to the camp, this time accompanied by Oswald Pohl, Ernst Kaltenbrunner, August Eigruber, Friedrich Rainer and Franz Kutschera on another inspection tour of the camp. Himmler also 'entertained' a number of Waffen-SS officers from 'Das Reich' on this particular visit to the camp facilities and they were given a comprehensive tour of the camp. Their numbers included such luminaries as Paul Hausser, Wilhelm Bittrich, Peter Hansen, Otto Kumm, Werner Ostendorff and Fritz Klingenberg. 'Das Reich' was resting in the Linz area after their Yugoslav campaign and soon they would be off to the Russian front.

On 6 June 1941, Himmler conducted an inspection of the Lodz ghetto where he met with the corrupt Jewish elder Chaim Rumkowski. Berlin beckoned once again and he returned the same evening, paying a visit to King Boris of Bulgaria at the Hotel Adlon on 7 June.

Marga notes in her diary for 11 June that she had an accident in her bath and received several injuries. She also recorded that young Gerhard's behaviour had declined further. There is no mention of either incident in Himmler's diary.

SEVEN

Barbarossa

Senior SS leaders were summoned to a meeting at Wewelsburg castle in Westphalia from 12 to 15 June 1941. There Himmler outlined the plans for the invasion of the Soviet Union which was to begin approximately one week later and he gave his instructions for the intended role of the SS. He highlighted the political war alongside the military objectives and indicated that the struggle would result in the mass deaths of millions of Slavs and Jews. Heydrich, Daluege, Jeckeln, Lorenz, Pohl, Johst, von dem Bach, Wolff and Rauter were among those left in no doubt as to the severity of the coming conflict.

With the major expansion of the war imminent, Himmler's daily routine gave no further indication of the impending conflagration. He found time to visit Gmund on 18 June and even to sit for his favoured photographer Friedrich Bauer the day before Barbarossa. There is no entry in Himmler's service diary on the day that Hitler unleashed the war against the Russians, but Himmler appears to have been in the capital and received a visit by State Secretary Schlegelberger from the Ministry of Justice. The following day, 23 June 1941, Himmler had various meetings before finishing his day with a game of tennis. At one of the meetings, with Heydrich and Wolff, the question of the eastern territories had been discussed and the result was a directive on 24 June for Professor Konrad Meyer to draw up a 'General Plan Ost' for the resettlement of the conquered territories.

On 25 June 1941, Himmler boarded his special train Sonderzug 'Heinrich' for the journey to Hitler's new field headquarters, Wolfsschanze at Rastenburg [*today Ketrzyn*] in East Prussia. He spent the following few weeks touring the east and inspecting various SS units including visits to Lodz, Bialystok, Stettin and to Pohl and Globocnik in Lublin on 20 July where he ordered Globocnik to create a new camp at Majdanek, and finally to Riga at the end of July. On 17 July 1941, Hitler entrusted Himmler with responsibility for security behind all front lines in the Soviet occupied territories. During this tour, Himmler ordered Fegelein to use his cavalry units to assist with 'pacification duties.' Himmler paid a fleeting visit to Berlin on 3 August before returning to Rastenburg two days later. His service diary entries again reflect his appointments from 13 August 1941.

Back in Berlin, Hermann Göring had charged Reinhard Heydrich on 31 July 1942 with seeking and implementing a 'final solution of the Jewish question.' The Himmler–Heydrich partnership used this instruction as a tool to stamp their authority on Jewish affairs over all government departments, a move which was made clear at the conference held at Berlin–Wannsee the following January.

Himmler arrived in Minsk on 14 August and the following day witnessed an execution of partisans and Jews in the morning prior to visiting a Soviet POW camp. This was Himmler's first experience of a mass execution up close and it had a profound effect on the Reichsführer-SS. Karl Wolff describes Himmler's reaction:

> An open grave had been dug and they had to jump into this and then lay face downwards. Sometimes when one or two rows had already been shot, they had to lie on top of the people who had already been shot and then they were shot from the edge of the grave. Himmler had never seen dead people before and in his curiosity he stood right up at the edge of this open grave—a sort of triangular hole—and was looking in. While he was looking in, Himmler had the deserved bad luck that from one or other of the people who had been shot in the head he got a splash of brains on his coat and I think it also splashed onto his face. He went very green and pale; he wasn't actually sick, but he was retching and turned round and swayed and then I had to jump forward and hold him steady and lead him away from the grave. After the shooting was over, Himmler gathered the shooting squad in a semi-circle around him and standing up in his car so that he would be a little higher and able to see the whole unit, he made a speech. He had seen for himself how hard the task which they had to fulfil for Germany in the occupied areas was, but however terrible it all might be, even for him as a mere spectator and how much worse it must be for them, the people who had to carry it out, he could not see any way around it. They must be hard and stand firm. He could not relieve them of this duty; he could not spare them. In the interests of the Reich, in this hopefully Thousand Year Reich, in its first decisive great war after the take-over of power, they must do their duty, however hard it may seem. He appealed to their sense of patriotism and their readiness to make sacrifices. Well, yes—and then he drove off. And he left this—this police unit to sort out the future for themselves, to see if and how far they could come to terms with this within themselves, because for some it was a shock which lasted their whole lives.

Einsatzkommando 8 under the command of Dr Otto Bradfisch was the unit involved and Himmler reassured the men that this order had come direct from the Führer and therefore had the rule of law.

After his inspection of the POW camp, Himmler visited an asylum at Novinki, just north of Minsk. There he ordered Arthur Nebe to liquidate the inmates, but to use a 'more humane' method than shooting. Nebe subsequently experimented with both high explosives and vehicle exhaust fumes.

After completing his inspection tour of Minsk, Himmler returned to his field headquarters near the Wolfsschanze. In order to be near the Führer, Himmler had established a site for his own field headquarters (just east of Rastenburg) which is referred to as 'Hegewaldheim' or 'Hegewald' [*not to be confused with Feldkommandostelle 'Hegewald,' south of Zhitomir in the Ukraine*] and also another new permanent site called 'Hochwald' near the village of Grossgarten [*today Pozezdrze.*] It was a quick drive to Hitler's FHQ and nearby was an airfield at Lötzen which provided quick access to air travel. It was also served by a rail link which enabled him to utilise his personal train Sonderzug 'Heinrich' and subsequently [*from February 1943*] Sonderzug 'Steiermark.'

The eventual SS-Standartenführer Josef 'Sepp' Tiefenbacher was responsible for Himmler's Feldkommandostellen, including his special trains and one of his deputies was Ludwig 'Lucki' Pemsel. Pemsel had direct responsibility under Tiefenbacher for the special trains and was the nominated commander of Sonderzug 'Steiermark.' Pemsel was a bank official by profession and had seen national service before the war with the army. He was a volunteer member of the Reichsarbeitsdienst and an early member of the SS. He was attached to the Personal Staff RFSS prior to the war and remained on the strength throughout the hostilities. Captured at war's end, he was interned by the British in various camps before his release from Dachau internment camp in 1948. He returned to banking and never spoke of his experiences with Himmler until his death at the age of ninety in 2003.

Hegewaldheim was a converted guest house in an area of woodland overlooking a lake and Himmler used this location to entertain guests. Apparently the building was demolished in January 1945 and the site is now occupied by a youth camp. The facility at Grossgarten, first constructed with wooden barracks in early August 1941, eventually consisted of five concrete air raid shelters built in 1942 by Organisation Todt and several wooden barracks, surrounded by minefields and security fencing. A rail spur allowed Himmler's train to be kept inside the perimeter. After it was evacuated, the facility was blown up by the Germans on 22 January 1945. The ruin of the biggest A-class air raid shelter still exists. From July 1941, this Feldkommandostelle was known by its codename 'Hochwald.'

Himmler was to spend a great deal of time at Hegewaldheim and Hochwald as Hitler remained at his favourite Wolfsschanze FHQ for much of the time over the next three years. However, Himmler's favoured overnight quarters was a large farm estate house called Friedrichsruh at Gansenstein [*now Brozowka*] near Kruglanken. For Himmler, these quarters provided more comfort than his other sites in the area and Felix Kersten mentions that he gave Himmler treatment at Friedrichsruh quite often. A rail line also passed nearby the estate and was only minutes away by car, allowing access by train when necessary.

By early September 1941, Himmler had begun to formulate a plan to deal with the Jewish question. In his role as head of the Four Year Plan, Hermann Göring had formerly ordered SS-Gruppenführer Reinhard Heydrich in the aforementioned directive dated 31 July 1941 to find a 'final solution' to the Jewish problem. This had been as a result of negotiations between Göring and Himmler and both Himmler and Heydrich accepted their new role with vigour. On 2 September 1941, Himmler had discussions with SS-Obergruppenführer Friedrich-Wilhelm Krüger regarding the Jewish question in the east and the resettlements from the Reich. By the middle of September, Hitler acknowledged Himmler's special role by admitting in private conversation:

> I've ordered Himmler, in the event of there someday being reason to fear troubles back at home, to liquidate everything he finds in the concentration camps. Thus at a stroke the revolution would be deprived of its leaders.

In August–September 1941, one of Himmler's HSSPF, Friedrich Jeckeln, energetically demonstrated his willingness to participate in the Jewish extermination process. From 27 to 29 August, SS and police units, supported by locally recruited auxiliaries and German military personnel, murdered 23,600 Jews in Kamenets-Podolsk in the Ukraine during an operation co-ordinated by Higher SS and Police Leader Ukraine, Friedrich Jeckeln. Also, from 29 to 30 September, under the leadership and with the co-ordination of Friedrich Jeckeln, German SS and police units supported by Ukrainian auxiliaries and German military personnel, shot approximately 33,000 persons, mostly Jews, at the Babi Yar ravine on the outskirts of Kiev, Ukraine. In the following months, German units shot thousands of Jews, Gypsies and Soviet prisoners of war at Babi Yar.

On 3 September 1941, SS functionaries at Auschwitz concentration camp experimented with the use of Zyklon B as a killing agent. Their victims were Soviet prisoners of war.

During the night of 9 to 10 September 1941, Himmler's mother died in Munich.

On 18 September 1941, Himmler wrote to Gauleiter Arthur Greiser in the Wartheland stating that Hitler had expressed a wish that the *Altreich* and the *Protektorat* be totally cleared of Jews and in consequence he would order their deportation initially to the Lodz Ghetto. Within weeks, the ghetto became overcrowded and Greiser delegated the local HSSPF SS-Gruppenführer Wilhelm Koppe to find a solution. Koppe ordered SS-Sturmbannführer Herbert Lange to eliminate the excess numbers and the use of gas vans was introduced at Chelmno. Between December 1941 and April 1943, nearly 150,000 people were exterminated by Lange's Sonderkommando.

Elsewhere, the situation in the *Protektorat* had begun to cause concern at Hitler's headquarters. Clearly, the *Reichsprotektor*, Constantin von Neurath, had not a firm grip on events. The underground movement was gaining in stature and black market trading had spiralled out of control. This was all having a detrimental effect on war production, the arms and munitions industry in the *Protektorat* being vital to the German war effort. The ambitious State Secretary Karl Hermann Frank joined Himmler and Heydrich for a working dinner with Hitler on the evening of 21 September 1941 in order to discuss the situation. The following day Himmler and Heydrich again called on Hitler for further discussions, this time without Frank. Heydrich laid out his ideas for future policies in Bohemia–Moravia. Himmler again met with Hitler on 23 September and it was decided that Heydrich, not Frank, would replace von Neurath as Acting Reichsprotector and that von Neurath would be placed on sick leave. On 24 September, Heydrich was promoted to SS-Obergruppenführer and formally appointed as Acting Reichsprotector, much to the obvious disappointment of the ambitious Frank.

One week later, Himmler was in the Ukraine. He visited the staff of Einsatzgruppe D from 4 to 5 October and addressed the officers of the group. The commander, Otto Ohlendorf, had agreed with local army commanders to exclude those Jews who were farmers from the executions. Himmler immediately countermanded this order and directed that all Jews be liquidated. At dinner, Ohlendorf brought the burden of mass killings felt by his men to the attention of the Reichsführer-SS. Ohlendorf later testified at Nuremberg that Himmler did not give him an answer and ignored his concerns.

On 7 October 1941, Himmler celebrated his 41st birthday and received personal congratulations from senior SS officers and members of his staff at Hegewaldheim. He called in on Hitler and in the evening he dined with senior members of the government and his SS organisation.

On 13 October 1941, Himmler held a meeting with Odilo Globocnik and Friedrich-Wilhelm Krüger at which Himmler directed Globocnik to build and administer a death camp at Belzec. This camp would receive and despatch deportees mainly from the southern General Government and in particular the Lublin area. Himmler discussed the Jewish emigration policy with Heydrich during a telephone conversation on 18 October and on 23 October 1941 a RSHA directive issued in Himmler's name ordered the total cessation of authorised emigration of Jews from within the German sphere of influence. At a stroke, the Jews within German occupied Europe became prisoners on death row.

Himmler spent much of the next days visiting some of his senior SS men in their seats of administration. He also engaged in a hunting trip with Count Ciano from 26 to 28 October. On 29 October he visited Heydrich in Prague before flying on to Rastenburg and reporting to the Führer. The following day Himmler entertained Baldur von Schirach at Hegewaldheim and the two men discussed how best the Hitler Youth and the SS could work together. Himmler spent several days at his field headquarters engaged with meetings and visiting Hitler at the nearby

Wolfsschanze. He took a day off on 3 November and went hunting at Haydtwald.

On 4 November 1941, Himmler spent the day with Reichsmarschall Göring at his headquarters before driving back to Friedrichsruh. He travelled to Munich on 8 November and that evening he dined with his Obergruppenführer and Gruppenführer. The following day was taken up with anniversary engagements for the 1923 Putsch commemoration before paying a flying visit to Gmund.

The Swedish masseur, Felix Kersten, notes in his diary on 11 November 1941 that he treated a depressed Himmler in Berlin on his return from the Reich Chancellery. According to Kersten, Himmler's low mood was because Hitler had ordered the physical extermination of the Jews. This provides a good example of why Kersten's testimony should always be treated with utmost caution. Himmler's service diary entries for this day do not include a visit by Kersten, nor do they indicate a visit by Himmler on his Führer. Most revealing is Himmler's location on this day which appears to be in East Prussia and not in Berlin. The diary notes a telephone call by Himmler to Paul Baumert in Berlin. Hitler also appears to be at his Rastenburg FHQ.

An unconfirmed discussion with Friedrich Jeckeln apparently took place on 12 November 1941 during which Himmler allegedly directed Jeckeln to liquidate the Riga Ghetto. Hans Prützmann had earlier indicated that the local governor, Hinrich Lohse, had objected to such an action, but an incensed Himmler demanded:

> You tell Lohse that is my order, which is also the Führer's wish!

Himmler remained in East Prussia until 20 November when he travelled to Danzig. Over the ensuing days, Himmler held meetings with Gauleiter Albert Forster, SS-Gruppenführer Richard Hildebrandt, Otto Hofmann and Ulrich Greifelt. On 23 November, Himmler inspected KL Stutthof [*Stutthof concentration camp*] before driving back to Rastenburg. There he remained until returning to Berlin where he attended the funeral of Luftwaffe ace Oberst Werner Mölders on 28 November.

Whilst present in Berlin, Himmler was unaware that a trainload of Berlin Jews had been mistakenly deported to Riga. The transport included German Jews who had been decorated during the First World War and should therefore have been sent to the model ghetto at Theresienstadt. Himmler discovered the mistake whilst visiting the Wolfsschanze on 30 November and immediately telephoned Heydrich from the field headquarters at 1.30 p.m. to order that no liquidation of the transport should occur. Himmler's telephone log is noted in his own hand 'Judentransport aus Berlin. Keine Liquidierung.' Both Heydrich and Himmler were unaware that the transport had already undergone 'special handling' before 9 a.m. that morning in the Rumbuli Forest outside Riga with all deportees having been shot on arrival. Friedrich Jeckeln subsequently reported proudly to Himmler that the action had gone smoothly and without incident. Himmler was furious and summoned Jeckeln to his field headquarters where on 4 December he rescinded a previous order to liquidate all Jews deported to Riga.

The Japanese attack on Pearl Harbour took place on 7 December 1941 and on 11 December Hitler declared war on the USA.

Himmler returned to Berlin by train on 9 December and carried on with his duties attending meetings with some of his departmental heads and senior NSDAP officials in addition to some foreign leaders. By 18 December he was back in East Prussia and that day attended an important meeting at 4 p.m. with Hitler at the Wolfsschanze. In his own handwriting, Himmler notes 'Führerhauptquartier Wolfsschanze 18.XII.41, 16h. Führer. Judenfrage. als Partizanen auszurotten.' Hitler ordered that Jews were to be eradicated as partisans. Reichsminister Hans Lammers testified that his attempt in early 1942 to investigate the 'final solution of the Jewish question' was cut short by Hitler who:

> … . refused to discuss these matters with me. He only said that he had given Himmler the order for the final solution, namely, for the evacuation of the Jews from Germany. He also said that Himmler was responsible to him alone and that he would inform me if my participation should turn out to be necessary.

Lammers' interpretation of Hitler's order only went as far as deportation, but it is clear from Himmler's own notes of his meeting with Hitler that Hitler ordered the physical obliteration of Jews by treating them as partisans. Partisans were killed, not deported.

Himmler went to Munich the following day after a flurry of meetings regarding the reorganisation of the Waffen-SS. He arrived in Gmund on 20 December and the Himmler family celebrated Christmas early as he could only stay for one day. He left for a tour of the Ukraine on 23 December, spending Christmas with the Leibstandarte at Taragnog and returned to Friedrichsruh on 28 December via Uspenskaya, Stalino and Poltava where they visited Generalfeldmarschall von Reichenau. The last days of 1941 were spent in the Rastenburg area, meeting and dining with von Ribbentrop and with Hitler. The war was still going well even though the initial plan for Barbarossa, a lightning strike with the intention of the campaign reaching a conclusion by winter, had not materialised and the industrial might of the powerful USA had entered the conflict. For Himmler there was still no doubt that the war would end successfully for the Axis powers and he would press on with his ordained mission.

Himmler spent the first day of 1942 at the Wolfsschanze with Hitler and 2 January was completely taken up with telephone calls before Himmler left on 3 January for an inspection tour of the eastern front. Accompanied by Friedrich Jeckeln, Himmler visited Eicke and the Totenkopf Division, Alfred Wünnenberg and the Polizei Division and finally a military hospital in Krasnogwardiesk just south of Leningrad. He returned on 6 January and reported his findings to Hitler before flying off on another inspection tour, this time secret, from 7 January to 9 January. It is more than likely that Himmler visited Globocnik in Lublin and could possibly have included an inspection of Trawniki and Belzec camps. Around this period, he was also investigating the corrupt activities of Governor Karl Lasch who was arrested on 24 January 1942 and later executed on 1 June 1942 in Auschwitz where his death certificate was subsequently discovered. The Lasch case highlighted the power struggle between Hans Frank and Himmler's SS. Whatever the reason for his trip, Himmler once again reported back to the Führer with his findings.

On 14 and 15 January 1942, Himmler entertained his senior SS colleagues at Hegewaldheim. On both days the group started with lunch and discussions lasted until the evening. These meetings, attended by all Hauptamt chiefs apart from Otto Hofmann and Ulrich Greifelt, included figures such as Daluege, Lorenz, Heydrich, Sachs, Jüttner, Meyszner, Pohl, Berger, Wolff and Grawitz, were convened to discuss policy in the east and the plans for the final solution of the Jewish question. Once again Himmler reported the results back to the Führer on 16 January. The next day Himmler went hunting with Gauleiter Koch and Reichsleiter Buch.

The Wannsee Conference, chaired by Heydrich, took place in the Berlin suburb at Am Grossen Wannsee 56-58 on 20 January 1942. Heydrich revealed the SS plans to other interested government departments. The surviving minutes, recorded by Adolf Eichmann, do not reflect accurately much of the top secret matters discussed. During a break in discussions, Heydrich telephoned Himmler to update him on the progress of the meeting and the initial reaction by other government officials.

The same day Himmler discussed the creation of the new SS rank of Oberst-Gruppenführer und Generaloberst der Polizei or Waffen-SS with Hitler. Daluege, Dietrich and Schwarz were the first to be promoted to the new rank on the occasion of the next Hitler birthday. Himmler discussed the outcome of the Wannsee Conference in full on the telephone with Heydrich at 3.30 p.m. the following day. Heydrich was able to report to his Reichsführer that all goals had been achieved and that the SS was in firm control of the Jewish question with the support of the necessary government departments. This conference marked the next and most strategic stage in the Third Reich policy towards European Jewry, that of systematic liquidation on an industrial scale.

On 25 January, Himmler met with Friedrich Jeckeln aboard Sonderzug 'Heinrich' prior to his usual drive over to the Wolfsschanze. At 5 p.m. that day he telephoned Heydrich in Prague and discussed the Jews held in concentration camps and the anticipated influx of new arrivals. This was followed by a telex message that Himmler sent Richard Glücks at midday on 26 January ordering him to prepare the camps for an anticipated additional 150,000 Jews.

Although heavily engaged in the promotion of the war and the Jewish policy, Himmler still found time for domestic politics and social issues. Of particular concern to him were the increasing reports of the influence on German youth resulting from American black music. This was predominantly evident in Hamburg where elements of 'swing' culture threatened acceptable German traditions among young people. Himmler directed Heydrich to stamp out this emerging culture by despatching the ringleaders to concentration camps for at least 2 to 3 years. If it was discovered that parents and teachers were in any way encouraging the playing of jazz or swing music, then they too should be incarcerated in a camp.

Himmler was back in Berlin for the anniversary celebrations marking the seizure of power on 30 January. Soon after he returned to Rastenburg in East Prussia and his daily HQ routine continued with telephone discussions, meetings and the odd lightning inspection visit. He lived at Friedrichsruh and directed his war from nearby Hegewaldheim or Sonderzug 'Heinrich,' all within easy reach of Hitler's Wolfsschanze FHQ. On 8 February 1942, the aircraft carrying Reichsminister Dr Fritz Todt out of Rastenburg mysteriously exploded and crashed to earth soon after take off. Todt was killed instantly. The same day, SS-Gruppenführer Paul Moder was killed in action fighting with the SS-Totenkopf Division, a bitter blow to the Reichsführer-SS.

On 15 February 1942 at 11.15 p.m., Hedwig Potthast gave birth to Himmler's son Helge at the SS clinic in Hohenlychen. Himmler was present at the clinic, accompanied by Wolff and SS-Hauptsturmführer Baumert from his staff. The ensuing weeks saw Himmler dividing his time between East Prussia, Munich, Gmund and Berlin. In addition to his official duties, he now had responsibilities towards two families, one in Gmund and the other in Berlin. He remained unreservedly loyal to his daughter Gudrun and held his wife Marga in high regard, even though he had fallen deeply in love with Hedwig who had given him a son. The wife of SS-Gruppenführer Theodor Berkelmann wrote to Marga Himmler on 1 March informing her that her own husband wanted a divorce in order to marry a younger woman who would bear him children. Marga comments that older women have to 'grin and bear it.'

1 March 1942 saw Himmler's orders for an expansion of the facilities at Auschwitz come to fruition with the opening of the camp at Auschwitz-Birkenau. The first selections for the gas chambers would begin in May, but the systematic killing by Zyklon B crystals would be delayed until July.

Himmler telephoned birthday greetings to Heydrich who was skiing at Oberjoch on 7 March 1942. From 9 to 10 March Himmler paid a visit to Weissruthenien and met with Gauleiter Wilhelm Kube in Minsk before flying back to the Wolfsschanze for his customary report to Hitler.

On his travels again, Himmler paid an inspection visit to the Generalgovernment from 13 to 15 March 1942, calling in on Eberhard Schöngarth, Julian Scherner, Friedrich-Wilhelm Krüger and Hans Frank in Krakau before moving on to Lublin to be entertained by Odilo Globocnik and Richard Wendler, the brother-in-law of his elder brother, Gebhard. Himmler's service diary does not indicate the subjects discussed, but the commencement of the deportation of the inhabitants of the ghettos at Lemberg and Lublin to the new death camp at Belzec at this time cannot be a coincidence. Himmler flew to Berlin on 15 March and back to Lötzen the next day. By 17 March, he was at the Wolfsschanze reporting to the Führer, just as the first major deportations from Lublin and Lvov to Belzec began.

Between 19 and 28 March, Himmler embarked upon a major inspection tour of the northern sector of the eastern front, visiting SA-Obergruppenführer Karl Litzmann, SS-Obergruppenführer Friedrich Jeckeln, General Eduard Dietl, Generalleutnant Ferdinand Schörner, Finnish General Hjalmar Siilasvuo and SS-Brigadeführer Karl-Maria Demelhuber. He flew back to East Prussia on 28 March and reported to Hitler the following day.

Yet another inspection tour took place from 31 March until 3 April when he went straight to report to Hitler on his return. The details or location of this tour are not recorded in Himmler's service diary apart from a note that Karl Wolff accompanied him.

Himmler visited his wife and daughter in Gmund from 10 until 13 April when he flew back to East Prussia. On 15 April, Himmler and Heydrich discussed the situation in France over the telephone. The next day Himmler flew to Posen where he had a lengthy meeting with Arthur Greiser and Wilhelm Koppe. On 17 April, The three men were joined for breakfast at the Ostland Hotel by Max von Herff before driving to Warsaw where Himmler visited the ghetto. That night he drove from Warsaw to Friedrichsruh arriving just before 4 a.m.

Hitler's 53rd birthday fell on 20 April 1942 and Himmler was in attendance at the Wolfsschanze to pass on the best wishes of the SS. Himmler remained in East Prussia until 24 April when, before an evening meal aboard Sonderzug 'Heinrich' with Lammers and Johst, his train left for Berlin, arriving at 9 a.m. the following day. He drove straight to his office at Prinz-Albrecht-Strasse and held an 11 a.m. meeting with Heydrich prior to calling upon Italian Ambassador Edoardo 'Dino' Alfieri at 1 p.m. On 26 April, Himmler and Heydrich had further discussions before attending the last Reichstag sitting at the Kroll Opera House at which Hitler was given sweeping powers over the rule of law.

Himmler flew to Munich on 27 April, staying at the Hotel Vier Jahreszeiten where he dined with Karl von Eberstein. He drove down to Gmund on 28 April and took lunch with Marga and Gudrun before returning to his hotel in Munich where he spent the entire evening in discussions with Heydrich. The next few days were occupied with meetings and visits, one of which was to Fridolfing where he spent the afternoon of 30 April with the Rehrls. From their farm Himmler drove back to Gmund where he spent the night.

On 1 May 1942, Himmler inspected Dachau concentration camp and witnessed high altitude experiments carried out by Dr Sigmund Rascher. The next day Himmler's diary notes a visit to a Friedhof. This is not the first such notation in his service diary during his visits to Munich and one can only assume that he regularly visited the grave of his parents. After this particular visit, he flew to Prague where he lunched with Heydrich before returning by air to East Prussia. His daily routine of meetings and shuttling between Friedrichsruh and the Wolfsschanze once again got underway. Marga noted on 7 May that Himmler was always with the Führer and Gudrun was in Gmund, whilst she was lonely in Berlin. The same day the gassings at Sobibor got underway.

On 8 May, Himmler flew to Kursk as the guest of Generaloberst von Weichs. A quick tour was followed by his return the following day to Friedrichsruh and his usual calendar of meetings and general office work once again resumed. Himmler visited Holland from 16 until 20 May and there he met Seyss-Inquart, Rauter, Mussert and Christiansen at various times before flying to Munich and then driving to Gmund where he spent the night of 20 May. The next day he drove back to Munich and again visited the grave of his parents. [*This particular visit is actually noted as such in his diary*.] That afternoon he flew to Berlin.

Kurt Daluege introduced Polizei Oberstleutnant Griese and Polizei Major Pannier to Himmler on the morning of 22 May. These two police officers were both awarded the Knights Cross to the Iron Cross in early May 1942 for gallant action whilst serving with police units on the eastern front. Himmler was photographed with them immediately before meeting with SS-Oberführer Hans Ring and then lunching with Prof. Gebhardt. In the afternoon, Himmler attended the funeral of Gauleiter Röver who had died on 15 May.

Heydrich and Himmler had talks again on 23 May and Himmler carried out an inspection of a unit in Berlin on 24 May. Himmler left for East Prussia on 25 May and immediately on arrival reported to Hitler. At 6.25 p.m. Himmler telephoned Heydrich in Prague. The two men held their last discussion over the telephone at 7.40 p.m. on 26 May 1942. They spoke about the shooting of Jewish hostages in retaliation for an arson attack on an exhibition in Berlin and also about the corruption case of Governor Karl Lasch. Heydrich then went off to a concert of his father's music in the Waldstein Palace in Prague.

Just after 10.30 a.m. on 27 May 1942, in a Prague suburb, two Czech army sergeants carried out an attack on Heydrich as he drove to his office. A grenade exploded against the rear wheel hub of his vehicle and Heydrich was severely wounded in his back. At about 11.45 a.m. the telephone rang in Himmler's field headquarters. Dr Achim Ploetz, Heydrich's adjutant, was trying to reach the Reichsführer-SS with urgent important news. Himmler took the call and was informed of the assassination attempt. Almost immediately, Karl Hermann Frank rang from his office in the Czernin Palace in Prague with the same news. Himmler reacted at once and telephoned SS-Hauptsturmführer Baumert, directing him to pass on the order to Prof. Gebhardt to fly immediately to Prague in order to treat the stricken Heydrich. Himmler then drove to the Wolfsschanze to report to Hitler who flew into a rage and ordered that Eric von dem Bach should proceed to Prague and exact revenge. Himmler suggested Daluege as an alternative as he was already in Prague on other business. Hitler agreed.

That evening, Himmler sent Frank a teleprinter message from Sonderzug 'Heinrich':

> No. 5745—27 May 1942
> 9.05 p.m.
>
> To: SS-Gruppenführer Frank
> Prague
>
> Immediately into his hands:
>
> Confidential.
> 1. I agree with the publication.
> 2. Among the ordered ten thousand hostages, arrest above all the Czech intelligentsia in opposition.
> 3. Out of the main body of this Czech intelligentsia, shoot one hundred of the most important this very night.
>
> I shall call you tonight.
>
> *Signed* H. Himmler.

During the following few days, Heydrich's condition first grew worse, but then seemed to improve. The eminent doctors in attendance agreed that recovery looked probable. Himmler received regular bulletins by telephone from Professor Gebhardt and left East Prussia for Berlin aboard Sonderzug 'Heinrich' on 28 May. On 29 May, after returning to Prinz-Albrecht-Strasse, he telephoned Lina Heydrich and held a personal conversation with her. He was informed by Gebhardt the next day that Heydrich's fever had dropped and so he decided to pay him a visit in the Bulovka Hospital. At 11.30 a.m. on 31 May, Himmler's aircraft took off from Tempelhof airfield and landed in Prague at 1 p.m. Himmler was greeted by Daluege and Frank and drove immediately to the Bulovka where he was updated on Heydrich's condition before visiting him. It was to be the last meeting between the two men.

After the visit, Himmler drove out to Panenske Brezany and had a late lunch with Lina Heydrich. This was followed by a further meeting with Daluege and Frank before Himmler boarded his aircraft for the flight to East Prussia where he immediately reported to Hitler. Himmler's usual itinerary resumed, but he received regular updates on Heydrich from Gebhardt. Heydrich's condition deteriorated again with a high fever, but then he rallied until finally succumbing to his wound on 4 June. Himmler's diary indicates he was at Friedrichsruh when he received a call at 9.24 a.m. informing him of Heydrich's death. In his own hand, Himmler inserted a death rune after Heydrich's name.

That morning Himmler visited his wife Marga who was in Tilsit and then flew to Prague, landing at 3.50 p.m. He drove to the Bulovka where he viewed Heydrich's corpse and received a report on his death. He also saw Lina Heydrich before attending an urgent meeting at the Hradschin with Daluege, Karl Hermann Frank and Bruno Streckenbach. He left Prague at 6.40 p.m. and arrived at Rastenburg at 9.50 p.m. where he visited Hitler and the two men discussed Heydrich's funeral and his replacement. At 11 p.m. Himmler telephoned Daluege in Prague to inform him of Hitler's wishes for a State funeral in Berlin and the donation of the villa at Jungfern Breschan [*Penanske Brezany*] to Heydrich's widow.

On 5 June, Himmler ordered Heinrich Müller to use all methods at his disposal to discover and apprehend the perpetrators of the attack on Heydrich. Himmler telephoned Gebhardt in Prague and was informed that Lina insisted that both Heydrich's sons should participate in his funeral as her representatives. The honour naming of the 6 SS-Infantry Standarte as 'Reinhard Heydrich' was also discussed. Himmler subsequently telephoned Bormann to discuss the Heydrich boys attending the funeral. On 6 June, Himmler telephoned Julius Schaub and discussed the draft of Himmler's funeral oration before confirming by telephone with Gebhardt that the Heydrich boys would participate in their father's funeral and receiving an update on the condition of Lina Heydrich who was heavily pregnant.

Himmler flew to Prague on 7 June, landing at 2.30 p.m. and then drove to Panenske Brezany to eat with Lina Heydrich. He then proceeded to the Hradschin for Heydrich's funeral departure to Berlin. The ceremony started at 6 p.m. in the courtyard of the Hradschin and Daluege gave a speech before the cortege left on the rail journey to the capital. Himmler flew back to Berlin. Heydrich's body arrived at the Anhalter station at midday on 8 June and was received by Himmler and a large contingent of senior SS officers. It was transferred to the Prinz Albrecht Palais to lie in state overnight before the funeral the next day.

The problem of Heydrich's successor as Chief of the Reichssicherheitshauptamt (RSHA) could not immediately be resolved. Himmler announced to the RSHA division heads at a meeting at 3.30 p.m. on 8 June 1942 that he himself would take charge of this important office until a more permanent successor could be found.

Himmler attended the state funeral of Heydrich at 3 p.m. on 9 June and gave the eulogy in the Mosaic Room of the Reich Chancellery. He followed the coffin to the Invalidenfriedhof where Heydrich's body was interred. Himmler returned to the Reich Chancellery and was present when Hitler received members of the Protectorate government. At 7.40 p.m. Himmler attended a meeting of Obergruppenführer and Gruppenführer in the Haus der Flieger where he delivered a lengthy address after dining with his men.

Himmler conducted an inspection tour on 11 and 12 June before flying to Munich on the 13th and staying at Gmund for two nights. He returned to Berlin on 15 June and carried out another inspection tour on 16 and 17 June. He stayed at Wewelsburg Castle from 18 to 20 June, visiting the officers of SS-Division 'Reich' on 19 June. He went to Munich on 21 June, visiting his parents' grave before meeting Daluege and Müller at the Hotel Vier Jahreszeiten. In the afternoon he attended the state funeral of Adolf Hühnlein before flying back to Berlin.

As chief of the RSHA, Himmler was engaged with additional meetings with divisional office heads of that department and this is reflected in his appointments diary over the ensuing few days. On 24 June, he flew back to Rastenburg and went straight to the Wolfsschanze for his customary report to the Führer. On 25 June he received Felix Steiner on Sonderzug 'Heinrich' and they watched the film of Heydrich's state funeral. This day also marked the start of Aktion Enzian, an operation aimed at destroying the partisan activity in Kärnten and Steiermark. Himmler was present at the FHQ when Hitler personally presented Theodor Eicke with the Oakleaves to the Knights Cross of the Iron Cross on 26 June.

The wide range of subjects discussed between Hitler and his Reichsführer-SS is well illustrated by Himmler's handwritten notes of their meeting at the Wolfsschanze on 1 July 1942. The meeting began at 4 p.m. after a late lunch. Himmler recorded eighteen various points discussed, including SS uniform insignia, awards, division renaming, Aktion Enzian, forged British currency, birthdays and partisan activity. Hitler turned down the award of the Kriegsverdienstkreuz 1st Class to Karl Wolff, but authorised the award of the Iron Cross 1st and 2nd Class Spange for Jüttner and the Deutsches Kreuz in Silber for Daluege.

Himmler stayed in East Prussia at his Friedrichsruh residence and carried out his usual duties of endless meetings and reports. On 7 July, Himmler ordered Wolfram Sievers of Ahnenerbe to establish an institute for military scientific research, to provide full support for the research of Professor Dr Hirt, to make use of the facilities at Dachau and to contact Oswald Pohl with regards to the financing of this project. On 8 July, he had lunch with Gottlob Berger, Richard Glücks, Karl Gebhardt and Professor Carl Clauberg. Clauberg received authority to experiment on Jewish women at KL Auschwitz I using x-rays.

In the afternoon of 9 July 1942, Himmler held a major meeting on the subject of anti-partisan warfare, possibly at Friedrichsruh. Present were not only SS and Police leaders but also several Waffen-SS senior officers. Also on the agenda was the use of foreign labour for the implementation of Generalplan Ost and Aktion Reinhard in the Generalgovernment.

The anti-British Indian leader, Subhas Chandra Bose, visited Himmler at Hegewaldheim on 15 July 1942 and they discussed the possible formation of an Indian unit in the Waffen-SS. Also present were SS-Standartenführer Walther Wüst, SS-Gruppenführer Kurt Knoblauch, Dr Adam von Trott and Dr Lösch.

EIGHT

The Auschwitz Factory

On 17 July 1942, Himmler made the second of two confirmed visits to Auschwitz concentration camp. He flew from Rastenburg (Lötzen Airfield) to Kattowitz, landing at 3.15 p.m. He was greeted at the airfield by Gauleiter Bracht, SS-Obergruppenführer Ernst-Heinrich Schmauser and SS-Sturmbannführer Rudolf Höss. They proceeded to Auschwitz, but according to Himmler's diary did not enter the camps, instead taking tea at the Führerheim (officers' mess) where Höss and Dr Hans Kammler had prepared plans and models of the area. Himmler held talks with Höss, SS-Sturmbannführer Caesar and SS-Obersturmbannführer Vogel before sitting down for a meal. In the evening, Himmler stayed with Gauleiter Bracht at his home in Kattowitz. The following day the two men took breakfast at 9 a.m. with Frau Bracht before driving back to Auschwitz where at 10 a.m. Himmler had a meeting with Schmauser, Caesar and Johanna Langefeld, the female leader of the women guards.

Himmler's service diary only records a visit to the I. G. Farben Bunawerke at Monowitz on the second day, but other sources indicate that Himmler's visit was more comprehensive and included a tour of the camp at Birkenau, including the gassing facilities. Höss describes this visit in his memoirs:

> [*Himmler made a*] ... trip through the whole area of interest ... farms and soil enrichment projects ... dam-building site ... orchards ... the Frauenkonzentrationslager (women's camp) ... Birkenau, the Russian camp, the Gypsy camp and a Jewish camp; [*Himmler*] watched the prisoners at work, inspected the housing, the kitchens and the sick bays. I constantly pointed out the shortcomings and the bad conditions. I am positive he noticed them. He saw the emaciated victims of epidemics. The doctors explained things without mincing words. He saw overcrowded sick bays and the child mortality in the Gypsy camp. Himmler also saw the overcrowded barracks, the primitive and totally inadequate toilet and wash facilities. He was told about the high rate of illness and the death rate by the doctors and their causes. He had everything explained to him in the greatest detail. ... Yet he said absolutely nothing. He really

> gave me a tongue lashing in Birkenau when I went on about the terrible conditions. He screamed, 'I don't want to hear anymore about any existing difficulties! For an SS officer there are no difficulties. His task is always to immediately overcome any difficulty by himself! As to how? That's your headache, not mine!'

Together with Gauleiter Bracht and his deputy, Albert Hoffmann, Himmler apparently witnessed the complete extermination process at Birkenau, from the selection of Jews [*from a recently arrived transport originating at Westerbork in the Netherlands*] to their murder with Zyklon B gas in Bunker II.

> He also looked on for a while during a selection of those who would work and those who would die without any complaint on his part. Himmler made no comment about the extermination process. He just looked on in total silence. I noted that he very quietly watched the officers, the NCOs and me several times during the process. ...

Höss describes the evening at the home of Gauleiter Bracht:

> Even though he had been in a very bad mood during the day and had hardly talked with civility to any of us, during the evening he was just the opposite in our small circle. He was in a very good mood that evening; charming and very talkative, especially with the two ladies, the wife of the [*Gauleiter*] and my wife. He discussed every topic that came up in conversation: the raising of children, new houses, paintings, and books. He told about his experiences with the Waffen-SS divisions at the front lines and about his front line inspection tours with Hitler. He carefully avoided mentioning, even with a single word, anything that he had seen during the day or any matters concerning official business. Any attempt by the [*Gauleiter*] to bring business into the conversation was ignored by Himmler. We broke up quite late. Himmler, who usually drank very little alcohol, that evening had a few glasses of red wine and smoked, which was another thing he didn't usually do. Everyone was captivated by his lively stories and cheerfulness. I had never seen him like that before ...

Höss describes the second day of the visit, following the meeting with Schmauser, Caesar and Langefeld as follows:

> Then he inspected the stables, the workshops, Canada [*the warehouses holding the clothing and other belongings of exterminated Jews*] and the DW [*German armaments factories*] the butcher shop, the bakery, the construction units, and the planning board for the troops. He examined everything thoroughly and saw the prisoners, asked about their reasons for being there and wanted an accurate count.

Höss continues:

> After the inspection, he held a final conference in my office and, in Schmauser's presence, addressed me more or less in the following words: 'I have now made a thorough inspection of Auschwitz. I have seen everything and I have seen enough of the deficiencies and difficulties and I have heard enough from you. I can, however, do nothing to alter them. You will have to manage as best you can. We are now in the middle of war and we must learn to think in terms of war. The actions which I have ordered the security police to carry out will not be stopped under any circumstances, least of all because of the lack of accommodation and so on, which I have been shown. Eichmann's programme will continue to be carried out and will be intensified month by month. You must see to it that swift progress is made with the building of Birkenau. The gypsies are to be destroyed. The Jews who are unfit for work are to be destroyed with the same ruthlessness. Soon the labour camps at the armament factories will absorb the first large contingents of able-bodied Jews and that will give you some breathing space again. Armaments factories will also be built in Auschwitz camp, so prepare for that. Kammler will give you far-reaching support in matters connected with their construction. ... The agricultural experiments will be intensively pursued, for the results are urgently required. ... I have seen your work and the results you have achieved and I am satisfied and thank you for your services. I promote you to Obersturmbannführer!'

On 18 July 1942, Himmler left Auschwitz and flew to Lublin from Kattowitz where he was met at 3.15 p.m. by SS-Obergruppenführer Friedrich-Wilhelm Krüger, SS-Brigadeführer Odilo Globocnik and SS-Standartenführer Walter Schellenberg. The following day, Himmler visited a SS cavalry unit and the training camp at Trawniki. [*There is an unconfirmed report that he also visited the death camp at Sobibor during this inspection tour.*] Himmler stayed in Globocnik's villa as his guest until his departure on 20 July. During this visit, Himmler ordered Krüger to clear the Generalgovernment of all Jews not in the ghettos of Warsaw, Lublin, Radom, Czestochowa or Krakau by 31 December 1942 at the latest.

Himmler carried out an inspection tour from 21 until 23 July, possibly in Berlin. On 24 July 1942, he flew from Berlin to Zhitomir in the Ukraine. Hitler was using a new FHQ at Vinnytsia which was codenamed 'Werwolf' and Himmler selected a site for his new field headquarters near the town of Zhitomir on an old Soviet airfield. He named the facility 'Hegewald' and it formed the centre of a small colony of that name south of Zhitomir. This was to be a German only area and Himmler ordered the forcible removal of 18,000 non-Germans, replacing them with 10,000 ethnic Germans. Himmler often used this new Hegewald over the next year as Hitler's armies pushed further into the southern USSR.

According to a post-war courtroom interrogation, SS-Gruppenführer Paul Scheer testified that Himmler ordered the complete destruction of the Ukrainian Jews at a meeting of local SS and Police Leaders in Hegewald on 26 July 1942. This meeting is not recorded in Himmler's Dienstkalendar.

On 28 July, Himmler left for an official visit to Finland, stopping at Reval *en route*. He arrived in Helsinki on 29 July and toured various units, meeting German and Finnish commanders until leaving on 6 August when he flew to Mogilew. There he met von dem Bach and Schimana to discuss anti-partisan measures before flying on to Zhitomir.

Himmler's routine at Hegewald-Zhitomir continued much in the same vein as in East Prussia ... meetings and reports. One meeting of note was at Hegewald on 11 August 1942 when, at 5.45 p.m., he saw Heinrich Müller and Adolf Eichmann. They discussed the progress of the final solution of the Jewish question and Himmler afterwards kept an appointment at 7.15 p.m. with SS-Brigadeführer Hans Kammler, the construction expert. Several days later, Kammler commenced the erection of four new crematoria at Auschwitz-Birkenau.

For much of the time around this period, SS-Gruppenführer Hanns Johst, the playwright and author, was with Himmler at Hegewald and on his journeys. Johst became a close friend of Himmler who respected his opinions. Johst was arrested and imprisoned after the war, serving a prison term of three-and-a-half years. He was unable to re-establish his career without Nazi patronage and died in 1978.

Himmler remained at Zhitomir until 17 August when he left for Lemberg accompanied by Johst and members of his staff. At the Haus der RFSS in Lemberg, Himmler held a meeting with SS-Brigadeführer Fritz Katzmann, Odilo Globocnik and Otto Wächter. They discussed the status of the Jews in Galicia and the discussion continued the following day when Himmler carried out an inspection of SS and Police facilities, including a labour camp. The same day, Hitler appointed Himmler as leader of all anti-partisan actions. In turn, Himmler nominated Eric von dem Bach as his personal representative for anti-partisan warfare. In late afternoon on 18 August, Himmler and Johst flew to Berlin where Himmler spent the next few days.

On the morning of 21 August, Himmler flew from Berlin to Lublin where he met with Globocnik before heading to Zamosc. He returned to Zhitomir that evening and dined with Johst at his Feldkommandostelle. On 24 August, Himmler entertained Gauleiter Eric Koch at Hegewald. The next day, Himmler found time between meetings to play handball and to take some shooting practice. He was at Hitler's headquarters on 26 August 1942 and had lunch with Hitler.

On 27 August 1942, Himmler flew to Prague. His diary lists his staff who accompanied him: SS-Obergruppenführer Prützmann, SS-Gruppenführer Johst, SS-Obersturmbannführer Tiefenbacher, SS-Sturmbannführer Schäfer, SS-Hauptsturmführer Grothmann, SS-Obersturmführer Dr. Wittmann, SS-Obersturmführer Kiermaier (Himmler's close protection officer,) SS-Scharführer Conrad and SS-Mann Schostal. They were met at the airfield in Prague by Daluege and Frank and the entourage drove at once to Hradcany Castle where Himmler dined with Daluege and his wife before visiting the widowed Frau Stahlecker. Himmler had further talks with Daluege, Frank and Horst Böhme before driving out to the Heydrich villa at Penanske Brezany. He stayed with Lina Heydrich overnight and returned to the city after breakfast for final talks with Daluege. The entourage took off at 11 a.m. and landed in Munich at 12.30 p.m.

Himmler had lunch with his wife Marga at the Hotel Vier Jahreszeiten before visiting his parents' grave. He then attended the Great German Art Exhibition prior to driving to Starnberg where he visited the grave of the recently deceased (29 July 1942) SS-Obergruppenführer Paul Scharfe before calling in on his widow. He spent the next three nights at Gmund.

On 31 August, Himmler started a tour of heavily bombed cities in the west of Germany. He flew from Munich to Wiesbaden and was greeted there by Gauleiter Sprenger, Gauleiter Bürckel, SS-Obergruppenführer Berkelmann and SS-Gruppenführer Berger. After talks with Bürckel at the airport, Himmler's entourage drove to Mainz where he met local police chiefs and officials. He returned to Wiesbaden and stayed at the Palast-Hotel.

On 1 September 1942, Himmler drove to Cologne and was joined by Gauleiter Grohé, SS-Brigadeführer Gutenberger and Generalmajor Lankenau. The city of Cologne had been the target of the first 1,000 bomber raid during the night of 30–31 May 1942 and had sustained serious damage. Himmler was conducted on a lightning tour of the damaged city. From there, he drove to Düsseldorf where he was greeted by Gauleiter Florian and SS-Brigadeführer Korreng. Again, he was shown the bomb damage to the city. At 5 p.m. he visited the widow of SS-Obergruppenführer Fritz Weitzel and then had a quick meeting with SS-Gruppenführer Schlessmann before driving to the city cemetery for a visit to the grave of Weitzel just before 7 p.m. After this he was shown unexploded British bombs before setting off towards Münster where he stayed at the Hotel Fürstenhof. On 2 September, Himmler was driven around the city and then moved on to Osnabrück where he was greeted by Gauleiter Wegener. The two men had a discussion *en route* to Bremen where they dined with other senior officials and officers at the famous ornate town hall. Himmler inspected the Bremen flak command post and then drove on to Hamburg.

He was entertained in Hamburg by Gauleiter Kaufmann and his wife before retiring to the Hotel Atlantik. From Hamburg Himmler drove to Lübeck with SS-Gruppenführer Querner and had lunch at the town hall. From Lübeck Himmler's entourage returned to Berlin by car. Following this inspection tour, Himmler ordered that prisoners from concentration camps were to be used to repair air raid damage and that replacement building materials would be provided by the camps.

On 6 September 1942, Himmler flew by Fieseler Storch from Hegewald to Göring's Sonderzug Asien where he spent the whole day in talks with the Reichsmarschall before flying back to his Feldkommandostelle near Zhitomir. Himmler's usual routine of meetings, working lunches and dinners, telephone conversations and reports continued at his Feldkommandostelle. His personal meetings with Hitler also continued, but not so frequently. He stayed in constant touch with his office in Berlin and spoke frequently by telephone to his private secretary, Erika Lorenz, and his adjutant in Berlin, SS-Sturmbannführer Paul Baumert. Baumert often updated Himmler with bulletins on air raid damage throughout Germany. His work fully occupied his waking moments and constantly kept him away from his family. Himmler regularly telephoned Hedwig at their homes in Berlin or Berchtesgaden-Schönau, or his wife and daughter in Berlin-Dahlem or Gmund am Tegernsee. He rarely saw them and had little time for himself, but found the odd moment to relax with a game of handball or to practise his shooting.

The flurry of comings and goings of silver braided field grey uniforms was quite marked during these weeks. Himmler would individually meet with his generals and staff before lunching or dining with them in the evenings in larger groups. At one such particular gathering on 16 September 1942, Himmler delivered a long speech to the SS and Police Leaders of southern Russia. In it he provided his views on ethnic cleansing of the Slavic people and the Germanisation of selected racially acceptable children with suitable German parents.

Himmler spent the day of 18 September in discussions with Reich Justice Minister Otto Thierack and his State Secretary Rothenberger. They formulated an agreement which clarified the role of the SS, Police and the legal system. Himmler gained the agreement that certain categories of prisoners serving terms of imprisonment would be made available to the Reichsführer-SS for resettlement or 'special handling.'

On 25 September, Himmler flew from Zhitomir to Interburg where he drove to Sonderzug 'Asien' at Eichkamp and spent the afternoon with Göring. The two men went hunting in Rominten for two days, sleeping in a hunting lodge and returning to Eichkamp on 27 September. Sonderzug 'Asien' made its way back to Berlin delivering the Reichsmarschall and Reichsführer at the Anhalter Station at 10.35 a.m. on 28 September. Later that day, Himmler attended the swearing-in of new SS officers at the Berlin Sportpalast.

On 29 September, Himmler inspected the concentration camp at Sachsenhausen with SS-Brigadeführer August Frank and Richard Glücks. He toured the whole facility including the cell block where several prominent prisoners were incarcerated. There is no record of any conversations Himmler had with any of them.

Himmler remained in Berlin until his visit to Krakau on 4 October 1942 where he had a meeting with Krüger, Becker, Globocnik, Schöngarth and Scherner before returning by air to Zhitomir.

7 October 1942 saw the occasion of Himmler's 42nd birthday. He spent the afternoon with Hitler and celebrated with all his SS officers present at Hegewald by dining with them in the officers' mess at 8 p.m. Himmler flew to Munich via Krakau on 9 October and stayed the night at Gmund. The following day he drove back to Munich, visited his parents' grave and took tea with SS-Obergruppenführer Josias Erbprinz zu Waldeck und Pyrmont at the Hotel Vier Jahreszeiten. At 6.40 p.m. he

boarded a train at Munich station and left for an official visit to Rome. There he had meetings with Mussolini, Count Ciano, Ambassador von Mackensen and various Italian dignitaries over the ensuing few days. At his meeting with the Duce, Himmler apparently informed him of the mass shooting of Jews as partisans in Russia. He took two tours around the city by car, taking in the sights accompanied by Eugen Dollmann. Himmler returned to Munich on 15 October and went to Gmund.

On 17 October, Himmler paid an inspection visit by air to the SS-Gebirgsdivision Prinz Eugen in Kraljewo. He also had a meeting with SS-Gruppenführer August Meyszner and flew back to Zhitomir on 18 October.

Himmler's diary notes that he received visits at Hegewald over the following days from numerous senior SS officers and there must have been a distinct lack of space around his dining table in the evenings with large groups being catered for. Among the guests were the ever present Johst, Prützmann, Rost von Tonningen, Karl Hermann Frank, Fritz Klingenberg, Gunter d'Alquen, Eric von dem Bach, Walter Krüger, Frau Bethge, Fräulein Hanstein, Fräulein Dreyer and many other SS officers. Of particular note among the guests is one name ... SS-Obersturmführer Alois Rehrl, Himmler's old friend and mentor. Rehrl arrived at Hegewald on 20 October 1942 and appears in the list of dinner guests at the Kommandostelle off and on until Himmler left for the Crimea on 27 October after attending and speaking at the funeral in Zhitomir of SS-Obersturmbannführer Carl Schnäbele, SS-Untersturmführer Johann Maurus and the Volksdeutschen woman Olga Bartz.

Schnäbele was Himmler's personal pilot and was killed in an ambush on his car by Ukrainian partisans near Zhitomir on 26 October 1942. He was travelling with his aid Maurus and two women when their vehicle was attacked. The partisans escaped and were never caught. Himmler was furious and ordered that hostages from the nearby villages where the attack occurred were to be shot. His wish was carried out. Also on 27 October, Himmler ordered the liquidation of the entire ghetto at Pinsk.

Alois Rehrl accompanied Himmler to the Crimea as part of his entourage. Himmler conducted a thorough inspection of units and installations throughout the Crimea which included a visit to the grave of SS-Untersturmführer Rehrl in Perekop. Whether or not this was the grave of Alois' son has not been confirmed, but Himmler went out of his way to visit this officer's grave, breaking his flight at Perekop in order to do so.

The party flew back to Zhitomir on 1 November 1942 and Himmler drove to Feldkommandostelle Hegewald. The morning of 2 November was occupied with packing up the quarters before leaving Hegewald at midday. Himmler visited the grave of Carl Schnäbele *en route* to the airfield at Zhitomir from whence Himmler flew to Lötzen in East Prussia.

Whilst Himmler occupied his Feldkommandostelle Hegewald near Zhitomir, it had been decided to erect and fortify the Hochwald facilities near the Wolfsschanze.

Organisation Todt erected several new concrete bunkers at the site near Pozezdrze and outer defences were also fortified. Himmler retained the name Hochwald for his improved Feldkommandostelle in East Prussia. He arrived at Hochwald around 4 p.m. on 2 November and was immediately shown around the new installations. His bunker, the largest, was an A-class bomb proof building of thick concrete and steel construction. There were four other concrete bunkers of lower grade resistibility and a number of wooden barracks. The compound was surrounded by wire fencing and a minefield, but there were no anti-aircraft gun emplacements as at the Wolfsschanze nearby. The entire area was heavily patrolled with guards at strategic locations. Whereas Himmler did not usually sleep at Hegewaldheim, he did have his train for overnight quarters at Hochwald and in fact he slept at the improved Feldkommandostelle the first night of reoccupation. According to Werner Grothmann, Himmler's adjutant, Sonderzug 'Heinrich' was kept in a rail siding within the area of the compound at Hochwald. Also, although Himmler had a designated concrete bunker, his day office was in one of the long wooden barracks, at one end.

On 4 November, Himmler flew from Lötzen to Berlin where he remained until flying to Prague on 6 November. He held meetings with Daluege, Frank and Graf Pückler before visiting the SS artillery school at Beneschau. He spent the night at the hunting lodge Schloss Doberschisch and flew to Munich the following day where he attended the funeral of Minister President Siebert. At the Hotel Vier Jahreszeiten, Himmler held meetings with Hausser, von Schirach, Eicke and Müller before attending an evening meal for Reichsleiter and Gauleiter at the Führerbau in Königsplatz. Himmler spent the night in Gmund, but returned to the Munich hotel for further meetings on 8 November.

At 6 p.m. Himmler attended the Löwenbräukeller for the speech by Hitler marking the anniversary of the 1923 Putsch. Himmler stayed at the hotel that night and at 12.30 p.m. on the 9th, attended the wreath laying ceremony at the Ehrentempeln in Königsplatz. He returned to his hotel and held further meetings throughout the afternoon and evening, taking a break at 8.30 p.m. for treatment from Kersten. The next few days were taken up with various meetings and commuting between Munich and Gmund. On a rare occasion, Marga Himmler accompanied her husband to Munich on 12 November.

On 13 November 1942, Himmler visited Dr Rascher in Dachau concentration camp and received a full update on the experiments he was conducting for the Luftwaffe. He also held meetings with the Standort commander SS-Oberführer Pfannenstiel and the camp commander, Martin Weiss. He then drove to Berchtesgaden, stopping off for lunch at Gmund. In Berchtesgaden he stayed at the Berchtesgadenerhof, but then moved to his Feldkommandostelle Bergwald on 15 November. Bergwald was the former mansion of the von Trapp family [*made famous by the 1965 film 'The Sound of Music'*] and was located at Salzburg-Aigen, giving Himmler easy access to the Berghof. He stayed at Bergwald for the next few days and visited the Rehrl family at Fridolfing on 21 November. He spent the night of 22 November at Gmund and carried out an inspection of the SS-Junkerschule Tölz on 23 November, returning to Bergwald that evening. From 24 to 27 November, Himmler went hunting at Hohentauern.

By 30 November, Himmler was again reporting to Hitler at Wolfsschanze in East Prussia and spent the night at Friedrichsruh. The service diary refers once again to Hegewaldheim for an evening meal on 2 December and thereafter for several meals. The Hochwald facility at Grossgarten does not reappear again until 25 December 1942. It seems that Himmler found the concrete bunkers too limited for space and he had ordered some alterations and new barrack construction with work being carried out in the first weeks of December. For whatever the reason, Himmler slept and worked mainly at Friedrichsruh throughout December 1942. During this period, Himmler held a meeting at Friedrichsruh on 3 December with Albert Ganzenmüller, the State Secretary in the Ministry of Transport. They discussed Jewish transports on the rail network, particularly in relation to the Generalgovernment. Without co-operation from the rail authorities, Himmler's plans for large scale deportations would not be possible.

On 11 December 1942, Himmler carried out an inspection tour of the secret facilities at Peenemünde and was fully briefed on the progress of rocket research and production.

Himmler flew from Lötzen to Munich on 16 December and after visiting his parents' grave he visited the SS office at Karlstrasse before driving down to Gmund, staying for three nights. On 19 December, Himmler flew to Prague and visited Lina Heydrich, spending the night at Panenske Brezany. The following day, he flew to Rechlin and paid a visit to the SS clinic at Hohenlychen before driving to Berlin. He was back at Friedrichsruh on 23 December where he stayed for Christmas. There is a note on 25 December 1942 'umzug in die neue Baracke' (move in the new barracks.) The next day Himmler's diary states he was at Hochwald where he remained for the last days of 1942.

It appears that Himmler spent the greater percentage of his time at Feldkommandostelle Hochwald and its subsidiary locations for the first months of 1943.

The winter of 1942–43 did not go well for Hitler's armies and the tide of war was turning against him. Hitler spent more and more time at his FHQ near Rastenburg and wherever his Führer went, the loyal Reichsführer followed. Hitler's style of leadership promoted intrigue and rivalry with his ministers and the top NSDAP officials. It did not pay to lose the confidence or the ear of the Führer and Himmler was no exception among the officials clambering for Hitler's attention.

Himmler received Walter Schellenberg in the evening of 4 January 1943 following his customary visit to Hitler at the Wolfsschanze earlier that day and on 6 January he left for Posen. On 9 January, he paid a fleeting visit to Warsaw and toured the ghetto before returning to Hochwald in the evening. During this visit, Himmler revealed that Hitler had ordered the dissolution of the ghetto and Himmler directed the local SS leader, SS-Oberführer Dr Ferdinand von Sammern-Frankenegg, to resettle the Jews serving the armaments industry in Auschwitz and Lublin.

Himmler was on the move again on 11 January, this time leaving for Berlin at 6.30 p.m. by his special train 'Heinrich,' arriving at 9.30 a.m. the following morning. It appears he only stayed in the capital for the day, departing for Lötzen the same evening. His schedule was as usual full of various meetings, but his diary notes that he found time for a sauna between 6 p.m. and 7 p.m. on 15 January and he was back at the Wolfsschanze on 16 January.

On 18 January 1943, Himmler commissioned the Korherr Report. He directed his statistician Dr Richard Korherr to research and report on the progress of the policy towards the Jews in Europe. Korherr reported on the shift in population within the areas of German influence and control. His figures included those Jews 'evacuated' from the Eastern Occupied Territories, the vast majority of whom had been killed by the Einsatzkommandos. He also included figures for the Jews who had been 'processed' through the camps in the Generalgovernment. The total number of Jews recorded as 'evacuated' reached 2.5 million.

The following day, 19 January, Himmler entertained Oberst Helmuth von Pannwitz at his Feldkommandostelle. Four days earlier, whilst receiving the award of the Oakleaves to his Knights Cross of the Iron Cross from Hitler, von Pannwitz had courageously voiced his opinion that the German policy towards the Slavic races which viewed them as sub-humans was fundamentally flawed. This controversial belief and the courageous voicing of his opinion did not apparently prevent von Pannwitz's subsequent promotion to the rank of Generalleutnant or his transfer from the Army to the Waffen-SS in February 1945.

On 23 January, Himmler met with Admiral Canaris, the head of the Abwehr, prior to a further audience with Hitler at the Wolfsschanze field headquarters. He left by train the next day and headed for Posen with Karl Wolff and his close protection officer from the RSD, Josef Kiermaier. Himmler's diary records a meeting on 25 January with Reichsminister for the Occupied Eastern Territories Alfred Rosenberg and his deputy Alfred Meyer. Himmler stayed in Posen for a few days before returning to Berlin on 29 January.

Back in Berlin, he was able to spend time at his office in Prinz-Albrecht-Strasse, but also had the opportunity for meetings with Reichsmarschall Hermann Göring and Reichsminister Dr Josef Goebbels on 30 January 1943, the tenth anniversary of the Nazi seizure of power. Following some time at his office the next day, Himmler visited the grave of the fallen SS-Obergruppenführer Reinhard Heydrich in the Invaliden Cemetery before leaving on another journey, this time accompanied by SS-Obergruppenführer Wilhelm Rediess, the Higher SS and Police Leader in Norway.

From 1 February 1943, Himmler's Sonderzug became known as 'Steiermark' and consequently his escort unit 'Heinrich' was renamed 'Steiermark.' All special trains in use as fieldheadquarters in the Third Reich changed their codenames the same day.

By 5 February, Himmler was again in Posen where he held a meeting with the Reich Youth Leader, Artur Axmann and was reporting once more to the Führer at the Wolfsschanze on 7 February. In turn, the next few days saw Himmler meeting with various senior SS personalities, including the Higher SS and Police Leader Rhine, SS-Obergruppenführer Theodor Berkelmann.

Berkelmann was a favourite of Himmler and was an old style SS leader. He had been a member of the SA and had held an instructor's position at the Reich SA Leadership School in Munich, before transferring to the SS. In early 1943, Berkelmann held the dual appointment of Higher SS and Police Leader in both Rhine and Westmark. On 21 May of that year, Himmler decided to combine the posts and created the single appointment of Higher SS and Police Leader Rhine-Westmark. Later in the year Himmler selected Berkelmann to replace Wilhelm Koppe in Posen as he was moving to Krakau. Berkelmann had hardly arrived when he was taken ill and finally succumbed to a brain tumour on 27 December 1943.

On 9 February 1943, Himmler also met with Oswald Pohl, the astute head of the SS economics empire governed by the SS main bureau for economic administration (SS-WVHA: SS-Wirtschafts-Verwaltungs Hauptamt) which oversaw the concentration camp system. Following his customary report to Hitler at the Wolfsschanze the following day, Himmler returned to Hochwald for his evening meal and the showing of a film on Leningrad.

Himmler flew to Lublin on 12 February, where he was entertained by the SS and Police Leader SS-Brigadeführer Odilo Globocnik and then inspected the Aktion Reinhard headquarters situated in the Julius Schreck Barracks in Lublin. He apparently included a lightning tour of the death camp at Sobibor. There is also speculation that he also visited Treblinka prior to his return to Hochwald on 14 February.

The following few days were occupied with office work and inspection tours, including meetings with SS-Gruppenführer Kurt Knoblauch, various other SS officers and the new chief of the Security Police and Security Service (Sipo und Sicherheitsdienst) SS-Gruppenführer Dr Ernst Kaltenbrunner on 18 February.

After Reinhard Heydrich had been assassinated the previous summer, Himmler was undecided over his replacement and temporarily took on the role himself. The Reichssicherheitshauptamt (RSHA) was the most important SS central office, controlling the Criminal Police (Kripo,) Security Police (Sipo,) better known by the term Gestapo, and the Security Service, more commonly referred to as the SD. This department more than any other, was both feared and envied by other government and party administrations. Through this instrument Himmler was able to govern everyday life in the Reich and its occupied territories. He could not afford to place this important tool in the hands of a rival as Heydrich had become and therefore he deliberated over Heydrich's replacement, finally deciding upon the less dangerous Kaltenbrunner who was also acceptable to Hitler.

On 20 February 1943, Himmler flew to Vinnytsia. That evening he received Hans Prützmann and Gerret Korsemann for a meal at Feldkommandostelle Hegewald when they appraised him of the current situation report for the Ukraine. On 22 February, Himmler visited Kiev before flying to Lötzen. His diary the next day notes an afternoon meeting with SS-Obergruppenführer Werner Lorenz. He was at Hochwald early on the morning of 24 February before flying from Lötzen to Prague where he held talks with SS-Gruppenführer Karl Hermann Frank.

Himmler then travelled the same day to Munich where he paid a visit to a cemetery, most likely the grave of his parents. That night he motored down to Gmund, spending the whole of the following day with his wife and daughter. On 26 February he returned to Munich and met with SS-Obergruppenführer Karl von Eberstein before flying once again to Prague where he stayed for just under four hours. He moved on to Weimar and at 5 p.m. arrived for a quick inspection tour of Buchenwald Concentration Camp. That night Himmler stayed at the Hotel Elephant in Weimar.

At 8 a.m. on 27 February, Himmler was informed that SS-Obergruppenführer Theodor Eicke had been killed in action the previous afternoon. Eicke had been carrying out an aerial reconnaissance for his SS-Totenkopf Division in his Fieseler Storch in the opening stages of the third Battle of Kharkov when his aircraft came under ground fire attack from Soviet forces approximately one kilometre south-west of Artelnoje near Lozovaya. The light aircraft crashed, killing all three aboard. Eicke's body, and those of his adjutant SS-Hauptsturmführer Otto Friedrich and the pilot Oberfeldwebel Michael Werner, was recovered and all three were buried with full military honours on 1 March in Otdochnina. When the Soviet army pushed the Germans back six months later, Himmler ordered that the remains of the Totenkopf commander be removed to the Hegewald Cemetery near Zhitomir. Eicke's grave was eventually abandoned in the spring of 1944 following the Soviet advance and his remains are today anonymously interred within a communal grave.

Himmler flew back to East Prussia and was at Hochwald on 28 February. The next day he had meetings with Gunter d'Alquen, the editor of the SS newspaper *Das Schwarze Korps,* and Reichsminister Hans Lammers, dining with him that evening. On 2 March, Himmler was back at the Wolfsschanze and again took an evening meal with Lammers, working late into the night.

Himmler's diary records almost a full day appointment with SS-Gruppenführer Gottlob Berger on 3 March which resumed in the afternoon of 4 March, this time joined by SS-Gruppenführer Hans Jüttner who returned the following day. The presence of these two officials indicates that the organisation of the Waffen-SS was high on the agenda. Lammers once again joined Himmler for his evening meal on 5 March and the Reichsführer worked on until late with further appointments.

The early evening entry for 6 March 1943 shows Himmler with SS-Obersturmbannführer Dr Rudolf Brandt, followed by his evening meal, again with Lammers. Himmler has written 'Heydrich Geburtstag' across the top of the page for 7 March as a reminder of the late Heydrich's birthday. On 8 March, Himmler had an appointment with Admirals Krancke and Voss who were both attached to the Führer's headquarters in addition to his usual appointments with various senior SS officers.

At Hochwald the following day, Himmler received a visit from SS-Gruppenführer Carl Oberg, the senior SS officer in northern France and Belgium. On 10 March at 3 p.m., Himmler saw Admiral Canaris, the head of military intelligence, followed by a 4 p.m. meeting with Kaltenbrunner and his chief of foreign intelligence, SS-Standartenführer Walter Schellenberg. Schellenberg had been mooted as a possible successor to Heydrich and he had an important role to play towards the end of Himmler's career, which will be mentioned later in this narrative.

On 12 March, Himmler notes that SS-Obergruppenführer Karl Wolff was in the SS clinic at Hohenlychen and on 13 March Himmler left Hochwald and flew from Lötzen to Riga where he was received by the local Higher SS and Police Leader SS-Obergruppenführer Friedrich Jeckeln. The following day, Himmler travelled on to Reval and visited SA-Obergruppenführer Karl-Siegmund Litzmann. He stayed in Reval, touring the local area, until he flew back to Lötzen and Hochwald on 16 March via Riga. Back at the Wolfsschanze on 17 March, he updated Hitler on his findings before returning to Hochwald in the evening with Hans Prützmann. Once more, back at his Feldkommandostelle, Himmler embarked on a merry-go-round of appointments and office duties until leaving for Berlin on 20 March.

Staying in the capital for one night, Himmler left Berlin on 21 March 1943 for Munich and immediately upon arrival he visited the cemetery, before driving to Gmund where he stayed throughout the next day and most of the 23rd. He was at Bergwald on 24 March and stayed there until 2 April as Hitler was in residence at the Berghof on the Obersalzberg. His diary entries for several days in this period are illegible, but he did spend a large part of the day on 28 March with Reichsleiter Martin Bormann at his home on the Obersalzberg. On 29 March, Himmler had appointments with SS-Obergruppenführer Josef 'Sepp' Dietrich, Reichsminister Albert Speer and Ernst Kaltenbrunner, all at Bergwald. On 30 March, he spent the majority of the day visiting his Führer's home at the Berghof and possibly discussed SS promotions for 20 April. [*The diary entry for 31 March 1943 is missing from the author's copies.*] On the evening of 1 April, he held a meeting at Bergwald with SS-Gruppenführer Max von Herff, the chief of the SS personnel office, no doubt to confirm forthcoming promotions for the Führer's birthday anniversary.

On 3 April, Himmler noted 'Angoulême' by the 9.30 a.m. entry. Angoulême is a French town in the south-west of the country in the area where Eicke's Totenkopf Division had conducted operations the previous winter. There is no other note or mention of what this entry means, but it preceded Himmler's visit to Paris, arriving at 12.30 p.m. the same day. He quickly set about his work with an appointment at

4 p.m. with Generalfeldmarschall von Rundstedt, General Blumentritt and General Stülpnagel. That evening Himmler dined with Oberg and René Bousquet, the Vichy police general secretary and he conducted a tour of inspection during the ensuing days.

Himmler was back at Bergwald on 8 April for meetings with Generalmajor Rudolf Schmundt, General Ziegler and SS-Gruppenführer Walther Krüger with whom he dined. On 9 April, Himmler held discussions with Bormann before joining Hitler probably at Schloss Klessheim in Salzburg. The diary notes that from 6 p.m. until 7.30 p.m. they were joined by another and the entry appears to read 'Duce,' indicating the presence of Mussolini.

Himmler required the healing hands of Felix Kersten on 10 April when he treated the Reichsführer at Bergwald between 12.30 p.m. and 1.45 p.m. That evening Himmler dined with Grossadmiral Karl Dönitz. The next day his appointments included Generaloberst Heinz Guderian. On 12 April Himmler visited the nearby small town of Berchtesgaden and his never-ending meetings continued the following day with appointments with SS-Obergruppenführer Lorenz, SS-Obergruppenführer Wilhelm Reinhard and SS-Brigadeführer Konstantin Kammerhofer. His stomach cramps appear to be particularly bad around this time as Kersten appears in the diary daily at 12.30 p.m. for several consecutive days until Himmler left Bergwald for Gmund on 17 April.

Haus Lindenfycht at Gmund am Tegernsee provided Himmler with a refuge away from the daily grind of office administration, meetings and inspection tours. It was situated close to the lakeshore and was set back from the road in a slightly elevated position. He had purchased the house with Marga in 1936 from Alois Burstaller after having rented it since 1934. They carried out some renovations in 1937-1938, using the same architect Himmler had engaged to build the SS officer cadet school at Bad Tölz. After selling the smallholding they owned at Waldtrudering in 1933, the Himmlers lived for a short period in a spacious apartment at Möhlstrasse in Munich, but this arrangement was only temporary. The larger house at Gmund suited family life and Marga remained there with Gudrun, even after the breakdown of their marriage.

The house had a separate smaller building at the entrance to the drive where a detachment of the SS security service was based to provide protection for the Reichsführer and his family in addition to office accommodation as required. Himmler's visits, infrequent as they were during the war years, were an opportunity to see his daughter and to relax. The atmosphere between Marga and her estranged husband remained cordial and their outward appearance was one of mutual respect. Marga resented Fräulein Potthast, but refrained from blatant hostility. Her diaries reflect the strain under which she lived. Himmler's relationship with his daughter remained one of a loving, caring father and he maintained regular contact with her by telephone, almost on a daily basis, whilst at his various Feldkommandostellen.

NINE

Rebellion

On 19 April 1943, Himmler drove to Bad Reichenhall where he stayed the night and worked the following day. On 19 April German troops entered the ghetto in Warsaw to complete the deportation of Jewish inhabitants that had begun some weeks before. Many Jews had realised that the deportations meant death and formed organised groups to offer armed resistance. They attacked the Germans who were forced to withdraw. The Warsaw ghetto uprising had begun. It was to last until 16 May 1943 and resulted in the deaths of 13,000 Jews and seventeen Germans. Himmler, dissatisfied with the way his SSPF Ferdinand von Sammern-Frankenegg was handling the uprising in its initial stages, replaced him with SS-Brigadeführer Jürgen Stroop. The ruthless Stroop was better organised and systematically destroyed the resistance along with many of the buildings.

The ever-present Kersten again attended Himmler on Hitler's birthday [*20 April*] and Himmler then called upon Reichsminister Joachim von Ribbentrop at his castle, Schloss Fuschl, east of Salzburg.

At 9.45 a.m. on 20 April 1943, Friedrich-Wilhelm Krüger left his residence at the Wawel Castle in Krakow to drive to his office at Weichselufer in his PKW car, registration OST31. As his vehicle turned into the Outer Ring Road, two men attempted to kill him. Krüger himself described the incident in a report to Himmler the same day:

> ... 2 men of good appearance and well dressed sprang out onto the footway from a shed which stood obliquely to the street ... and threw, within an interval of seconds, 2 bombs which were shaped something like a short thermos flask. I could see the first bomb exactly as it came flying towards my vehicle. It was coloured black. Both bombs exploded immediately behind my vehicle, with the result that my right wheel and tyre were damaged and the petrol tank holed.
>
> While the second bomb was thrown, I ducked and grasped my pistol. After the explosion, when I realised that I had not been wounded, I shouted to my driver to

> stop at once and he pulled over to the right. I turned round, meanwhile and saw the two men disappearing in the same direction, roughly into the middle of the shed.
>
> I could no longer see them exactly, since I had already gone past the corner. When I ran to the shed myself, there was no longer any sign of the two would-be assassins. Now various Germans came running up to me, both from the direction of the 'Press Centre' and from the cul-de-sac which runs near the shed. In addition, all the windows in the vicinity were damaged by the two explosions. …

Krüger also reported that a discarded pistol, a British Colt, was recovered from the roadside and handed to the police. He stated that both he and his driver were unscathed and he concluded with a scant description of the culprits.

The report is dated the day of the attack and is signed by him. There followed a thorough investigation by the Security Police and SD in Krakow which culminated in the two would-be assassins being captured. Krüger visited them in prison before they were executed. As a result Martin Bormann ordered that an armoured car be placed at the disposal of the HSSPF. The press agency Reuters mistakenly reported that Krüger ' … renowned for his cruelty in Poland' had died from bullet wounds.

Around this time, Himmler was severely troubled with his stomach cramps and Kersten earned his fees, attending the Reichsführer again on 21 and 22 April. Himmler had discussions with the Reichsminister for Justice, Otto Thierack, on 21 and then spent the evening of 22 with von Ribbentrop at Hitler's Salzburg HQ Schloss Klessheim.

From 23 to 26 April 1943, Himmler was in Kharkov where he addressed a meeting of the command corps of the Waffen-SS. He touched upon the racial struggle for the Germanic people and impressed on those gathered that the SS remained the main weapon against the spread of non-Aryan blood. What the officers of fighting units who had made so many sacrifices in the battlefields of the eastern front thought of his words, one can only speculate. Many were still 'believers,' but a growing number realised that they were now in a battle for survival. Himmler finished his tour of inspection with a visit to SS-Panzer Division Wiking on 26 and 27 April.

Two days of travelling saw him back in Bad Reichenhall on 30 April before paying a 50th birthday visit to von Ribbentrop at Schloss Fuschl. On 1 May, Kersten was again in attendance amid a flurry of official appointments. Himmler visited Millstattersee, Veldes [*today Bled, Slovenia*] and Klagenfurt on 2 May. After a night in Klagenfurt, Himmler toured the south of Carinthia and into northern Croatia, taking in Agram [*today Zagreb*] before heading back to Graz where he stayed on 5 May.

Hitler was back in Berlin now and Himmler headed to the Reich capital to report to his Führer over the following few days before taking his special train overnight on 10 May back into East Prussia, arriving at Hochwald at 10.45 a.m. on 11 May. His usual agenda of meetings and office work kept him occupied before his next visit to the Wolfsschanze on14 May where he had meetings with Bormann, Dönitz and Speer respectively. On 15 May in the evening Himmler visited Hegewaldheim and the next day travelled to see Gauleiter Koch in Königsberg.

SS-Gruppenführer Hans Jüttner was summoned to Hochwald on 17 and 18 May when the two men discussed administrative matters pertaining to the Waffen-SS. Himmler dined with Lammers on 18 May and the following day the Reichsführer received the artist Professor Conrad Hommel. Hommel's paintings were approved by the Nazi regime and he had produced portraits of both Hitler and Göring. Himmler had chosen Hommel to paint him in a striking pose as a war leader. The finished work of art depicted a full figure Himmler standing, legs slightly apart with his arms resting across his front, in full uniform with boots and cap. Hommel stayed for lunch and they were joined by Kaltenbrunner who briefed Himmler on security matters at an afternoon meeting.

Reichsminister Hans Lammers appears to have been a frequent visitor to Himmler's Feldkommandostelle Hochwald and most likely used Sonderzug 'Steiermark' as a temporary base, sleeping in one of the compartments. The two men regularly dined together and Lammers was present once again on 20 May.

Gottlob Berger and the Flemish fascist politician Jef van der Wiele attended Hochwald in the afternoon of 21 May for a 3 p.m. meeting when the formation of a Waffen-SS unit of Flemish volunteers was discussed. It was decided that the Walloon Battalion under the Belgian Rexist leader Leon Degrelle should transfer to the Waffen-SS, culminating in its transfer to SS command in June 1943. Immediately after this meeting, Himmler had an appointment with Admiral Canaris to discuss Abwehr and other intelligence matters. Berger and van der Wiele returned the next day for lunch and a further appointment where details were finalised for the transfer of the Flemish unit. They were joined by Hans Prützmann and then SS-Brigadeführer Karl Cerff after van der Wiele had departed. On 23 May Himmler left Hochwald at 10 p.m. by train accompanied by Leon Degrelle and Berger. In a three hour meeting the men ironed out the practical details of forming a new Waffen-SS Flemish volunteer unit, the finer points being decided by the time the train reached Meseritz where he conducted an inspection visit of the Flemish troops.

Himmler continued to suffer badly with stomach cramps at this time. He had two sessions in one day with Kersten on 24 May, one in the morning and the other in the evening. One can only assume that he had a lot on his mind, the consequences of which resulted in stress and severe abdominal discomfort. He remained on his train and it appears that Kersten was a travelling guest as Himmler had another session with him on the morning of 25 May before arriving in Berchtesgaden via Bad Reichenhall. He worked in his makeshift office aboard the train until driving to Fridolfing for an evening visit to the Rehrl farm. He motored on to Bergwald and had yet another session with Kersten on 26 May before going to Munich where he met with Reichsleiter Franz Xaver Schwarz. That night he drove down to Gmund where he was to spend the following few days.

Whilst staying in Gmund, Himmler was able to visit the SS-Junkerschule at Bad Tölz on 27 May. He spent time with his family the next day and may have taken the opportunity for some wild boar hunting on 29 May before heading to Kassel and Arolsen where he stayed at the Schloss of SS-Obergruppenführer Josias Erbprinz zu Waldeck und Pyrmont. Himmler flew from Kassel at 5.30 p.m. on 30 May and landed at Staaken airfield in Berlin soon after.

The following days Himmler was on the move, presumably carrying out inspection tours. He arrived in Freiburg im Breisgau on the first anniversary of Heydrich's death, 4 June 1943, duly noted as such in his diary. On 5 June, Himmler moved north to Strasbourg and then returned to spend the night at Feldkommandostelle Bergwald near Salzburg. He made a quick visit to Gmund on 6 June and stayed overnight, leaving the next morning for Berchtesgaden where he met Kaltenbrunner in the late afternoon.

At 10.30 p.m. on 7 June, Himmler had a meeting with SS-Brigadeführer Dr Hans Kammler, the chief of construction and buildings in Department C of the SS-WVHA. No doubt Kammler briefed Himmler on the progress of the building work being carried out at Auschwitz-Birkenau. In late March–early April 1943, three new crematoria with incorporated gassing facilities (crematoria IV, II and V) had opened for operation and the fourth (crematorium III) was nearing completion. (Crematorium III opened on 25 June 1943.) The four purpose built facilities increased the possible daily capacity in the ovens to 4,756 victims.

Himmler's schedule of meetings continued at Bergwald with SS-Gruppenführer von Herff and SS-Gruppenführer Oberg, both attending on 8 June. Himmler spent most of the next day at Bormann's house on the Obersalzberg and discussed police affairs with SS-Gruppenführer Otto Winkelmann during the early evening of 10 June. On 12 June, Himmler visited von Ribbentrop at Fuschl before driving to Gmund for a few days rest. By 16 June he was back at Bergwald.

On 17 June 1943, Himmler went to the Obersalzberg and congratulated Bormann on his 43rd birthday before having a private discussion with Hitler. He then drove down the mountain to Berchtesgaden for an evening meal with SS-Gruppenführer Leonardo Conti, the Reich health leader, and Himmler's police adjutant Willy Suchanek. Kersten treated Himmler in Berchtesgaden the following day and Himmler stayed overnight in town. He called on Hitler at the Berghof for most of the afternoon of 19 June and left by train at 8 p.m. bound for East Prussia.

Himmler spent the day of 20 June on his train and was accompanied by SS-Gruppenführer Karl Hermann Frank from midday for the rest of the journey to Hochwald where the train arrived in the early evening.

On 21 June 1943, Himmler was treated by Kersten in the morning and was briefed by Kaltenbrunner before lunch and then he held an afternoon conference of senior SS men. The attendees included Himmler (as Chair), Prützmann, Kaltenbrunner, von dem Bach, Pohl, Winkelmann, Katzmann, Krüger and Knoblauch. Himmler confirmed that von dem Bach would henceforth be responsible for all anti-partisan measures. There is no doubt that the question of Krüger's role in the General Government was also discussed in private, for two days later, Himmler and Dr Hans Frank held talks at Hochwald. As a result, Krüger was ordered to make more of an effort to reconcile his differences with Dr Frank.

On the same day of the conference, 21 June 1943, Himmler ordered the chief of the SS economic empire Oswald Pohl and local Higher SS and Police Leader Friedrich Jeckeln to erect a new concentration camp at Riga and to transport all remaining Jews within ghettos in 'Ostland' to concentration camps. He forbade any Jews in camps being taken for work outside the camps and directed that any Jews not used for work within the camps '... are to be evacuated to the east,' setting the date for compliance with his orders as 1 August 1943.

On 22 June, Himmler had one of his regular appointments with Kersten and then received a delegation of medical men, including Professor Max de Crinis. The professor had been a close friend of Heydrich and was heavily implicated in the euthanasia programme. After they had departed, Himmler saw SS-Gruppenführer Kurt Knoblauch and SS-Obergruppenführer Hans Prützmann respectively.

The diary entry for 23 June 1943 indicates that Himmler continued to be treated at Hochwald by his masseur for stomach cramps. After this he worked in his office until 1.15 p.m. when he had the aforementioned meeting with General Governor Dr Hans Frank who possibly stayed for lunch and was also present during the rest of the afternoon. That evening, Himmler drove across to Hegewaldheim for his evening meal with SS-Obergruppenführer Friedrich Jeckeln and SS-Gruppenführer Graf Pückler.

Himmler took lunch on 24 June with Under-Secretary of State Albert Ganzenmüller who also stayed for an afternoon meeting with other officials. Ganzenmüller was an official at the Transport Ministry with responsibility for railways and had co-operated with Himmler to organise the train schedules and rolling stock which allowed the deportation of thousands of Jews initially to Theresienstadt, then to the Aktion Reinhard death camps in Poland and finally to the death factory at Auschwitz-Birkenau. Without his collaboration, the Himmler plans for resettlement and consequently liquidation would have been extremely difficult, probably impossible. Himmler's recent resettlement order required further ministry co-operation.

Himmler embarked on an inspection tour from 25 June, taking off from Lötzen airfield at 6 p.m. His destination is not recorded, but he spent two days from 28 June carrying out a thorough inspection of the rocket research facilities at Peenemünde before returning to Lötzen on the evening of 29 June.

On 30 June, Himmler was back at Hochwald carrying out his usual office work and had a 7.30 p.m. appointment with Karl von Eberstein who stayed for the evening meal. Throughout the entire diary for 1943, apart from very few deviations, Himmler recorded that he took his meals regularly at 2 p.m. and 8 p.m. and this can almost certainly be attributed to his constant battle with abdominal problems. No doubt his doctors and Kersten had advised him to keep a regular routine within his busy schedule. It should be noted, however, that Himmler's health remained reasonably good despite his stomach cramps and the odd common cold. There is no real evidence in later life of the weak constitution that had plagued him as a young man and which certainly did not interfere with his extremely busy workaholic lifestyle and his constant travelling.

[*The pages of Himmler's diary for the period 1 July 1943–20 July 1943 are missing from the copy held by the Imperial War Museum, London.*]

Himmler received Haj Amin al-Husseini, the Grand Mufti of Jerusalem, at Hegewaldheim on 4 July 1943. The men discussed the policy on the Jews and the use of Muslim volunteers for the Waffen-SS.

On 9 July 1943, Reichsmarschall Hermann Göring, as head of the Four Year Plan, delegated responsibility for all matters appertaining to the production of natural rubber to Himmler. Hitler personally appointed Himmler as his special representative for all matters concerning the mass production of natural rubber on 23 July 1943.

On 12 July, Himmler commissioned SS-Obergruppenführer Erich von dem Bach (-Zelewski) with responsibility for the entire campaign for anti-partisan warfare in Belgium, France, Belarus, the Generalgovernment, Holland, Norway, Ukraine, Yugoslavia and parts of the Bezirk Bialystok. In practice, von dem Bach's main centre of operations was confined to Belarus.

By 21 July, Himmler was at Hochwald and still receiving daily soothing treatment from Kersten to combat his abdominal cramps. SS-Obergruppenführer Oswald Pohl attended a meeting on 22 July and Himmler left the following day by aircraft for another inspection tour, the results of which he reported back to Hitler at the Wolfsschanze on 26 July, spending the whole day with the Führer. He returned to the Wolfsschanze again the next day and then drove back to Hochwald in the afternoon. His evening meal he took at Hegewaldheim. On 28 July at Hochwald, Himmler noted his diary that the following day was Mussolini's birthday, but he had been arrested on orders of King Victor Emmanuel III on 25 July and was being held prisoner.

The Japanese ambassador Hiroshi Oshima visited Himmler at Hochwald on 29 July and then took lunch at Hegewaldheim. That afternoon Himmler was in conference with Kaltenbrunner, SS-Gruppenfüher Heinrich Müller and Walter Schellenberg. Kaltenbrunner and Himmler had a further meeting at 9 p.m. after dinner. Over the next two days, Himmler had meetings with Bormann and Hitler at the Wolfsschanze. There is little doubt that the incarceration of Mussolini was high on the agenda.

On 30 July 1943, Himmler took control of the Hauptamt Ordnungspolizei as SS-Oberst-Gruppenführer Kurt Daluege had suffered a second heart attack. Himmler appointed Alfred Wünnenberg as his permanent successor on 31 August 1943.

For an unknown reason, the diary entries for 1 August 1943 are written in an unidentified hand, other than that of Himmler; probably that of his adjutant or secretary. The reason remains a mystery, but could possibly be as a result of some form of minor incapacity. The entries indicate that Himmler continued with his schedule at Hochwald, meeting SS-Sturmbannführer Herbert Kappler at 1.30 p.m. and again at 3.45 p.m. followed by a drive to the Wolfsschanze and an evening meal as a guest of Bormann. Kappler was a senior SD officer in Rome and had information regarding the whereabouts of the Duce. The details were passed on to Hitler who personally authorised Mussolini's rescue.

On 2 August 1943, SS-Gruppenführer Odilo Globocnik was at Hochwald when news filtered through that there had been an armed insurrection at Treblinka death camp. Himmler was furious and issued orders that those responsible should be rooted out and executed. That evening he reported the facts to Hitler at the Wolfsschanze. Many of the leaders of the revolt were killed in the fire fight before escaping and those who were successful were tracked down and killed. Serious extensive damage had been done to the camp structures, but the gas chambers had survived and continued to operate for several weeks until Himmler finally gave the order to close the camp and obliterate all signs of its existence. On 19 October 1943, the camp ceased operations after having claimed the lives of approximately 900,000 men, women and children. The gas chambers and barracks were bulldozed and trees planted in their place.

The Reich NSDAP leader of women, the wife of SS-Obergruppenführer August Heissmeyer, Gertrud Scholtz-Klink, spent the afternoon of 3 August at Hochwald. That evening Himmler went to the Wolfsschanze and had an evening meal with Bormann, as he did the following day. Himmler's abdominal complaint seems to have improved as Kersten is not mentioned in the diary around this time. Between appointments at his field headquarters, Himmler paid daily visits to Hitler at the Wolfsschanze and dined regularly with Bormann until 8 August when he flew to Munich and journeyed on to Gmund where he spent the night. Unable to stay for longer, he flew to Prague and visited Daluege after discussing his condition with his doctors. Himmler then flew back to Rastenburg and reported to Hitler on Daluege's condition and his future suitability as Acting Reichsprotector of Bohemia-Moravia. Daluege's appointment as Acting Reichsprotector as a replacement for the assassinated Heydrich had only been temporary and Hitler decided, almost certainly after advice from Himmler, to install a permanent governor in

Prague. Constantin von Neurath was still officially the *Reichsprotektor* in name only and Daluege's health prompted Hitler to come to a decision on a permanent replacement. He chose Wilhelm Frick.

A secret order was issued by Himmler to all HSSPF on 10 August 1943, prohibiting the interference of police when local German residents clashed with Allied aircrew who had bailed out of their aircrafts. There had been several incidents where the German population had attacked bomber crews and the police had intervened.

Once again, Himmler's daily routine of meetings, office duties dealing with correspondence and daily visits to Hitler's FHQ where he had meetings and meals with Bormann and von Ribbentrop continued until 13 August when he left for a visit to Hamburg. He returned on 15 August when his daily trips to the Wolfsschanze recommenced. Kersten also reappeared for treatment on 16 August as did Lammers as a guest for meals. Daluege was well enough to travel by 17 August as he appeared at Hochwald as a dinner guest along with SS-Obergruppenführer Karl Wolff and the following day Himmler consulted Dr Stumpfegger, one of his SS doctors, but the reason is unknown. He had by now recommenced his regular daily treatment with Kersten.

Another unknown hand made the diary entries for 19 August, recording meetings with Kaltenbrunner and Winkelmann plus an evening meal with Bormann. 20 August was occupied with several meetings, including Reichsminister Speer, Reichsminister Frick and Friedrich Jeckeln, followed by a visit to Hitler.

On 21 August 1943, Hitler appointed Himmler as head of the A4 research project. This covered the research and production of V1 and V2 rockets. Himmler delegated direct responsibility to the SS-Wirtschafts-Verwaltungshaupamt (Amt C) under the direction of Dr Hans Kammler who reported to Oswald Pohl. That day Pohl and Kammler presented themselves to Himmler at Hochwald where they were briefed on their new responsibilities and Himmler reported his actions and intentions to Hitler on 22 August. There is little doubt that Hitler had by now informed Himmler of his decisions regarding his cabinet reshuffle which were to become common knowledge over the ensuing days.

On 23 August, Himmler flew from Rastenburg to Berlin and that afternoon at Prinz-Albrecht-Strasse appraised Kaltenbrunner, Wolff and Müller of the changes in government. Himmler officially replaced Wilhelm Frick as Reich and Prussian Minister of the Interior on 25 August 1943 and this elevation saw him reach the pinnacle of his powers. Frick was moved sideways to become the new *Reichsprotektor* in Prague, but in effect this was a demotion as Karl Hermann Frank administered the real power in the Protectorate. Himmler spent the day on an inspection tour taking in his new Interior Ministry. On 26 August Himmler addressed a gathering of civil servants and officials in the Interior Ministry situated in Unter den Linden at the junction with Wilhelmsrasse. He remained in

Berlin until leaving for Hochwald by train on 27 August. That afternoon he had a meeting with Prützmann and Erich von dem Bach.

Himmler was back at Hochwald on 28 August and reported dutifully to Hitler at the Wolfsschanze in the evening. The omnipresent Kersten attended his patient again on a daily basis. On 29 August, Himmler's old family friend, SS-Gruppenführer Prof. Dr Karl Gebhardt, visited the Feldkommandostelle and joined Himmler for lunch with Prützmann before Himmler left for the Wolfsschanze where he dined with the Führer. Gebhardt was still at Hochwald on 30 August and was joined by Prützmann, SS-Gruppenführer Prof. Dr Ernst-Robert Grawitz and possibly SS-Gruppenführer Dr Karl Genzken for an afternoon conference. That evening Himmler received Renato Ricci, the Italian politician and Nazi sympathiser, at Hegewaldheim for an evening meal.

Himmler had lunch with Hitler the following day at the Wolfsschanze before meetings with Generalleutnant Walter Warlimont and Generalfeldmarschall Wilhelm Keitel prior to returning to Hochwald for evening meetings and another meal with Ricci who stayed for several days. Himmler remained at his Feldkommandostelle until arriving in Berlin during the night of 7 to 8 September. During this period his routine of working at his desk, meetings and the odd visit to the Wolfsschanze continued as normal. The diary entries are difficult to read, but he did have a meeting with State Secretary of the Interior Ministry SS-Gruppenführer Dr Wilhelm Stuckart on 4 September. Himmler did not stay long in Berlin, leaving by air on 8 September and flying to Munich where he had lunch with Reichsleiter Schwarz before motoring down to Gmund where he stayed overnight. He held a quick meeting with von Eberstein back in Munich on 9 September and then flew to Rastenburg for a meeting with Hitler and then SS-Brigadeführer Werner Naumann of the Propaganda Ministry, Reichsleiter Bormann and Reichsminister von Ribbentrop.

Himmler was a frequent visitor to the Wolfsschanze around this time, regularly attending conferences and taking meals with Hitler and his inner circle. The names of Bormann, Lammers and Prof. Dr Karl Brandt appear alongside those of Vice-Admiral Voss and others.

On 12 September 1943, a detachment of paratroopers and SS troops under the command of Luftwaffe General Kurt Student, were dropped on to the mountain top of Gran Sasso in the Dolomites where Kappler had discovered Mussolini was being held prisoner. The operation, codenamed 'Oak' was led by Major Otto-Harald Mors supported by SS-Sturmbannführer Otto Skorzeny who took the credit when the Duce was successfully freed.

On 13 September, Himmler left by air for another inspection tour and returned to Rastenburg on 15 September. That evening he was a guest of the Führer for dinner with Mussolini, Wolff and Ricci. Himmler's usual routine of office duties, meetings and visits to Hitler continued apace over the subsequent days until 23

September when Himmler travelled to Riga for a meeting with Jeckeln, Gauleiter Hinrich Lohse and Latvian General Rudolf Bangerskis. Himmler moved on to Reval and spent the night of 23 September as a guest of Litzmann. He flew back to Rastenburg the next day and visited Hitler that evening before his normal routine was resumed at Hochwald.

Himmler Flew to Debica on 28 September and carried out an inspection at the SS military training area of Heidelager where he stayed as a guest of SS-Standartenführer Franz Augsberger, the commanding officer of 3 Estonian SS-Volunteer Brigade. Himmler returned to Hochwald the following day and stayed until flying to Berlin on the afternoon of 30 September. He paid a rare visit to his office at Prinz-Albrecht-Strasse on 1 October and flew back to Lötzen on 2 October after a morning meeting at his office with Berger, Jüttner and SS-Obergruppenführer Alfred Wünnenberg. Himmler spent the night and next day back in East Prussia before he left in his special train at 12.20 a.m. on 4 October to Posen.

TEN

Posen

In October 1943, Himmler attended three major conferences in Posen, speaking at all three. The first, on 4 October in the Golden Hall of the Posen City Hall, was attended by almost one hundred senior SS officers of Gruppenführer and Obergruppenführer rank. His diary entry shows the speech lasting from 5.30 p.m. until 9 p.m. followed by a meal at 9.30 p.m.

Himmler's speech was recorded and was used in evidence at the Nuremberg trials. In part, he stated:

> ... we must be honest, decent, loyal, and comradely to members of our own blood, and to no one else. What happens to the Russians, the Czechs, is totally indifferent to me. Whatever is available to us in good blood of our type, we will take for ourselves, that is, we will steal their children and bring them up with us, if necessary. Whether other races live well or die of hunger is only of interest to me insofar as we need them as slaves for our culture; otherwise that doesn't interest me. Whether 10,000 Russian women fall down from exhaustion in building a tank ditch is of interest to me only insofar as the tank ditches are finished for Germany.
>
> ... I want to mention another very difficult matter here before you in all frankness. Among ourselves, it ought to be spoken of quite openly for once; yet we shall never speak of it in public. Just as little as we hesitated to do our duty as ordered on 30 June, 1934, and place comrades who had failed against the wall and shoot them, just as little did we ever speak of it, and we shall never speak of it. It was a matter of course, of tact, for us, thank God, never to speak of it, never to talk of it. It made everybody shudder; yet everyone was clear in his mind that he would do it again if ordered to do so, and if it was necessary. I am thinking now of the evacuation of the Jews, the rooting out of the Jewish Folk as an ethnic nation. It is one of those things that's easy to say. The Jewish nation will be rooted out, says every Party Comrade, that's quite clear, it's in our program: shutting the Jews down and out, rooting them out; that's what we're doing. And then they all come along, these 80 million good

> Germans, and every one of them has his decent Jew. Of course, it's quite clear that the others are pigs, but this one is one first class Jew. Of all those who speak this way, not one has looked on; not one has lived through it. Most of you know what it means when 100 bodies lie together, when 500 lie there, or if 1,000 lie there. To have gone through this, and at the same time—apart from exceptions caused by human weaknesses—to have remained decent, that has made us hard. This is a chapter of glory in our history which has never been written, and which never shall be written; since we know how hard it would be for us if we still had the Jews, as secret saboteurs, agitators, and slander mongers, among us now, in every city—during the bombing raids, with the suffering and deprivations of the war. We would probably already be in the same situation as in 1916–1917 if we still had the Jews in the body of the German Folk.

His diary entries for 5 October 1943 are like a who's who of the most senior SS personalities. From midday until the evening, there is a long list of names, all Obergruppenführer or Gruppenführer rank.

On 6 October, Himmler addressed a large meeting in the same Golden Hall, consisting of senior NSDAP and government officials. This speech is noted in the diary from 5.30 p.m. until 7.30 p.m. The conference is shown as a Reichs-und Gauleiter meeting starting at 3 p.m. and had been convened by Reichsleiter Martin Bormann in order to discuss the policy of total war. Controversy over whether or not Reichsminister Albert Speer was present and heard Himmler's speech (thereby implicating him in the policy of Jewish annihilation) raged on into the decades after the war. Speer denied being present, but when faced with proof he had been at the meeting, he stated he had left prior to Himmler's speech. Subsequent evidence produced in 1971, proved that Speer had been present throughout and had heard Himmler's words:

> ... I want to speak now, in this most restricted circle, about a matter which you, my party comrades, have long accepted as a matter of course, but which for me has become the heaviest burden of my life—the matter of the Jews. You all accept happily the obvious fact that there are no more Jews in your province. All Germans, with very few exceptions, realize perfectly well that we couldn't have lasted through the bombs and the stresses of the fourth, perhaps in the future the fifth and even sixth year of war, if this destructive pestilence were still present within or body politic. The brief sentence 'The Jews must be exterminated' is easy to pronounce, but the demands on those who have to put it into practice are the hardest and most difficult in the world.
>
> You see, of course they are Jews; obviously, they are only Jews. But think for a moment how many people—including party comrades—have addressed one of those famous petitions [*to us*] in which was written that of course all Jews are pigs, but so-and-so is a decent Jew who should be exempted from whatever was being done.

I daresay that according to the number of such petitions ... there must have been more decent Jews in Germany than there were Jews altogether. I'm only mentioning this because you will know, each of you, that in your own province there are good respectable National Socialists, each of whom knows one decent Jew.

I ask that you only listen but never speak of what I am saying to you here today. We, you see, were faced with the question 'What about the women and children?' And I decided, here too, to find an unequivocal solution. For I did not think that I was justified in exterminating—meaning kill or order to have killed—the men, but to leave their children to grow up to take revenge on our sons and grandchildren. The hard decision had to be taken to have this people disappear from the face of the earth. For the organization which had to carry out this order, it was the most difficult one we were ever given ... I think I can say that it has been carried out without damaging the minds or spirits of our men and our leaders. The danger was great and ever present. For the difference between the two possibilities ... to become cruel and heartless and no longer respect human life, or to become soft and succumb to weakness and nervous breakdowns ... the way between Scylla and Charybdis is appallingly narrow.

The immense fortunes we requisitioned from the Jews have been handed over to the last penny to the Reich Minister for Economics. My position has always been that while we have done our duty here, toward our people, our race ... and our Führer who this once in two thousand years has been given to us ... we do not have the right to keep one penny of this requisitioned Jewish wealth. My order has been from the start, that any SS man who steals even one single mark, is to be put to death. And I can tell you that I have signed about a dozen death sentences precisely for this in these last days. ...

I considered it my duty to speak to you, who are the highest dignitaries of the party, of our political order which is the Führers' political instrument, for once quite openly about this question ... to tell you how it was.

By the end of this year, the matter of the Jews will [*also*] have been dealt with in the countries under our occupation. ... You will not doubt that the economic aspect presented many great difficulties, above all with the clearing of ghettos: in Warsaw we fought street battles for four weeks in the ghetto, four weeks of clearing seven hundred bunkers, one after the other. Because that ghetto produced fur coats and textiles, we were prevented from taking it over when it would have been easy: we were told we were interfering with essential production. 'Halt!' they called, 'This is war production!'

Of course, this has nothing to do with party comrade Speer: it wasn't your doing. It is precisely this kind of so-called war production enterprise which party comrade Speer and I will clean out together over the next weeks. We will do this just as unsentimentally as all things must be done in this fifth year of the war: unsentimentally, but from the bottom of our hearts, for Germany. ... And with this I want to finish about

> the matter of the Jews. You are now informed, and you will keep the knowledge to yourselves. Later perhaps we can consider whether the German people should be told about this. But I think it is better that we- we together- carry for our people the responsibility … responsibility for an achievement, not just an idea…and then take the secret with us to our grave. …'

There is little doubt that, to speak so openly about the liquidation of the Jews, would have required Hitler's prior approval. Himmler reported back to Hitler immediately on his return to East Prussia on 7 October (Himmler's 43 birthday) before going to his own Feldkommandostelle. Had the tribunal at Nuremberg known of Speer's presence when these words were uttered by Himmler, there is also little doubt that Speer would have joined his subordinate, Gauleiter Fritz Sauckel, on the steps of the gallows.

Himmler compounded his own guilt by calling for:

> … merciless execution for defeatism, in particular among well-educated and well-to-do classes; espionage carried out mainly by Jews and Freemasons; sharp distinction to be drawn between Germans and Slavs; harsh measures and death penalty in the case of undesirable fraternization; on the other hand, forcible removal of Slav children from their parents in order to gain so-called 'Good Blood'. …

This was in a speech delivered to senior Wehrmacht officers on 14 October 1943 during another inspection tour after leaving Hochwald on 10 October. Himmler was in Rechlin on 13 October and then flew to Friedrichshafen in the afternoon. He was a guest of General Reinecke in Lindau that night and delivered his speech to a large gathering of senior Wehrmacht officers at Bad Schachen before continuing his flying tour of south-west Germany, including Stuttgart. He returned to Rastenburg on 15 October and held a meeting at Hochwald with SS-Brigadeführer Hermann Priess.

On 16 October, he received Eric von dem Bach and SS-Brigadeführer Hans Lammerding before his now daily visit to the Wolfsschanze. The next day he met with the Chief of Staff of the Army General Staff, General Kurt Zeitzler. Since replacing Franz Halder, Zeitzler had several meetings with Himmler. Karl Wolff was at Hochwald on 18 October and when Himmler attended the Wolfsschanze the following day, he met with Sepp Dietrich.

Himmler went to Posen on 23 October and after visiting Berger at one of his residences called Gluckshöhl, Himmler stayed as a guest of Gauleiter Arthur Greiser. On 24 October, Himmler gave his third important speech in Posen when he addressed a gathering of the political and administrative staff of the Warthegau. He left Posen that afternoon and arrived in Danzig on 25 October before heading back to Hochwald.

At about 5.15 p.m. on Sunday 24 October 1943, Himmler's Godson, Klaus Heydrich, the elder son of the late Reinhard Heydrich, was riding his bicycle in the grounds of the Heydrich mansion at Panenske Brezany near Prague when he strayed outside the gates and was accidentally struck by a truck carrying the local football team. The boy was killed instantly. Himmler was genuinely upset when given the news and immediately transmitted a telegram of condolences to Lina Heydrich. On 28 October he flew to Prague from Lötzen and accompanied Karl Hermann Frank to visit Lina Heydrich. He reappeared at the Heydrich house the following day before flying back to Lötzen. Returning to Hochwald, he had meetings with Oswald Pohl, Hans Kammler and SS-Brigadeführer Georg Lörner. Himmler also arranged for a local flower firm in Prague to send a wreath on his behalf to the boy's funeral on 9 November.

Operation Harvest Festival was implemented by SS-Gruppenführer Jakob Sporrenberg on 3 November 1943 when approximately 42,000 Jews were killed at Majdanek concentration camp in Lublin and its sub-camps. This was the largest single action to be completed in one day by German troops during the entire holocaust. It came about to prevent any possible further revolt by Jewish prisoners, following the uprisings at Sobibor and Treblinka.

By 19 October 1943, Odilo Globocnik had terminated Aktion Reinhard in the Generalgovernment and he notified Himmler in his final report on 4 November 1943:

Trieste, 4 November 1943
The Höherer SS- und Polizeiführer in the Operationszone Adriatische Küstenland
Gl./Go. Diary No. 225/43 [*initialled*] H. H. [*Himmler*]

To the Reichsführer-SS and Chief of the German Police, Heinrich Himmler, Berlin

I concluded Aktion Reinhard, which I have been directing in the Generalgouvernement, on 19.10.1943, and have dissolved all camps.

I take the liberty of submitting the attached portfolio to you, Reichsführer, as my final statement.

My observations on Lublin showed that a special center of radiation existed in the Generalgouvernement and particularly in the Lublin district, and I have tried, therefore, to capture these dangerous tendencies graphically. It may prove to be a good thing for the future if we can point to the elimination of this danger. I have, however, also endeavored to give a picture of the employment of labor, from which one can not only gather the extent of the work, but also with how few Germans this fatal effort was made possible. It has at any rate grown to such proportions today, that well known industries are interesting themselves in it.

I have meanwhile handed these labor camps over to SS Obergruppenführer Pohl. Please, Reichsführer, look through this portfolio.

During a visit, you, Reichsführer, held out to me the prospect that a few Iron Crosses might be awarded for the special performances of this hard task after the work had been concluded. Please advise me, Reichsführer, whether I may submit suggestions in this connection.

I beg to point out that such an award to the forces of the local SS- und Polizeiführer was authorized for the work in Warsaw, which formed only a comparatively small part of the total work.

I should be grateful to you, Reichsführer, for a positive decision regarding this matter, as I would like to see the hard work of my men rewarded.

Heil Hitler!

[*signed*] Globocnik
SS-Gruppenführer und Generalleutnant der Polizei'

Himmler replied on 30 November 1943:

Dear Globocnik,

I confirm receipt of your letter dated 4.11.43 and your notification regarding the termination of Aktion Reinhard. Also I thank you for the portfolio you sent me.

I express to you my thanks and my acknowledgement for the great and unique services which you have performed to the entire German people by carrying out the Aktion Reinhard.

Heil Hitler!
Sincerely Yours

[*signed*] H. H.

On 6 November 1943, Himmler flew to Munich in preparation for the anniversary celebrations to commemorate the 1923 Putsch. Immediately following his arrival, he paid his customary visit to his parents' grave. At 5 p.m. on 8 November he attended the anniversary meeting in the Löwenbräukeller and heard Hitler's speech. In the evening of 9 November, Himmler motored to Gmund where he stayed until 12 November, returning to Hochwald.

Himmler embarked on a quick visit to the Baltic States from 14 November until the night of 16 November when he returned to Hochwald. He had the usual meetings on 17 November and took an evening meal with Grossadmiral Dönitz.

On 18 November, Himmler flew to Krakow for discussions with Dr Hans Frank. Himmler and Frank were bitter rivals and the atmosphere between the two men must have been something to behold. For outward appearances, they remained cordial towards each other, but Frank was antagonistic at his perception of Himmler trying to undermine his authority in the Generalgovernment. Frank vehemently disliked Himmler's representative in Krakau, the Higher SS and Police Leader SS-Obergruppenführer Friedrich-Wilhelm Krüger and the feeling was mutual.

Krüger had strong suspicions that Frank was illegally plundering goods for his own benefit; with some justification. Frank placed obstacles in Krüger's way when he attempted to implement the orders of the Reichsführer-SS and made regular complaints to Hitler and Himmler that he, as Governor General, was the only law in the name of the Führer, in the Generalgovernment. Something had to give. Krüger was desperate for a frontline posting and Himmler finally agreed to replace him. Krüger was posted to the SS-Führer Reserve on 9 November 1943 and served with the 7 SS-Division 'Prinz Eugen' and subsequently the 6 SS Mountain Division. He was later awarded the Knights Cross of the Iron Cross. His replacement in Krakow from 9 November 1943 was SS-Obergruppenführer Wilhelm Koppe.

Himmler stayed overnight with Frank on 18 November at the Wawel Castle and the following day left for Breslau by his special train. In Breslau he met Jüttner and spent the evening of 20 November with Generalfeldmarschall Erhard Milch. Himmler's train left Breslau the following evening at 7 p.m. bound for East Prussia and Hochwald. The Austrian Edmund Glaise-Horstenau visited Hochwald on 23 November and the following day Himmler attended a high level conference at the Wolfsschanze with Hitler, Göring and Keitel.

On 25 November, Himmler received a visit from SS-Obergruppenführer Wilhelm Rediess and the next day he held a meeting with Wünnenberg, Winkelmann and SS-Gruppenführer August Frank in the afternoon before an evening meeting with SS-Gruppenführer Curt von Gottberg. Himmler remained at Hochwald over the following days, working at his paperwork, receiving visitors for meetings and motoring to the Wolfsschanze. During this period, Prützmann was a regular visitor and others included Gunter d'Alquen, Ulrich Greifelt and Hans Kammler.

Himmler flew to Berlin on 2 December and spent a couple of days at his office in Prinz-Albrecht-Strasse. He left on an inspection tour on 4 December, calling first at Weimar and returning to Rastenburg on 7 December. Back at Hochwald, his diary for 8 December is illegible. He chaired a meeting on the afternoon of 9 December where the participants included Kaltenbrunner, Prützmann, von Gottberg and d'Alquen. Kersten reappeared to administer treatment on 10 December prior to an afternoon conference. The list of attendees is almost illegible, but Kaltenbrunner and Greifelt were present. Himmler appears to have been very active with meetings at this time, but his diary entries are almost indecipherable. He was at Hegewaldheim at 7 p.m. on 13 December and departed that night for Posen. The next days in the diary are impossible to read, but Himmler did meet

Kammler in Weimar at 11.45 a.m. on 16 December. The final entry for 1943 is at the foot of 16 December which reads 'Midnight departure.'

[*There are no pages for the remainder of 1943.*]

The explanation for the lack of diary entries for the Christmas period is explained by Marga Himmler in her own diary entry for 15 January 1944:

> Christmas and New Year passed. H. was here for 8 days before Christmas and then again on 8 January.

The first Himmler diary entry for 1944 is on 3 January. It shows Himmler to be at Hochwald where his evening meal guests included Milch, Reichsminister Funk, Lammers and SS-Gruppenführer Franz Hayler. His daily routine of continual paperwork and meetings relentlessly controlled his activities. Nothing unusual appears in the diary until 8 January when he departed Hochwald for Gmund. He left Gmund on 10 January and flew to Berlin where he later boarded his special train towards Breslau. It appears he stayed aboard his train in Breslau on 11 January, holding meetings and taking his meals. In attendance were Wünnenberg and Kersten, among others.

On 13 January 1944, Himmler originally planned to visit Lina Heydrich at Panenske Brezany, but this whole afternoon is crossed through and replaced by work and an evening meeting with Hitler. He kept his engagement with Lina Heydrich the following day, arriving in Prague in the morning and driving out to visit the Heydrich family for lunch. He left at 3 p.m. and headed for Hochwald, arriving at Rastenburg just after lunch on 14 January. He used his train over the next few days and was in Königsberg on 20 January.

The entries are illegible until 23 January when he was back at Hochwald receiving treatment from Kersten and meeting Friedrich Jeckeln. In the evening he attended the Wolfsschanze and on 24 January he met with Jüttner and Kammler. Himmler departed from Hochwald on 30 January, but his destination is unreadable. However, he is shown as visiting Rost von Tonningen in Amsterdam in the early evening and on 31 January Himmler had a meeting with Anton Mussert, the Dutch National Socialist in Den Haag. [*According to information from Himmler's daughter via the late Stuart Russell, Himmler detested Mussert, but recognised that he had to deal with him for the sake of policy.*] Himmler was accompanied by the Higher SS and Police Leader in Holland, SS-Obergruppenführer Hanns Albin Rauter and Gottlob Berger.

On 30 January 1944, Himmler introduced an award in recognition of the dangerous work in combating partisans in the occupied territories. Award of the Anti-Partisan War Badge was delegated to commanders of the army, navy, airforce and Higher SS and Police Leaders (HSSPF.) The previous summer had seen the introduction of another badge by Himmler and he personally presented the first of these Germanic Proficiency Runes Badges on 1 February 1944 during his visit to the Netherlands. His visit lasted several days and he met with Reichskommissar SS-Obergruppenführer Arthur Seyss-Inquart, SS-Brigadeführer Erich Naumann and SS-Gruppenführer Karl Maria Demelhuber, also inspecting the Dutch SS School at Avegoor.

During Himmler's visit to Holland, more problems arose in Warsaw. Franz Kutschera had replaced Jürgen Stroop as SS and Police Leader (SSPF) in Warsaw in September 1943. Kutschera was a ruthless man, employing brutal methods against the civilian population of Warsaw to minimise resistance and sabotage. At 9.09 a.m. on the morning of 1 February 1944, Franz Kutschera was travelling in his car for the short journey between his residence and SS headquarters. At the gate of the SS headquarters, his car was blocked off and Kutschera was attacked with gunfire. He lay seriously wounded in his car when one of the attackers gave him the *coup de grâce*. The following day, one hundred civilian hostages were publically shot in Warsaw as retribution.

Himmler was back at Hochwald by 8 February and Prützmann is shown as attending upon his Reichsführer that day and the next. Other diary entries are illegible around this time, apart from a viewing of the film 'Titanic' on the evening of 10 February. This film had been produced as a propaganda film with changes to the plot illustrating how the British capitalists valued financial gain above human life. It was commissioned by Dr Goebbels, but by the time of completion Germany was suffering almost daily bombing raids resulting in great loss of life. Goebbels was so worried that a film which portrayed multiple deaths would have an adverse effect on German morale, he therefore banned it from being shown in the Greater Reich. The ban did not extend to the occupied territories where the film was well received with good reviews.

Hitler appointed Himmler as chief of a new unified German Secret Intelligence Service on 12 February 1944 and this signified the death of the Abwehr the following June when all its functions were transferred to the SD Foreign Intelligence Service under Schellenberg.

Himmler was in Posen on his train on from 12 to 14 February 1944 as the guest of Arthur Greiser. This resulted in the following letter dated 14 February 1944 from Greiser to Oswald Pohl:

> On the occasion of the visit of the RFSS in Posen yesterday and the day before I had an opportunity to discuss and clarify two questions which concern the area of your work.
>
> The first question is as follows:

The ghetto in Litzmannstadt will not be converted into a concentration camp, as was emphasized at the discussion on 5 February, held at my office, the Reichsstatthalter in Posen, by SS-Oberführer Baier and SS-Hauptsturmführer Dr. Volk, who had been sent to my Gau by your office. The order of the RFSS of 11 June 1943, will therefore not be carried out. I have agreed the following with the RF:

1. The population of the ghetto is to be reduced to a minimum, and only those Jews are to remain who are absolutely required in the interests of the armaments industry;
2. The ghetto thus remains a Gau ghetto of the Reichsgau Wartheland;
3. The reduction of the population will be carried out by the Sonderkommando of SS-Hauptsturmführer Bothmann, which operated in the area previously [*at Chelmno*]. The RF will issue an Order instructing SS-Hauptsturmführer Bothmann and his Sonderkommando to leave their station in Croatia and be available for service in the Wartheland;
4. The disposal and use of the property of the ghetto will remain the responsibility of the Reichsgau Wartheland;
5. After the removal of all the Jews from the ghetto and its demolition, the entire area of the ghetto will become the property of the city of Litzmannstadt.
   The RF will then give appropriate orders to the Haupt-Treuhandstelle Ost.
   May I request you to convey your proposals to me on this subject.

[*Signed*] Greiser'

Himmler's train left Posen on 14 February and headed west towards Berlin. *En route*, Himmler visited Müncheberg during the afternoon of 14th. At this location was situated the Kaiser Wilhelm Scientific Research Institute which was involved in the research, experimentation and production of new weapons. Its board of directors had at one time included the nuclear scientists Albert Einstein and Otto Hahn.

On 15 February 1944 Himmler's house in Berlin-Dahlem was damaged in an air raid. The roof was badly burnt requiring a complete replacement.

The next two days in Himmler's diary are noted with the single letter 'B' and one concludes that this signified Berlin. On 17 February, he returned to Hochwald, meeting Hans Kammler the following day. Leon Degrelle's Flemish volunteers had been in action, fighting on the Eastern Front under Army Group South and Himmler was in attendance at the Wolfsschanze on 20 February when Hitler personally presented Degrelle with the Knights Cross of the Iron Cross. The following day Himmler spent some time, including lunch, with his SS adjutant, SS-Sturmbannführer Werner Grothmann. Later that day Himmler also had an appointment with his police adjutant Willy Suchanek.

Grothmann was typical of the young SS officers with whom Himmler surrounded himself on his personal staff. Born in 1915 in Frankfurt-am-Main, Grothmann entered banking as a profession and joined the SS in 1933. He received a commission on 20 April 1936 having previously attended an officers' course at the SS-Junkerschule Braunschweig. He was attached to SS-Standarte 'Deutschland' and was promoted to SS-Obersturmführer on 11 September 1938. Grothmann's unit saw active service on the Western Front and he was seriously wounded in France on 17 June 1940. He was appointed as 2. Adjutant to the Reichsführer-SS on the Personal Staff RFSS on 15 August 1940 and was promoted to SS-Hauptsturmführer on 9 November 1940. From 1 April 1942 until he was captured, he was the Chief SS Adjutant of the Reichsführer-SS. Promoted to SS-Sturmbannführer 21 June 1943 and SS-Obersturmbannführer on 21 June 1944, after the war Grothmann was interned by the Allies (British) and spent some time in the camp at Fallingbostel where he came across Gebhard Himmler and Ludwig Pemsel of the Personal Staff Reichsführer-SS. Grothmann was also held in the witness wing at Nuremberg where he appeared as a witness during the trial of doctors.

Grothmann submitted an affidavit on 27 January 1947 which is noted in the introduction of this study. He was eventually released by the British and became a merchant. He died in 2003.

Himmler's police adjutant was Oberstleutnant der Schutzpolizei und SS-Obersturmbannführer Willy Suchanek. Born in Berlin in 1905, Suchanek joined the police service in 1925 and was promoted to Leutnant on 18 December 1930 and Oberleutnant on 9 November 1933. In 1935 he was also a member of the Reichs Arbeitsdienst. The same year he was attached to the adjutancy of the Gestapo and followed this by spending some time in 1936 as an adjutant of Heydrich and was promoted on 1 July 1936 to Hauptmann. Suchanek joined the NSDAP in 1937 (NSDAP no. 4 691 083) and was appointed as a police adjutant to Himmler in 1938. On 6 October 1940, he was promoted to Major and was accorded the SS rank of Sturmbannführer on 9 November 1940 (SS no. 290 461.) At some point during the war (most likely 1940) Suchanek became Himmler's chief police adjutant, attached to the RSHA. He was promoted to Oberstleutnant der Polizei on 1 March 1943 and to SS-Obersturmbannführer und Polizei Oberstleutnant on 21 June 1943. Suchanek commanded a unit in the SS Police Regiment and saw active service. He appeared as a witness in various trials from 1946 until 1949, including that of SS-Gruppenführer Hanns Johst. He was not considered as a war criminal and therefore did not face criminal charges. His fate is unknown.

Himmler travelled by rail to Munich on 23 February where he saw Reichsleiter Schwarz. There is no entry for 24 February, but Himmler was at Gmund on 25 February, returning to Berlin on 29 February. He did not stay long and was back in Bergwald on 2 March as Hitler was in residence at the Berghof. Kaltenbrunner was summoned to Bergwald on 4 March and Himmler continued his routine of office work, meetings, inspections and visits to the Berghof. This was an extended stay at

Bergwald throughout the month of March and into the first week of April and there is little doubt that Himmler took the opportunity to spend time with his second family at Schneewinkellehen. Häschen was six months pregnant with the couple's second child and the overjoyed father-to-be would not have missed the prospect of visiting his beloved second family. There is no mention of Gmund at this time.

[*Himmler's diary is extremely difficult to decipher during these weeks as the entries are very faint.*]

A meeting at Bergwald with Schellenberg appears on 24 March 1944 and Jüttner is mentioned several times. It appears that Himmler conducted a meeting with Pohl on 30 March, but the location is not noted. Himmler was at Bergwald on 1 April until 4 April when he drove to Gmund, staying there until 7 April. He was at Bergwald on 8 and 9 April, but then left on an inspection tour. His destination is illegible as are the entries for several days until 16 April when he is shown as returning to Salzburg.

It would appear that Himmler remained at Feldkommandostelle Bergwald as Hitler was at the Berghof for an extended period. He had left the Wolfsschanze for the Berghof at the end of February and did not return until July. Unfortunately, the diary is mostly indecipherable apart from a visit noted on 1 May to Königsee. It is known that on 26 April 1944 Himmler attended the funeral in Berlin of Generaloberst Hans Hube who had been killed five days earlier in an aircrash at Salzburg. Himmler was travelling in the first week of May and appeared at the Ordensburg Sonthofen on 5 May to address a gathering of Generals.

Beginning on 15 May 1944, the deportation of Hungarian Jews commenced. Their destination was Auschwitz-Birkenau and the vast majority of the approximately 440,000 souls were despatched to the crematoria upon arrival. For this major operation, trains were diverted inside Birkenau and unloading was carried out on a new 'ramp' installed for the purpose. The deportations continued until 9 July 1944.

On 15 May, Himmler gave a speech at the annual convention of Abwehr and SD officials in Salzburg. Himmler left Bergwald on 16 May and headed to Lemberg, stopping at Neuhammer to address the officer corps of the Galician SS-Division. He returned to Bergwald on the evening of 21 May. He was at Sonthofen again on 24 May and in Kochem the following day. It appears that he again returned to Bergwald where he remained, but all diary entries are too faint to read and the copies of the Himmler desk diary held by the Imperial War Museum comes to an end on 31 May 1944.

On 3 June 1944, Himmler was a witness at the civil wedding in Salzburg of SS-Brigadeführer Hermann Fegelein and Gretl Braun, the sister of Eva Braun. Himmler officiated at the SS ceremonial section of the proceedings. The same day, Hedwig Potthast gave birth to a daughter at Hohenlychen SS clinic. Nanette Dorothea was Himmler's second daughter.

ELEVEN

Warlord

As Allied troops were landing and fighting their way off the beaches in Normandy on 6 June, Himmler attended a meeting at Schloss Klessheim in Salzburg with Göring, von Ribbentrop and Kaltenbrunner at which it was decided that 'lynch justice' would apply to any Allied airmen who were captured on German soil. Himmler agreed that enemy airmen would be handed over to the SD for 'special handling.'

Himmler made another speech at the Ordensburg Sonthofen on 21 June. In order to bring his Higher SS and Police Leaders under the protection of the Hague Convention, on 1 July 1944 Himmler issued a directive that they could hold Waffen-SS General rank in addition to their Allgemeine-SS rank. On 13 July at the Berghof, Hitler announced to the commanders and officers of the newly formed Volksgrenadier Division that Himmler would henceforth be placed in overall command.

On 14 July 1944, Hitler left the Berghof for the last time and headed back to the Wolfsschanze. On 20 July, Oberst Claus von Stauffenberg unsuccessfully attempted to kill Hitler by exploding a bomb during a conference at the field headquarters. The Reichsführer was not at the Wolfsschanze at the crucial moment, but he appeared very soon after, rushing to declare his loyalty to his Führer. Himmler ordered Kaltenbrunner to take charge of the investigation and the 'Sonderkommission 20. Juli 1944' was set up under Heinrich Müller to co-ordinate the operation. Himmler is believed to have been in Berlin soon after and may have personally questioned some of the suspects during the ensuing investigation. Hitler ordered that Himmler should take over immediate command of the Replacement Army, replacing the heavily suspected Generaloberst Fromm. With a single stroke, Himmler for the first time had a senior post in the Army High Command. He delegated everyday responsibilities to Jüttner as his representative. Himmler was also appointed as Chief of the Army Armaments Branch, holding this post until 7 January 1945. Himmler addressed a gathering of officers from the Office of Military Armament, commanders of the Replacement Army and the Army headquarters staff on 21 July.

On 24 July, Hitler ordered that Himmler be responsible for all customs and frontier protection matters. Kaltenbrunner was delegated to act on Himmler's behalf. The next day Himmler made a speech in Grafenwöhr to the officers of the 544 Volksgrenadier Infantry Division and then another speech on 26 July in Bitsch to the 545 Volksgrenadier Infantry Division. This was followed on 27 July by a third speech in Münsingen to the officers of 543 and 547 Volksgrenadier Infantry Divisions.

As part of Operation Tempest, nationwide uprisings by the Polish Home Army, General Bór-Komorowski ordered that irregular Polish troops should revolt in Warsaw. At 5 p.m. on 1 August 1944, fighting broke out on the streets of Warsaw. Himmler took immediate charge of the counter measures and flew to Posen to direct the campaign. The next day SS-Obergruppenführer von dem Bach took command. He wrote his account for his interrogators post-war:

> When I heard about the uprising over the radio, I wondered why I was not immediately called to take over. I therefore called up the Operational Staff at Reichsführer Himmler's headquarters and questioned them about it. I was told Himmler had personally gone to Posen in order to start counter measures from there. …
>
> … Only a few days after that I was called up by Fegelein's staff and told that I was to take over immediately the Supreme Command against the Warsaw uprising. I was also told, that the situation in Warsaw had definitely turned to the worse. …
>
> … Himmler's counter measures had failed to be successful and had already been stopped in the outskirts of the city. I was told furthermore that the full power which I had asked of the Führer was given, and that I should put down the uprising quickly and forcefully. …
>
> … I immediately flew ahead into the area of Warsaw. …
>
> … Using Posen as a base Himmler had done everything to mobilize all forces which could possibly be put at his disposal behind the rear echelon. … Due to the fact that Himmler had no idea of the correct methods of leading troops into battle, no clear battle directives were issued. One had also failed to clarify the order of rank which caused a general confusion of command.
>
> … Following my arrival in Warsaw all commanding officers assured me unanimously that Himmler had merely ordered to shoot down everything ruthlessly, that no prisoners were to be taken. Warsaw was to be wiped out as an example and a warning for all large occupied cities. …
>
> … This was the situation when I arrived in Warsaw. It was a wild confusion, there was shooting everywhere, no one knew who was friend and who was foe. … I gave the order to cease the executions. Himmler's orders were herewith repealed. … I met with Heinz Reinefarth and told him that I was herewith taking over the command of all operations. … Reinefarth was glad to learn of my instruction, made no difficulties whatsoever and stressed, that … these orders of Himmler had caused discipline to break down. …

Himmler's version of events is recorded in a speech on 21 September 1944 to Army district commanders and commanders of military training schools:

> For the past five weeks we have been fighting for Warsaw. I have appointed SS-Obergruppenführer von dem Bach as my commander there. It is the hardest battle we have fought since the beginning of the war. ... When I heard the news of the Polish Uprising I went at once to see the Führer. ... I said: 'My Führer the timing is unfortunate, but from a historical point of view it is a blessing that the Poles are doing this. We'll get through the four and five weeks and Warsaw, the capital city, the brain, the intelligence of the 16–17 million-strong Polish nation will have been obliterated. ... Then the historic problem will no longer be a major one for our children, for all those who come after us and for us too. Moreover, I simultaneously gave orders for Warsaw to be totally destroyed. You may think I am a fearful barbarian. If you like, I am one if I have to be. My orders were to burn down and blow up every block of houses. As a result, one of the biggest abscesses on the Eastern Front has been removed.

The fighting continued until Bór-Komorowski was forced to surrender on 2 October 1944.

Hitler decided that he wanted a total reform of the Wehrmacht after the attempt on his life by Army officers and who better with whom to trust the task than the loyal 'Reichs-Heini?' On 2 August 1944, Himmler was appointed as Reich Plenipotentiary of the Führer for Reformation of the Wehrmacht. By 5 August, Himmler had delegated Pohl in this role. On 3 August, Himmler addressed a gathering of Reichsleiter and Gauleiter in Posen where he declared that all family members of those involved in the attempt on the life of the Führer were liable to arrest. Himmler himself ordered the widow of von Stauffenberg be removed to a concentration camp and his children to an orphanage. He declared '... The family of Graf Stauffenberg will be wiped out down to the last member.' He followed this with a directive on 17 August that all Reich and local representatives of the SPD and KPD were to be detained in an operation codenamed 'Thunderstorm.'

On 2 August 1944 the Gypsy family camp at Auschwitz-Birkenau was liquidated and from 9 August to 28 August, SS and police units liquidated the Lodz ghetto and deported around 60,000 Jews and Gypsies to Auschwitz-Birkenau.

On 31 August, Hitler placed Himmler in charge of the entire V2 rocket programme and its operational staff and Himmler delegated responsibility to Hans Kammler. Hitler also appointed Himmler as his representative for all security measures and defence of the Reich in the West on 1 September. Himmler created a special staff for this purpose, headed by General Karl Kitzinger. Himmler was also appointed as the titular commander of 'Führungstab Nordsee' on 13 September.

Himmler held a meeting at his Feldkommandostelle with General Andrei Vlasov on 16 September. Vlasov was the commander of the collaborating anti-Bolshevik Russian Liberation Army. Following their meeting, Vlasov observed of Himmler:

> ... Quiet, modest, nothing of the gangster boss like Dr. Ley. On the contrary, he was none too self-assured. ... I do not think he is intelligent. He seemed limited, narrow, pedantic ...

Hitler signed an order dated 25 September 1944 which commissioned Himmler with responsibility for all prisoner-of-war matters from 1 October 1944 and Himmler delegated this particular task to Gottlob Berger who carried out the job with integrity, gaining the respect of Allied commanders in the process. Upon Berger's death in 1975, a plaque was attached to his headstone recording the appreciation and thanks of the US POWs in his charge.

On 25 September, Hitler also ordered the creation of the Volkssturm, the units of men too young or too old to enlist in the regular forces. Himmler attended a ceremony in Königsberg on 10 October marking the creation of the local unit, where he delivered a stirring speech. He was placed in command of all Volkssturm units on 18 October 1944. The establishment of such units clearly indicated that the Third Reich leadership accepted that the war was not going well, many logically realising that the war was lost by 1943. Although not voicing his thoughts publicly, by now Himmler knew that an Allied victory was inevitable. The best he could hope for was that the western Allies would negotiate a separate peace and turn against the Soviets, join forces with the Reich and defeat the Bolshevik threat in the east.

With this in mind, in October 1944 Himmler ordered a halt to the gassing of Jews. The previous year he had tried to obliterate all signs of his crimes at Treblinka and now he embarked on a damage limitation policy. According to the post-war testimony of SS-Standartenführer August Becher, Himmler's order to Pohl and Kaltenbrunner clearly stated:

> Effective immediately I forbid any liquidation of Jews and order that, on the contrary, hospital care should be given to weak and sick persons. I hold you personally responsible even if this order should not be strictly adhered to by lower echelons.

Becher's testimony continued:

> ... I personally took Pohl's copy to him at his office in Berlin and left the copy for Kaltenbrunner at his office in Berlin. In my opinion Kaltenbrunner and Pohl bear the full responsibility after this date for any further killings of Jewish prisoners. ...

There had been a serious revolt at Auschwitz-Birkenau on 7 October 1944 where the Sonderkommando IV (Jewish prisoners tasked with the removal of corpses from the gas chamber and cremation of the bodies in crematorium IV) blew up crematorium IV and killed the guards. This resulted in a bloody battle, the death of around 450 prisoners and serious damage to the gassing facility.

Around this time, Himmler involved Walter Schellenberg with the first negotiations surrounding the release and exchange of Jews for materials the Reich could use in its war effort. As head of foreign intelligence in the SD, Schellenberg had numerous foreign contacts within the neutral countries of which Himmler was to take advantage. Much of what transpired in the final months of the war is well recorded for posterity and access is freely available in numerous publications.

The first of these negotiations appears to be in late October 1944 when Himmler held a secret meeting, at Schellenberg's instigation, with the right-wing Swiss politician Jean-Marie Musy. Himmler was indecisive at Musy's suggestion of the release of all Jews from camps in the Greater Reich in exchange for tractors and trucks. The meeting ended with no decisions.

On 3 November at Klein Berkel, Himmler delivered a speech to representatives of the Party, armed forces and industry with the aim of reassuring those elements of a successful outcome to the war. He was back in Posen on 5 November to address locals on the fifth anniversary of the incorporation of the Warthegau. On 8 November, Himmler spoke at a gathering of the Volkssturm where he read from the proclamation of the Führer on the foundation of the Volkssturm.

On 26 November 1944, Himmler ordered the physical destruction of the crematoria at Auschwitz-Birkenau. The dismantling of crematoria II and III began in early December 1944. The Sonderkomando revolt on 7 October 1944 had partially destroyed crematorium IV and the demolition of the walls of crematorium IV had commenced in mid-October of 1944. The demolition with explosives of crematoria II and III by a SS unit under SS-Rottenführer Perschel were carried out on 20 January 1945 and crematorium V, which was operational until the end, was blown up in the early hours of January 26, 1945.

Himmler gained his first combat command on 2 December 1944 when he was nominated as Oberbefehlshaber Oberrhein Reichsführer-SS, commander-in-chief of Army Group Oberrhein for the defence of the Colmar region and recapture of Strasbourg. He took over formally on 10 December from General Friedrich Wiese in Army Group G. Himmler had absolutely no combat experience and his short tenure until 23 January 1945 proved a total disaster. It appears that Bormann may have instigated the appointment of Himmler in order to illustrate his shortcomings and to strengthen his own position with Hitler. Himmler failed to recognise the threat from Bormann, being totally swept up in his daydreams of being a military field commander. Himmler appointed the aged First World War Pour le Mérite holder SS-Obergruppenführer Heinrich von Maur as his military adviser.

On Christmas Day 1944, Himmler made a speech in Gebweiler to the Waffen-SS commanders of Army Group Oberrhein.

Himmler was on his Sonderzug 'Steiermark' on 1 January 1945 and arrived at Pforzheim-Weissenstein where he was based for three days. He gave another speech to Waffen-SS commanders on 3 January in Sassbachwalden before returning to Pforzheim-Weissenstein. He then travelled to Triberg on 5 January and moved on to Trossingen the following day where he took afternoon tea with the family of Fritz Kiehn, SS-Obergruppenführer Karl Hermann Frank, his adjutant Major Hoffmann and Frau Lina Heydrich. Kiehn was a member of the Reichstag, the local Kreisleiter, SS-Obersturmbannführer, a member of the *Freundeskreis Reichsführer-SS* and the owner of the cigarette paper manufacturing company Efka-Werke GmbH. Frank, Hoffmann and Lina Heydrich were apparently visiting the area.

From 7 January until 12 January 1945, Himmler was at Triberg and visited Hitler at his Adlerhorst fieldheadquarters near Ziegenberg on the afternoon of 10 January. That night, Himmler played card games with his close staff, *Referent* Dr Brandt, adjutant Suchanek and bodyguard Kiermaier. Himmler was visited by Baldur von Schirach on 11 January.

12 January 1945 saw the massive Soviet military offensive commence with swift victories for the three million Russian troops against 750,000 poorly equipped Germans at the Baranow bridgehead. On 13 January, Himmler set up temporary headquarters at Forbach-Gausbach where he remained busy with various meetings until leaving for Berlin on 19 January by train upon which during the journey he conducted a presentation ceremony for winners of the Oakleaves to the Knights Cross. Also on this day, Gauleiter Greiser abandoned Posen under imminent threat of occupation by the Soviet army and Lodz was liberated by Marshal Zhukov.

Himmler did temporarily leave Forbach-Gausbach for a significant meeting with ex-Swiss President Dr Jean-Marie Musy at the Hotel Post in Wildbad, accompanied by SS-Brigadeführer Walter Schellenberg, on 15 January. The men discussed the Jewish problem and the possible exchange of Jewish prisoners for tractors, trucks and machine tools. Events elsewhere were spiralling out of control. During the night of 17 to18 January 1945, the guards at the Gestapo prison in Radogoszcz set the building ablaze with one thousand detainees still inside and the last surviving forty prisoners at Chelmno death camp were shot.

Himmler travelled by train to Schneidemühl [*today Pila, Poland*] on 21 January, arriving at 1 p.m. At 4.30 p.m., his train left for Deutsch-Krone [*today Walcz, Poland*] via Marienburg and he arrived at his destination at 4 a.m. on 22 January. Hitler issued a teleprinter order on 21 January, informing all parties that Himmler had been appointed as the commander of the newly formed Army Group Weichsel [*Vistula*] and that he would take up his new command as soon as possible in order to protect Danzig and Posen. Himmler's first order, the same day, was to direct the local commander in Posen to defend the city '... to the last breath.' By 22 January, the Russians were at the River Oder and the evacuation of Memel had commenced.

On 23 January 1945, Himmler was replaced as commander of Army Group Oberrhein by SS-Oberst-Gruppenführer Paul Hausser and on 24 January Himmler took up his new posting as commander of Army Group Weichsel [*Vistula.*] He received a visit to his train parked in a siding at Deutsch-Krone by Reichsminister Albert Speer who noted in his memoirs an overheard unfriendly telephone threat from Himmler to General Weiss to the effect that he would answer with his head if he abandoned his position. Army Group Vistula had been formed at the instigation of Generaloberst Heinz Guderian who suggested to Hitler that Generalfeldmarschall Maximilian von Weichs should take command. Hitler insisted on Himmler as the new commander, much to the dismay of Guderian, but Himmler did appoint the efficient SS-Gruppenführer Heinz Lammerding as his Chief of Staff.

Around this time, Himmler's attitude towards concentration camp inmates began to show further signs of relaxation. Robert Schirmer of the International Red Cross delegation in Berlin attended a meeting at the 'T' building in Oranienburg. This building housed the head offices of the Concentration Camp Inspectorate under SS-Gruppenführer Richard Glücks. Schirmer met Glücks, SS-Standartenführer Dr Enno Lolling and SS-Obersturmbannführer Rudolf Höss. Agreement was reached that parcels of the IRC (International Red Cross) could be distributed to certain nationalities of inmates. Elsewhere though, orders concerning the liquidation of foreign workers agreed at a security police meeting in Düsseldorf on 19 January were confirmed.

Himmler directed combat operations from Deutsch-Krone until the morning of 27 January when Sonderzug 'Steiermark' steamed towards Falkenburg where Himmler utilised the luxury villa occupied by Reichsleiter Dr Robert Ley, but retained Sonderzug 'Steiermark' as his Feldkommandostelle and even took his meals aboard the train. According to one source [*Duffy, Christopher*]:

> ... the train was unsuitable for a military field headquarters, had only one telephone line, inadequate maps, no signal detachment and insufficient radio transmitters with which to establish communication and relay military orders. Himmler seldom left the train, only working about four hours per day and insisted on a daily massage and a lengthy nap afterwards.

Himmler left for Ordensburg Crössinsee at 3 p.m. that afternoon, just as the Soviet army was liberating the camps at Auschwitz.

On 28 January, Himmler issued a secret directive that SS-Gruppenführer Dr Hans Kammler would take command of a newly formed unit designated A.K.z.V. responsible for rocket warfare. Hitler would also appoint Kammler as Special Plenipotentiary for Jet Aircraft on 31 January and ordered that the V1 and V2 programmes both be placed under Kammler's command.

On 29 January, Himmler sent a teleprinter message to all heads of military and civilian offices reminding them that abandoning their places of work without orders would make them liable to the death penalty. On 30 January 1945, Himmler issued an order which appeared in all German newspapers on the 8 February. The first paragraph declared:

> I have degraded the former SS-Standartenführer and Police President of Bromberg von Salisch for forgetting his duties and for cowardice. He is to be shot immediately. ...

It wasn't only men attempting to save themselves that felt the wrath of the Reichsführer-SS. Six hundred inmates of the Sonnenburg Prison were liquidated on orders of Himmler during 30 to 31 January. Himmler also ordered the evacuation on foot of concentration camps, resulting in the deaths of hundreds by the enforced conditions of the so-called 'death marches.'

Himmler left Crössinsee on 1 February and his train travelled from Falkenburg to Feldkommandostelle Birkenwald at Birkenhain near Prenzlau, arriving at 3 p.m. the same day. Birkenwald was situated near the airfield at Prenzlau and had good road and rail connections close by. The site had been chosen in the summer of 1943 after Himmler directed on 6 July 1943 that suitable premises must be found near Berlin, but away from the danger of air attacks. In September 1943, construction had begun using concentration camp labour numbering approximately three hundred workers. A new sub-camp of Ravensbrück was opened nearby at Hindenburg [*today Lindenhagen*] for the purpose. The wooden barrack used by Himmler still stands today and was called the 'R hut.' In total there were nearly twenty buildings over an area of 290,000 square metres. The cost of the 'R hut' to erect amounted to 930,000 Reichsmarks and was ready for occupation by the Reichsführer by the turn of the year. The complex was occupied by General Heinrici as his field headquarters after Himmler, but the SS remained until finally evacuating the site on 26 April 1945.

The commandant of Sachsenhausen concentration camp, SS-Standartenführer Anton Kaindl, subsequently reported under interrogation that he had received an order from Himmler on 1 February 1945 via SS-Gruppenführer Heinrich Müller to destroy Sachsenhausen camp, but the feasibility of such a task was impossible. During the night of 1–2 February, 150 prisoners were liquidated and by the end of March, 5,000 had been killed. The same night 400 Soviet POWs escaped from Mauthausen concentration camp, resulting in a mass round-up and execution of those recaptured. However, Himmler also showed his compassionate side, allowing the deportation of 1,200 Jews from Theresienstadt across the border into neutral Switzerland.

Birkenwald remained Himmler's field headquarters of choice throughout February 1945 and he stayed there apart from visits to the Reich Chancellery in

Berlin where Hitler had settled from 16 January. Himmler continued his rounds of meetings and constantly issued orders concerning the need for courage and that deserters and looters must be dealt with using the harshest methods. That the situation had deteriorated to a campaign of barricade warfare and threats of execution was obvious to everyone. It was only a matter of time before total collapse was inevitable. Outwardly Himmler gave the impression of steadfast defence and belief in final victory, but he was no fool. He had, however, underestimated the attitude of the Allies towards him. Believing that last minute displays of compassion would be his salvation and that his authority in a post-war defeated Germany was absolutely essential to the victorious Allies, particularly the Western Allies, he decided to take a path toward reconciliation.

Contact had already been made indirectly with the neutral Swedish Count Folke Bernadotte with the idea of negotiating the release of prisoners from concentration camps. Bernadotte was Vice-President of the Swedish Red Cross and was known to Himmler, but the men had not met. He was ideally placed for Himmler's purposes and the Reichsführer gave his tacit approval for initial negotiations to be opened. On 17 February 1945, Bernadotte had a meeting in Berlin-Wannsee with Ernst Kaltenbrunner and Walter Schellenberg at which Bernadotte requested a personal meeting with the Reichsführer-SS. The next day he met von Ribbentrop, but kept his mission secret, other than alluding to some work his Red Cross workers could carry out in the camps. During the evening of 19 February 1945, Himmler had his first personal meeting with Count Bernadotte at the Hohenlychen SS clinic. The meeting lasted 2 hours and 30 minutes and at Schellenberg's suggestion it was agreed that Danish and Norwegian prisoners would be concentrated in one single camp at Neuengamme, south-east of Hamburg.

On 20 February, Himmler had a short meeting with one of Heydrich's old adjutants, SS-Obersturmbannführer und Oberstleutnant der Polizei Kurt Pomme. Pomme slept on Himmler's train before going on to Rheinsberg. On 23 February, Posen fell to the Soviet advance. Himmler attended a meeting in Berlin the following day where all Reichsleiter and Gauleiter were appraised of the current situation by Hitler. During his speech, Hitler alluded to the use of newly invented weapons, new submarines, new aircraft and newly formed divisions to be used on the Eastern front. It was the last large gathering of Hitler's lieutenants.

Himmler's brother Gebhard, now a SS-Standartenführer, paid Himmler a visit at Birkenwald on 27 February and on the last day of February 1945, Himmler took to his bed with a heavy cold.

Himmler moved his headquarters to the SS clinic at Hohenlychen on 2 March 1945. Why he chose Hohenlychen remains a mystery. At the end of February he had suffered from a bad head cold which confined him to his bed and he was bedridden again on 4 March, but his ailments appear to have been minor. His old friend SS-Gruppenführer Prof. Dr Karl Gebhardt was still in charge and possibly

Himmler was buckling under the realisation that a combat command was above him. The reappearance of Felix Kersten is another indication that Himmler was suffering from stress.

On 5 March 1945, Count Bernadotte flew to Berlin where he continued negotiations with Kaltenbrunner and Schellenberg. At this meeting Kaltenbrunner openly admitted that he was opposed to any agreement and refused to co-operate. Bernadotte angrily retorted that he was not prepared to allow a subordinate of Himmler to sabotage an agreement between himself and Kaltenbrunner's boss. He was walking a dangerous tightrope.

On 7 March, Himmler received Dr Goebbels at Hohenlychen for a talk lasting two hours. Goebbels noted in his diary on 8 March that Himmler had been ill with angina and although still quite frail, he was now on the mend. This is the one and only mention of Himmler suffering from angina and one suspects that Himmler's complaint was more a suggestion of angina than the real thing. Goebbels continued that SS-Obergruppenführer Curt von Gottberg had been ordered by Himmler to comb railway stations for unattached itinerant soldiers and that he had experienced substantial success. Elsewhere, in Holland on 7 March, terrorists attacked the Higher SS and Police Leader SS-Obergruppenführer Hanns Albin Rauter leaving him seriously wounded and on 8 March, SS-Obergruppenführer Karl Wolff entered Switzerland and met the US intelligence officer Allen Dulles. They discussed a possible surrender of all German forces in Northern Italy.

Himmler was informed that there had been an outbreak of typhus at Bergen-Belsen and on 10 March he ordered that the disease must be contained and eradicated using all medical means before it could spread into the local populace. The diary entry by Goebbels on 12 March indicates that Hitler's faith in Himmler was beginning to wane.

Apparently, on 12 March 1945 Himmler signed an agreement with his masseur Felix Kersten in which he gave assurances that Hitler's orders to destroy all concentration camps and their inmates on the approach of Allied troops would not be acted upon. Himmler also declared that no further killing of Jews would be permitted, that Jews would henceforth be treated as other prisoners and that the evacuation of camp inmates would cease forthwith. Kaltenbrunner confirmed these instructions under interrogation post-war, but insisted that, in his opinion, all Jews should have been released immediately.

Although the date is not certain, according to a post-war interrogation of Hedwig Potthast, she saw Himmler for the last time at Hohenlychen around this time. She suggested that it was around 22 March 1945, but stated that Himmler had taken to his bed with an attack of grippe (former name for influenza.) This suggests that it was almost certainly earlier in the month when he was bedridden with the flu.

Himmler returned to Birkenwald on 14 March for a quick visit, but was back at Hohenlychen before the day was out. That same day Dr Rudolf Brandt alluded to

Himmler's recent health problems in a letter to Himmler's old friend Hanns Johst, pointing out that Himmler had been suffering from influenza, but was improving. On 15 March, Himmler was in Berlin for a couple of days before returning to Birkenwald on 18 March and then Hohenlychen on 19 March. At a meeting with Hitler on 16 March, Himmler received a fierce dressing down. He was again in Berlin for two days until returning to Birkenwald on 22 March when he relinquished command of Army Group Vistula to Generaloberst Gotthard Heinrici.

Once again Himmler's abilities as a combat commander had proved more than wanting. His command had begun well, mainly due to the competent General Walter Wenck, but then had drastically deteriorated after Wenck was involved in a serious car accident. Guderian had vehemently disagreed with Hitler over the appointment of Himmler and had attempted to get Himmler to admit that he had failed as a combat commander. He reported:

> After the disappearance from the scene of General Wenck, Himmler had proved a complete failure so far as the offensive in the Arnswalde area went. Conditions at his headquarters grew steadily more chaotic ... I therefore drove, in mid-March to his headquarters near Prenzlau in order to find out what the situation was. Himmler's chief of staff, Lammerding, greeted me at the entrance with the words: 'Can't you rid us of our commander?' I told Lammerding that this was purely a matter for the SS. When I asked for the Reichsführer I was told that he was suffering from influenza and was being treated by his personal physician, Professor Gebhardt, in the Hohenlychen sanatorium. I immediately drove there, where I found Himmler in apparently robust health ... he must have realized by now that a command of troops at the front is no easy matter. I therefore proposed to him that he give up his command of the army group and concentrate on his other offices. Himmler ... hesitated: 'I can't go and say that to the Führer. He wouldn't approve of my making such a suggestion.' I saw my chance and took it: 'Then will you authorize me to say it for you?' Himmler now had to agree. That same evening I proposed to Hitler that the overburdened Himmler be relieved of his command of Army Group Vistula and that in his place Generaloberst Heinrici ... be appointed to succeed him. Hitler disliked the idea, but after a certain amount of grumbling finally agreed.

An Allied intelligence report dated 27 March 1945 suggested that Himmler was at the Bregenz Gestapo HQ around 20 March and that his family was residing at the Villa Maund in Hopfreben, but this cannot be confirmed and seems unlikely.

On 23 March, Himmler temporarily moved his Feldkommandostelle to Schloss Wustrau at Fehbellin. (Grothmann believes this to have been a day earlier.) The imposing building had for a short period housed the offices of the SS Military Finance Office and the SS Leadership Central Office and there is also a suggestion that the concentration camp inspectorate at Oranienburg and Ravensbrück camp had been temporarily directed from here. Himmler stayed overnight and drove to Berlin the next day for a meeting with Kaltenbrunner and Wolff at the home of Hermann Fegelein. They discussed the meeting between Wolff and Allen Dulles. Himmler returned to Wustrau on 25 March, but was back in Berlin at the Reich Chancellery on 26 and 27 March. Frustrated by the efforts of Göring and Speer, Hitler made sweeping changes to the production of air armaments and placed Hans Kammler in charge of all modern aircraft on 27 March 1945. Already responsible for all matters of rocket weapons, Kammler now controlled what Hitler saw as Germany's salvation. Hitler promoted Kammler to SS-Obergruppenführer und General der Waffen-SS on the spot.

TWELVE

The Lost Soul

Having relinquished his command of Army Group Vistula, Himmler now had more freedom of movement and once again adopted a mobile approach. In Eisenstadt, south of Vienna, on 28 March, Himmler delivered a speech to Army Group South and met with SS-Oberst-Gruppenführer Josef Dietrich. During the same visit, which ended on 29 March, Himmler chaired a conference of Austrian Reichsstatthalter in Vienna where he gave authority for the introduction of martial law. Reichsleiter Baldur von Schirach recalled:

> Himmler came to Wien ... to talk to the Commander of Army Group South ... he had ordered all the Reichsstatthalter of the Ostmark up to Wien and granted them full authority to enforce martial law in the future, since Wien and some of the other Ostmark Gaue had by that time become almost front-line zones. At this conference Himmler told his adjutant to call Ziereis in while the papers for full powers were being typed in the next room. That is how I came to meet Ziereis for the second time in my life. And now Himmler did not, as Marsalek [*IMT witness*] said, tell Ziereis that the Jews were to be marched on foot from the south-east wall [*south-east front*] to Mauthausen, but he did say something else which surprised me enormously. He said: 'I want the Jews now employed in industry to be taken by boat, or by bus if possible, under the most favourable food conditions and with medical care, etc., to Linz or to Mauthausen.' I do not quite remember whether he said they should be taken to Mauthausen, but he also said to Ziereis: 'Please take care of these Jews and treat them well; they are my most valuable assets.' From this declaration I assumed, in the very beginning—it was my very first, fleeting impression—that Himmler wished to deceive me in some way or another and then it became clear to me that with these instructions he was following certain foreign political intentions, in the last moments of the war, in emphasizing the excellent treatment of the Jews.

Himmler then returned to Berlin via Wiesbaden. He was at Prenzlau [*most likely Birkenwald nearby*] on 30 March where he issued personal orders to SS-Sturmbannführer Heinz Macher to proceed to Wewelsburg and blow up the castle. Himmler was back with Hitler at the Reich Chancellery on 31 March. On Easter Sunday 1 April 1945, Himmler telephoned Wolff and warned him against returning to Switzerland. By way of a threat to ensure Wolff complied, Himmler advised Wolff that his wife and two sons had been placed under Himmler's personal protection. Himmler then made a quick visit to Hamburg on the afternoon of 1 April, returning to Hohenlychen on 2 April where he had a four hour discussion with Count Bernadotte. The Swedish diplomat subsequently reported that Himmler appeared very nervous and had admitted that the situation was grave, but not hopeless. Himmler agreed that immediate surrender was the best course, but that Hitler had refused to consider such a move. Himmler still felt obliged by his oath of allegiance and refused to act contrary to Hitler's orders. He also admitted that he knew himself to be top of the Allied wanted war criminals list, but insisted that he abhorred violence and cruelty. Himmler also advised Bernadotte to be wary of Kaltenbrunner.

Himmler may have spent the night back in Berlin to attend the Reich Chancellery on 3 April, but there is also a suggestion that he had another meeting with Bernadotte at Hohenlychen. The following day he was in Rheinsberg near Neuruppin where he had a conference with SS-Standartenführer Kaindl.

On 5 April 1945, SS-Gruppenführer Heinrich Müller issued instructions to the camp commandant at Dachau, SS-Obersturmbannführer Eduard Weiter:

> On the orders of the RFSS and after obtaining the decision of the highest authority, the prisoners listed below are to be immediately admitted to KL Dachau:
>
> Former Generaloberst Halder
> Former General Thomas
> Hjalmar Schacht
> Schuschnigg with wife and child
> Former General von Falkenhausen
> The Englishman Best (Wolf)
> Molotov's nephew Kokorin
> Oberst von Bonin General Staff
>
> I know you already have limited space in the cell block, but I request that these prisoners are kept together after examination. However, please ensure that the prisoner Schuschnigg codenamed Oyster is registered under his own name and is allotted a larger cell. His wife is a voluntary prisoner and is to be treated accordingly. The RFSS instructs that Halder, Thomas, Schacht, Schuschnigg and von Falkenhausen are well treated.

I request that on no account is the prisoner Best (codenamed Wolf) to make contact with the Englishman Stevens who is already there.

von Bonin was employed at Führer Headquarters and is now in honourable detention. He is still an Oberst on the active list and is expected to remain as such and I request that he be well treated.

The question of special protective custody prisoner Eller [*Georg Elser, Hitler's would-be assassin*] has again been discussed at the highest level and the following direction issued:

During one of the next terror attacks on Munich or the area of Dachau, it will be alleged that Eller was fatally injured. I request therefore, when such an occasion occurs, that Eller is liquidated as discreetly as possible. Steps must be taken to involve as few people as possible and all must be specially pledged to silence. ... After noting the contents of this instruction and after execution of these orders, please destroy this letter.

Signed SS-Gruf. Müller.

Himmler is known to have been in Berlin on 6 April when he lunched with Speer and attended the daily Führer conference at 3 p.m. He also appointed SS-Standartenführer Kurt Becher as Reich Special Commissioner for the Affairs of Jewish and Political Prisoners. On 8 April, Himmler attended a Führer conference in Berlin at which Gauleiter Karl Kaufmann declared that he was not in a position to defend Hamburg. Hitler dismissed his protestations and insisted that Hamburg be defended at all costs.

At about 6 a.m. on 9 April, Admiral Wilhelm Canaris, Generalmajor Hans Oster, Pastor Dietrich Boenhoffer, Hauptmann Ludwig Gehre, General Friedrich von Rabenau, Dr Karl Sack and Hauptmann Theodor Strünck were all hanged in the cellblock yard at Flossenbürg concentration camp. The orders came from Hitler via Himmler; old scores were being finally settled.

Himmler visited the Ruhr pocket on 11 April and at 3.15 p.m. the camp at Buchenwald was liberated by US forces. He gave his authority the same day to hand over the camp at Bergen-Belsen without a fight.

Schellenberg reports that on 13 April he was summoned to Schloss Wustrau by Himmler and in a private chat during a walk in the nearby forest, Himmler first broached the subject of dismissing Hitler. Schellenberg had been approached by Professor Max de Crinis who had noticed that Hitler was exhibiting symptoms of Parkinson's disease. This information Schellenberg passed on to Himmler who circled around his options, remaining undecided and unwilling to act. Himmler also discovered that Wolff had betrayed him and Hitler, and had proceeded with his negotiations in Switzerland. Himmler summoned Wolff immediately, but Wolff replied that he was 'otherwise engaged.' Kammler also informed Speer that he was willing to hand over the entire rocket project to the Americans in exchange for assurances of safety and offered Speer the opportunity to join him. It seems that everything was falling apart.

Himmler was resident at Schloss Wustrau from 13 April to 15 April, issuing an order on 14 April to the respective camp commandants at Dachau and Flossenbürg in response to their suggestion that the camps be handed over to the Americans:

> There is no question of a handover. The camp is to be immediately evacuated. No prisoner shall fall into the hands of the enemy alive. The prisoners behaved atrociously against the civilian population at Buchenwald.
>
> [*Signed*] H. Himmler.

Himmler changed his mind on the subject of evacuations after hearing that liberated prisoners from Buchenwald had entered Weimar and committed criminal acts of revenge including rape and looting. On the afternoon of 15 April, the camp at Bergen-Belsen was handed over to the British where they discovered appalling scenes of disease and death. Around 13,000 unburied corpses littered the camp compound. That same day Himmler held a series of meetings with Kurt Becher, August Heissmeyer, Adolf Eichmann and Hermann Pister (former commandant of Buchenwald.) Eichmann received orders to clear his offices of all documents and hand them over to the Gestapo who would destroy them.

On 16 April, Hitler's escort physician SS-Gruppenführer Dr Karl Brandt was arrested on Hitler's orders for defeatism. Apparently he had left his wife and child in Thuringia where they were certain to fall into the hands of the advancing Americans. Hitler was furious. Brandt was held in the luxury villa at Schwanenwerder owned by Dr Goebbels and it was here the following day that a court martial was quickly held and found the unfortunate doctor guilty. He was sentenced to death. Brandt had been a member of Hitler's close circle since 1934 and was very popular with Hitler's staff. Hitler's chief secretary, Johanna Wolf, was extremely upset and declared, 'I no longer understand him [*Hitler.*]' Himmler appeared at the Reich Chancellery on 17 April and reassured the occupants. [*In fact Brandt was saved by the intervention of Himmler and Speer, but fell victim to Allied justice on 2 June 1948 when he was hanged at Landsberg Prison.*]

Back at Hohenlychen on 16 April, Himmler held conferences with Kaltenbrunner and Karl Wolff. Wolff justified his meeting with Allen Dulles and suggested that Himmler ask Hitler for a Führer-Order to surrender all forces in Italy. Himmler declined and Wolff left with Kaltenbrunner to return to the Reich Chancellery where they met Hitler early the following day in his garden bunker. Accompanied by Schellenberg, Himmler attended a meeting with Graf Schwerin von Krosigk and Franz Seldte on 19 April. That evening, Himmler returned to Hohenlychen from where he telephoned Hedwig Potthast; their last conversation. As usual, Himmler only spoke of personal matters, but he did say that the general situation was extremely grave and that he would call again the following day. She never spoke to him again. She received one last letter in which he hoped God would protect her and the children, but he made no mention of his plans or what she should do.

Himmler attended Hitler's last birthday celebrations at the Reich Chancellery on 20 April where he also had private conversations with Göring. Himmler tried to obtain assurances from the Reichsmarschall that in any post-Hitler government, Himmler would have a senior role, but Göring refused to commit himself. After passing on birthday greetings, most ministers and senior officials left Berlin. Himmler headed for Schloss Wustrau where Schellenberg awaited his arrival. Schellenberg urged Himmler to bring the war to an end, but Himmler hesitated again, deciding to drive to Gut Hartzwalde, the country residence of Kersten. They arrived at 2.30 a.m. and conferred with Kersten and Norbert Masur of the World Jewish Congress. After a few hours, Himmler drove to Hohenlychen for a breakfast meeting with Bernadotte. Himmler then retired to his bed, feeling unwell.

According to Grothmann, Himmler's Sonderzug 'Steiermark' left for Bavaria on 21 April 1945 with the intention of awaiting the arrival of the Reichsführer at either Berchtesgaden or Bayrisch Zell. It reached Pilsen where it was held up by aerial bombing. On board were the train commander SS-Hauptsturmführer Ludwig Pemsel, Oberstleutnant Suchanek, Major Vollmar, SS-Oberführer Bender and other train personnel.

Himmler hurriedly abandoned Schloss Wustrau on Sunday 22 April and drove to Hohenlychen along roads packed with Wehrmacht columns and under constant air attack. He spent the night at the SS clinic and on 23 April he drove to the Reich Chancellery with Gottlob Berger. They were received by Hitler who had decided to remain in Berlin contrary to the advice of his generals, including Himmler. At 3 p.m. Schellenberg had a meeting with Count Bernadotte at the Swedish consulate in Flensburg to discuss a further meeting with Himmler later that day. At this meeting Schellenberg stated that Hitler was finished and Himmler desired a meeting with General Eisenhower in order to capitulate all German forces in the west. Schellenberg enquired if Bernadotte would be willing to deliver this message to Eisenhower. Schellenberg telephoned Himmler's Feldkommandostelle to ask if Himmler could come to Lübeck to meet Bernadotte. Dr Brandt advised him that Himmler was unavailable at that moment, but that he would inform the Reichsführer of his request. Brandt returned the call at 6 p.m. and told Schellenberg that Himmler would be in Lübeck at 10 p.m.

Hans Prützmann accompanied Himmler to Lübeck where they met Count Bernadotte at the Swedish Consulate. The proceedings were conducted by candlelight as a result of a power cut and they were delayed when a heavy air raid targeted a local airfield. The men discussed the formal method by which the offer of surrender could be made and it was decided to put the offer in writing to the

Swedish Foreign Minister. Himmler left at 1.30 a.m. in the morning of 24 April and drove himself to the Hotel Danziger Hof in Lübeck where SS-Obergruppenführer Alfred Wünnenberg had his field headquarters. Himmler's letter dated 24 April 1945 to the Swedish Foreign Minister stated:

> Excellency!
> I have asked Count Bernadatte [*sic*] to inform you of a number of problems which I had the opportunity of discussing with him today. Please accept in advance my genuine appreciation for your kind attention to these matters.
> With the expression of my highest respects,
> I remain Your Excellency's
> Very devoted,
> [*signed*] H. Himmler

On 25 April Bernadotte called upon the US ambassador to Sweden in Stockholm and informed him of his meeting with Himmler and Himmler's offer of capitulation in the west. Ambassador Herschel Johnson immediately informed Washington.

By this time most SS central offices had either been evacuated out of Berlin, or were in the process of doing so. Himmler's older brother Gebhard was attached to the SS-Führungshauptamt and this department evacuated its offices between 22 and 24 April. By chance, on the road to Schwerin, Gebhard encountered his brother accompanied by his driver SS-Sturmbannführer Franz Lucas and his bodyguard SS-Sturmbannführer Josef Kiermaier. The Himmler brothers stopped only briefly to discuss personal matters and then went their own way. It was the last time they met.

Himmler returned to Hohenlychen after his night time meeting with Bernadotte where he received a visit from Reichsminister Albert Speer. Himmler admitted to Speer that he expected to be running the government within days. Generalfeldmarschall Wilhelm Keitel also arrived and professed undying support for the Reichsführer-SS.

Without delay, all three major Allied powers rejected Himmler's proposal of a western surrender of German forces and insisted on an unconditional surrender on all fronts.

On 27 April, Himmler attended a situation conference called by Grossadmiral Karl Dönitz at Supreme Headquarters in Neuroofen. There Himmler asked Dönitz if he had Dönitz's support if Hitler entrusted the government to him. Dönitz replied that he would serve in any legal government to prevent chaos and bloodshed. That same day Himmler ordered the arrests of Generalmajor Dornberger and SS-Obergruppenführer Kammler for failure to carry out orders. Both men escaped. Also that day, Bernadotte informed Schellenberg of the Allied rejection of Himmler's proposal and requested a further meeting with Himmler. Schellenberg passed on the news to Dr Brandt. Himmler rejected the notion of another meeting and ordered Schellenberg to report in person to him south of Lübeck on the morning of 28 April. Himmler's party, consisting of Grothmann, Tiefenbacher, Dr Brandt, Kiermaier and Dr Müller, moved from Hohenlychen on 28 April to a villa near Krakow-Mecklenburg where they would stay for a night or two.

Deep in his bunker in Berlin, Hitler was informed of radio news broadcasts revealing the peace negotiations and offer of surrender by his Reichsführer-SS. Hitler flew into a rage declaring Himmler a traitor. When it was discovered that SS-Gruppenführer Hermann Fegelein had absconded from the bunker and contents of his briefcase revealed Himmler's previous peace feelers, Fegelein was arrested, sentenced to death and executed in the gardens above before midnight on 28 April. The same night, 28–29 April 1945, Hitler married Eva Braun.

At 4 a.m. on 29 April 1945, Hitler dictated his last will and political testament to one of his secretaries, Traudl Junge. The second part contained the following declarations:

> Before my death I expel from the Party the former Reichsmarschall Hermann Göring and deprive him of all rights which he may enjoy by virtue of the decree of 29 June 1941 and also by virtue of my statement in the Reichstag on 1 September 1939. I appoint in his place Grossadmiral Dönitz, President of the Reich and Supreme Commander of the Armed Forces.
>
> Before my death I expel the former Reichsführer-SS and Reichsminister of the Interior Heinrich Himmler from the Party and all offices of State. In his place I appoint Gauleiter Karl Hanke as Reichsführer-SS and Chief of German Police and Gauleiter Paul Gieseler as Reichsminister of the Interior. ....

Hitler then gave his reasons for the two dismissals as treachery and secret attempts to seize power. He followed this with a list of nineteen further appointments in Dönitz's new government which the new Reich President duly ignored.

On 30 April Himmler was *in situ* at Dobbin village, the estate of the late Dutch oil magnate Henri Deterding, but he agreed to vacate the mansion house to make way for the new headquarters staff of the OKW and he moved to Schloss Kalkhorst, east of Travemünde. Himmler was invited to a meeting with Grossadmiral Karl Dönitz at the police barracks in Lübeck after Dönitz was informed of Himmler's treachery. At this time Bormann failed to inform Dönitz of his nomination as Hitler's successor, but ordered him to take ruthless action against traitors:

> New treason afoot. According to enemy radio Reichsführer has made surrender proposal via Sweden. Führer expects you to act against all traitors with lighting speed and as hard as steel.
>
> [*signed*] Bormann.

Dönitz was understandably mystified by the ambiguous and meaningless message. Once in Lübeck, Himmler kept Dönitz waiting. Himmler had been made aware by telephone that Hitler had received the news of his peace negotiations badly. Dönitz asked Himmler if the rumours were true and Himmler flatly denied them.

Dönitz writes of this meeting with Himmler:

> As far as I myself was concerned, to maintain order and to be able to get on with my job was the only thing that mattered. In any case, how could I be expected 'to take instant and ruthless action against' the Reichsführer who had the whole of the Police and the SS at his disposal? I was quite powerless to do so. For the protection of my staff and myself at Plön not one single man had been detailed. To use force against Himmler was therefore quite impossible. Nor did I wish to do so, for chaos would have been the inevitable result. The decision I reached was simple and swiftly taken. I invited Himmler to a meeting for I wanted to know what game he was playing. We agreed to meet at the police barracks in Lübeck. About midday, as I was about to set out, Admiral Meisel, the Naval Chief of Staff, and Gauleiter Wegener came to see me and told me that they feared for my personal safety if I went to visit Himmler. I did my best to allay their anxieties. Meisel declared roundly that it was just not good enough that my sheep dog should be my only guard, and he asked permission to be allowed at least to transfer Commander Cremer and his submariners to Plön for my protection. To this I agreed. When I reached the police barracks in Luebeck I found that every available senior SS leader had apparently been summoned to the meeting. Himmler kept me waiting. He seemed already to regard himself as head of the state. I asked him whether the report was true that he had sought contact with the Allies through the medium of Count Bernadotte. He asserted that it was not true, and that in his opinion it was essential, in these last days of the war, that discord among ourselves should not be allowed to create further chaos in the country. We parted amicably.

At approximately 2.30 p.m. on 30 April 1945, Hitler and his new wife bid farewell to the remaining circle of followers and staff in the underground Führer bunker below the grounds of the Reich Chancellery in Berlin. They then retired into Hitler's sitting room and closed the door. Witnesses reported hearing a single gunshot at about 3.30 p.m. Reluctant to enter, a few minutes passed before Heinz Linge and Bormann opened the door. Linge states there was an obvious odour of almonds, a clear indication that hydrogen cyanide had been exposed to the air. Otto Günsche entered the room to find Hitler and Eva both sitting on the sofa, Eva's legs drawn up under her slumped body. Hitler to her right was slumped over the armrest and blood was dripping to the floor from his head. Both were obviously dead.

Upon his return to his headquarters at Plön, Dönitz received the all important message that Hitler had appointed him as his successor:

> Berlin 1807hrs. Grossadmiral Dönitz. Instead of the former Reichsmarschall Göring the Führer has appointed you, Herr Grossadmiral, as his successor. Confirmation in writing is on way to you. You now have all the necessary measures for the current situation.—Bormann.

Bormann failed to mention that Hitler was dead and Dönitz was the new Reich President and Supreme Commander. Dönitz summoned Himmler to his Plön HQ and he arrived at midnight with a body of large SS men. Dönitz handed Himmler the telegram with the words, 'Please read this.' The blood visibly drained from Himmler's face and after a few awkward moments, Himmler offered his services to the Dönitz government. The admiral declined the offer and made it clear that he could not use Himmler in any capacity in his new government. Himmler withdrew from the room a defeated man and returned to Kalkhorst where at some point he learned of the death of Hitler.

Schellenberg arrived at Kalkhorst at about 4 a.m. on 1 May and learned of the startling events of the previous 24 hours from Dr Brandt. Himmler had retired at 3 a.m. and arose a few hours later looking pale and unshaven, taking breakfast with Schellenberg at 9 a.m. Although Schellenberg appraised Himmler of his latest negotiations, Himmler stopped him short and told him that he was no longer in a position to have any influence. At 11 a.m., the two men drove back to Plön to visit Dönitz, arriving at 2 p.m. after a difficult journey. Later that day, Himmler's Feldkommandostelle moved to Gutshof Neversfelde near Malente and he was visited there by Graf Schwerin von Krosigk.

Himmler's new status was confusing. He had been stripped of the title Reichsführer-SS along with all his government and party functions by Hitler, but Dönitz still considered him to be an important and dangerous character who commanded a large body of troops. Therefore, for the time being, he was allowed the respect and treatment of a high profile figure. Dönitz did not like him and had no intention of using his skills, but Himmler was allowed into headquarters and was invited to dine with Dönitz. Himmler appointed Hans Prützmann as his personal representative with the Dönitz administration.

On 2 May, Himmler arrived unannounced at a meeting of Dönitz's new government at Plön where he was confronted by the aviatrix Hannah Reitsch. She took him to task over the revelations of his secret peace negotiations which she considered as a betrayal of the Führer. Himmler defended himself declaring that he considered Hitler a madman leading Germany into the abyss. Himmler dined with Dönitz and Speer before Dönitz moved his headquarters to the Marine School Mürwick at Flensburg.

At about 3 p.m. on 2 May, Leon Degrelle states he ran into Himmler driving his own car, dressed in leather driving helmet, on the road from Eutin at the Bad Segeburg junction. Apparently, Himmler's staff at Neversfelde had been surprised by the rapid advance of the enemy and had abandoned the Feldkommandostelle with a move to Flensburg. Himmler and his staff were billeted in the Lorenzen farmhouse in the village of Ausacker on the outskirts of Flensburg. However, Himmler spent the night of 2 May at the farmhouse of Johannes Festesen in the village of Esgrus, east of Flensburg. He took up residence at the Lorenzen farmhouse on 3 May and it was at this location that a post-war interrogation of Wilhelm Walther, one of Himmler's bodyguards, revealed that important documents were buried. Extensive searches failed to recover them, but Lorenzen and his daughter both admitted that Himmler and his staff had lived at the farm from 3 to 7 May 1945.

Himmler continued to turn up uninvited at Mürwick and on 3 May he had a final meeting with what remained of his concentration camp inspectorate team, Richard Glücks, Gerhard Maurer and Rudolf Höss. He bade them farewell with the parting orders that they should disguise themselves with Glücks and Höss crossing into Denmark whilst Maurer and the remaining staff should mingle with army and naval personnel.

On 4 May, Himmler turned up at the farm of Johannes Christiansen in the village of Kollerup which had been sealed off and turned into the headquarters of C-in-C North West, Generalfeldmarschall Ernst Busch. Himmler asked Busch for a Wehrpass to assist him disguise himself. Busch refused. At Lüneburg Heath, the site of Bernard Montgomery's headquarters, the German surrender in north and north-west Europe was signed by Admiral Hans-Georg von Friedeburg at 6.30 p.m., signalling a capitulation effective at 8 a.m. on 5 May 1945.

During the evening of 4 May, Himmler held a meeting with Gauleiter Ernst Bohle where he confirmed that he wished to retain his position as Reichsführer-SS and Chief of the German Police in order to maintain law and order.

On 5 May, Himmler held his last staff conference at Flensburg, most probably at Wünnenberg's new Ordnungspolizei headquarters in the fireman's training school at Harrisleefeld in Flensburg. Lasting a maximum of 45 minutes, it was attended by:

SS-Obergruppenführer Alfred Wünnenberg, head of the Ordnungspolizei Office;
SS-Obergruppenführer Maximilian von Herff, head of SS Personnel Office;
SS-Obergruppenführer Werner Lorenz, VOMI;
SS-Obergruppenführer Hans Jüttner, head of the SS Leadership Office;
SS-Obergruppenführer Hans Prützmann, special representative of the RFSS;
SS-Obergruppenführer Udo von Woyrsch, HSSPF Wehrkreis IV;
SS-Obergruppenführer Karl Demelhuber, head of SS training;
SS-Obergruppenführer Curt von Gottberg, staff GFM Busch;

SS-Gruppenführer Karl Gebhardt;
SS-Gruppenführer Otto Ohlendorf;
SS-Gruppenführer Georg-Henning von Bassewitz-Behr, HSSPF Hamburg;
SS-Gruppenführer Hermann Behrends, HSSPF Kurland;
SS-Gruppenführer Fritz Katzmann, HSSPF Danzig;
SS-Standartenführer Dr Rudolf Brandt, Personal Referent RFSS;
SS-Obersturmbannführer Werner Grothmann, adjutant RFSS.

Himmler informed the group that he had been rebuked for his unofficial peace negotiations and that it was his intention to form a new government if possible. He gave an unrealistic situation report and allotted certain tasks to several of those present before dismissing all but the Obergruppenführer. Von Herff asserted that he added nothing new to the remaining Obergruppenführer and the men dispersed with a feeling of uncertainty, most to fall into Allied hands very soon after.

Hans Jüttner described in a subsequent interrogation that Himmler had said he had no intention of committing suicide and that he desired a personal meeting with Montgomery to discuss a policy of western opposition to the Russians. This idea was also confirmed by a Grothmann interrogation. Rudolf Höss asserts that on 5 May the camp inspectorate team received their false papers and took false identities. He was to be known as Franz Lang and Glücks took the name Sonnemann.

THIRTEEN

The Curtain Falls

On 6 May at 5 p.m., Dönitz finally dismissed Himmler and severed all ties with him. Himmler retired to his temporary headquarters at the fireman training school in Harrisleefeld although it appears he used the Lorenzen farm near Ausacker to sleep. The following day in Reims, France, at 2.41 a.m. Generaloberst Alfred Jodl signed the instrument of unconditional surrender on behalf of Grossadmiral Dönitz and the German government. On 8 May 1945 at 11.01 p.m. Central European time all hostilities in the European theatre of war came to an end.

Around this time, Himmler still surrounded himself with a large group of loyal SS men and his escort protection unit, but he decided to reduce his motorcade to four vehicles. Himmler and his staff moved out of the town on 8 May having given orders that all troops under his command were to lay down their arms. He left a letter with Generaloberst Jodl for Montgomery which Jodl promised to deliver. At the IMT in Nuremberg, Jodl told Speer that he reneged upon his word and destroyed the letter.

On 9 May, or possibly 10 May, Himmler shaved off his moustache and secretly left the Flensburg city area with the intention of remaining a free man in order to speak with Montgomery. He was accompanied by a reduced staff and escort of around fourteen men travelling in four PKW vehicles. They included Werner Grothmann, Josef Kiermaier, Dr Rudolf Brandt, Heinz Macher and Oberfeldarzt Dr Müller, plus several escort personnel. Himmler had disguised himself in a marine artillery uniform as had Grothmann, Macher and Brandt. Others wore green police uniforms all of junior rank.

On 10 May at about 3 p.m., SS-Gruppenführer Richard Glücks, who had been admitted to the naval hospital in Mürwick under the name of Sonnemann, bit his glass vial of cyanide and killed himself. On 11 May, Gebhard Himmler turned up at the fireman training school in Flensburg looking for his brother, but only encountered the remnants of his staff (Baumert, Tiefenbacher, Gutgesell and Fälschlein) who advised him that the Reichsführer had already left and was on the move. Gebhard was later arrested with Hans Jüttner in Schleswig on 16 May.

It appears that the Himmler group stayed close to Flensburg and did not strike out away from the immediate vicinity until after 11 May. Macher states with some uncertainty that it was about 13 or 14 May that they left in a vehicle driven by him which contained Himmler, Grothmann and Feldwebel Siegfried Lüngen and they took the side roads towards Friedrichskoog where they planned to stay until they could safely cross the River Elbe estuary. It is possible they stayed in the Friedrichskoog area for a few days until the weather was suitable for a river crossing and until they could hire a boat. They abandoned their vehicles in Friedrichskoog and made their way on foot to the estuary of the Elbe where, during the night of 15–16 May, they paid 500 RM to a local fisherman called Willi Pett to take the whole group and some refugees across to Otterndorf on the southern bank. Lüngen left the party at Otterndorf. By now the entire party had changed into civilian clothes and Himmler had donned a patch over his left eye. He carried papers in the name of Feldwebel Heinrich Hitzinger of the Geheime Feld-Polizei (GFP-Secret Field Police.)

Elsewhere, Major Norman Whittaker noted in his diary on 15 May 1945 at 31a Uelzener Strasse in Lüneburg that SS-Obergruppenführer Hans Prützmann had been brought in. Whittaker also noted on 16 May that Prützmann had been taken away at 11 a.m. that morning. His diary records on 17 May:

> I heard this morning that Prützmann has committed suicide—poison concealed in a cigarette lighter. Thank God he didn't do it while in my charge. ... At 2000hrs Karl [*sic, correct Kurt*] Daluege who is another SS-Obergruppenführer and a General of Police ... [*arrived*] together with Dr Meissner ... after the Prützmann episode I was taking no chances so I had them stripped and their clothes thrown out on the landing and gave them blankets to wrap themselves in. ...

The Himmler party made their way on foot towards Bremervörde where they stopped at the farmhouse of Hinrich Dankers, Waldstrasse 165 and the house next door, in the northern outskirts of the town on about 17 or 18 May. The group consisted of:

Reichsführer-SS Himmler;
SS-Standartenführer Dr Brandt;
SS-Obersturmbannführer Grothmann;
SS-Sturmbannführer Kiermaier, RSD;
SS-Sturmbannführer Macher;
Oberfeldarzt Dr Müller;
SS-Obersturmführer Schmidt, RSD;
SS-Untersturmführer Lorenz, RSD;

SS-Oberscharführer Müller, RSD;
SS-Untersturmführer Baumann;
SS-Untersturmführer Ehm;
SS-Unterscharführer Haushalter;
SS-Unterscharführer Erdt;
SS-Unterscharführer Queisser;
SS-Unterscharführer Rudolf.

At approximately 10 a.m. on 20 May, Kiermaier and Dr Müller went into the town to request assistance from the Landrat Wilhelm Dorhmann to obtain authority for the group to travel to Lüneburg as a party of discharged wounded soldiers. Himmler became nervous when the two had not returned by midday and decided that he would leave with Grothmann and Macher and head south. An hour after they left, a British army lorry pulled up outside the houses and the remainder of the party were all detained.

Himmler, dressed in civilian clothing and a blue raincoat, with Grothmann and Macher, both dressed in civilian trousers with military tunics and rubberised greatcoats without insignia, trudged down lanes and across fields towards the village of Meinstedt. There, at about 7 p.m. on 21 May, they emerged from a hedgerow and encountered two Russian soldiers, Vasilij Gubarev and Ivan Sidorov. They were both liberated POWs who were attached to a British security patrol under Corporal Morris of 73 Assault Regiment. The British were brewing up tea when the Russians stopped the three men and demanded their papers for examination. The papers of one were found to be not in order and all three were detained and put into an army vehicle which took them to the camp at Seedorf where they spent the night in the guardhouse. The next morning they were taken under escort to the bridge control point in Bremervörde where arrest reports were created and initial interrogations carried out.

In 1964, a Russian newspaper reported the statement of Vasilij Gubarev on the initial detention of Himmler:

> … the two had shortly before been released from a German prisoner of war camp and brought them to an assembly point; the following day they were on patrol in vicinity of Meinstedt village near Bremervörde. The report continued, while the British drank tea, the two Russians maintained their patrol: 'Five hundred meters off the road, three Germans appeared out of the woods. We noticed, and got behind them. When we were two hundred meters distant, we called on them to stop. One stopped, the two other went further on. We then called loudly: "Stop!" raised out rifles and brought all three to a standstill. We asked: "Soldiers?" One answered: "Yes!" To our question: "Have you identity cards?" One answered with: "Jawohl!" They showed us one identity card. It had neither stamp nor signature. They wore officers' coats and

> boots. One of the Germans, later found to be Himmler, had civilian shoes and a hat. His left eye was covered by a black bandage, he had no mustache. He carried a stick.
>
> We led the detainees into the village and handed them over to the English soldiers. The three Germans told the English they had recently been released from hospital. One had been injured in the eye and foot. The English patrol wanted to let them go. But we insisted they should not be released and be brought to the camp. Together with two English soldiers we took the detainees. At the camp an English officer-interpreter received us. He took over the detainees and sent them to the guard house.
>
> A few days later we heard that a British officer and interpreter were looking for us. They asked: "Where are the Russians who captured the three Germans on 21 May? What badges did they have?" We asked them: "Do you know if they have been arrested?" "No," the interpreter explained. "You arrested the head of the Gestapo, Himmler, right-hand man of Hitler."'

Himmler's arrest report, dated 22 May and signed by Staff-Sergeant John Hogg of 1003 Field Security Detachment based at Westertimke Cage, indicates that Hizinger [*sic, correct Hitzinger*] was formally arrested at 5 p.m. and had been interrogated by Sergeant Arthur Britton of 45 Field Security Section. It shows that Hizinger had been demobilised on 3 May 1945 and was claiming to be a former Feldwebel with a Panzer Company attached to the GFP for special duties. This in itself was grounds for immediate arrest as the GFP was recognised as an arm of the SD. Grothmann used his brother Eduard's identity and Macher gave his correct name, but false rank and unit.

Himmler, Grothmann and Macher were given mugs of tea on the orders of Sergeant Ken Baisbrown of the Intelligence Corps and searched by Corporal Richard Forrest before being housed in the Wilhelm Lohse mill occupied at the time by 1003 Field Security Detachment for the night. That night they slept in a first floor grain storeroom, still unrecognised by the British security detachment. The site is today occupied by a hotel, the original buildings having been demolished.

At 7 a.m. on 23 May 1945, the three prisoners left by army truck driven by Sergeant Britton and an escort of two guards, the intended destination was the civil internment camp at Westertimke. At Zeven a stop was made at 45 Field Security Section HQ to report the arrest of three suspected SD men to Captain Excell. He told Sergeant Britton to continue to Westertimke to register the prisoners. At around 2 p.m. that day, the three prisoners and their escort made their way to Civilian Interrogation Camp 031 at Kolkhagen near Barnstedt, finally arriving after several stops to collect other prisoners at approximately 6.40 p.m. The subsequent events at Kolkhagen are described in a report held at the National Archives, Kew:

Secret Report dated 23 May 1945 by Capt. C A Smith, Chief Interrogation, 031 Camp:

Subject: Identification of HEINRICH HIMMLER.
To: GSO 2 I (b) Ops and Policy
HQ 2 Army Main

1. At 1840 hrs today twenty German civilian and military prisoners arrived at 031 Civilian Interrogation Camp from the internment camp at Westertimke.

2. While they were being searched, I was informed that one of them wished to speak urgently with the Camp Commandant. I went to the camp office and saw the man who had made the request. His arrest report gave his particulars as: Uffz. Grothmann Eduard, a suspected member of the GFP; arrested by 1003 FSRD on 22 May 45 at Bremervorder [*sic*].

3. Grothmann said that he was a member of the SS and that he and two others would like to speak privately with me. I took him apart with the other two men whose arrest reports showed them as: Feldwebel Hizinger Heinrich, and Obergfr. Macher Horst. The details of arrest were the same as for Grothmann.

4. The man who called himself Hizinger then told me that he was Reichsführer SS Heinrich Himmler and that the other two were officers of his staff. He wished to speak to an officer on the staff of Field Marshal Montgomery.

5. I asked the other two men their real names and they gave them as follows:
   Obersturmbannführer Werner Grothmann and
   Sturmbannführer Heinz Macher.
   The three men were immediately taken into a room and a guard was posted, while I advised you of their arrival by 'phone.

6. Himmler was immediately searched with the utmost thoroughness by Capt. Selvester, Lieut. Findlay and myself. He was made to strip entirely and don a complete change of underwear which was examined minutely beforehand. His other clothes were also carefully examined and all his effects, which were contained in a rucksack.

7. The only unusual article we found was a small glass phial containing a colourless liquid and enclosed in a small metal tube. Himmler explained that he suffered from cramps in the stomach and the phial contained a medicinal remedy. I handed the phial to you later on in the evening.

8. The three men were dressed in a miscellaneous assortment of German army uniform and civilian clothes. Himmler wore horn-rimmed glasses, and on his arrival at the camp had a black patch over his right eye. He removed this patch on his first being searched.

9. Himmler and the other two men were kept in the room under constant supervision until you arrived with Major Rice.

Signed C A Smith Capt.
Chief Interrogator
031 Camp

A similar version of events is provided by Captain Thomas Selvester the commanding officer of 031 Civil Interrogation Camp in an undated statement. This has slight variations from the Smith version, but is also quoted here for reference purposes:

On the 23 May 1945, I was the Commandant of 031 Civilian Interrogation Camp, near Luneburg.

About 2-0 p.m. on that day, a convoy arrived at the Camp with a party of suspected persons, who I understood had been arrested at a check point on a bridge near Bremervorde. At that time, large numbers of German troops were endeavouring to make their way home, and were carrying in most cases documents issued by senior officers of their respective regiments. These troops were being stopped, and placed in ordinary P.O.W. cages, but if there was any doubt as to their identity they were sent to my Camp for further interrogation. On arrival at my Camp, the drill was for such prisoners to be paraded outside my office, and then allowed to enter singly, when it was my duty to obtain from them their names, addresses, ages, and any documents carried. I was also responsible for the searching of the prisoners, and the listing of the personal property in their possession.

It will be appreciated that such procedure took some little time, and somewhere about 4-0 p.m. it was reported to me that the troops guarding the prisoners outside the offices were having some little trouble with three men in the party, who were insisting on seeing me immediately. This was most unusual, as normally these prisoners were most apprehensive, and only too anxious to please, and as a result I ordered that they be brought before me one at a time. The first man to enter my office was small, ill-looking and shabbily dressed, but he was immediately followed by two other men, both of whom were tall and soldierly looking, one slim, and one well built. The well built man walked with a limp. I sensed something unusual, and ordered one of my Sergeants to place the two Tall [*sic*] men in close custody, and not allow anyone to speak to them without my authority. They were then removed from my office, whereupon the small man, who was wearing a black patch over his left eye, removed the patch and put on a pair of spectacles. His identity was at once obvious, and he said 'Heinrich Himmler' in a very quiet voice. At that time only myself and a Sergeant were present in the room, so I ordered the sergeant to notify Captain Smith of the Intelligence Corps that I would like to see him in my office, and arranged for an armed guard to be posted outside the room to prevent any person entering.

On Captain Smith's arrival, I told him what had transpired, (but I don't think he needed to be told the identity of our prisoner), and he asked Himmler to sign his name in order to compare with a copy we had in our possession. Himmler was most reluctant to write his name, and was under the impression that we wanted it as a souvenir, but eventually agreed on condition that the paper was torn up immediately.

The next step was to search the prisoner, & this I carried out personally, handing each item of clothing as it was removed to my Sergeant, who re-examined it. Himmler was carrying documents bearing the name of Heinrich Hizinger, who I think was described as a postman. In his jacket I found a small brass case, similar to a cartridge case, which contained a small glass phial. I recognised it for what it was, but asked Himmler what it contained, and he said, 'That is my medicine. It cures my stomach cramp.' I also found a similar brass case, but without the phial, and came to the conclusion that the phial was hidden somewhere on the prisoner's person. When all Himmler's clothing had been removed and searched, all the orifices of his body were searched, also his hair combed and any likely hiding places examined, but no trace of the phial was found. At this stage he was not asked to open his mouth, as I considered that if the phial was hidden in his mouth and we tried to remove it, it may precipitate some action would be regretted. I did however send for thick bread and cheese sandwiches and tea, which I offered to Himmler, hoping that I would see him if he removed anything from his mouth. I watched him closely but did not notice anything unusual.

In the meantime, information had been sent to 2 Army Headquarters, and whilst we were waiting for Senior Intelligence Officers to arrive, I arranged for clothing to be provided for the prisoner. The only clothing available of course was British Army uniform, and on seeing it Himmler refused to put it on, with the exception of the shirt, underpants and socks. He seemed to be under the impression that we would photograph him in the uniform, and use it for Press purposes. He was then provided with a blanket to wrap on top of the underwear.

If memory serves me correctly, it would be about 7-30 or 8-0 p.m. when Colonel Murphy arrived at the Camp to interrogate the prisoner, and I was present during that interrogation. I have no knowledge of the actual conversation, as I was still obsessed with the thoughts of the missing phial, and watched Himmler closely. I had informed other Intelligence Officers of my fears regarding the poison, and they had been in touch with senior medical officers to try and discover if there was any method of giving Himmler a drug to make him lose consciousness and enable us to search his mouth. We were told that it was impossible to administer a drug to any

> person which would act so quickly that the person would be unaware that he had been drugged, so the idea was abandoned. During the interrogation, Himmler was again asked to sign his name, this time by Colonel Murphy, and he did so, but again he tore the paper into small fragments after the signature was examined. During the course of the evening, the prisoner was again served with sandwiches and tea, and none of the five or six officers present saw him make any unusual move.
>
> About midnight Colonel Murphy issued orders for Himmler to be removed to 2 Army Headquarters, and he was escorted there by Intelligence Officers. I have no further knowledge of later events.
>
> During the time Himmler was in my custody he behaved perfectly correctly, and gave the impression that he realised things had caught up with him. I was rather surprised when I heard of his death so soon after leaving my camp, but as I said earlier, although I have no knowledge of what transpired when he was interrogated by Colonel Murphy, I did gain the impression that he was quite prepared to talk, and indeed at times appeared almost jovial. He looked ill when I first saw him, but improved tremendously after a meals and a wash (he was not permitted to shave). He was in my custody for approximately eight hours, and during that time, whilst not being interrogated, asked repeatedly about the whereabouts of his 'Adjutants,' appearing genuinely worried over their welfare. I have no reason to believe that Himmler was successful in passing any check points prior to being detained at Bremervorde. His simple disguise was extremely effective, but once the eye patch was removed his identity was obvious. I found it impossible to believe that he could be the arrogant man portrayed by the Press before and during the war.

Colonel Michael Murphy, Chief of Intelligence for the Second British Army, arrived at Kolkhagen at some time between 8 p.m. and 9.45 p.m. to take charge of the prisoner. He recognised that it was still possible for Himmler to have poison secreted about his body orifices and he ordered a further search which proved negative. Mindful of the empty brass case found earlier, Murphy ordered a doctor to be on standby at 31a Uelzener Strasse in Lüneburg, a house prepared for the reception and interrogation of high profile Nazis. Himmler's outer clothing was taken from him and he was dressed only in a shirt, underpants, socks and boots. He was offered a British battledress, but refused, almost certainly avoiding the ignominy of a possible media report of the Reichsführer-SS being captured in British uniform. He accepted an army blanket and was then bundled into the rear of Murphy's staff car next to Colonel Bernard Stapleton at just after 10.30 p.m. for the short drive to Lüneburg. During the journey, Murphy was unsure of the route and asked Stapleton for directions, but he too was not sure. Their passenger confirmed that they were on the correct road to Lüneburg.

The Second Army HQ medical officer, Captain C. J. Wells, had been summoned to 31a Uelzener Strasse by Major Norman Whittaker to await the arrival of

Himmler. Dr Wells and Whittaker discussed the possible hiding places suitable for a poison vial whilst Company Sergeant-Major Edwin Austin awaited the arrival of their guest. At about 10.45 p.m., Himmler arrived and was asked to wash his hands prior to being submitted to an immediate body search by the doctor. Dr Wells' subsequent description of the events is probably the most accurate:

> I was polite and gentle. He was quiet and co-operative. I examined his heart and chest and the webs of his hands and feet. With exaggerated care. I noticed that his fingernails were cut to a point. ... His hands were small and sensitive. I examined his axilla [*armpits*] between his buttocks, his nostrils, his external auditory meatus [*ear canals*] and each time I shook my head dismally. Last I came to his mouth and I asked him casually to open it.
>
> In doing this he threw his head a little backwards and away, but only in the same way that many other people do when asked to show their teeth. There was nothing exaggerated in the movement. They were goodish teeth with a certain number of gold fillings and some small round amalgam ones in the fissures of his molars, the cusps of which were rather unduly flattened I thought, but I may have been wrong. But what I did see was a small blue tit-like object sticking out of the lower sulcus [*gap between inner cheek and gum*] of his left cheek. That was something abnormal. That more than likely was it. What on earth was I going to do now? The real question, and I realised it, was not what I had seen—but whether Himmler knew what I had seen? Had my face given me away? He must have been watching me carefully. Did he feel the object slip into view as he opened his mouth?

Major Whittaker was shining a standard lamp into Himmler's face to provide the doctor with more light. Dr Wells continued:

> Without waiting, I slipped my finger into the sulcus to sweep out what I had seen. Himmler, who had been watching me acutely, saw what was happening and immediately clamped down on my finger. We struggled for a moment. He wrenched my hand out of his mouth ... swung his head away and then with an almost deliberate disdain faced me, crushed the glass capsule between his teeth and took a deep inhalation.
>
> His face became immediately deeply suffused and contorted with pain. His vena cavo [*neck veins*] stood out; his eyes stared glassily, his head fell forward and he crashed to the ground ... There was a slowing series of stertorous [*heavy snoring respiration*] breaths, which may have continued for half a minute and the pulse for another minute after that.

Major Whittaker stated that the doctor shouted, 'My God, it's in his mouth—he has done it on me!' The major also reported that he smelled cyanide and knew that it must have been a strong dose. He later wrote:

> ... We immediately upended the old bastard and got his mouth into the bowl of water which was there to wash the poison out. There were terrible groans and grunts coming from the swine. Colonel Murphy and I were taking it in turns to get hold of his tongue. All this time the doc was working on artificial respiration and calling for cardiac stimulants. ...
>
> We had now procured a needle and cotton to fix his tongue, but the first thing we did was to get the needle through his lip so we had to get it out. Finally we got his tongue fixed, but it was a losing battle and this evil thing breathed its last at 2314 ... We turned it on its back, put a blanket on it and came away.

Those present in the front room at 31a Uelzener Strasse at the time of death were Colonel Michael Murphy, Major Norman Whittaker, Captain Clement 'Jimmie' Wells and Company Sergeant-Major Edwin Austin. In the hallway outside were Major Keith Randall and Major Storm Rice. According to one version by Captain Wells, Colonel Murphy and Major Whittaker were not present during the body search, but this seems unlikely.

The actual device used by Himmler was almost certainly from a batch manufactured at Sachsenhausen concentration camp and probably supplied to him by Dr Stumpfegger. Evidence of this was provided by Albert Widmann who was chief of the Chemical Department of the KTI (who himself had served rather light sentences for developing the technical means of the euthanasia program). Dated Feb 15, 1973 his testimony in a letter reads:

> On orders of our Department Chief, SS-Gruppenführer Nebe, Reich Director of Criminal Investigation, self-destruction devices were developed and manufactured. They were intended for distribution to German agents. It might have been 1943 or 1944, when approximately 950 of these devices were ordered by the Reich Chancellery for distribution to the senior leadership. For that reason the filling operation was supervised personally by Senior Criminology Secretary Karl Sacks. The self-destruction devices were given over to the courier from the Reich Chancellery by me. They were obviously in fact distributed, as they were used.
>
> Our Department Chief Nebe gave the order to manufacture self-destruction devices that were infallibly effective. Potassium cyanide tablets, according to his statement, were disapproved from the medical end, for the reason that in cases of subacid stomach and with diabetics due to synthesis of cyanohydrin, they may fail to function. This gave a clear directive for production of the self-destructor. As an effective agent anhydrous hydrocyanic acid was used as a filler. For stabilization, 2 percent oxalic acid was added. For this reason the liquid is still in perfect condition today. It was neither polymerized, coloured brown nor turned resinous, as was the case with the Polish ampoules. The dosage per ampoule was an even cubic centimeter. The lethal dose on inhalation, as I recall, is around 8 mg. The hydrocyanic acid was made from

pure sodium cyanide. This work was done by a prisoner, Dr Kramer, who was a chemist. Manufacture of the hydrocyanic acid and loading the ampoules was done in a small building in the RKPA plant in the Sachsenhausen concentration camp. Supervision was by Senior Criminology Secretary Sacks and SS-Hauptscharführer Gerhard Maier. There were no accidents. Some 3,000 to 4,000 were made. We made the glass ampoules to fit the containers. The diameter was 9 mm and the total length after annealing about 35 mm. The bottoms of the ampoules were flat. The annealed top was tinted blue for reinforcement. Ampoules that had been tested for hermetic seal in a vacuum were marked with a small read spot on the blue.

As containers for the self-destructors, spent infantry rifle cartridges were fashioned into small cases. The cartridge cases were cut away on a lathe below the narrowing point. Their length came to about 41 cm. The 9 mm long caps were also made from cartridge cases. The caps were simply pushed down over the cases. The total length of the self-destructor therefore came to 46 mm, the diameter about 11 mm.

It should be added that we probably received 1,000 empty ampoules from the Army Medical Centre, each at three different times. I do not know which lot went to the Reich Chancellery.

On the subject of the ampoules used by high profile members of the Nazi government, the famed Nazi aviatrix Hanna Reitsch subsequently declared:

... The description of the cartridge case agrees completely with the account given by Dr Widmann on page 2 of his letter of February 15 in the indentation beginning with 'Zur Aufbewahrung' ... and ending at '11 mm.' I know this so precisely because I sewed the capsule inside the cartridge case myself into the lining of a uniform skirt. That was how I came to measure the size in comparision with my little finger, then immediately measured it. When Hitler gave me the capsule, he said that I was free to use it. General von Greim had asked for capsules for himself and me. Hitler further said words to the effect that we should not be put to any disadvantage with respect to the other people in the bunker.

Finally, the dentist Dr Kunz who served since 23 April 1945 as dental officer in the infirmary bunker of the Reich Chancellery stated on 21 February 1973:

I can say nothing about the glass, colour and the shape of the capsules on hand in the bunker. I was given to read the last passage, but three, in what Dr Widmann wrote on Febrary 15 1973. I should like to comment that the containers I saw in the possession of Frau Goebbels and Eva Braun might easily have been made from an infantry rifle brass cartridge case. The total length might have been about 46 mm. I myself had no such container in my possession. Besides, I never had one in my hand. I do not know if Dr Stumpfegger had any capsules in his possession, Frau

> Goebbels had several in the jacket of her suit. I am convinced, however, that it was Dr Stumpfegger or Dr Frau Goebbels or both who gave the Goebbels children poison.

The day following his successful suicide attempt, 24 May 1945, Himmler's body was photographed *in situ* and Colonel Murphy held a press conference. At 6.15 p.m., a Russian delegation attended the house and viewed the body. Grothmann and Macher were still at Barnstedt unaware of Himmler's suicide when photographed outside a hut still wearing the clothes in which they were arrested. Oswald Pohl heard the news and informed Hedwig Potthast at Achensee. She was subsequently arrested and taken to Munich for interrogation. Marga and Gudrun were already in custody in Italy.

On 25 May, various doctors, pathologists and dentists examined the corpse and took measurements and impressions. Two criminal police officers from Lüneburg, Musgiller and Wichmann, made a cast of Himmler's face in death and took his fingerprints.

Colonel Murphy ordered Major Whittaker to bury the body secretly in an unmarked grave and on 26 May it was wrapped in a camouflage net and grey blanket and thrown into the rear of a lorry. Without any ceremony, the body was dumped into a hastily dug grave on Lüneburg Heath, not far from the town. Those present were Major Whittaker, CSM Austin and the actual gravediggers, Sergeants Bill Ottery and Ray Weston. The location was kept secret and Ray Weston returned to the site over the following few days to check it remained undisturbed. The remains are still there, in an unmarked secret location, recorded only by a map reference which remains classified. Post-war attempts by Gudrun Burwitz to recover her father's remains and provide him with a proper burial have proved unsuccessful.

Bibliography & Sources

Heinrich Himmler, Peter Longerich, 2012
Himmler—Reichsführer-SS, Peter Padfield, 1990
Heinrich Himmler, Roger Manvell & Heinrich Fraenkel, 1965
Die Dresdner Bank und der Reichsführer-SS, Peter-Ferdinand Koch, 1987
Himmlers Graue Eminenz—Oswald Pohl, Peter-Ferdinand Koch, 1988
Reinhard Heydrich—Road to War, Max Williams, 2001
Reinhard Heydrich—Enigma, Max Williams, 2003
The SS Leadership Corps, volume 1, Max Williams, 2004
Das Braune Heer, 1932
Reichsführer! Briefe an und von Himmler, Helmut Heiber, 1968
Der Dienstkalendar Heinrich Himmlers 1941/42, 1999
The Architect of Genocide, Richard Breitman, 1991
Die Generale der Waffen-SS und der Polizei, Band 2, Andreas Schulz, Günter Wegmann, Dieter Zinke, 2005
Heinrich Himmlers Burg, Stuart Russell, Jost Schneider, 1989
Himmler, Willi Frischauer, 1953
Heinrich Himmler: A Nazi in the Making, Bradley Smith, 1971
The Himmler Brothers, Katrin Himmler, 2007
Das Führerhauptquartier 1939-1945, 1983
Hitler's Personal Security, Peter Hoffmann, 1979
Himmler Geheim Reden, Joachim C. Fest, 1974
Allgemeine-SS, Mark C. Yerger, 1997
Red Storm on the Reich, Christopher Duffy, 1991
Order of the Deaths Head, Heinz Höhne, 1967

Other Published Sources

After the Battle magazine, number 14, 1976
After the Battle magazine, number 17, 1977
After the Battle magazine, number 128, 2005
After the Battle magazine, number 142, 2008
Illustrierte Beobachter, various editions

Unpublished Sources (at time of writing)

Manuscript of Himmler's schedule 1945, compiled by Stephen Tyas and Peter Witte
Manuscript of Himmler's schedule from his 1943/1944 diaries
Manuscript of Leaders of the SS and German Police, volume 2, Michael D. Miller

World Wide Web

Axis History Forum
Focal Point

Sources

Institutions and Archives

Author's Archive
Bundesarchiv, Berlin-Lichterfelde (formerly the Berlin Document Centre)
Bundesarchiv, Koblenz
Hoover Institute, Stanford University, California
Imperial War Museum, London
Landesarchiv, Berlin
National Archives, Kew
National Archives, Washington DC
Pemsel Collection, now in private hands
Private Archives
Staatsarchiv, Munich
Staatsbibliothek, Munich
Stadtarchiv, Fridolfing
USHMM, Washington DC
Wegmann Archive, Kassel

APPENDIX ONE

Glossary of Terms

Abschnitt Sector; district
Abwehr Wehrmacht intelligence service
Adjutantur
i. Staff department dealing with routing personnel and administrative matters;
ii. The earlier title of the Persönlicher Stab RfSS
Ahnenerbe Society for Research into and Teaching of Ancestral Heritage. Administered by the Pers.Stab RfSS, this office promoted research of family and national hereditary history and dissemination of racial theories.
Aktion Reinhard The programme of systematic murder by gassing of the Polish Jews
Allgemeine-SS The general body of the SS, composed of part-time, full-time, and honorary members
Amt Department or section
Befehlshaber der Sicherheitspolzei und des Sicherheitsdienstes Commander of the Sipo and SD in a Wehrkreis or similar territory
Braunschweig The German town of Brunswick
Bund League
Bund Oberland A Wehrverband (paramilitary formation) of predominantly Bavarian membership formed from the Freikorps Oberland. Under the leadership of Dr. med. vet. Friedrich Weber, it was the primary ally of the Nazi Party during the Munich Putsch of.11.1923
Bürgermeister Mayor of a mid-size town or smaller community
Chef der deutschen Polizei (Ch.d.Dt.P.; ChdDtP; ChdDtPol.) Commander-in-Chief of the German Police (Heinrich Himmler)
Chef der Heeresrüstung und Behfehlshaber des Ersatzheeres (Ch.H.Rü.u.B.d.E.)
Chief of Army Equipment and Commander of the Replacement Army (Generaloberst Friedrich Fromm until 07.1944, then Heinrich Himmler)
Chef der Ordnungspolizei (CdO) Chief of the Order Police (Kurt Daluege, then Wünnenberg assumed duties due to Daluege's illness)
Chef der Sicherheitspolizei und des SD (CSSD) Chief of the Security Police and SD (Reinhard Heydrich until 4.06.1942, then Himmler until 30.01.1943, and finally Dr. jur. Ernst Kaltenbrunner)
der Reserve (d. R.) of the Reserve

deutsch German

Deutsche Arbeitsfront (DAF) The German Labor Front. Largest of the NSDAP's affiliated organizations comprising all the corporations, guilds, and professional associations. Led by Reichsleiter Dr. Robert Ley

Deutsche Arbeiterpartei (DAP) German Workers' Party

Deutsche Ausrüstungswerke (DAW) German Equipment Works, SS enterprise founded in 1939

Deutsche Erd- und Steinwerke GmbH (DEST) German Clay and Brickworks Ltd. SS enterprise established in 1938, primarily to construct brickworks and exploit quarries by the use of prisoner labor

Deutschland Erwache Germany awake! DE standards were presented to town SS units and to various Waffen-SS units, consecrated by touching the standard with the sacred Blood Flag from the failed 1923 Beer Hall Putsch

Dienststelle Headquarters, administrative office, station, or depot

DKiG and DKiS Award of the German Cross in Gold or Silver

Ehrenführer Honorary leader. Distinction accorded by Himmler to leading NSDAP and State figures nominally attached to his staff

Einsatz Action, operation, employment

Einsatzgruppe Operational group or task force of the Sipo and SD for special missions (particularly liquidiations of Jews, communist officials, etc.) in occupied territory

Einsatzkommando Detachment of the Sipo and SD; subordinate element of an Einsatzgruppe

Fähnrich Officer candidate (second stage)

Fahnenjunker Officer candidate (first stage)

Feldgendarmerie Military police

Feldkommandantur Administrative headquarters in occupied countries (of regimental status)

Feldlazarett Field hospital

Feuerschutzpolizei Fire Protection Police; a branch of the Orpo

Freiherr Baron (aristocratic title)

Freikorps Temporary and voluntary paramilitary formations created by the German Army and Navy during the 1918/1919 revolutionary period in Germany

freiwilligen volunteer

Führer Leader; commander; chief. The title *"Der Führer"* was only used in reference to Adolf Hitler.

Führerhauptquartier (FHQ) Hitler's Field Headquarters

Gau Main territorial division of the NSDAP. There were 42 Gaue in the Reich and annexed territories, with a further 43rd Gau comprising the Auslandsorganisation (AO; Foreign Organization of the Nazi Party)

Gauleiter Highest ranking NSDAP official in a Gau, with responsibility for all matters of politics, economics, labour mobilization, and civil defence

Gebirgs-Division Mountain Division of the Heer or Waffen-SS

geheim secret

Geheime Feldpolizei (GFP) Secret Field Police

Geheimes Staatspolizei (Gestapo) Secret State Police; Amt IV of the Reichssicherheitshauptamt from 1939

Gendarmerie Rural police, including motorized traffic control units

Generalgouvernement Government General. German-occupied Poland and the

administration thereof under Dr Hans Frank
GFP Geheime Feldpolizei Secret Field Police. Came under the umbrella of the SD.
Gottgläubig Lit.: "God-believing". Essentially a form of agnosticism, this designation was used in place of a religious denomination after one had left the church ("Kirchenaustritt"). This action was strongly encouraged and expected of SS members by Himmler, however it was not mandatory.
Graf Count (aristocratic title)
Gruppe Group; section.
Gymnasium Type of secondary school in German-speaking countries. Its primary purpose was preparation for university study and positions of higher administrative work
Hauptamt (HA) Main or central office
Heer Army
Heeresgruppe Army Group
Hitler-Jugend (HJ) Hitler Youth. The Nazi youth organization
Höhere SS- und Polizeiführer (HSSPF) Higher SS and Police Leader
Junkerschule Officer cadet school
Kaserne Barracks
Kavallerie Cavalry
Kavallerie-Division Cavalry division
Kavallerie-Regiment Cavalry regiment
KL Konzentrationslager or concentration camp
Kommandant Commandant
Kommandantur Administrative HQ; Garrison HQ
Kommandeur Commander
Kreis District
Kreisleiter District Leader; Head of an NSDAP Kreis
Krieg war
Kriminalpolizei (Kripo) Criminal Police; Amt V of the Reichssicherheitshauptamt from 1939
Landwirtschaft Agriculture
Lebensborn The "Fountain of Life" society. Established by the SS in 1936. Attached to the Personal Staff of the Reichsführer-SS and affiliated with the SS-RuSHA. Main functions of the society were adoption of "racially suitable" children for childless SS families, encouragement and facilitation of procreation between "Aryan" men and women, and the promotion of the racial policies of the SS.
Leiter chief; head
Ministerialdirektor (Min.Dir.)
A senior civil service official. Department head in a ministry with the approximate equivalent of Generalleutnant
Ministerialrat (Min.Rat)
Senior ministerial counselor in civil service; usually head of a section within a ministry; approximately equivalent to an Oberst
Ministerpräsident Minister-President; Prime Minister of a Land government
München Munich. Capital city of the German state of Bayern (Bavaria)
Nachrichten Signals
Nationalsozialistische Deutsche Arbeiter Partei (NSDAP) National-Socialist German Workers' Party (commonly known as the Nazi Party).

Nationalsozialistische-Kraftfahrkorps (NSKK) National-Socialist Motor Corps. Played an important role in the military and paramilitary training.

Nord North

Nordost Northeast

Nordwest Northwest

Ober higher; senior

Oberbürgermeister Lord Mayor of a large town or city

Oberste SA Führer (OSAF) Supreme SA Leader

Ordnungspolizei (Orpo) Order Police. Regular uniformed police force of the Reich, consisting of the Schutzpolizei, Gendarmerie, and Feuerschutzpolizei as well as various technical and auxiliary services (such as the Technische Nothilfe [TeNo])

Ost East

Polizeipräsident Police President. Head of the regular police in a large city

Rasse- und Siedlungshauptamt (RuSHA) SS Race & Settlement Main Office. Responsible for racial purity of the SS and settlement of SS colonists in occupied territories.

Realschule A type of secondary school, less prestigious than the Gymnasium, with the purpose of preparing students for employment in practical or technical fields

Referat A sub-section or "desk" within an Amtsgruppe

Referent Official in charge of a Referat or personal advisor

Reichsarbeitsdienst (RAD) Reich Labour Service. A national compulsory labour service, organised along paramilitary lines (superseded the earlier Freiwilligen-Arbeitsdienst [FAD])

Reichsführer-SS (RFSS) Reich Leader of the SS

Reichsführer-SS und Chef der Deutschen Polizei "Reich SS Leader and Chief of the German Police"

Heinrich Himmler's title from 17.06.1936 to 28.04.1945.

Reichsführung-SS Supreme command of the SS, comprising the Persönlicher Stab RfSS and the Hauptämter

Reich Chancellery Reich Chancellery

Reichskommissar für die Festigung Deutschen Volkstums (RKFDV) Reich Commissioner for the Strengthening of Germanism. Title given to Heinrich Himmler in 1939 when Hitler entrusted him with the repatriation of Volksdeutsche ("racial Germans") and the settlement of German colonies in the East. A Stabshauptamt RKFDV was established under Ulrich Greifelt to put Himmler's plans for Germanic mastery into effect

Reichskriminalpolizeiamt (RKPA) The headquarters of the Kriminalpolizei (Amt V of the RSHA)

Reichsleiter The highest rank in the NSDAP hierarchy

Reichsministerium des Innern Reich Ministry of the Interior

Reichssicherheitshauptamt (RSHA) Reich Security Main Office RSHA

Reichstag The German National Parliament. Largely a figurehead body after its legislative powers were taken away and granted to the Reich Government by way of Hitler's "Enabling Act" of 24.03.1933

Reichsstatthalter Reich Governor; Hitler's representative in a German Land or Reichsgau

RFSS Reichsführer-SS

RSD Reichssicherheitsdienst (Reich Security Service.) The unit made up of mainly police officers tasked with the close protection of Hitler and other high profile dignitaries.

Schar An SS or SA unit consisting of 3 to 13 men

Schutzpolizei Protection Police. The regular uniformed municipal and country police forces, comprising most of the membership of the Ordnungspolizei

Schutzstaffel (SS) Protection or Guard Detachment. Officially established in 1925, the SS became under Heinrich Himmler the most powerful organization in the Third Reich

SD Sicherheitsdienst des RfSS The SS Security Service established by Reinhard Heydrich in 1931 as the intelligence organization of the Nazi Party

Sicherheitspolizei (Sipo) Security Police, composed of the Gestapo and Kripo

Sigrunen The runic double "S" insignia of the Schutzstaffel

Sonderkommando Special commando of the Sipo or SD

Sonderzug Special train

Special handling Euphemism for physical extermination

SS- und Polizeiführer (SS-u.Pol.F.; SSPF) SS and Police Commander in the occupied territories, subordinate to an HSSPF

Staatssekretär State Secretary in a Reich or Land Government Ministry

Stab staff

Stabschef Chief of Staff of the SA

Sturmabteilungen (SA) Storm Troops. The original defense formations of the NSDAP, founded in 1921. Purged in June/July 1934 when it became too radical and unwieldly for Hitler's tastes, prompting him to wipe out numerous members of its leadership, including SA-Stabschef Ernst Röhm. The purge of the SA was carried out by Himmler's SS, initially a sub-unit of the SA and in its wake the SS gained considerable power

Sturm A company-sized unit of the SS, SA, or NSKK, consisting of several Truppen

Sturmbann A battalion-sized unit of the SS, SA, or NSKK consisting of several Stürme

Totenkopfverbände (SS-TV) Death's Head units, employed in the concentration camps as guards. Formed the nucleus of the SS-Totenkopf-Division when it was formed in 1939

Unternehmen Operation; undertaking; enterprise

Vernichtungslager Extermination camp (designation applied to the death camps in Poland- Belzec, Treblinka, and Sobibor)

Verwaltung Administration

Volksdeutsche Ethnic German

Volksdeutsche Mittelstelle (VoMi) Ethnic German Assistance Office. Established as the Büro von Kursell in 1936 and renamed in 1937. Led by SS-Obergruppenfuhrer Werner Lorenz, it obtained the status of a Hauptamt of the SS in 1941.

Volksgruppe An ethnic group

Waffen-SS (W-SS) Fully militarized combat formations of the SS

Wehrkreis A Military District

Wehrmacht The German armed forces, consisting of the German Army (Reichsheer), Navy (Kriegsmarine), and Air Force (Luftwaffe.)

Wirtschafts-Verwaltungshaupamt (WVHA) Central Office for Economics Administration

APPENDIX TWO

Comparison of Officer Ranks

SS	German army	British army
Reichsführer	Generalfeldmarschall	Field Marshal
Oberst-Gruppenführer	Generaloberst	No equivalent
Obergruppenführer	General	General
Gruppenführer	Generalleutnant	Lieutenant General
Brigadeführer	Generalmajor	Major General
Oberführer	No equivalent	No equivalent
Standartenführer	Oberst	Colonel
Obersturmbannführer	Oberstleutnant	Lieutenant Colonel
Sturmbannführer	Major	Major
Hauptsturmführer	Hauptmann	Captain
Obersturmführer	Oberleutnant	Lieutenant
Untersturmführer	Leutnant	Second Lieutenant

Clockwise from top left:

Heinrich Himmler was born on 7th October 1900, the second son of schoolmaster Gebhard Himmler and his wife Anna.

Heinrich von Wittelsbach, Prince of Bavaria, agreed to his former tutor's new baby being named after him and acted as his Godfather. The prince was killed by a sniper's bullet in November 1916.

A young Heinrich Himmler with his schoolteacher father. Heinrich's distinctive features are already recognisable.

The Himmler family. Heinrich stands on the left with his mother's hand gently placed on his right shoulder. Thilde, the nanny, sits with baby Ernst on her lap and older brother Gebhard stands on the right with his father behind.

Schoolboy Heinrich Himmler.

Himmler's school class in his second year at the Wilhelm Gymnasium. He is second from right in the second row and his lifelong friend, Falk Zipperer, sits in the front row, third from left.

Summer 1917. Gebhard visits the family on home leave. The 16 years old Heinrich stands behind his father.

Ehrenurkunde der D. E. d. W.

J. V.

Der Ordensrat

des Verbandes nationalgesinnter Soldaten

verlieh

Herrn Heinrich Luitpold Himmler

Diplomlandwirt zu Schleißheim

auf Grund nachgewiesener Würdigkeit

die

Deutsche Ehrendenkmünze des Weltkriegs

(D. E. d. W.) am schwarzweißroten Bande.

20. 12. 22.

Franz Stassen

Verlagsanstalt für Vaterländische Geschichte und Kunst, G. m. b. H.
Berlin NW 23, Schleswiger Ufer 10.

In the summer of 1919 Heinrich completed his school education in Landshut. He is front row, second from left and his father sits three places to his left.

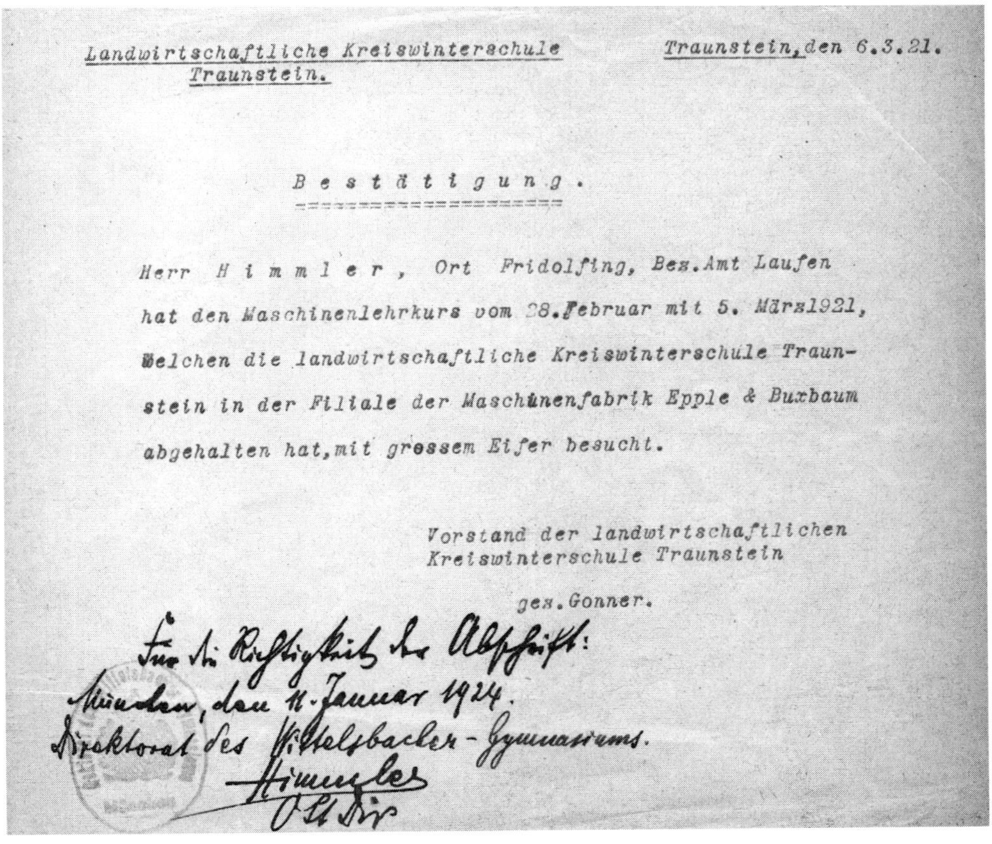

Landwirtschaftliche Kreiswinterschule Traunstein. — Traunstein, den 6.3.21.

B e s t ä t i g u n g .

Herr H i m m l e r , Ort Fridolfing, Bez.Amt Laufen hat den Maschinenlehrkurs vom 28.Februar mit 5. März1921, welchen die landwirtschaftliche Kreiswinterschule Traunstein in der Filiale der Maschinenfabrik Epple & Buxbaum abgehalten hat, mit gressem Eifer besucht.

Vorstand der landwirtschaftlichen
Kreiswinterschule Traunstein

gez. Gonner.

Für die Richtigkeit der Abschrift:
München, den 11. Januar 1924.
Direktorat des Wittelsbacher-Gymnasiums.
Himmler
OStDir

Gebhard Snr. testifies that his son attended a machine instruction course at the agricultural school in Traunstein. His handwritten note and signature confirm the details.

Opposite: The German Commemorative Medal of Honour for the 1914-1918 war awarded to Heinrich Luitpold Himmler.

Landshut 23. Juni 1919
München,

Ausweis

Vorzeiger dieses Ausweises gehört einem der mir unterstellten Verbände an. Ich ersuche alle militärischen Dienststellen und Polizei-Organe, ihn in jeder Beziehung zu unterstützen. Der Vorzeiger ist berechtigt, Waffen zu tragen.

Der Oberbefehlshaber.

(Stempel)

Unterschrift des Inhabers:

Vor- und Zuname: Heinrich Himmler

Truppenteil: FREIKORPS „OBERLAND" Ergänzungskompagnie

Dienstgrad:

Unterschrift des Kompagnie usw. Führers

Himmler's membership card for the Freikorps Oberland dated June 1919.

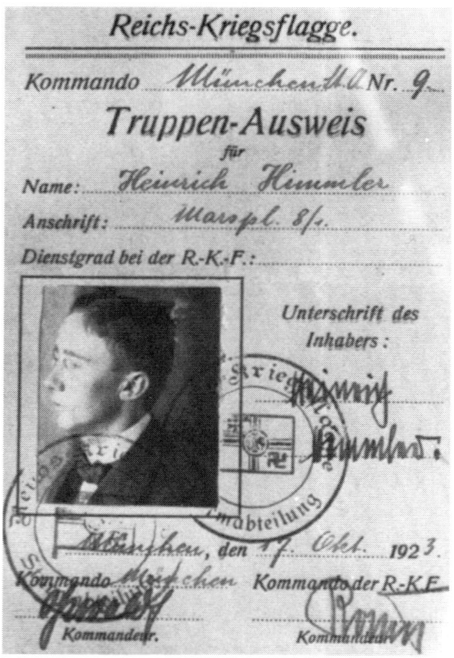

Reichs-Kriegsflagge.

Kommando München Nr. 9

Truppen-Ausweis

für

Name: Heinrich Himmler

Anschrift: Marspl. 8/I.

Dienstgrad bei der R.-K.-F.:

Unterschrift des Inhabers: Heinrich Himmler

München, den 17. Okt. 1923.

Kommando München Kommandeur.

Kommando der R.-K.F. Kommandeur.

Left: Himmler's identity card for the Reichs-Kriegsflagge. Ernst Röhm's signature is bottom right.

Right: Himmler carries the banner at the barricade outside the Bavarian War Ministry in Munich, November 1923.

Members of Stosstrupp "Adolf Hitler" awaiting sentencing for their participation in the Beer Hall Putsch. Among those present are Hansgeorg Maurer (in uniform 4th from left) Hermann Fobke (front, 5th from left) Josef Gerum (12th from left, in light jacket and moustache) Walther Hewel (rear centre) Erhard Heiden (11th from right) and Karl Fiehler (10th from right behind Heiden.)

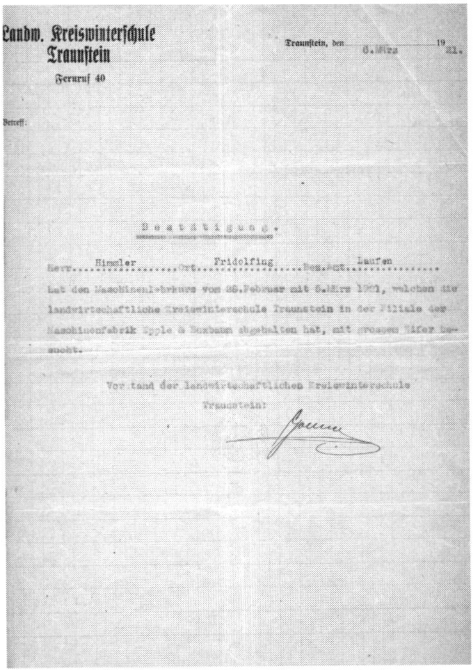

Landw. Kreiswinterschule
Traunstein
Fernruf 40

Traunstein, den 5. März 1921.

Betreff:

Bestätigung.

Herr Himmler Ort Fridolfing Bez. Amt Laufen
hat den Maschinenlehrkurs vom 28. Februar mit 5. März 1921, welchen die landwirtschaftliche Kreiswinterschule Traunstein in der Filiale der Maschinenfabrik Epple & Buxbaum abgehalten hat, mit grossem Eifer besucht.

Vorstand der landwirtschaftlichen Kreiswinterschule
Traunstein:

Left: 1923. As a young man, Himmler already had strict ideas about correct behaviour.

Right: Original reference confirming Himmler had attended a course of instruction at the Traunstein agricultural school from 28th February to 5th March 1921.

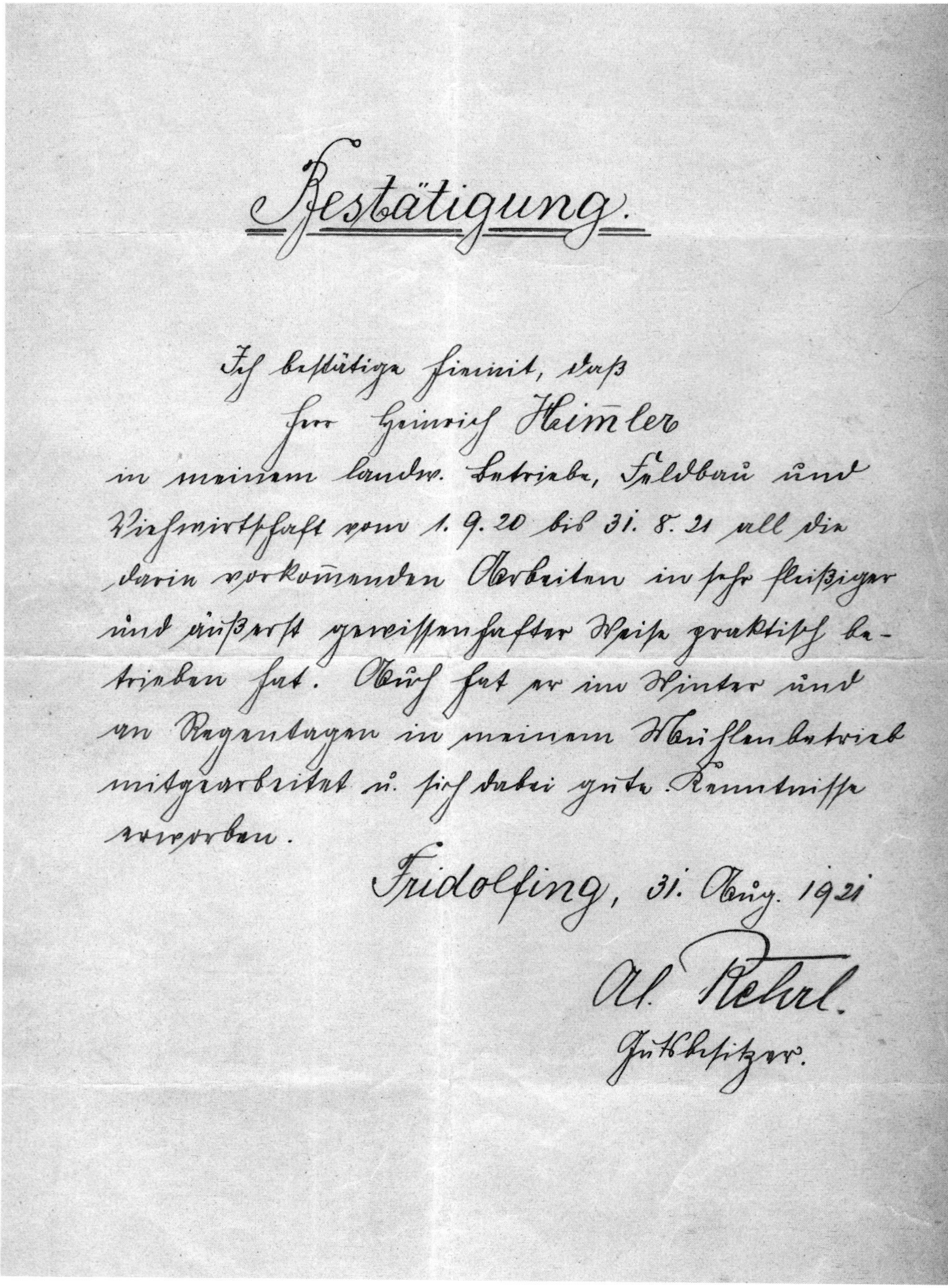

Bestätigung.

Ich bestätige hiermit, daß
Herr Heinrich Himmler
in meinem landw. Betriebe, Feldbau und Viehwirtschaft vom 1. 9. 20 bis 31. 8. 21 all die darin vorkommenden Arbeiten in sehr fleißiger und äußerst gewissenhafter Weise praktisch betrieben hat. Auch hat er im Winter und an Regentagen in meinem Mühlenbetrieb mitgearbeitet u. sich dabei gute Kenntnisse erworben.

Fridolfing, 31. Aug. 1921

Al. Rehrl.
Gutsbesitzer.

Handwritten reference from farmer Alois Rehrl in Fridolfing attesting that Himmler had worked on his farm from 1st September 1920 until 31st August 1921 and that he was conscientious and practical, working in all weathers in the mill and on the farm.

Right: Farmer Alois Rehrl in SS uniform. On his left sleeve is the odal rune, signifying attachment to the SS-Race and Settlement Central Office. Rehrl exerted a strong influence on the young Himmler and the men remained friends until the end of the war. Rehrl was subsequently transferred to the Personal Staff of the RFSS.

Below: The Rehrl family from Fridolfing. It appears that the eldest son was killed in action in the Crimea whilst fighting for a SS division.

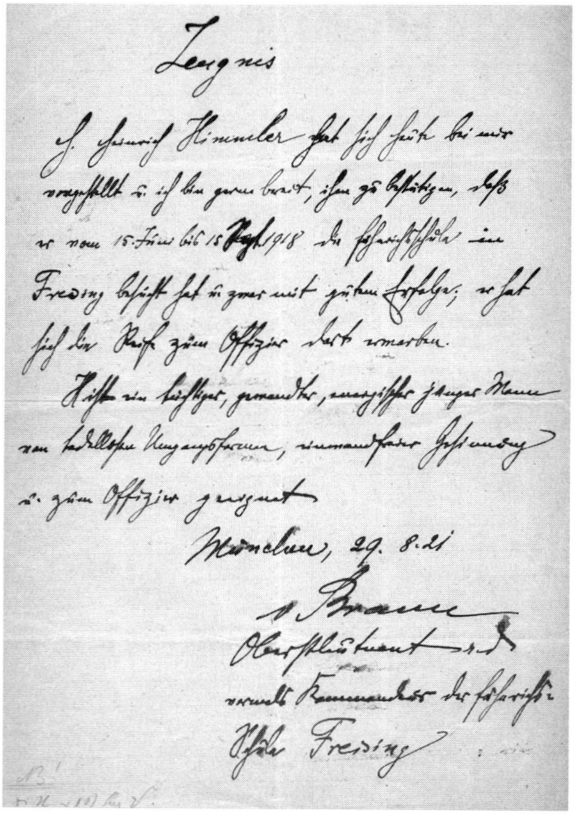

Zeugnis

H. Heinrich Himmler hat sich heute bei mir vorgestellt u. ich bin gerne bereit, ihm zu bestätigen, daß er vom 15. Juni bis 15. Sept. 1918 die Fahnenjunkerschule in Freising besucht hat u. zwar mit gutem Erfolge; er hat sich die Reife zum Offizier dort erworben.

Himmler ist ein tüchtiger, gewandter, energischer junger Mann von tadellosen Umgangsformen, einwandfreier Gesinnung u. zum Offizier geeignet.

München, 29. 8. 21

v. Braun
Oberstleutnant a.D.
vormals Kommandeur der Fahnenjunkerschule Freising

Certificate of confirmation that Himmler attended the officer candidate school in Freising from 15th June 1918 until 15th September 1918 and successfully completed the course, proving himself to be an excellent candidate, mature, active and energetic.

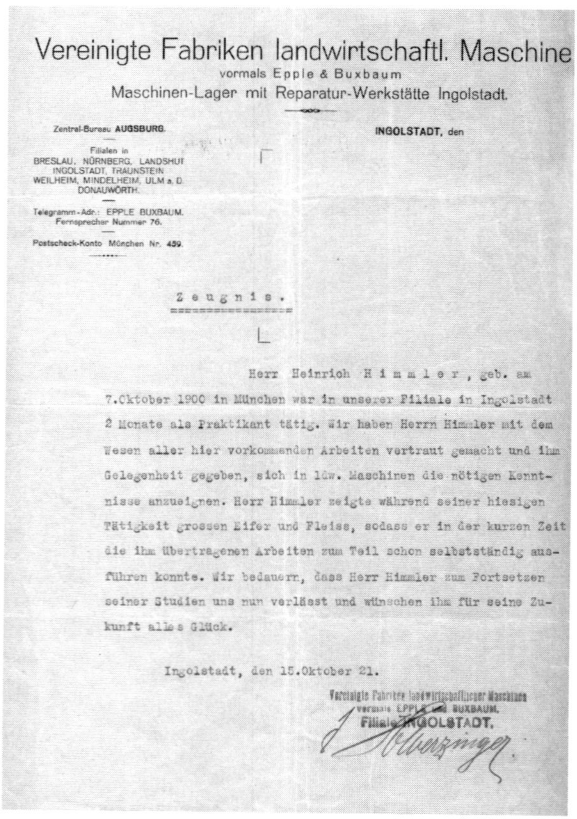

Vereinigte Fabriken landwirtschaftl. Maschine
vormals Epple & Buxbaum
Maschinen-Lager mit Reparatur-Werkstätte Ingolstadt.

Zentral-Bureau AUGSBURG.

Filialen in
BRESLAU, NÜRNBERG, LANDSHUT
INGOLSTADT, TRAUNSTEIN
WEILHEIM, MINDELHEIM, ULM a. D.
DONAUWÖRTH.

Telegramm-Adr.: EPPLE BUXBAUM.
Fernsprecher Nummer 76.

Postscheck-Konto München Nr. 459.

INGOLSTADT, den

Z e u g n i s .

Herr Heinrich H i m m l e r , geb. am 7.Oktober 1900 in München war in unserer Filiale in Ingolstadt 2 Monate als Praktikant tätig. Wir haben Herrn Himmler mit dem Wesen aller hier vorkommenden Arbeiten vertraut gemacht und ihm Gelegenheit gegeben, sich in ldw. Maschinen die nötigen Kenntnisse anzueignen. Herr Himmler zeigte während seiner hiesigen Tätigkeit grossen Eifer und Fleiss, sodass er in der kurzen Zeit die ihm übertragenen Arbeiten zum Teil schon selbstständig ausführen konnte. Wir bedauern, dass Herr Himmler zum Fortsetzen seiner Studien uns nun verläßt und wünschen ihm für seine Zukunft alles Glück.

Ingolstadt, den 15.Oktober 21.

Vereinigte Fabriken landwirtschaftlicher Maschinen
vormals EPPLE und BUXBAUM.
Filiale INGOLSTADT.
J. Oberzinger

Original reference for Himmler's employment at the agricultural machine factory in Ingolstadt.

Besitzzeugnis.

Für ehrenvolle Teilnahme am Weltkriege 1914/18
ist auf Antrag des Bayerischen Kriegerbundes (Landeskriegerverband gegr. 1874) dem Kameraden
Herrn Heinrich Himmler, Fähnrich a. D.
Mitglied des Kyffhäuser-Bundes der Deutschen Landes-Kriegerverbände
die Kriegsdenkmünze 1914/18 des Kyffhäuser-Bundes
unter dem 18. März 1922 verliehen worden.

Kyffhäuser-Bund der deutschen Landes-Kriegerverbände

Vorstand des Kyffhäuserbundes der Deutschen Landes-Krieger-Verbände Berlin

von Hindenburg — von Heeringen

Generalfeldmarschall, Ehrenpräsident — Generaloberst, Präsident

Für den Vorstand des Bayerischen Krieger-Bundes

Award certificate for the War Commemorative Medal 1914/18 of the War Veterans Association given to Heinrich Himmler, former officer candidate, on 18th March 1922.

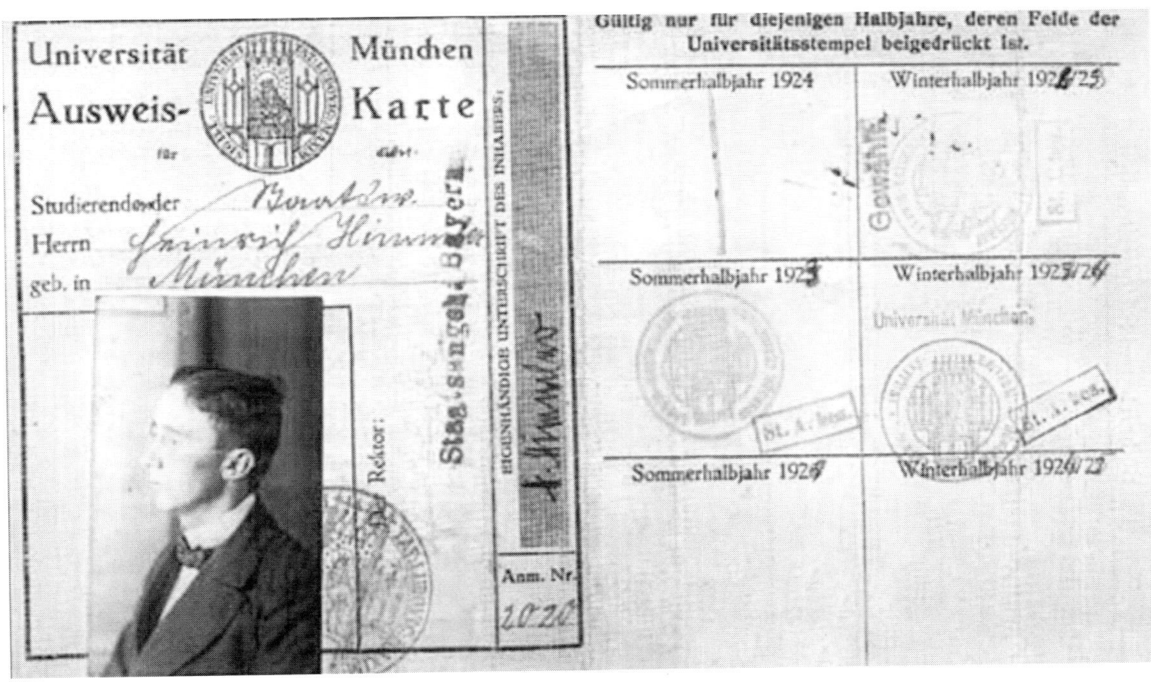

Universität München
Ausweis-Karte
für den
Studierenden der Landw.
Herrn Heinrich Himmler
geb. in München

Rektor:

Eigenhändige Unterschrift des Inhabers:

Anm. Nr. 2020

Gültig nur für diejenigen Halbjahre, deren Felde der Universitätsstempel beigedrückt ist.

Sommerhalbjahr 1924	Winterhalbjahr 1924/25
Sommerhalbjahr 1925	Winterhalbjahr 1925/26
Sommerhalbjahr 1926	Winterhalbjahr 1926/27

Munich University identity card.

Left: Gregor Strasser's secretary in Landshut.

Below: The Himmler family. A photo taken in the Munich apartment of the boys' parents.

Right: Julius Schreck, Hitler's chauffeur and bodyguard, formed the nucleus of the infant SS.

Below: Hitler's early close aides included Wagener, Schwarz, Bouhler, Esser, Schaub, Himmler, von Salomon and Schreck.

Clockwise from top left:

Josef Berchtold.

Erhard Heiden.

Party member Heinrich Himmler wearing an early SS cap.

SA-Stabschef Ernst Röhm. The homosexual chief of the SA was Himmler's superior until deposed in 1934. In the immediate aftermath of the "Night of Long Knives" Röhm was shot in his Stadelheim prison cell by Theodor Eicke and Michael Lippert.

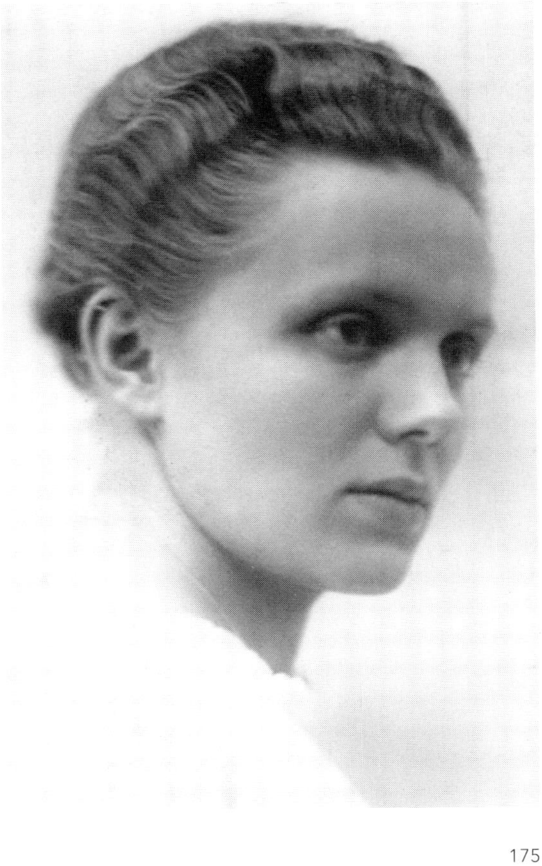

Margarete Boden. At their chance meeting in December 1926, Himmler was captivated by her beautiful hair.

Heinrich married Marga on 3rd July 1928.

The Himmler couple at home in Waldtrudering.

Left to right: Gebhard, Mathilde, Heinrich, Marga, Ernst, Anna and Gebhard Senior. Mathilde was the sister of Richard Wendler, later SS-Gruppenführer and Governor of Krakow. Ernst subsequently met and married Paula Melters.

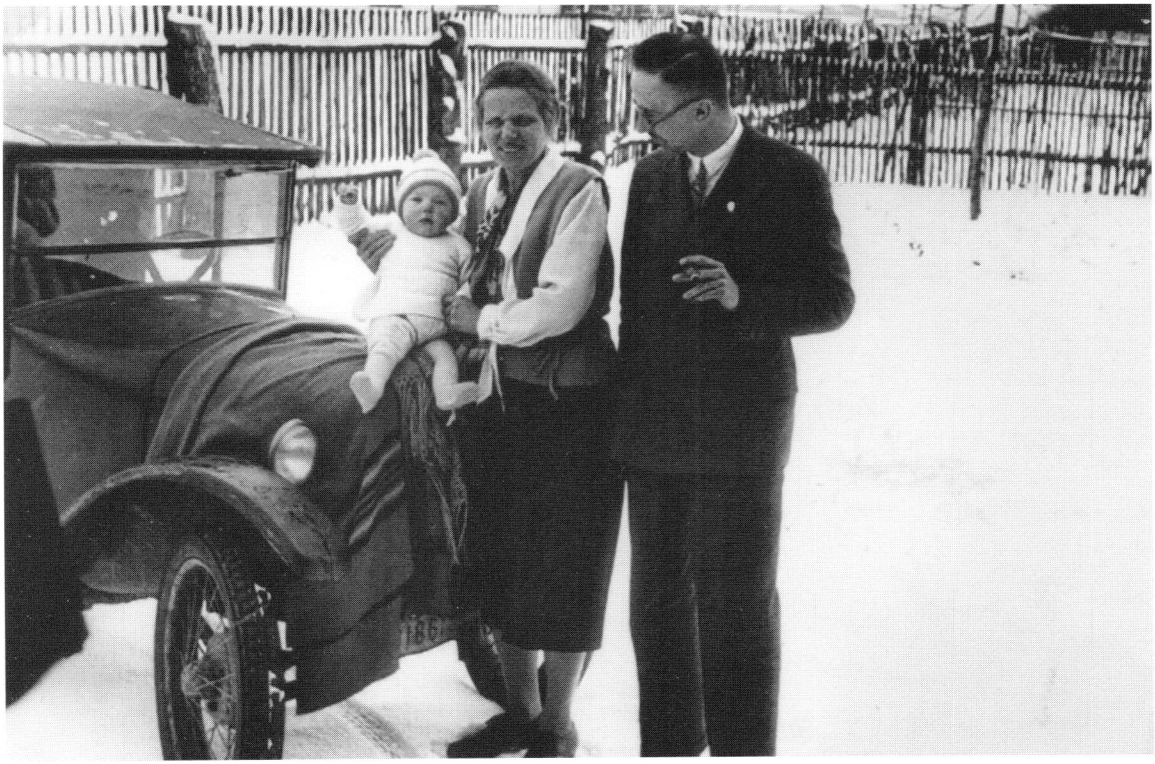

In the garden at Waldtrudering, winter 1929/30.

Proud grandparents 1930.

Marga and Heinrich proudly show off their new daughter inside the house at Waldtrudering.

Marga and Heinrich pose in front of their house in Waldtrudering.

Himmler at the wheel of one of his first cars.

Reichsführer-SS.

An early undated photo of Himmler, probably during the period of the prohibition on wearing political uniforms.

Above: Another photo from the uniform prohibition era. Himmler leads a column of SS men. Front row, left to right: Carl Zenner, Fritz Weitzel, Himmler and Fritz Engel.

Right: The young Reichsführer-SS in civilian attire.

At the time of the public uniform ban, 1931. Left to right, Himmler, Wahl, Schaub, Graf, Hitler, Schwarz, unident. and Schreck.

Düsseldorf, 8th August 1931. Seated (left to right) are Fritz Schlessmann, Fritz Weitzel, Karl Florian, Himmler, unident. and Fritz Engel.

Düsseldorf, 8th August 1931. Left to right: Fritz Schlessmann, Fritz Engel, Himmler, Wilhelm Rediess, Fritz Weitzel, Hans Döring, Carl Zenner and Karl Zech. A pencilled cross appears on the face of Engel, added after he left the SS under dubious circumstances in 1934.

Left: Himmler wearing Gruppenführer rank insignia.

Right: A relaxed Himmler is photographed in a swimsuit with a friend. The slightly knocked knees and splayed feet are obvious in this image.

Left: Himmler wearing his trademark pince nez.

Below: The time of political struggle witnessed violent conflict between the extreme right and left parties, often resulting in deaths on both sides. Here early SS men carry the coffin of one of their fallen comrades.

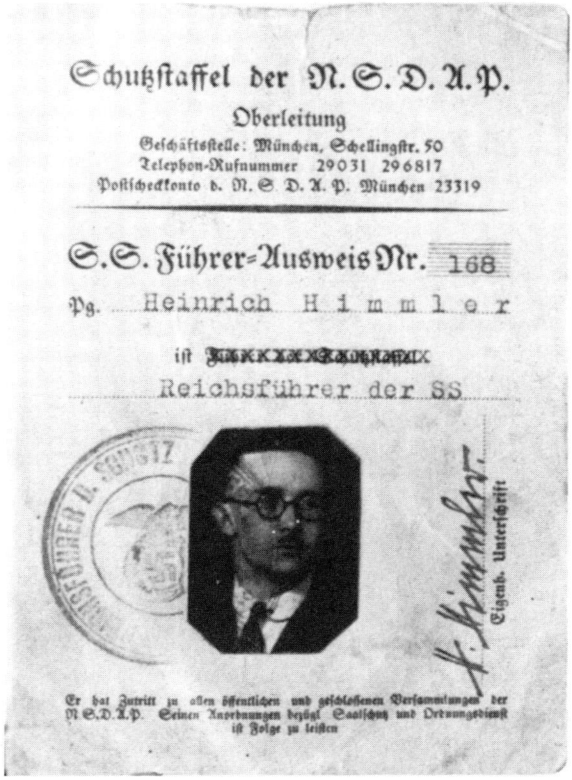

Schutzstaffel der N.S.D.A.P.
Oberleitung
Geschäftsstelle: München, Schellingstr. 50
Telephon-Rufnummer 29031 296817
Postscheckkonto d. N.S.D.A.P. München 23319

S.S. Führer-Ausweis Nr. 168
Pg. Heinrich Himmler
ist Reichsführer der SS

Eigenh. Unterschrift

Er hat Zutritt zu allen öffentlichen und geschlossenen Versammlungen der N.S.D.A.P. Seinen Anordnungen bezügl. Saalschutz und Ordnungsdienst ist Folge zu leisten

Right: Himmler's SS identity card as Reichsführer-SS, bearing his image, signature and SS number 168.

Below: Himmler's membership card for the Munich Light Aircraft Club 1931/32.

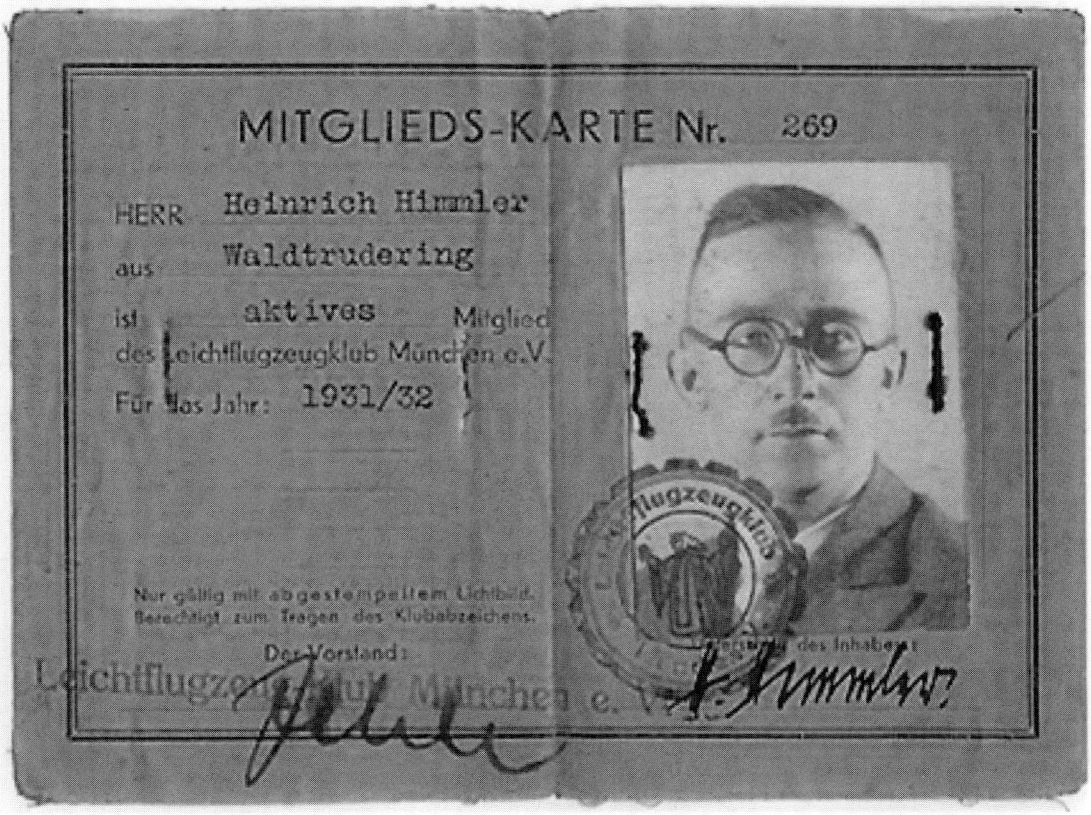

MITGLIEDS-KARTE Nr. 269
HERR Heinrich Himmler
aus Waldtrudering
ist aktives Mitglied
des Leichtflugzeugklub München e.V.
Für das Jahr: 1931/32

Nur gültig mit abgestempeltem Lichtbild.
Berechtigt zum Tragen des Klubabzeichens.
Der Vorstand:
Leichtflugzeugklub München e.V.

Unterschrift des Inhabers:

The RFSS as a family man in his garden at the smallholding in Waldtrudering. Note the house keys hanging from Marga's waist.

The devoted father 1933.

In this family photo, Himmler appears rather uncomfortable displaying his bare knees in front of the camera.

Little Gudrun pulls a face for the camera. Often described as a precocious child, Himmler would not tolerate any criticism of his beloved daughter.

Marga Himmler 1933. This photograph clearly shows the severe scar on her left cheek, the cause of which remains a mystery.

Friedrich Karl Freiherr von Eberstein.

Reinhard Heydrich was discharged from the navy as a result of his behaviour at a hearing called to hear a complaint about ungentlemanly conduct towards a young woman. He subsequently approached von Eberstein, a family friend, to recommend his application to join the SS.

Left: Official portrait of the Reichsführer-SS, 1932, now in his familiar black uniform.

Below: February 1934. Surrounded by SS officers, Himmler checks the time. In the group are Wolff, Heydrich and Pohl.

Right: Göring and Himmler making their way to a Reichstag sitting in 1932.

Below: Himmler and his senior SS commanders in the Brown House in 1932.

Clockwise from top left:

From 1st January 1933 Himmler was authorised to wear Obergruppenführer rank insignia.

The Reichsführer strikes a pose for the camera at his desk.

A smiling Reichsführer.

Clockwise from top left:

Wilhelm Keppler.

Kurt von Schröder.

Deputy Führer Rudolf Hess wearing the uniform of a SS-Obergruppenführer.

Opposite: In 1933, Himmler opened the first concentration camp at Dachau. He chose Hilmar Wäckerle as the first commandant, but soon replaced him with Theodor Eicke. Eicke introduced strict rules for both prisoners and guards which formed the basis of regulations for all camps. He later headed the concentration camp inspectorate and commanded the SS-Totenkopf Division. He is pictured here as a SS-Gruppenführer.

Left: Fritz Kranefuss.

Below: Hitler's close collaborators at the time he acceded to power. Left to right (back row) Kube, Kerrl, Goebbels, Röhm, Darré, Hess (front row) Frick, Hitler, Göring and Himmler.

A rare photo of Himmler escorting his boss, Ernst Röhm, around Dachau concentration camp. Between them is Viktor Lütze, Röhm's successor.

Röhm's visit to Dachau 1933. In the middle of the three SS men on the left is Theodor Eicke. On his left is Michael Lippert. This is the only known photograph of Röhm with his two executioners. Just visible over Himmler's shoulder is Ernst Heinrich Schmauser who was also at the Stadelheim Prison when Eicke and Lippert shot Röhm. On Himmler's left is Dietrich von Jagow and behind him is Siegfried Seidel-Dittmarsch. Note also that Himmler and Seidel are both wearing the rare white collar patches.

Right: Himmler's only real rival for power in the SS was Kurt Daluege, the Berlin SS leader. He was no match for the cunning Himmler-Heydrich partnership and was quickly out-manoeuvred.

Below: Hitler was one of the first politicians to widely use aircraft to cover the country. His flight entourage here includes Esser, Bormann, Schaub, Brückner, Röhm, Himmler and Dietrich. Note Himmler wears a field grey greatcoat, unusual for this early date.

Above: Karl Wiligut-Weisthor (centre) looks on as Darré and Himmler discuss a find at an archeological site near Wewelsburg.

Left: Georg Aumeier; an early adjutant of the RFSS.

Right: Siegfried Seidel-Dittmarsch; Himmler's chief of staff in the SS-Hauptamt, a staunch supporter of the Bavarian Himmler, died unexpectedly in February 1934.

Below: The original 1933 document appointing Karl Wolff as adjutant to the RFSS.

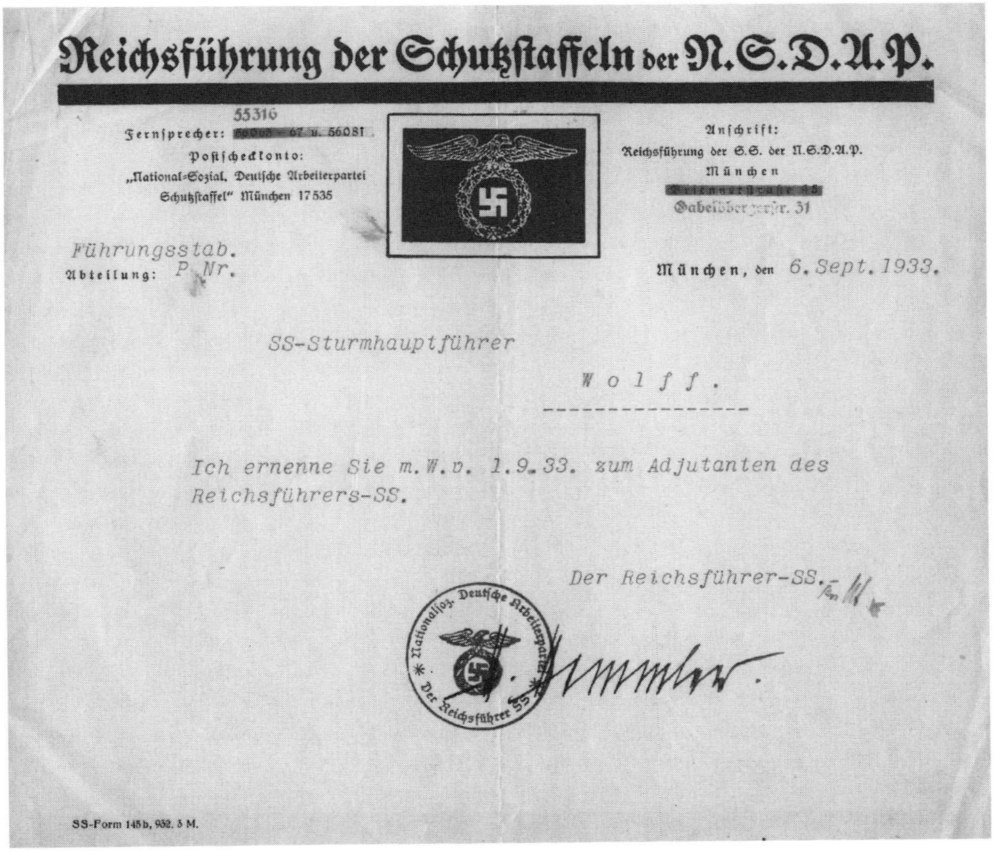

Reichsführung der Schutzstaffeln der N.S.D.A.P.

Fernsprecher: 55316 67 u. 56081
Postscheckkonto:
„National-Sozial. Deutsche Arbeiterpartei Schutzstaffel" München 17535

Anschrift:
Reichsführung der S.S. der N.S.D.A.P.
München
Gabelsbergerstr. 31

Führungsstab.
Abteilung: P Nr.

München, den 6. Sept. 1933.

SS-Sturmhauptführer

Wolff.

Ich ernenne Sie m.W.v. 1.9.33. zum Adjutanten des Reichsführers-SS.

Der Reichsführer-SS.

H. Himmler.

SS-Form 145b, 932. 3 M.

Above: Marga takes breakfast with her husband who appears to be amusing his adjutant Wolff.

Left: Himmler and Wolff in Munich, 9th November 1933.

Röhm is flanked by Himmler and Hitler. On the right is Gauleiter Martin Mutschmann, with Otto Dietrich visible over Hitler's left shoulder and Wilhelm Brückner over Himmler's right shoulder.

An early 1934 photograph showing Heydrich, Prützmann, Himmler and von Gottberg who wears the very rare "Württemberg" cuff title denoting his attachment to the Politische Bereitschaft Württemberg.

In August 1933, SS-Gruppe Ost held a mass rally in Berlin. Left to right: Himmler, Röhm, Seidel-Dittmarsch and Bergmann (Röhm's adjutant.)

Left to right: Engel, Breithaupt, Daluege, Himmler, Waldeck und Pyrmont, Seidel-Dittmarsch and Körner.

The RFSS studies a map, joined by Prützmann, Schmitt, Wolff, Heydrich and Pohl.

Himmler practices his shooting skills with what seems to be a kind of percussion pistol. His surroundings do not appear to be conducive to firearms practice, looking more like the rear veranda of a private house.

Left: Oswald Pohl was a member of the Marine SA when Himmler recognised his talent for accountancy. He immediately arranged for Pohl's transfer to the SS where he subsequently controlled the vast SS business empire, including the concentration camps.

Below: Rudolf Hess visits Dachau 1934. The party enters through a gate topped with barbed wire. Note the SS guard saluting wears early fatigue uniform. Hess is flanked by Himmler and Pohl.

Above: Prinz-Albrecht-Strasse 8, Berlin; a former music school and the site of Himmler's Berlin offices and headquarters of the SS and Gestapo.

Below: A view inside the main entrance hall of the Gestapo building. The busts are of Göring (left) and Hitler (right.)

Göring's man in charge of the Gestapo, Rudolf Diels.

Göring shakes the hand of Rudolf Diels on the occasion of Himmler taking official control of the Prussian State Police.

Heydrich based his SD at Wilhelmstrasse 102 in the Prinz Albrecht Palace.

Röhm and Himmler lead the mourners at the funeral of Seidel-Dittmarsch who died on 20th February 1934.

Above: Himmler inspects a troop of SS men with Prützmann. Among those behind are Wolff, Heydrich and Schmitt.

Left: Reichsführer-SS Heinrich Himmler wearing the rank insignia of an Obergruppenführer.

Above: Wewelsburg castle in Westphalia.

Right: The south wing and moat of Wewelsburg castle.

Above: Wewelsburg, undated. Left to right: unidentified RAD man, Dr Peter des Coudres, Manfred von Knobelsdorff, Hans Prützmann, Himmler and Heydrich.

Left: Not far from Wewelsburg, just outside Detmold is a dramatic formation of rocks into which caves have been created. This site holds significance for pagan worshippers and reliefs have been carved into the rock face. Himmler's party inspects one of the reliefs.

Above: At an archeological site. Left to right: Pohl, Himmler, Wiligut (with stick) and Wolff (wearing adjutant cords.)

Right: Himmler at the Externsteine.

Richard Walther Darré; the Reichsminister for Food and Agriculture, National Farmers' Leader and chief of the SS Race and Settlement Central Office.

SA-Obergruppenführer Friedrich-Wilhelm Krüger was head of SA training. He passed on information to Himmler about the machinations in the SA. Following the Röhm purge, Krüger transferred permanently to the SS and gave up his SA rank. A senior member of Himmler's associates, he was considered a traitor by many SA members. Here he wears SA uniform.

Right: The SS attracted many members of the German aristocracy, the most senior of whom was Josias Erbprinz zu Waldeck und Pyrmont.

Below: Himmler's personal car in the spring mountain snow of 1934. Note the RFSS car pennant and the SS bonnet ornament on this right hand drive Maybach Zeppelin.

Some of the close associates of the RFSS 1934. The group includes Walter Schmitt (in cap,) Hans Prützmann, Oswald Pohl and Erasmus Malsen-Ponickau.

Himmler addresses a mass meeting of SS-Standarte 63 in Reutlingen. Behind him is his personal standard.

Right: Himmler in conversation with Malsen-Ponickau and Prützmann.

Below: The personal standard of the Reichsführer-SS. The eagle, wreath and swastika are hand stitched in high quality silver bullion on a black and white background.

Left: A candid shot of Himmler addressing his men.

Below: 9th June 1934, Hanau. On the right is SS-Sturmbannführer August Jakober.

Feldherrnhalle, Munich, 9th November 1934. Left to right: Wolff, Maurice, Hess, Weber, Himmler, Hitler, Lütze and Schaub.

At a sports shooting range in Berlin-Wannsee, October 1934. Left to right: Daluege, Wolff, Himmler, Bonin, Milch, Heydrich, Krüger and von Schutz.

Krüger with Himmler, Wolff and von Blomberg.

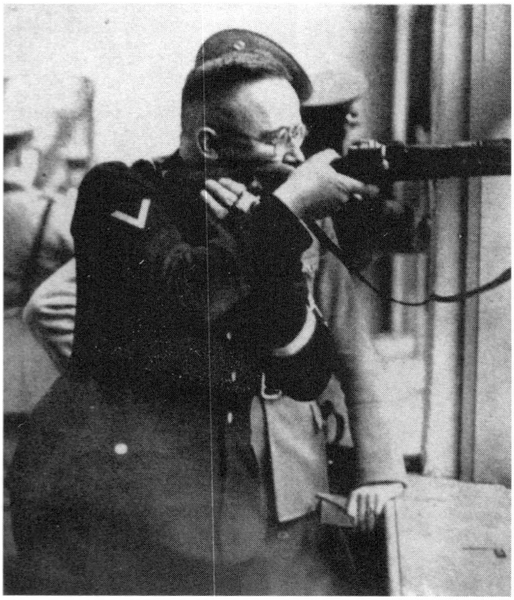

Left: Himmler uses the range at Wannsee.

Right: Himmler's routine at his office in Prinz-Albrecht-Strasse was one of endless meetings and dealing with the numerous files which landed upon his desk. He insisted on reviewing many files personally.

Himmler relaxes with an after-dinner cigar and a chat with von Ribbentrop.

Landhaus "Lindenfycht" at Gmund on the shores of the Tegernsee in Bavaria. The Himmlers lived here from the mid-1930s and carried out improvements to suit the family and lifestyle of an important member of the regime. (Photo 1997.)

The rear aspect of Haus "Lindenfycht" rarely seen. (Photo 1997.)

Haus "Lindenfycht" side elevation. (Photo 1997.)

Above: An annex was subsequently added a few metres from the main building which served as office space and accommodation for Himmler's RSD escort. (Photo 1997.)

Right: Haus "Lindenfycht" 1934. The children are Gudrun and Gerhard von der Ahe. Himmler stands in the background with a member of the household staff on the left and an unidentified woman on the right.

Haus "Lindenfycht" 1934. Marga cuddles her own daughter whilst the body language between Marga and Gerhard von der Ahe speaks volumes. The scar on Marga's cheek is just visible in this photo.

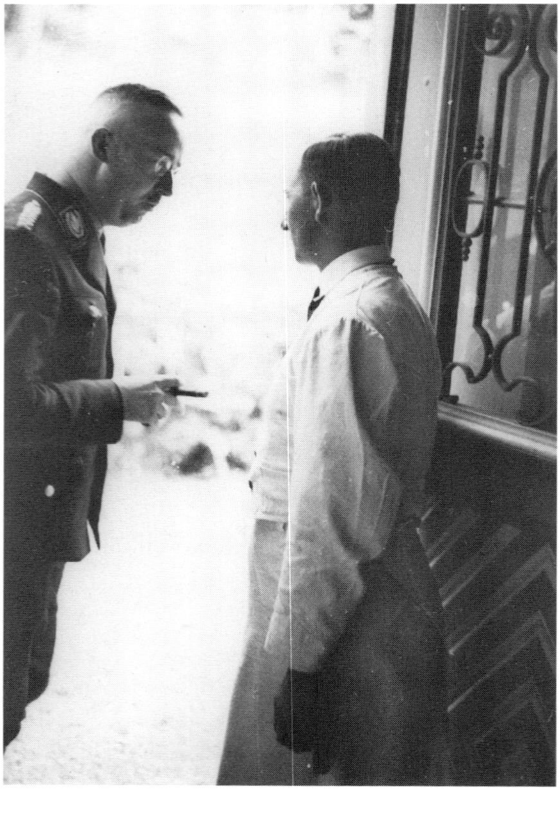

Himmler instructs one of the household staff at Gmund. Marga constantly complained about the staff which frequently changed.

The Himmler couple take afternoon coffee and cake.

Himmler has decided to plant a young tree in the front grounds of his house. The Tegernsee can just be seen through the bushes and trees. The woman carrying the support pole is Inez von Woyrsch. Her husband, Udo von Woyrsch, is on the left helping to push the cart with bodyguard Josef Kiermaier. Himmler, dressed in uniform riding breeches and boots with civilian top, holds the tree upright in the cart.

Having selected the spot, Himmler digs the hole. Left to right: a family friend, house maid, family friend, Inez von Woyrsch, then Kiermaier, SS aide and Udo von Woyrsch.

Now it's Himmler's turn to watch von Woyrsch with the shovel. The SS aide on the right wears a motorised insignia on his sleeve above the RFSS cuff title, indicating he is almost certainly Himmler's chauffeur.

When at "Lindenfycht" for any length of time, Himmler took the opportunity to hunt. The children are probably those of von Woyrsch (in dark trilby hat.)

Himmler reaches for his jacket from von Woyrsch. Inez follows her husband.

Clockwise from top left:

In this 1937 private snapshot, Himmler stands in a small boat he used for game shooting.

An interior shot of the house at Gmund.

Guests at Gmund – Karl Wolff and Reinhard Heydrich pay a social visit with their wives.

Above: The Reichsführer enlists the help of several aides when Heydrich's car needs a push to start. Frieda Wolff and Lina Heydrich are just visible in the rear seat.

Right: Tegernsee 1934. A photograph taken by Gebhard Himmler of Wolff, Heydrich, Himmler and probably Mathilde Himmler.

Above: Reinhard Heydrich.

Opposite: Werner Lorenz.

Clockwise from top left

Karl Wolff.

August Heissmeyer.

Walter Schmitt.

Clockwside from top left:

Fritz Weitzel.

Hanns Johst.

Udo von Woyrsch.

Himmler takes the salute with Gauleiter Sprenger. Wolff is in front with Heydrich, Hildebrandt, Pohl and Schmitt.

Opposite above: Himmler with von Woyrsch, 21st January 1935.

Opposite below: Himmler in Rosenheim 1935 with Ernst Heinrich Schmauser.

Hans Adolf Prützmann.

Left: Himmler wore unique collar insignia from autumn 1934. His decorations are the Blood Order ribbon in his right breast buttonhole, the NSDAP Golden Party Badge on his left breast pocket, the Honour Chevron on his right upper sleeve and his NSDAP pin on his tie. Note he also wears a brown shirt.

Himmler wore his hair with a severe style, almost shaved bald at the back and sides. His secretary, Hedwig Potthast, later convinced him to grow his hair slightly longer.

Right: Himmler remained faithful to old friends after he rose to command the SS. Prof. Dr Karl Gebhardt was appointed as Chief SS Surgeon.

Below: The three Himmler brothers in SS uniform; Ernst, Heinrich and Gebhard.

Clockwise from top left:

A picnic in 1936 with Marga and friends. Karl Gebhardt is top right.

As the SS gained power, many men who would later become notorious were recruited. Among them was a criminal police officer, Heinrich "Gestapo" Müller.

To consolidate the power of the SS, Himmler offered SS membership to senior NSDAP members and important businessmen. The Nazi party treasurer, Franz Xaver Schwarz, poses in his SS uniform.

Clockwise from top left:

Another such recruit, here resplendent in his SS-Gruppenführer uniform, was Joachim von Ribbentrop.

Reichsleiter Philipp Bouhler joined the SS in April 1933.

The chief NSDAP judge and father-in-law of Martin Bormann, Reichsleiter Walter Buch, seen here in SS uniform.

Left: A senator in Danzig, Arthur Greiser was typical of the young Nazis who worshipped Hitler and embraced Himmler's SS. In this photo Greiser wears early pattern cap eagle and skull with early collar patches for a SS-Standartenführer.

Below: Himmler recognised the importance of good uniform design and contracted the fashion designer, Hugo Boss, to devise new SS uniforms with the assistance of the insignia created by Prof. Karl Diebitsch. A new white summer tunic was introduced, here being worn in Himmler's Berlin office. Behind Himmler are Wolff and Chief Adjutant Ludolf von Alvensleben.

Clockwise from top left:

Himmler and Wolff wear the white collar patches, only in use for a very short period.

Himmler chose the highly decorated Curt Wittje to command the important SS-Hauptamt. Wittje would later leave the SS in disgrace.

Members of Hitler's staff began joining the SS. Here Hitler's personal pilot, Hans Baur, stands with Himmler.

Clockwise from top left:

Hitler's original bodyguard, Ulrich Graf, seriously wounded at the Beer Hall Putsch, in the uniform of a SS-Brigadeführer.

Julius Schaub, Hitler's personal adjutant, as a SS-Standartenführer.

Hitler's press chief, Dr Otto Dietrich, was rarely seen out of SS uniform.

Clockwise from top left:

Reichsleiter Max Amann, Hitler's former sergeant in World War One.

The most famous Waffen-SS officer, Josef "Sepp" Dietrich, was an early follower of Hitler and one of his favourites. He commanded the Leibstandarte-SS "Adolf Hitler" which was the initial unit responsible for the protection of the Führer. He later proved himself to be a brave and efficient military commander, loved by his men. Dietrich found Himmler's interfering intolerable and often failed to carry out his orders and flaunted regulations.

Hans Heinrich Lammers, chief of the Reich Chancellery and always close to Hitler, only wore SS uniform. Himmler liked Lammers and allowed him to share his special train.

Opposite above: Himmler visited Sachsenburg concentration camp on 16th February 1935. SS-Totenkopf guards demonstrate a machine gun watched by Eicke and Schmitt.

Opposite below: On 29th April 1935, the Himmler couple were guests at the wedding of Hans Prützmann and Christa von Boddien in Leissienen.

Right: A happy Reichsführer-SS in 1935.

Below: Himmler insisted that all SS men had to compete for the SA Sports Badge, including himself. A shirtless Himmler and Wolff listen to the instructor at Bad Tölz.

Above: Wolff strides out with Himmler behind.

Left: The long jump.

He also expected his officers to take part in pack marches.

Proficiency with a handgun was also expected, using both hands. Normally right handed, Himmler tries his left on the range.

Himmler found relaxation in a game of tennis.

Himmler prepares to race against younger and fitter SS men at Bad Tölz 1935.

Jogging at Bad Tölz, 1935.

Himmler and Heydrich at a ski meeting. The figure on the left looks remarkably like Hitler.

Himmler's blue eyes peer through his pince nez.

Above: Whenever the Reichsführer (third from left bareheaded) motored across country, he was accompanied by an entourage of staff and senior officers.

Right: A smiling RFSS in 1935. Wolff in the background in adjutant cords.

Left: Himmler in conversation with Constantin von Neurath and Rudolf Hess, 1935.

Below: Himmler joins the ranks of the "old fighters" to commemorate the Beer Hall Putsch. This march was on 9th November 1935.

Above: Unlike the relatively shy Heydrich, Himmler had no problem with speaking in public or giving a live radio address.

Right: Himmler could relax at home in Bavaria, 1937.

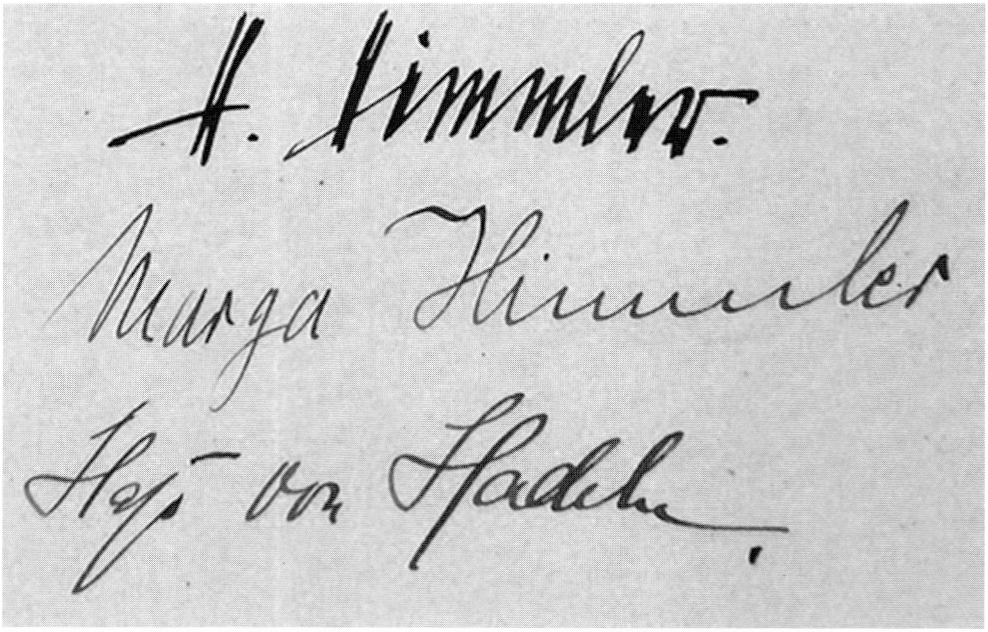

Above: The signatures of Himmler, Marga Himmler and adjutant Hajo von Hadeln as they appear on a page of a visitors' book.

Left and below: Examples of Himmler's distinctive handwriting and a variation of his signature. The rear of the envelope shows the sender as "H. Himmler, member of the Reichstag, Waltrudering near Munich."

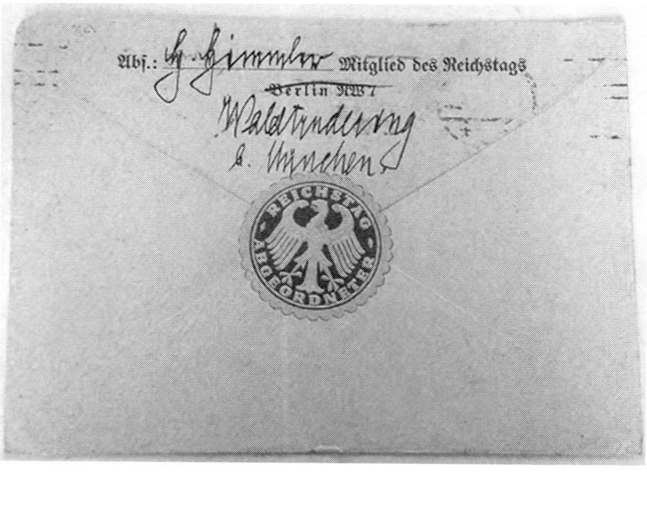

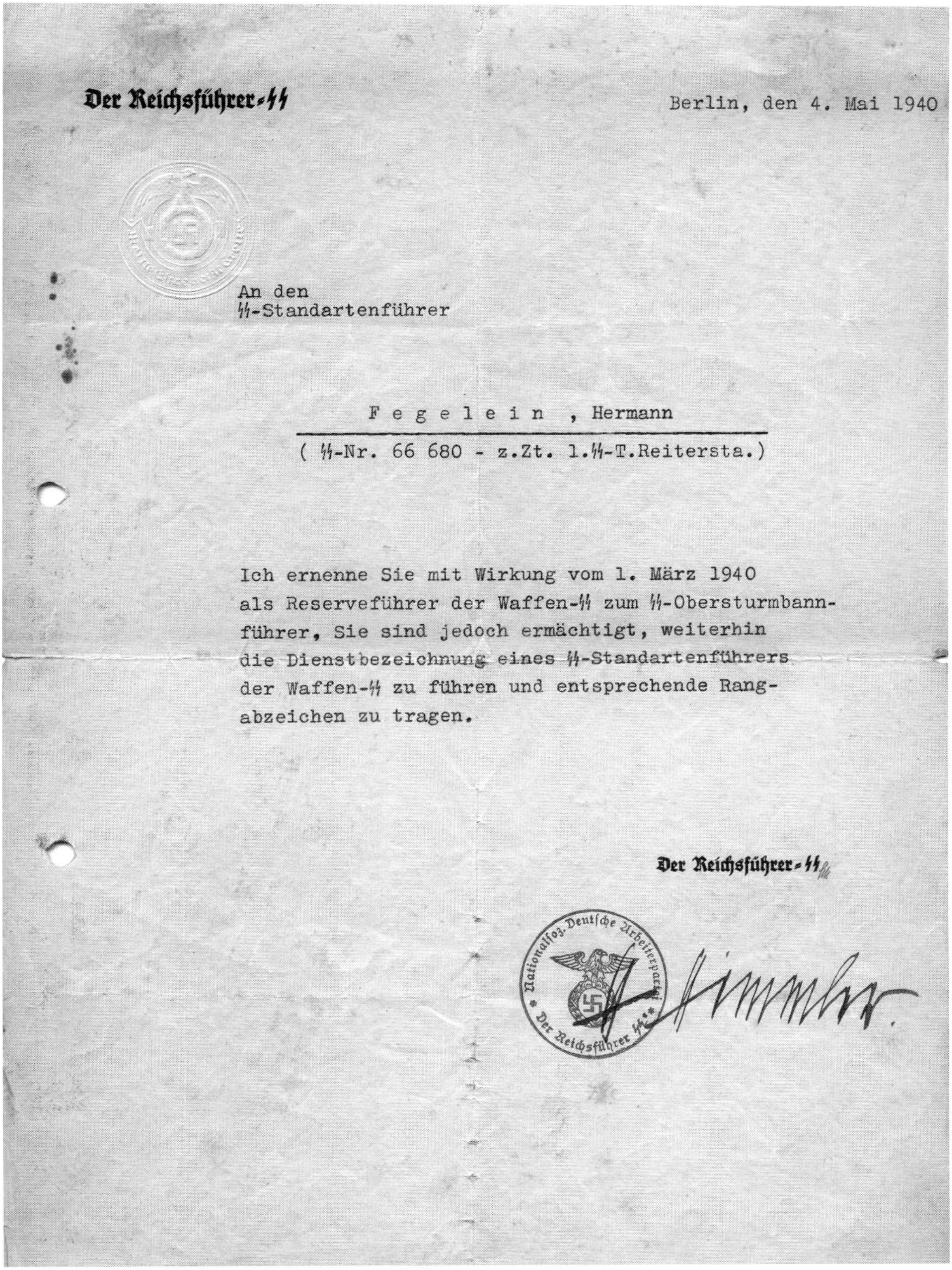
Der Reichsführer-SS

Berlin, den 4. Mai 1940

An den
SS-Standartenführer

F e g e l e i n , Hermann

(SS-Nr. 66 680 - z.Zt. 1.SS-T.Reitersta.)

Ich ernenne Sie mit Wirkung vom 1. März 1940
als Reserveführer der Waffen-SS zum SS-Obersturmbann-
führer, Sie sind jedoch ermächtigt, weiterhin
die Dienstbezeichnung eines SS-Standartenführers
der Waffen-SS zu führen und entsprechende Rang-
abzeichen zu tragen.

Der Reichsführer-SS

Nationalsoz. Deutsche Arbeiterpartei * Der Reichsführer SS *

H Himmler.

This document informs Hermann Fegelein that he has been appointed as SS-Obersturmbannführer der Reserve in the Waffen-SS prior to his promotion to SS-Standartenführer der Waffen-SS. Fegelein already held the rank of Standartenführer in the Allgemeine-SS. The document is on personal stationery and bears Himmler's characteristic signature.

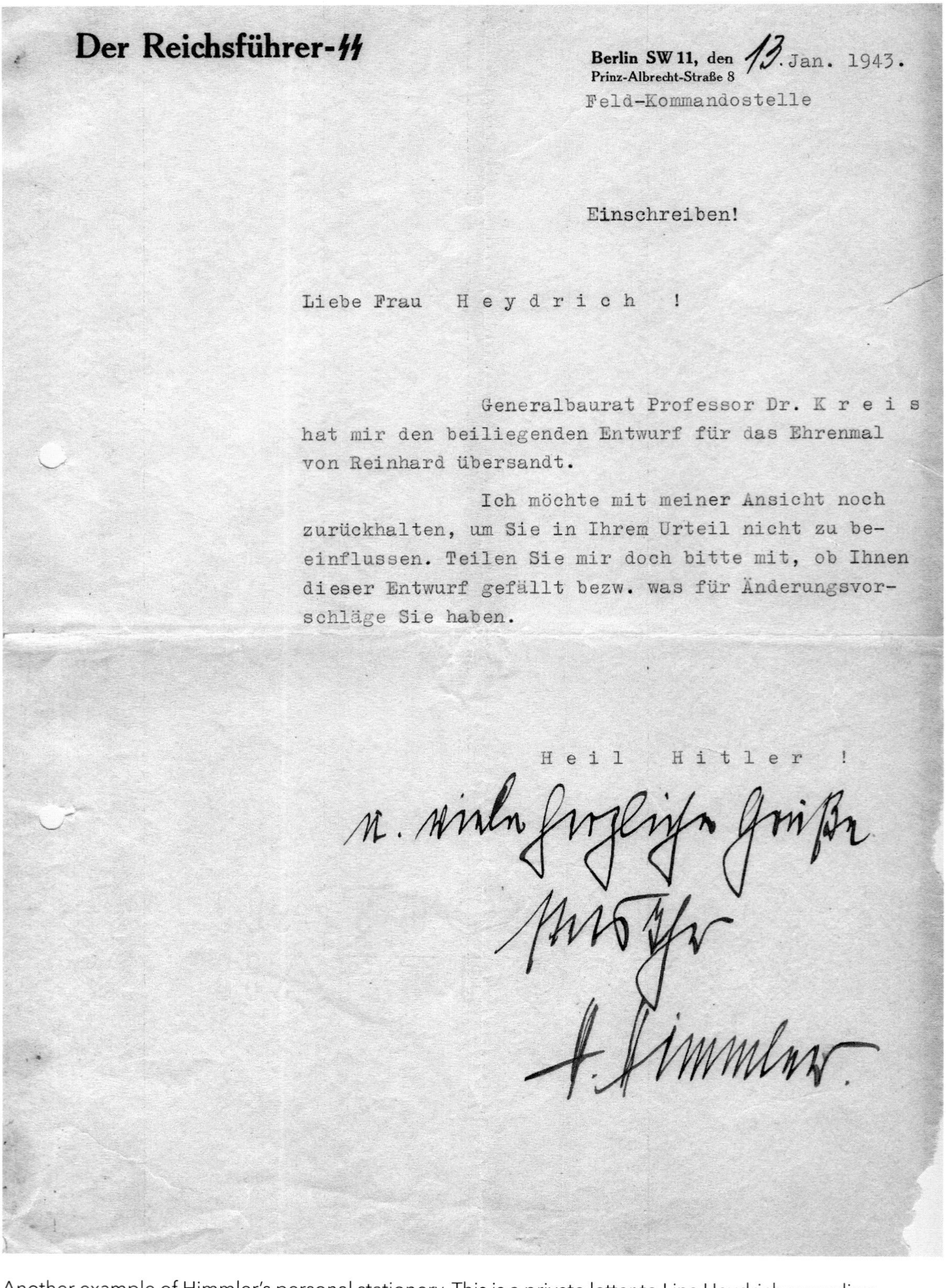

Der Reichsführer-SS

Berlin SW 11, den 13. Jan. 1943.
Prinz-Albrecht-Straße 8
Feld-Kommandostelle

Einschreiben!

Liebe Frau H e y d r i c h !

Generalbaurat Professor Dr. K r e i s hat mir den beiliegenden Entwurf für das Ehrenmal von Reinhard übersandt.

Ich möchte mit meiner Ansicht noch zurückhalten, um Sie in Ihrem Urteil nicht zu beeinflussen. Teilen Sie mir doch bitte mit, ob Ihnen dieser Entwurf gefällt bezw. was für Änderungsvorschläge Sie haben.

H e i l H i t l e r !

u. vielen herzlichen Grüßen

Stets Ihr

H. Himmler.

Another example of Himmler's personal stationery. This is a private letter to Lina Heydrich regarding a permanent monument for her late husband. Himmler adds additional greetings in his own hand.

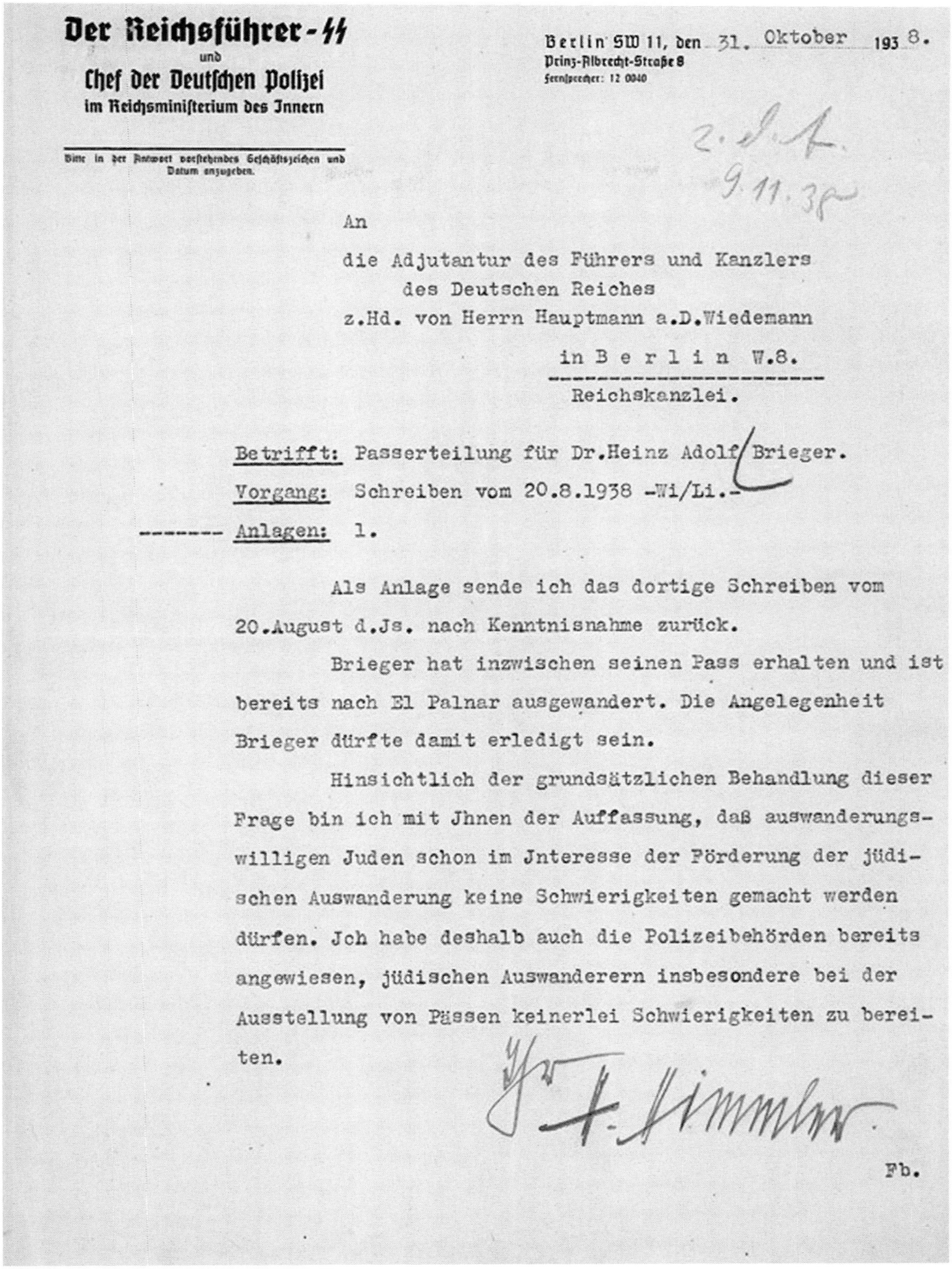

Der Reichsführer-SS
und
Chef der Deutschen Polizei
im Reichsministerium des Innern

Bitte in der Antwort vorstehendes Geschäftszeichen und Datum anzugeben.

Berlin SW 11, den 31. Oktober 1938.
Prinz-Albrecht-Straße 8
Fernsprecher: 12 0040

z. d. A.
9.11.38

An

die Adjutantur des Führers und Kanzlers
des Deutschen Reiches
z.Hd. von Herrn Hauptmann a.D.Wiedemann

in B e r l i n W.8.

Reichskanzlei.

Betrifft: Passerteilung für Dr.Heinz Adolf Brieger.
Vorgang: Schreiben vom 20.8.1938 -Wi/Li.-
-------- Anlagen: 1.

Als Anlage sende ich das dortige Schreiben vom 20.August d.Js. nach Kenntnisnahme zurück.

Brieger hat inzwischen seinen Pass erhalten und ist bereits nach El Palnar ausgewandert. Die Angelegenheit Brieger dürfte damit erledigt sein.

Hinsichtlich der grundsätzlichen Behandlung dieser Frage bin ich mit Jhnen der Auffassung, daß auswanderungswilligen Juden schon im Jnteresse der Förderung der jüdischen Auswanderung keine Schwierigkeiten gemacht werden dürfen. Jch habe deshalb auch die Polizeibehörden bereits angewiesen, jüdischen Auswanderern insbesondere bei der Ausstellung von Pässen keinerlei Schwierigkeiten zu bereiten.

H. Himmler

Fb.

A letter from Himmler to Fritz Wiedemann, Hitler's military adjutant, regarding a request concerning Dr Heinz Brieger, a Jew. Himmler confirms he has arranged for a passport for Brieger who will be able to leave Germany. A remarkable letter indicating that favours were being allowed for certain Jews to leave Germany. Note the date and the official headed stationery.

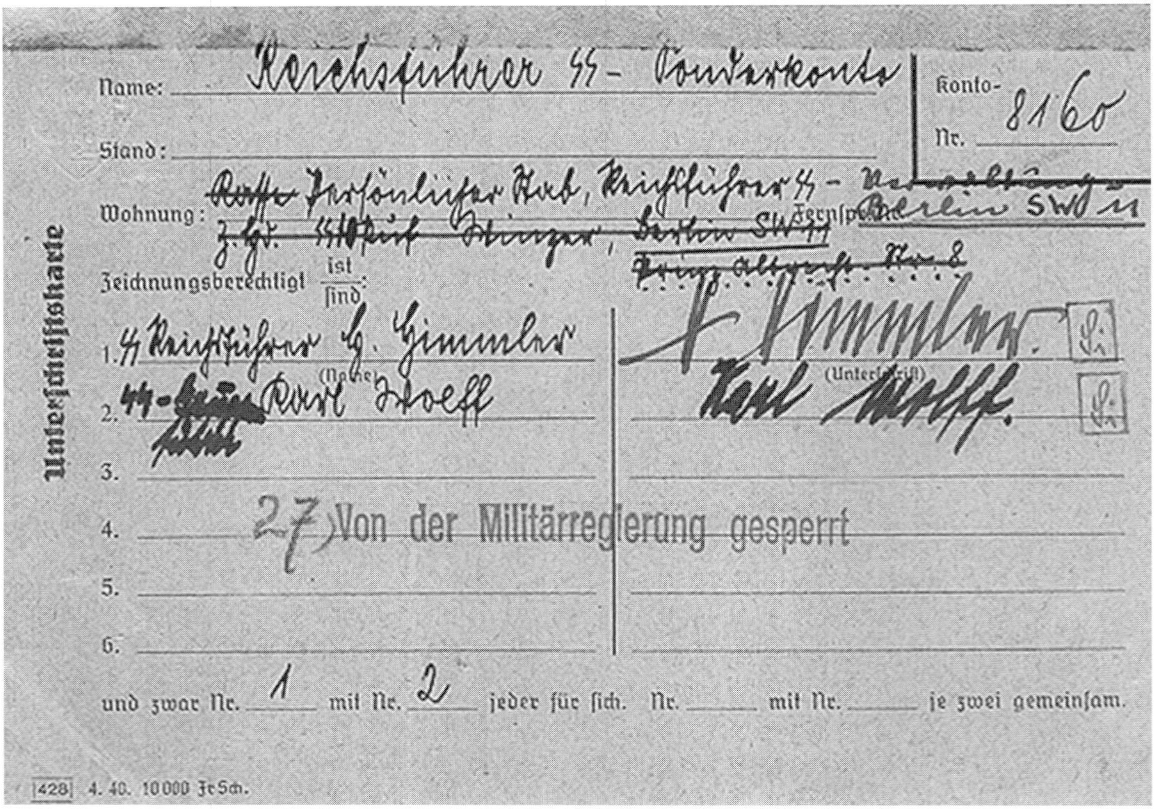

Unterschriftskarte

Name: Reichsführer SS-Sonderkonto | Konto-Nr. 8160

Stand:

Wohnung: Persönlicher Stab, Reichsführer SS – Berlin SW 11 | Fernsprecher:

Zeichnungsberechtigt ist/sind:

1. SS Reichsführer H. Himmler | H Himmler
2. SS-Karl Wolff | Karl Wolff
(Name) | (Unterschrift)
3.
4. 27 Von der Militärregierung gesperrt
5.
6.

und zwar Nr. 1 mit Nr. 2 jeder für sich. Nr. ____ mit Nr. ____ je zwei gemeinsam.

428 4. 40. 10000 Fr Sch.

Above: There were several personal bank accounts held by the SS in Himmler's name. This is the signature authority for Special Account number 8160. The only two authorised signatories are Himmler and Wolff. A similar account was opened for the proceeds of valuables appropriated from the Jews.

Left: For a man who closely monitored the smoking habits of his SS men, he was often pictured with a cigar, such as here at his hunting lodge at Valepp.

Clockwise from top left:

Plainly enjoying himself in a boat used for hunting.

A close friend of the Himmler family, Wilhelm Graf von Wedel.

Himmler chose the young Rudolf Brandt as his personal referent or advisor. He is photographed here without his trademark spectacles.

Left: With Himmler's backing, Heydrich began recruiting young intellectuals for the SS and in particular the SD. They included theologians, such as Albert Hartl who left the catholic priesthood to join the SD. By 1936, Himmler actively encouraged men to leave the Church.

Below: Himmler at Schloss Arolsen, the family seat of the royal family of Waldeck und Pyrmont and the headquarters of the area SS, March 1936.

Himmler at Schloss Arolsen with the royal family of Waldeck und Pyrmont in March 1936. The baby is Wittekind, the newborn son of Erbprinz Josias, holding his son. The head of the family, Fürst Friedrich zu Waldeck und Pyrmont, stands third from left.

Familien-Anzeigen

Die Geburt ihres dritten Kindes zeigen in froher Dankbarkeit an

Albrecht - Wieland

Richard Hildebrandt
SS-Brigadeführer und
Frau Johanna, geb. Fischer

z. Z. München 59 Häherweg 32 — Im Heumond 1936 — Wiesbaden Taunusstraße 54

Die Geburt eines Sohnes zeigen an

Udo v. Woyrsch
SS.-Obergruppenführer im Stabe des Reichsführers SS.
Inez v. Woyrsch
geb. Freiin von Tschammer und Quaritz

Breslau - Südsanatorium — Schwanowitz, Bez. Breslau

Doris

Unseren beiden Buben wurde heute das erhoffte Schwesterchen geboren.
Das zeigen in dankbarer Freude an

Käthe Floegel, geb. Loref
Rechtsanwalt Dr. Martin Floegel
Sturmführer i. St. d. Motorgruppe Schlesien

Breslau, den 3. Juli 1936
Kaiserstraße 77

Heute nachmittag verstarb durch Unglücksfall unsere teure, in aufopfernder Liebe und Hingabe für uns lebende und sorgende Frau und Mutter, unsere liebe Tochter, Schwiegertochter, Schwester und Schwägerin

Frau Gustava Skowronski
geb. Lippold

im Alter von 35 Jahren.

Osterode, den 4. Juli 1936

Himmler authorised the SS to have its own newspaper, "Das Schwarze Korps" edited by Gunter d'Alquen. SS men of all ranks could make announcements. This particular edition carried news of the birth of children to the von Woyrsch and Hildebrandt couples. The newspaper was carefully monitored by Heydrich's SD.

Gunter d'Alquen at his editorial desk.

On 16th May 1936, Julius Schreck died.

Julius Schreck was buried at Grafelfing with full SS honours. Hitler was devastated by the loss of his loyal companion and ordered that Schreck be accorded the privilege of a near state funeral.

Himmler speaks at the grave side.

1936 / Folge 22 Illustrierter Beobachter Seite 841

Julius Schreck

wird von seinem Führer zu Grabe geleitet.

Vorwärts! Und wenn auch der Feind sich verstieg
und zum Ziele den Weg dir vertrat!
Das Steuer in deiner Faust, Kamerad,
hieß: Sieg!

Pidder Lüng

Aufbahrung des Sarges im Friedhof von Gräfelfing bei München.
Im Hintergrund der Führer, links von ihm sein Stellvertreter Rudolf Heß,
rechts: Generaloberst Göring, Gauleiter Streicher, Reichsschatzmeister Schwarz,
Reichsleiter Buch, Reichsminister Dr. Frick.

Der Sarg Julius Schrecks wird, begleitet von alten Kämpfern, von SS.-Führern, Blutordenträgern, zum Grabe getragen.
Aufnahmen: Heinrich Hoffmann (3), Bayerischer-Bildbericht Fischer (2).

Der Führer grüßt zum letztenmal seinen alten Freund und Mitkämpfer.
Links: Lutze, Goebbels, Heß, Schaub, Brückner, Streicher, Bormann, Frick; rechts: Amann, Himmler, Ley.

Opposite above: The Illustrierte Beobachter report of Schreck's funeral. Schreck had been the founder of the infant SS.

Opposite below, left: Hitler pays his respects to his long term bodyguard.

Opposite below, right: Schreck's coffin is lowered into the grave.

Himmler's SS took control of the successful Allach porcelain factory in 1936. Prof. Karl Diebitsch examines the fencer.

In this war date photo, Himmler shows Hitler some of the Allach military figures. In the background hovers Julius Schaub, whilst Himmler's liaison officer at the Führer headquarters, Hermann Fegelein, looks on.

Above: One of the items manufactured at the Allach porcelain factory was the Julleuchter. Made from hardened clay, it signified the strength of the SS family. It would be used on special occasions and at the summer and winter solstice celebrations. Here the Julleuchter is used for the marriage ceremony of a junior SD officer, conducted by SS-Brigadeführer Wilhelm Harster.

Left: Wolfram Sievers. Himmler and Darré's interest in ancestral heritage manifested in 1935 in the formation of the Ahnenerbe Foundation. Himmler selected a Dutch historian, Hermann Wirth, as president and Sievers as its director. Its brief was the research of ancient German history. Wirth was quickly found to be a crank and was replaced by Prof. Walter Wüst in 1937.

Himmler replaced the traditional religions with his own brand of SS religion. Central to his beliefs were the ancient pagan principles and the chronicles of King Heinrich I who reigned from 912 until his death on 2nd July 936. He was the first king to unite all the German peoples. He was buried in the crypt of St. Servatii church at Quedlinburg. A rare photo of the church from the 1930s. After the war, the twin steeple roofs were demolished and replaced with two lower pyramid shaped steeple roofs.

Another rare photo from the same period with a swastika flag being displayed from one of the church bell towers. Today church officials refer to the period under Himmler's influence as "....the church being misused by the Nazis."

The church interior with SS banner. The entrance to the crypt is via the central archway.

The crypt of St. Servatii with tombs at the far end. Himmler discovered the tombs to be empty and set about trying to discover the whereabouts of the last resting place of King Heinrich. His team of historian archaeologists was unsuccessful.

SS sentries stand guard over the empty tomb of the king. Note the wreath from Himmler.

The view of the crypt from the position of the SS sentries.

Above: Leaving the main gate of the castle.

Right: Goslar, July 1936. A meeting with Darré's Race and Settlement Office staff.

Opposite above: Himmler, Gauleiter Rudolf Jordan and August Heissmeyer lead the way into Quedlinburg Schloss through the main gateway. Heydrich peers over Heissmeyer's shoulder. The church is situated within the walls of the Schloss.

Opposite below: Himmler lays a wreath on the empty tomb. Behind Himmler are Wolff, Jordan, Heydrich, Heissmeyer and Jeckeln.

Left: SS-Obersturmbannführer Georg Martin on the right. The cart carries heavy timber rings that will be stuffed with hay, set ablaze and rolled down a local hillside outside the town of Detmold. A local custom.

Below: The timber ring on the left has been stuffed with hay and the farmers are jamming hay into the ring on the right.

As part of the traditional fun and games, SS General Otto Hofmann takes part in the egg and spoon race in full SS uniform. In contrast, Hofmann was a participant at the infamous Wannsee conference in January 1942 which formalised the fate of the European Jews.

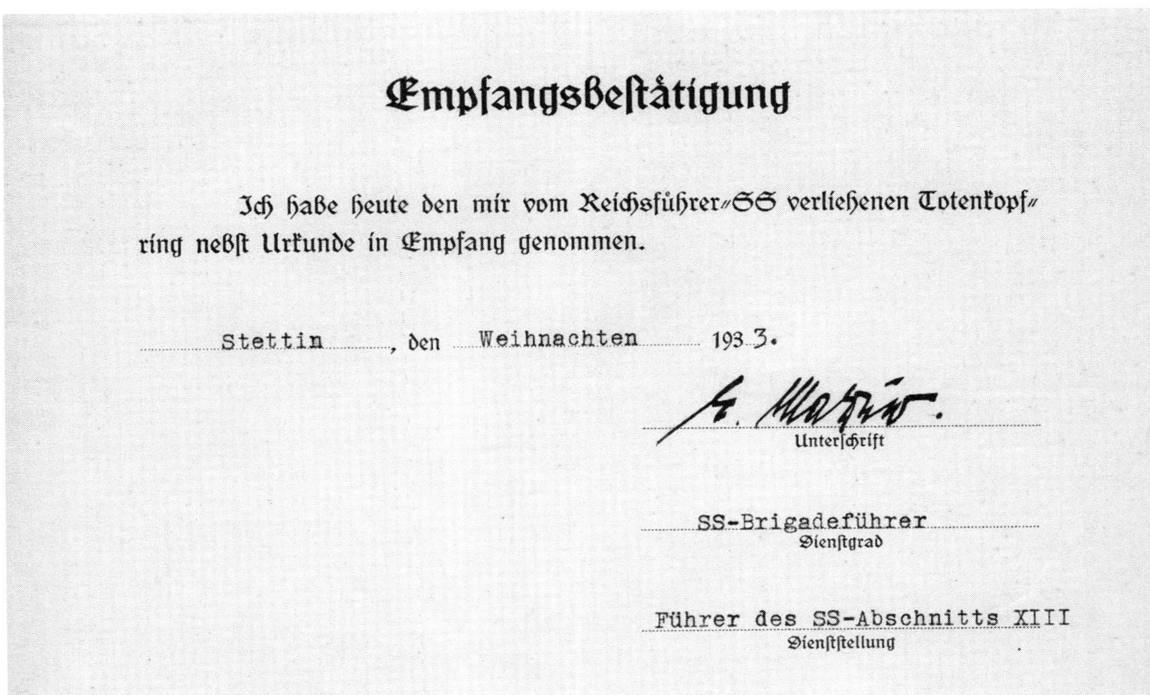

Empfangsbestätigung

Ich habe heute den mir vom Reichsführer-SS verliehenen Totenkopf-ring nebst Urkunde in Empfang genommen.

Stettin, den Weihnachten 1933.

Unterschrift

SS-Brigadeführer
Dienstgrad

Führer des SS-Abschnitts XIII
Dienststellung

Himmler introduced the SS-Totenkopfring (death's head ring) for his officers as an award. When presented, the recipient had to notify the SS personnel office to update the SS records. A printed proforma was created for the purpose and here is the one submitted by Emil Mazuw.

Left: Himmler and Hitler during an official visit.

Below: Himmler plays the role of loving father.

Right: The Himmler family at home in Gmund. Himmler lays a fatherly hand on the young Gerhard von der Ahe, adopted by the Himmlers. His poor behaviour soon caused Himmler to largely ignore him. He later joined the Waffen-SS.

Below: A breakfast guest at Heydrich's summer house on the Baltic island of Fehmarn.

Clockwise from top left:

Summer 1935. Himmler autographs a photo of himself.

Himmler, von Woyrsch and Weitzel in an undated photograph.

An early supporter of Himmler, Paul Moder was often in the company of the RFSS.

Erasmus von Malsen-Ponickau, whose career promotions slowed after a promising start. He served with Odilo Globocnik in Trieste towards the latter stages of the war.

Emil Mazuw; looked upon by Himmler as solid and reliable, but not considered among the most dynamic SS leaders.

Hess looks on as Himmler speaks to Karl Maria Demelhuber, the commander of SS-Standarte "Deutschland." Centre is von Eberstein, the local area SS commander and far right at the back is Wolff.

Opposite above: By 1936, Dachau concentration camp was considered a model camp and would be used as a template by other camp commandants. On 8th May 1936, Himmler welcomed Rudolf Hess on an inspection visit and conducted him around the entire facility. Visible in this photo are von Eberstein, Hess, Waldeck, Himmler, Hildebrandt, Heydrich, Loritz and Frank.

Opposite below: Himmler and Hess in a sombre mood. The monument is for SS men killed on 25th July 1934 in Vienna during the attempted coup against the government of Engelbert Dollfuss. Note the SS belt buckle emblem and the swastika and SS runes in the railings.

An official portrait of Reichsführer-SS Heinrich Himmler by his favoured photographer, Friedrich Franz Bauer.

Chatting with local children who had just presented the Reichsführer with a bouquet.

Himmler with Udo von Woyrsch. Behind stands adjutant Hajo von Hadeln.

Opposite above: In June 1936, Himmler was appointed Chief of the German Police. This photo shows the most important police officials. Left to right: Daluege, Stuckart, Frank, Himmler, Heydrich, Best, von Helldorf and unident.

Opposite below: Himmler addresses the meeting. All the men on the top table, apart from Werner Best, suffered unnatural deaths; Stuckart - car accident, Heydrich - assassinated, Himmler - suicide, Frank, Daluege and von Helldorf - all hanged.

Right: Kurt Daluege was nominally Himmler's deputy in the SS. An ex-refuse engineer in Berlin, he gained the nickname "Dummi Dummi," but soon showed this to be unjustified by efficient command of the Ordnungspolizei after Himmler delegated responsibilities. Heydrich was handed the more important police departments, but Daluege took his role seriously, rarely appearing in SS uniform after 1936, preferring that of a police general.

Below: Duties permitting, Himmler found time for his daughter Gudrun.

Opposite above: Himmler in traditional Bavarian attire.

Opposite below: Himmler covers his eyes against the glare of the sun to look at the mountains. On his right is Heydrich and on his left in uniform is Wolff.

Left: The Himmlers' marriage was put under great strain by his constant absences.

Below: Marga and her husband walk almost unnoticed in a street in Wiesbaden.

Left: The RFSS at Hohenlychen SS clinic in 1936. In whites with spectacles is Prof. Dr Karl Gebhardt.

Below: Women found the Reichsführer polite and good company. On his left is Frau von Ribbentrop.

As a young man, Himmler exhibited his prudish nature when his brother Gebhard became engaged to Paula Stölzl, a banker's daughter. Heinrich did not approve of her and interfered to such an extent that Gebhard called off the engagement.

A rare photo of Nini Rascher, the wife of Dr Sigmund Rascher. There was an unconfirmed rumour that she had a brief affair with Himmler before marrying the infamous doctor. As the former singer, Karoline Diehl, she became acquainted with the Reichsführer-SS during the 1930s and remained on good terms with him until a scandal involving children.

Dr Sigmund Rascher conducted high altitude experiments on inmates at Dachau. He gained access to the RFSS through his wife's friendship with the chief of the SS.

Reichsführer-SS and Chief of the German Police in the Reich Ministry of the Interior.

Right: The first SS officer training school was set up in the military academy in Munich in 1934. By 1936, Himmler had appointed Paul Hausser as the Inspector of the SS-Verfügungstruppe, the forerunner of the Waffen-SS. The first two SS officer cadet schools were opened at Bad Tölz and Braunschweig. This is the new iconic archway entrance at Tölz.

Below: The RFSS on an official visit to the SS officer cadet school at Braunschweig. Behind him are Dietrich Klagges, Friedrich Jeckeln and Karl Wolff.

Above: Inspection of the school at Braunschweig. Left to right: Hausser, Jeckeln, Klagges and Himmler.

Left: Hausser presents the school parade to Himmler at Braunschweig. In the background the columns of the imposing Residenzschloss.

Above: Himmler always took a personal interest in his officer corps. Here he interviews an officer candidate at Braunschweig. He sits between Schmitt and Heissmeyer.

Right: Welcome to the SS elite.

Above: A visit to SS barracks.

Left: Leaving a building at the SS complex. Schmitt, Pohl and Heissmeyer behind Himmler. The SA General is Max Jüttner.

Opposite above: Himmler (left) takes a look at the Nuremberg arena with Ernst Heinrich Schmauser (back to camera) and Karl Wolff (second from right.)

Opposite below: At the Nuremberg rallies, Himmler would lead his SS contingent in the town market square where Hitler took the salute and then stand with the Führer before the main body of SS troops marched past. Here Himmler and Wolff arrive at the market square.

Café
Café
ZIGARRE
Cigarren

Left: Himmler at Nuremberg. In the background is the men's clothing store Marmorecke, owned by the Jewish businessman Ludwig Levy.

Below: The press and newsreels cover Hitler's arrival at Nuremberg airfield. Left to right: Benno Martin, Julius Streicher, Willy Liebel, Hitler, Wolff and Himmler.

Right: Nuremberg, 1935, Reichsparteitag. Himmler in the motorcade.

Below: Hitler reviewing a guard of honour. On the left is Gauleiter Jakob Sprenger.

On an official visit to the town of Braunschweig. Left to right: Wolff, Klagges, Jeckeln, Himmler and von Alvensleben.

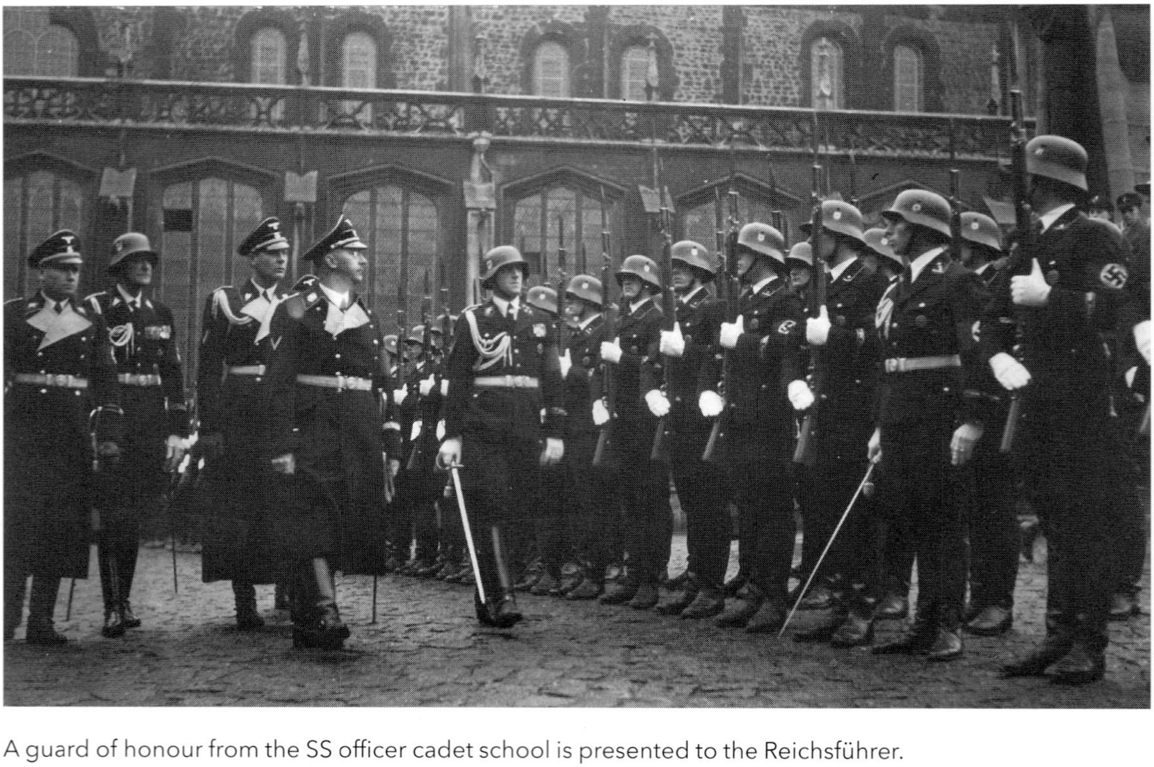

A guard of honour from the SS officer cadet school is presented to the Reichsführer.

Curt Kaul accompanies Himmler on this official visit.

Heinrich Koeppen of SS-Germania salutes Himmler beside Curt Kaul.

Official portrait of Reichsführer-SS Heinrich Himmler by his favourite photographer, Friedrich Franz Bauer. The detail of Himmler's epaulette and collar patches, unique to his position, are clearly visible. The epaulette is constructed of entwined silver bullion with a single silver oakleaf. The collar patches are silver bullion thread comprising three oakleaves enclosed in a wreath with tiny coloured glass or brass beads at the base of each sprig in the wreath.

Clockwise from top left:

Enjoying a glass of local wine with Darré.

Newly commissioned officers are presented with their SS swords.

A visit to SS-Standarte "Franken" on 23rd July 1936.

Above: Faces in the crowd: Franz Gürtner, Darré, Lütze, Himmler, Hühnlein, Heydrich, Jurgensen.

Left: A tradition of the SS was to put items for future generations sealed inside foundation stones. Here Himmler watches as a metal case containing such items is sealed before it is entombed within the foundations of a new building, possibly one at the SS riding school at Munich-Riem.

Schmitt, Wolff and Himmler on 26th February 1936.

Himmler and Prützmann, 26th February 1936.

The Heinrich Hoffmann series postcard of Himmler.

An earlier image reproduced in postcard form.

Himmler replaced Curt Wittje as Chief of the SS-Hauptamt in May 1935 as a result of homosexual activity. He was placed on "gardening leave," but was arrested by the Hamburg Gestapo in February 1938. Himmler finally ousted him from the SS on 12th November 1938.

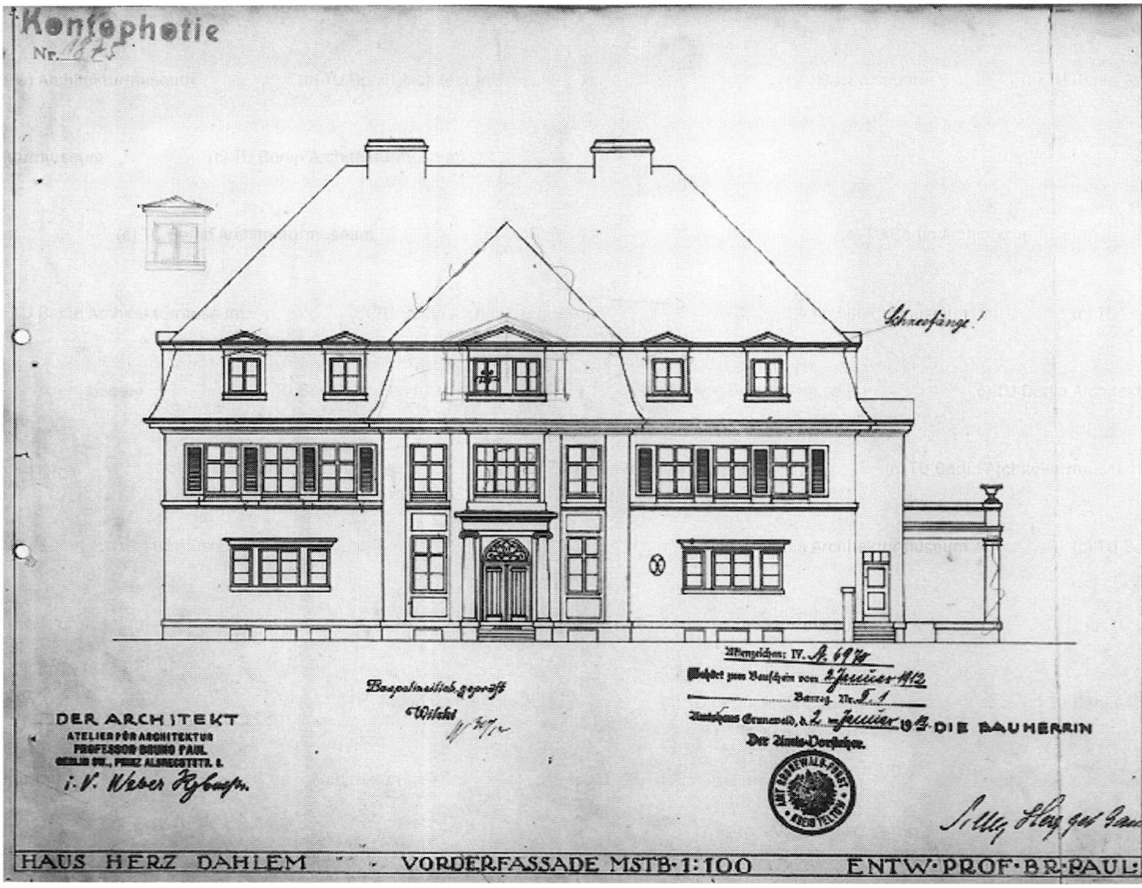

The Himmlers needed a home in Berlin and they finally settled on a large house at Dohnensteig 10 in Berlin-Dahlem. Prior to this they lived at Tiergartenstrasse 6a and Hagenstrasse 22. The house in Dohnensteig was originally called Haus Herz and it went through several renovations, including one following serious bomb damage to the roof during an Allied air raid on Berlin.

Opposite above: An immediate post-war photo of Himmler's family house at Dahlem. Note the alterations since the architectural drawing.

Opposite below: A US serviceman grabs a photo of the former home of the chief of the Gestapo. The house has since been demolished.

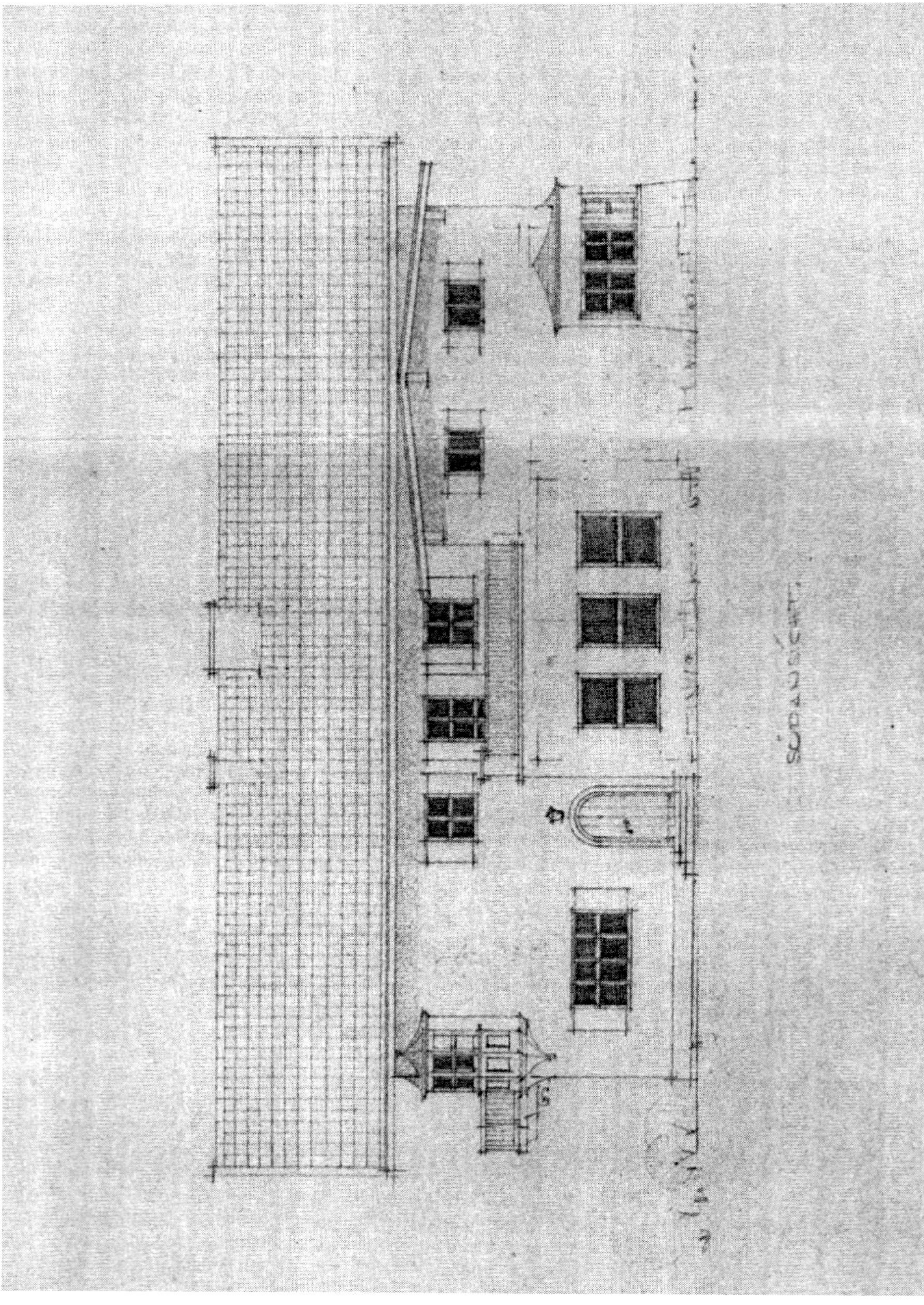

Architect plans of Himmler's family home at Gmund. Note the architect used by Himmler is the same he used to design the SS officer cadet school at Bad Tölz.

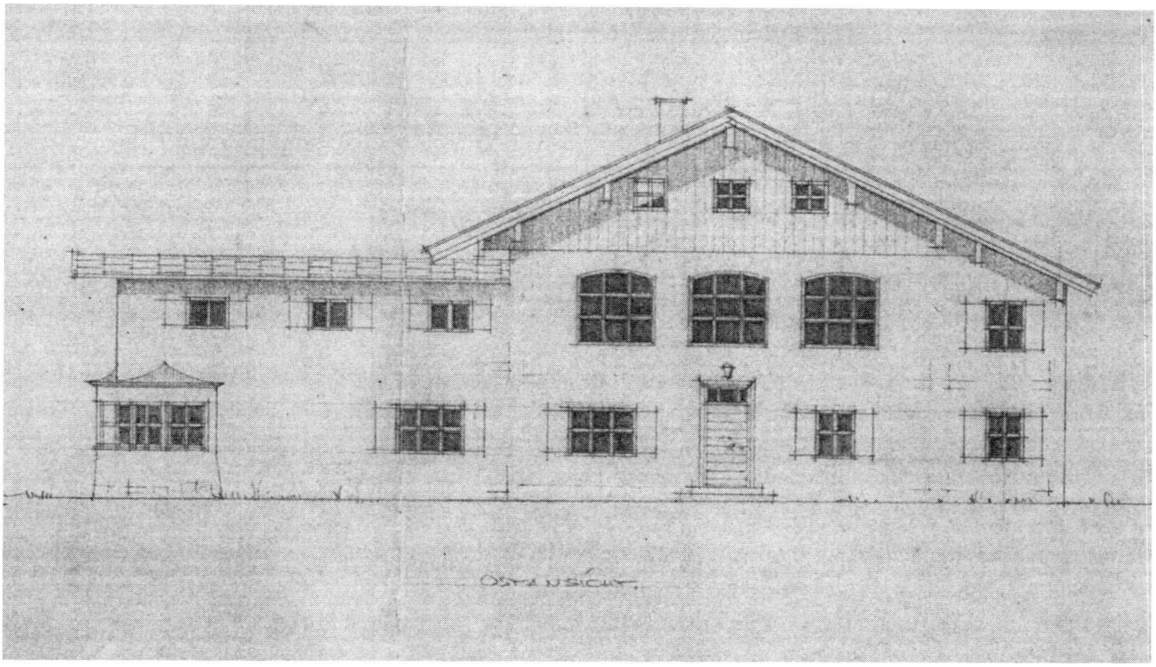
OSTANSICHT

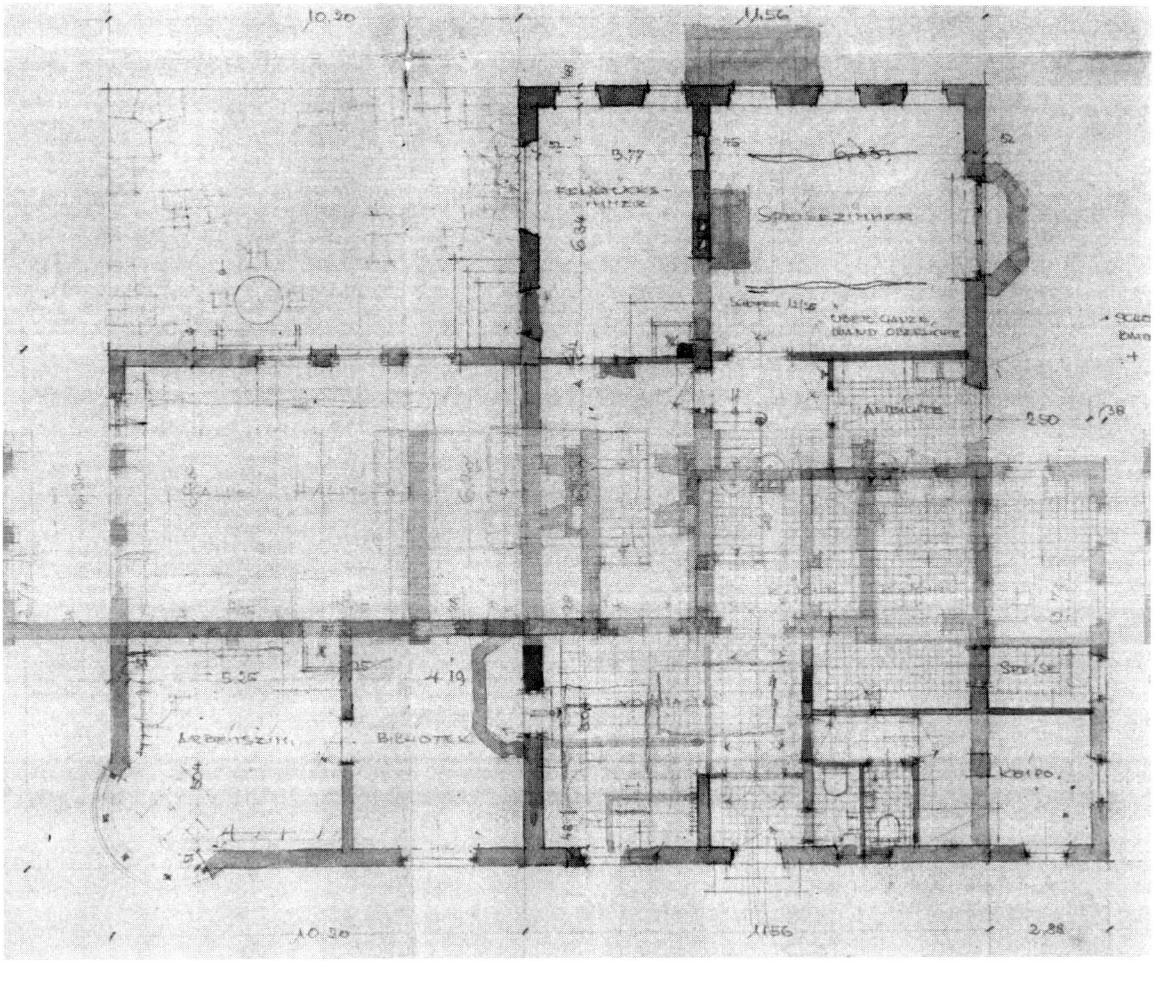
10.20
11.56
SPEISEZIMMER
ANRICHTE
VORPLATZ
ARBEITSZIM.
BIBLIOTEK
SPEISE
KORR.
10.20
11.56
2.38

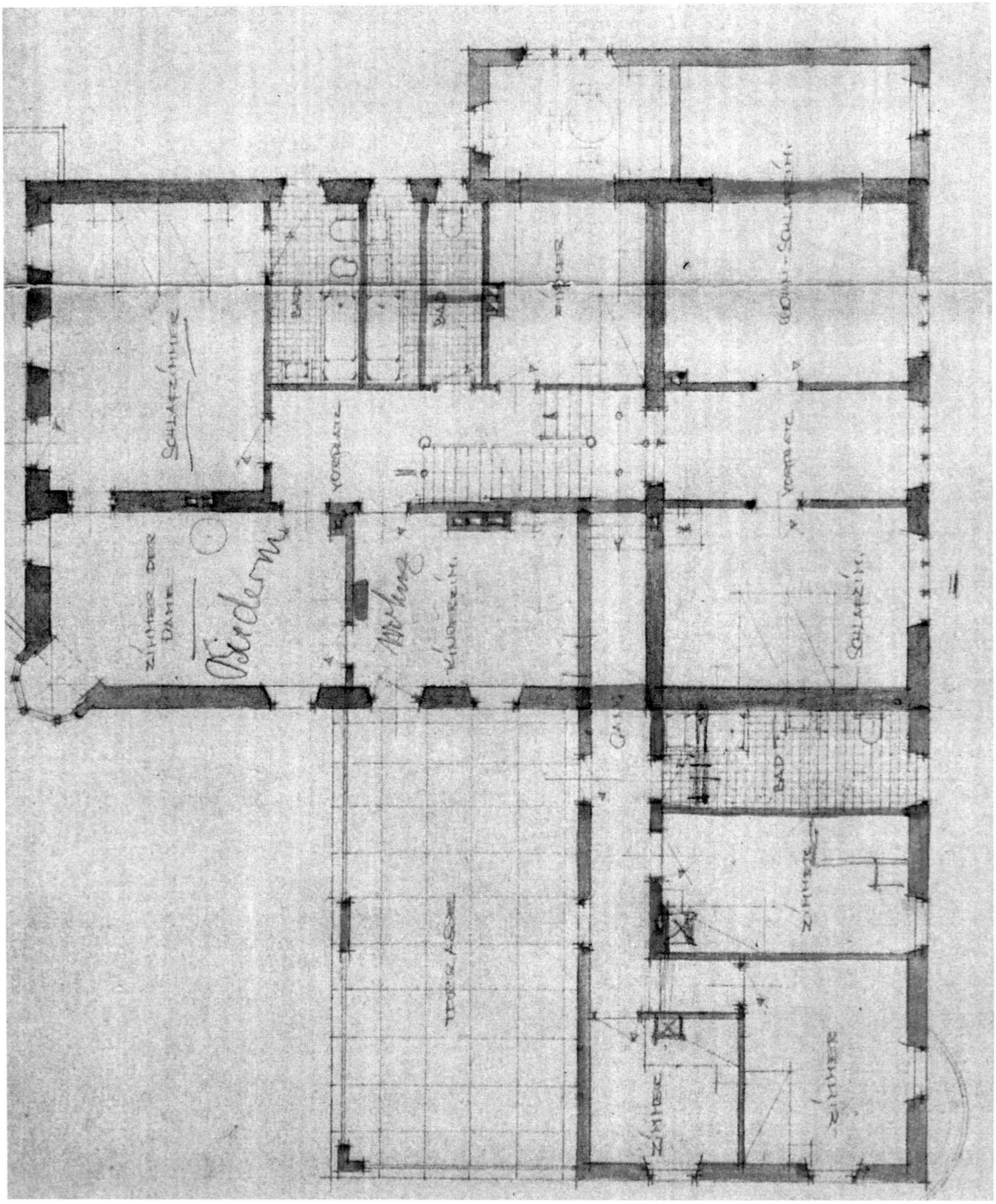

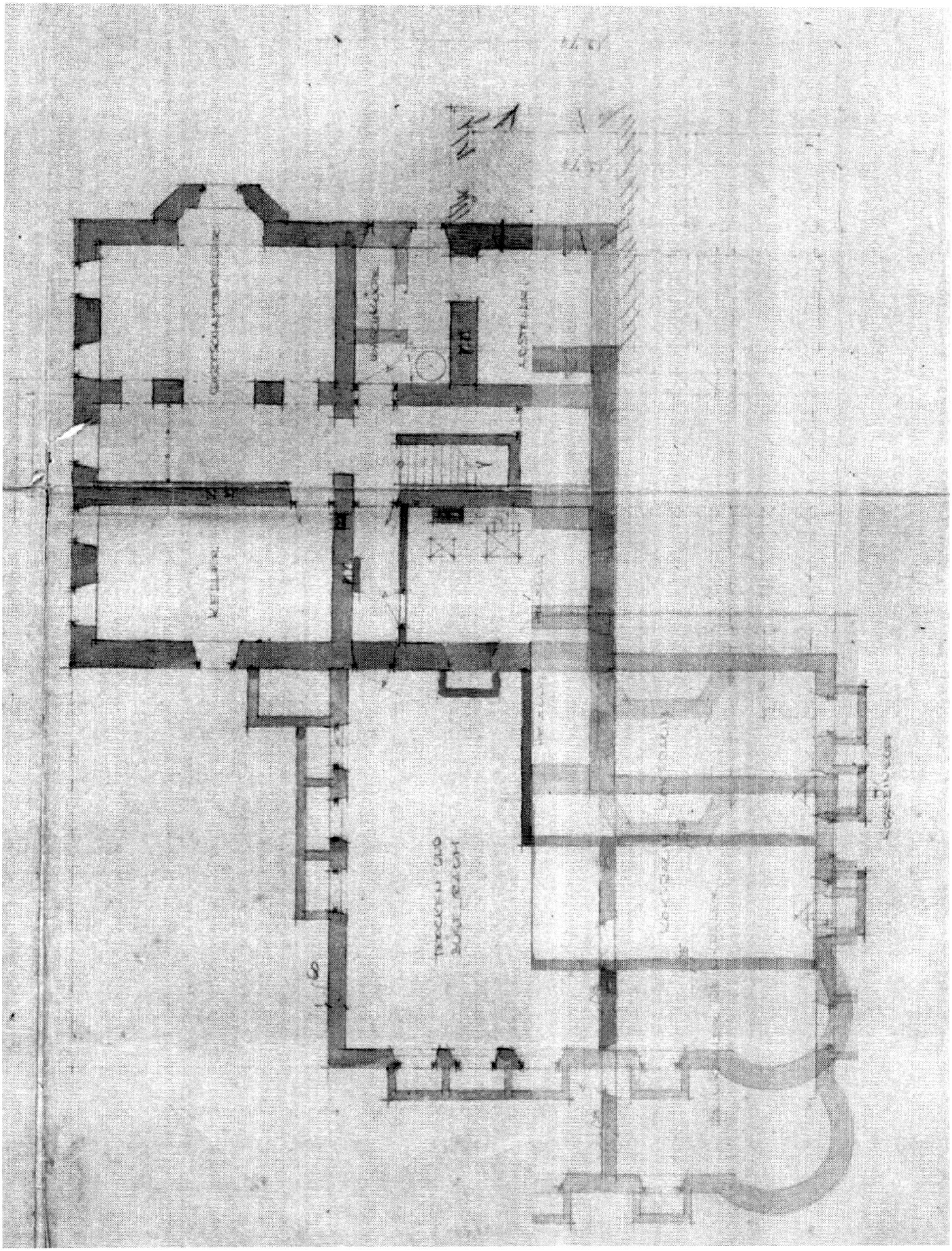

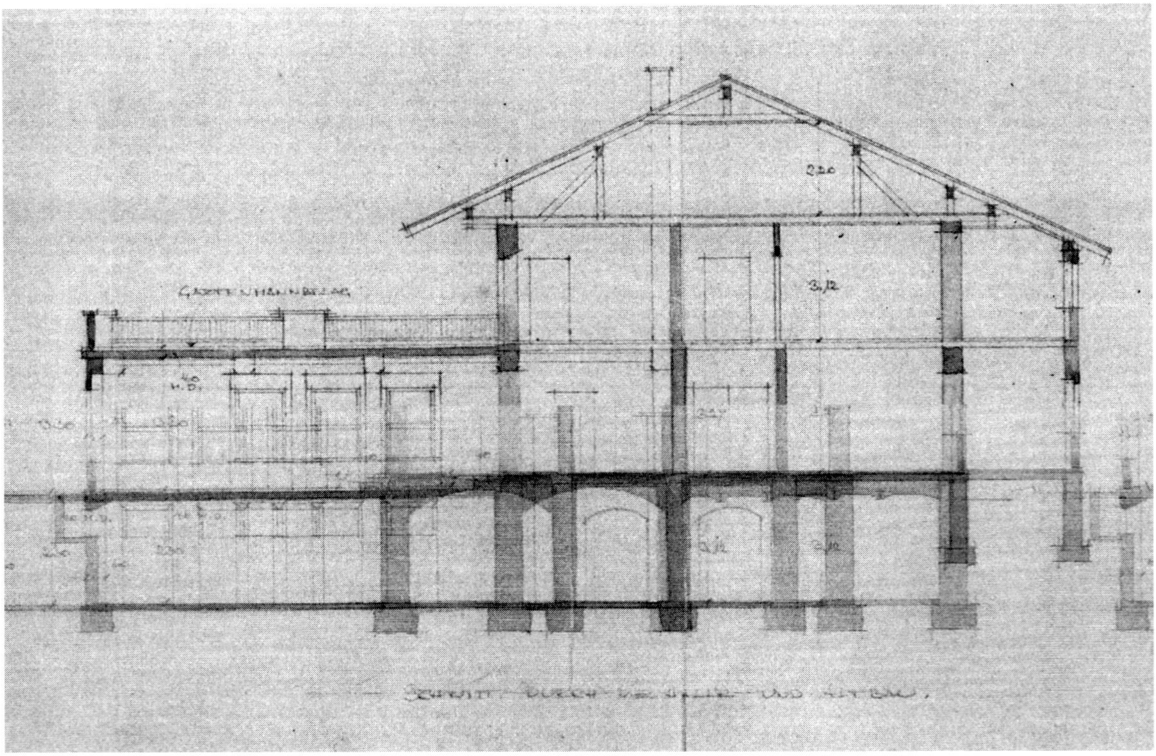
2,20
3,12

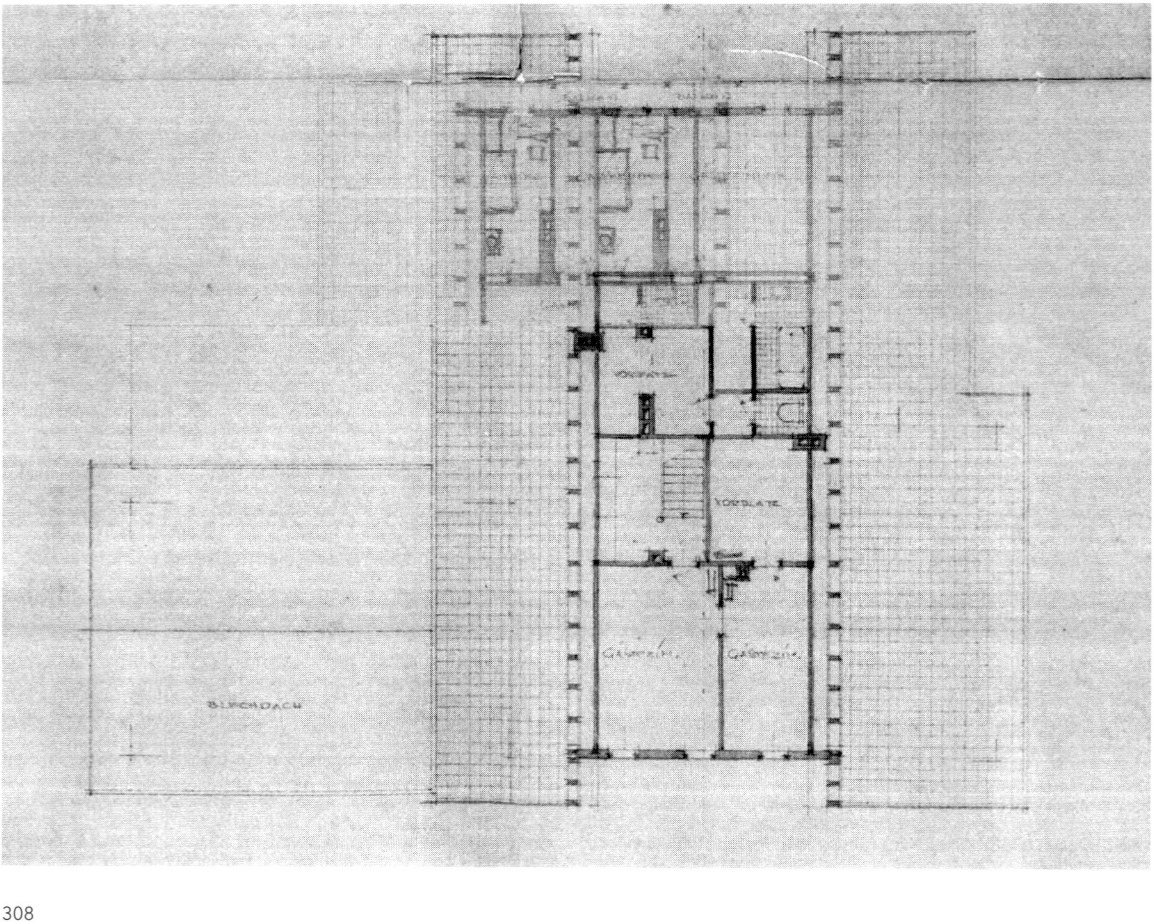
VORPLATZ
GASTZIM.
GASTZIM.
BLECHDACH

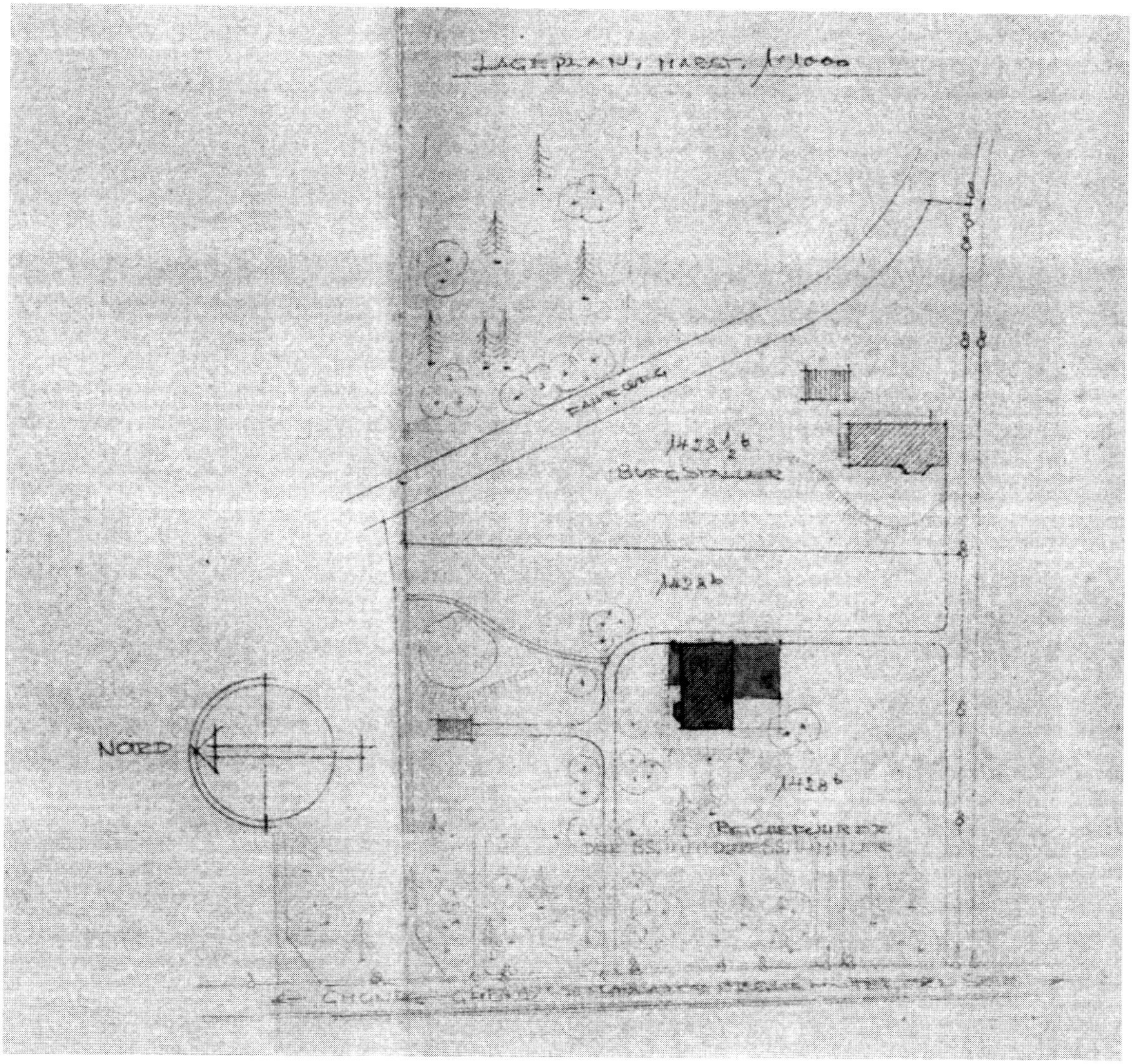
NORD

A rare photo of Himmler at Haus "Lindenfycht" with Wiligut-Weisthor (right) and Karl Wolff. Gudrun stands in front of her father and Marga is in the middle of the three women.

According to his wife, Himmler loved the house at Gmund in the snow.

Above: In this immediate post-war image taken inside "Lindenfycht," US soldiers billeted in Himmler's former home relax on his furniture and carpets whilst listening to his radio. Interior photos are extremely rare.

Right: Himmler in conversation with Burghauptmann Manfred von Knobelsdorff in the castle gardens at Wewelsburg. In the latter half of the 1930s, Himmler was a frequent visitor.

Above: Having just arrived in the inner courtyard of Wewelsburg castle, Himmler stands between Wolff and von Knobelsdorff.

Left: In the courtyard at Wewelsburg with Wolff.

Right: A local band welcomes the Reichsführer.

Below: Marga accompanied her husband to Wewelsburg on 25th May 1935. In one of the few images of Marga at the castle, Himmler escorts his wife from the castle. On his right is Heissmeyer and Heydrich is behind.

Opposite above: Himmler and Marga at Wewelsburg in 1935. The castle walls and windows are in the background, as gifts are distributed to local children.

Opposite below: Himmler and his guests in the village of Wewelsburg. On the right is Heydrich next to Marga Himmler and Hermann Bartels. Over Himmler's shoulder is Heissmeyer.

Right: The Reichsführer-SS, believed photographed in his private study at Wewelsburg. Note the rustic timber cupboards, indicative of Himmler's taste.

Below: Exiting a doorway in the castle. On the left are members of his personal staff, including his driver.

During construction work at Wewelsburg castle, Himmler listens to Hermann Bartels.

In this 1935 photo at Wewelsburg, Himmler speaks to Dr Bernhard Frank who was placed in command of the Obersalzberg complex during the war.

Himmler was happy to play host to visitors at Wewelsburg. In 1937, one such high profile visitor was Reichsleiter Dr Robert Ley.

Looking over the dry moat. Bartels on the right.

Dr Ley flanked by Himmler and Wolff in the castle gardens.

A short drive outside the village with a view of the castle's imposing position in the background.

Himmler took Dr Ley to an archeological site of a Germanic burial ground in the nearby forest at Böddeken.

Himmler arrives for a double wedding reception at the Dorfgemeinschafthaus, now known as the Ottenshof. The building in the background was then Ebbers Bakery and still stands in the village today. Above the windows are carved heads, some say depicting the SS staff from the castle.

Above: Inside the building, Himmler with von Knobelsdorff.

Left: Himmler enjoys a cigar in the gallery of the Wewelsburg Dorfgemeinschafthaus.

Right: Himmler chats with the Wewelsburg village postman.

Below: The arrival of the two brides and their grooms, both of whom were attached to the staff of the SS School Wewelsburg.

Above: The guest of honour sits between the two brides.

Left: Reinhard Heydrich with an SS aide walking in the village at Wewelsburg.

Himmler not only ordered extensive building work on the castle, but also construction and renovations in the village itself.

Here men of the Reichs-Arbeitsdienst seem to be enjoying their labours renovating a village roof.

Left: When the time came to replace von Knobelsdorff as Burghauptmann, Himmler selected a member of Heydrich's staff from the SD. Siegfried Taubert fitted the requirements and he was duly installed at the castle.

Below: Siegfried Taubert wears a white SS summer tunic in this 1943 photo. Next to him is his son-in-law, Ernst-Robert Grawitz, with the castle housekeeper, Elfriede Wippermann between him and Max von Herff.

Clockwise from top left:

Himmler's father died in October 1936. At his funeral in Munich on 31st October, Himmler and his brother Ernst follow their mother out of the chapel. Marga Himmler is behind her husband.

Anna Himmler is assisted at her husband's gravesite. Behind her are Ernst Himmler, Paula Himmler and Heinrich Himmler. Note the attendance of men from the SS-Totenkopf Standarte.

The mourners pay their respects after the internment.

Opposite above: Himmler's hunting companions on this trip include Kurt Daluege, Sepp Dietrich and Reinhard Heydrich.

Opposite below: Himmler (centre, in light raincoat) in conversation with Heydrich. In the foreground is Daluege and left, with the spaniel dog, is Dietrich.

Left: Himmler's favourite pastime was hunting and he took every opportunity to hunt in what little spare time his duties allowed.

Below: Himmler owned a private hunting lodge at Valepp on the German-Austrian border, south of Tegernsee. (Modern photograph.)

Dietrich and Himmler chat while Heydrich listens far right.

The group move off for the shoot. Far right is Daluege, next to Wolff, Dietrich and Himmler.

The hunting party. Daluege centre, Dietrich left and Heydrich right centre.

Himmler examines the kill.

Opposite above: An off-duty moment with Marga.

Opposite below: This photograph at an unidentified location was taken on 24th or 25th April 1937.

Left: Himmler with an unidentified hunt companion.

Below: Himmler takes the wheel with Wolff as a front seat passenger.

Himmler takes a meal with Walter Krüger, Wolff and Schmitt.

Opposite: Sepp Dietrich, Hitler and Himmler listen to the band of the Leibstandarte-SS "Adolf Hitler" in the doorway of the old Reich Chancellery in Berlin, 20th April 1937.

Left: Hitler receives a gift of a painting from his loyal Reichsführer, with Dietrich and Wolff looking on.

Below: As Hitler salutes the Leibstandarte-SS "Adolf Hitler" in Wilhelmstrasse, Berlin, Himmler and Sepp Dietrich stand in front of the Führer's car.

Right: With the Reich Youth Leader, Baldur von Schirach.

Below: Mussolini arrived in Berlin in September 1937.

Above: Seated are Ritter von Epp, Himmler, Gauleiter Otto Hellmuth and Ernst Heinrich Schmauser.

Left: A photo from 1937/38 showing Himmler inspecting SS men with Theodor Eicke and Max Simon, probably at Dachau. Note the smoking furnace stack and camp entrance in the far background.

Opposite above: On 29th April 1938, Gauleiter Josef Terboven was injured when his aircraft crashed at Essen-Mülheim airport. The pilot was killed, but Terboven and the radio operator were hospitalised. The deputy Gauleiter, Fritz Schlessmann, escaped with minor injuries. Hitler visited Terboven in hospital accompanied in this photo by Sepp Dietrich, Dr Karl Brandt, Himmler, Otto Dietrich, Wolff, Gauleiter Grohe, Bodenschatz and Schaub.

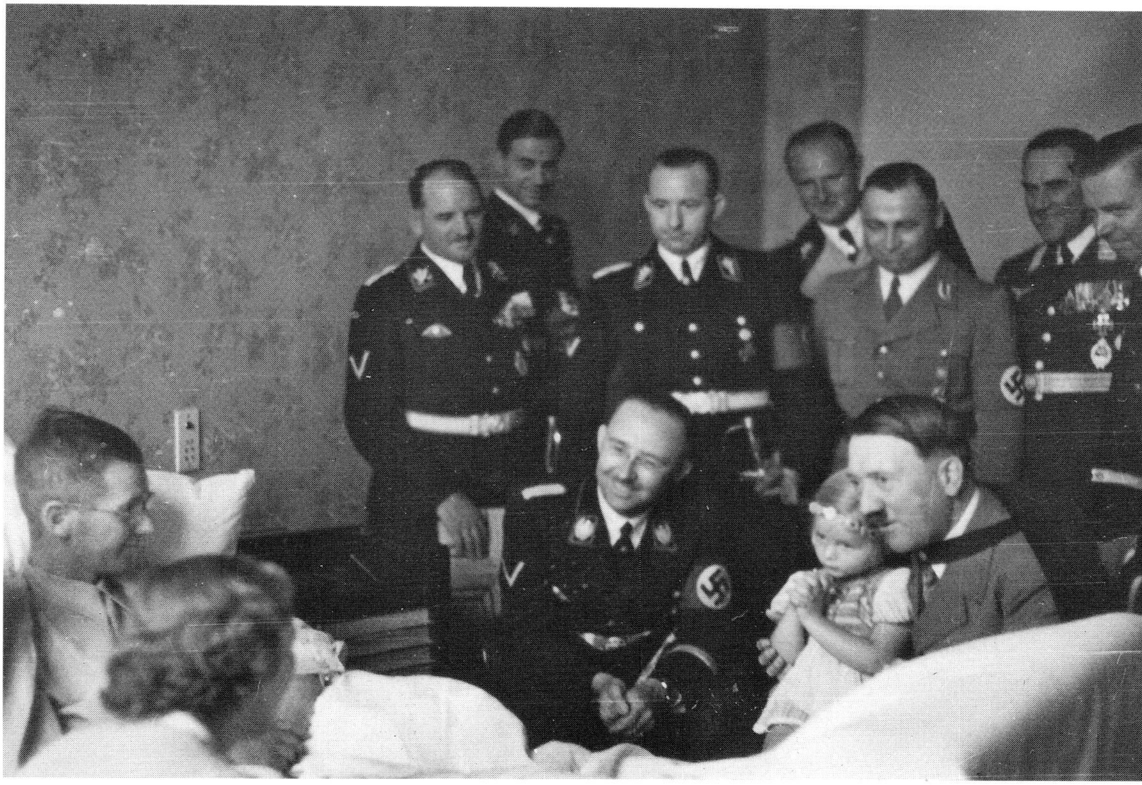

Below: Hitler pulls a funny face for Terboven's young daughter as Terboven, Himmler, the doctors, Schaub and Weitzel look on amused.

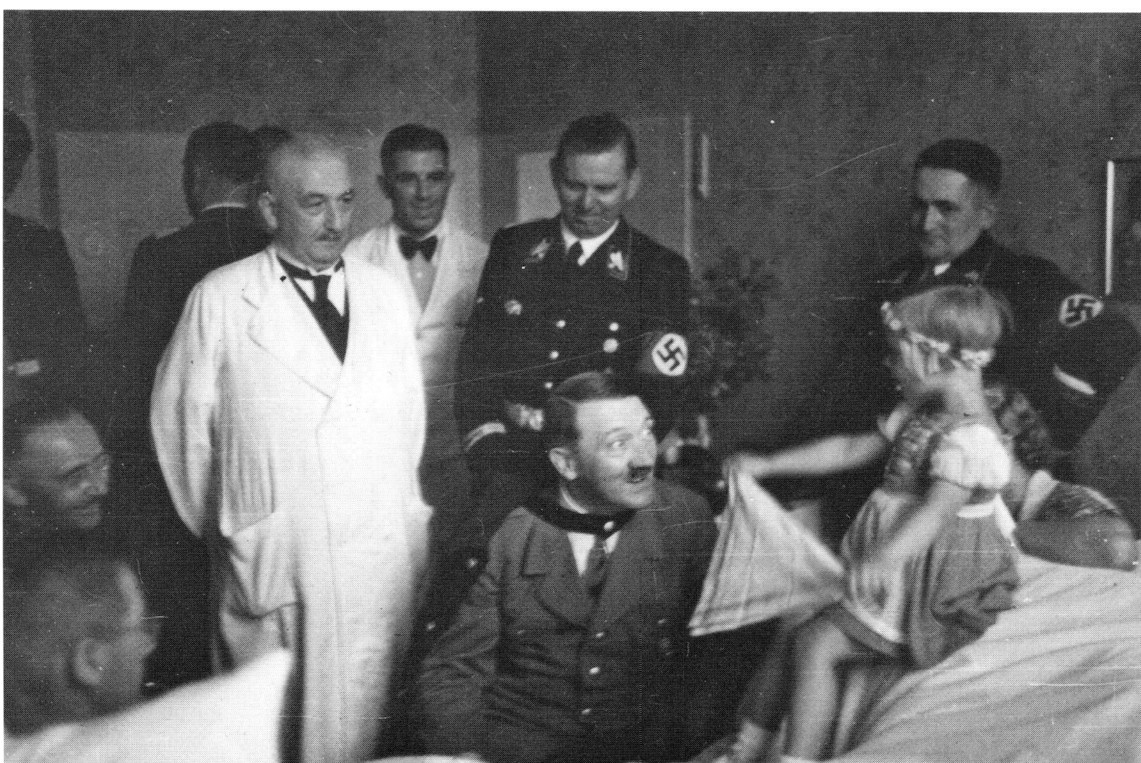

Clockwise from top left:

As Himmler's public profile heightened, so did the threat of assassination. He chose a police detective, Josef "Sepp" Kiermaier, as his personal close protection officer. Kiermaier was attached to the RSD (Reichssicherheitsdienst) which was responsible for guarding all high profile Nazi leaders including Hitler. The RSD wore SS uniform and held SS or police rank. It was commanded by Johannes Rattenhuber who was subordinate to Himmler, but in effect the Reichsführer had little control over the RSD.

Himmler and Paul Hausser at a march past of SS-Standarte "Deutschland," commanded by Felix Steiner (in helmet, right.) Wollf stands on the left.

Another photo of Himmler with Felix Steiner.

Himmler, Wolff and Jeckeln in conversation with NSDAP functionaries.

A relaxed and smiling Himmler enjoying the sun.

Darré and Himmler.

Guest of the navy in Wilhelmshaven.

Himmler chats to the commander of the SS mounted unit of SS-Abschnitt IV. Note the sleeve insignia of a cavalry unit.

Himmler (far left) watches as Hitler greets several SS generals in dress uniform.

Gertrud Scholz-Klink, the Nazi women's leader, sits next to Hitler during the festival for German Women during a Nuremberg rally. A postcard from the time.

An undated photo of a smiling Himmler as dinner guest.

Himmler listens as Hitler addresses the gathered SS men. The location of this photograph is in dispute. Some suggest it is Wewelsburg, but there is no evidence to suggest that Hitler ever visited the castle. Some suggest it is Quedlinburg, but the staircase cannot be located there. This particular photograph bears the original pencil signature of the photographer, Friedrich Franz Bauer.

Hitler inspects a guard of honour formed by the Schutzpolizei.

Hitler takes the salute at the march past of the Leibstandarte-SS "Adolf Hitler" on 30th January 1938 in Wilhelmstrasse. Hess, Dietrich and Himmler stand beside the car.

Hitler arrives for a session of the Reichstag at the Kroll opera house, accompanied by Himmler and Wolff.

Hitler receives the adulation of the crowd at an unidentified location, possibly Nuremberg. Far left is Fritz Weitzel.

The RFSS in Hamburg. Next to him in the car is Gauleiter Karl Kaufmann, with Prützmann and Lorenz beside it.

Above: A motorcycle unit put on a display. Left to right: Lorenz, Himmler, Bassewitz-Behr, Prützmann and Pancke.

Right: Werner von Blomberg with his new wife, Erna Gruhn, a typist with whom he had fallen in love. Hitler and Göring had been witnesses at their wedding.

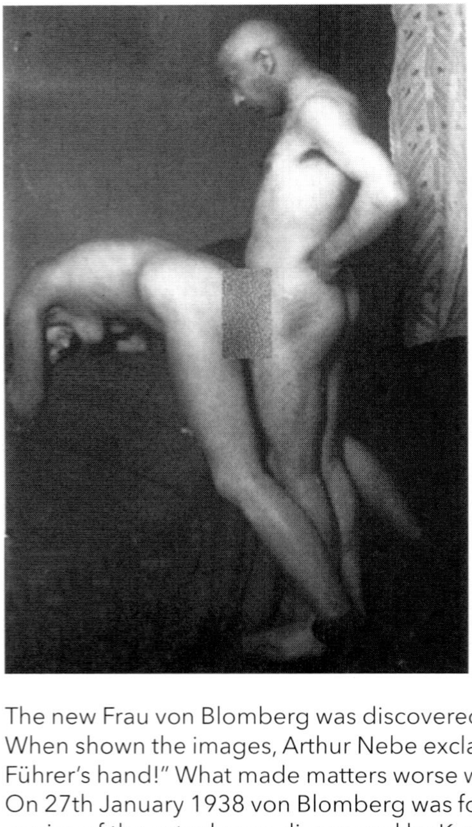

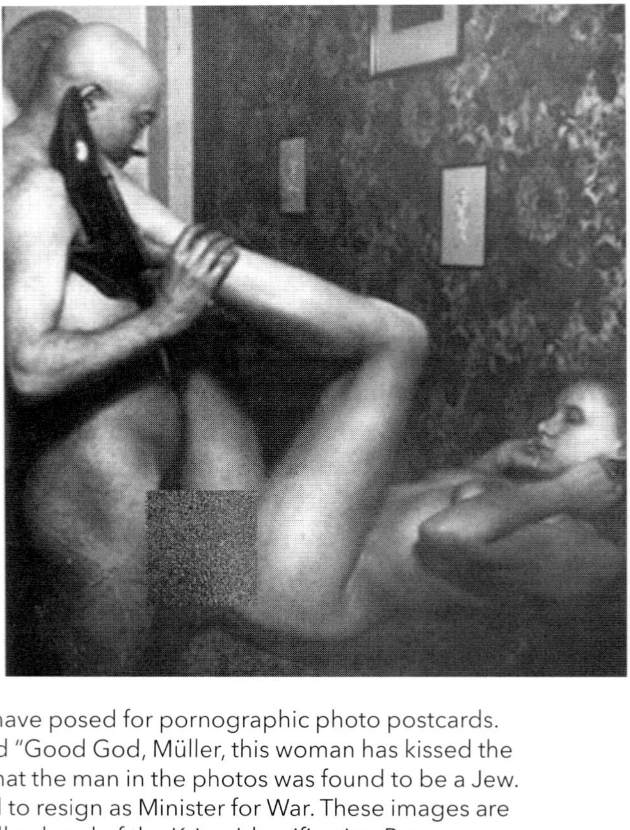

The new Frau von Blomberg was discovered to have posed for pornographic photo postcards. When shown the images, Arthur Nebe exclaimed "Good God, Müller, this woman has kissed the Führer's hand!" What made matters worse was that the man in the photos was found to be a Jew. On 27th January 1938 von Blomberg was forced to resign as Minister for War. These images are copies of the actual ones discovered by Kurt Müller, head of the Kripo Identification Bureau.

Left: The head of the army, Generaloberst Werner von Fritsch, was an old school officer of the Reichswehr. When falsely accused by Himmler and Heydrich of homosexuality, he did not shrink from a fight and insisted on a court of honour where he was exonerated. The SS was shown to have falsified evidence and Himmler's position became very tenuous. The honourable general was killed in action in Poland.

Right: Himmler photographed in Rome on 18th October 1937 with the German ambassador Ulrich von Hassell and Italian Chief of Police Bocchini. Daluege, Wolff and Heydrich behind.

Himmler and his party are taken to historical sites and memorials in Rome.

Mussolini and Himmler during a visit to Italy. Far right is Heydrich.

On the right in this war date photo is Eugen Dollmann, standing on the rail platform at Hitler's headquarters in East Prussia. Dollmann was Himmler's and Hitler's interpreter in Italian. He was also the German officer secretly recorded in conversation with Karl Wolff at the Allied interrogation centre on 22nd May 1945.

Above: In July 1937, Himmler established the Buchenwald concentration camp on the Ettersberg near Weimar. In this photo Himmler visits the small zoo at the camp which the commandant, Karl Otto Koch, set up just outside the protective custody compound. Left to right are Paul Hennicke, Himmler, Ludolf von Alvensleben, Theodor Eicke and Karl Koch. The camp perimeter wire is just visible behind them and a prisoner can be seen between Eicke and Koch.

Right: Karl Otto Koch was typical of the men selected by Himmler to command his camp empire. Koch had seen previous service at the infamous Columbia House wild camp in Berlin and had also served at Esterwegen and Sachsenhausen. He married Ilse Köhler, a secretary who had worked at Sachsenhausen. She later gained notoriety as the infamous "Bitch of Buchenwald."

Above: The NSDAP had many branches in other countries other than Germany. It was particularly strong in Austria where it was a prohibited party and therefore political uniforms were not allowed. Himmler inspects a parade of SS men, most likely Austrians.

Left: The staunch Austrian Nazi, Arthur Seyss-Inquart, was appointed as Austrian Chancellor on 11th March 1938. Two days later he invited Hitler to take the reigns of power and the Greater Reich was born. He later held high positions in occupied Poland and Holland.

Above: Himmler, Wolff and Schaub accompany Hitler during a visit. Behind Hitler are Josef Bürckel and Arthur Seyss-Inquart.

Right: Himmler and Heydrich leave the Hotel Metropole in Vienna having arrived immediately to establish a foothold in power. Both wear the new field grey uniform which soon was to become Himmler's everyday dress.

Hitler salutes at a military march past. Also in attendance are Keitel, Himmler, von Brauchitsch, Milch and Seyss-Inquart.

Vienna, March 1938. Himmler inspects units of the Austrian police. Left to right: Wolff, Steinhäusl, Heydrich, Kaltenbrunner, Bürckel, Fitzhum, Himmler and Daluege.

Above: Himmler takes the salute in Vienna.

Right: Himmler visits the graves of the "July martyrs" executed for the attempted Putsch in July 1934 when Engelbert Dollfuss was murdered. Behind him is Dr Ernst Kaltenbrunner.

Left: The most powerful SS man in Austria was Dr Ernst Kaltenbrunner.

Below: Recruiting for the SS. Medical examination of candidates. Below left is Werner Lorenz and behind Himmler sits Arthur Seyss-Inquart. Far right is a very young adjutant, Jochen Peiper.

Above: Himmler attends an evening function of the Vienna NSDAP. In the centre, in brown shirts, are Josef Fitzhum and Odilo Globocnik. Far right is Seyss-Inquart and the ever-present Wolff is just visible bottom left.

Right: Heydrich and Himmler went about setting up an office in Vienna to administer emigration of Jews. Adolf Eichmann was selected to take charge.

Himmler photographed in Hof where Richard Wendler (right) was mayor. Behind Wendler is Heydrich.

Hitler arrives by train to the sounds of a military band. Following him are Schmundt, Engel, Himmler, Heissmeyer and Wolff.

Right: Hitler greets the Reichsführer-SS on the steps at the Berghof.

Below: Himmler went to great lengths to mark the birthdays of senior Nazi figures and on special occasions. This particular event was Göring's 46th birthday in January 1939 when he presented representatives of the SS senior leadership. Left to right: Heissmeyer, Daluege, Himmler, Heydrich, Nebe, Wolff, Best, Lorenz, von Alvensleben and Pancke.

Opposite above: This time the congratulations are for Hitler on his birthday. Himmler looks on as Hitler greets Heissmeyer. Also watching are Meissner, Heydrich, Wolff and Daluege.

Opposite below: In the anteroom at the Reich Chancellery, Otto Meissner explains something to Himmler, Wolff, Heydrich, Heissmeyer and Daluege. Note the detail on the SS swords worn by Heissmeyer and Daluege, the latter in police uniform with SS runes below his left breast pocket denoting full membership of the SS. Also of interest is Himmler's leather pistol holder, indicating that weapons were not removed at this time.

Himmler offers Göring a personal greeting. The two men were bitter rivals for power in Hitler's regime.

Mussolini relied a great deal on his son-in-law, the dashing and handsome Count Galeazzo Ciano.

Hitler courted the support of Mussolini and both leaders exchanged diplomatic visits. Here Mussolini is in Munich with Ciano.

The Munich crisis brought Europe close to war. During a pause in negotiations in the Führerbau, the main Axis partners discuss the carving up of Czechoslovakia. Left to right: Keitel, Mussolini, Hitler, Morell, Bormann, Göring, Himmler, Hess and Bodenschatz.

Hitler leaves the Führerbau.
Himmler talks to Krause.

Himmler and Sir Neville Henderson, the British ambassador in Berlin from 1937 until 1939. Henderson totally misjudged Hitler's intentions and encouraged Neville Chamberlain to agree to Hitler's demands at Munich. He died from cancer in December 1942.

The Sudeten Germans were led by Konrad Henlein and his deputy Karl Hermann Frank. Frank joined the SS on 1st November 1938 and was attached to the Staff of the RFSS with the rank of SS-Brigadeführer. Three days later he was appointed as Deputy Gauleiter of the Sudetenland.

Konrad Henlein was appointed Gauleiter of the Sudeten Gau on 30th October 1938. He had already joined the SS on 9th October 1938 and was accorded the rank of SS-Gruppenführer.

Above: Himmler's relationship with von Ribbentrop (far right) in the late 1930s can be described as cordial and Marga Himmler got on well with Annelise von Ribbentrop (third from left.) During his time as German Ambassador in London, von Ribbentrop developed a rapport with highly placed pro-Nazi British citizens. In this photo Lord and Lady Londonderry (centre) visit the von Ribbentrops. These connections would become useful when relations between the two countries subsequently became strained.

Right: Herschel Grynzpan, a young Jew of Polish descent living in Paris, was incensed by the treatment of his family by the German government, resulting in him entering the German embassy in Paris on 7th November 1938 and fatally shooting a legation third secretary, Ernst vom Rath. Goebbels used the assassination as an excuse to unleash the attacks on Jewish property and synagogues known as "Krystallnacht" or the "night of broken glass." This photo shows vom Rath (X) as a member of the SA.

Albert Sauer. In August 1938, Oswald Pohl, acting on orders from Himmler, opened a new camp at the Wiener-Graben quarry in Mauthausen near Linz, Austria. The first commandant, Sauer, was ordered to provide stone for the SS company DEST (Deutsche Erd-und Steinwerke GmbH) of which Pohl was chief executive.

Oswald Pohl, chief of the SS-Wirtschafts-Verwaltungshauptamt (SS Main Economic and Administrative Department) was the brain behind the SS economic empire. All concentration camps were placed under his jurisdiction in Amt D of his central office.

The Inspector of Concentration Camps in Amt D of the SS-WVHA was Richard Glücks. He was deputy inspector under Theodor Eicke and replaced Eicke when the latter transferred to combat duty commanding the SS-Totenkopf units in the SS-VT and Waffen-SS.

Himmler visits Totenkopf. Behind him is Theodor Eicke.

An extremely rare photograph of the "T" building in Oranienburg at the time it housed the inspectorate of concentration camps. Glücks ruled the entire camp system from his office on the first floor of this building above the main entrance. Note the two sentry boxes either side of the entrance. The building has a further wing at the rear in the centre, at 90 degrees to the front, giving rise to its nickname. It is situated around 500 metres from the gatehouse of Sachsenhausen concentration camp and today it is occupied by a local government office. On the far left of the photo one can see the trees in the garden of the Glücks villa.

Opposite below: In 1939, Pohl replaced Sauer as commandant of Mauthausen with Franz Ziereis. He remained in charge until the camp was liberated in 1945. Here, Ziereis (centre) shows Himmler around a camp workshop.

Right: Himmler with his wife at an exhibition. Peiper is on the right.

Below: Himmler is shown an unusual sculpture at an art exhibition.

There is little doubt over how much Himmler cared for his daughter, taking opportunities to return to Gmund when duties allowed. It is difficult to equate the conscientious father with the man who held power of life and death over thousands.

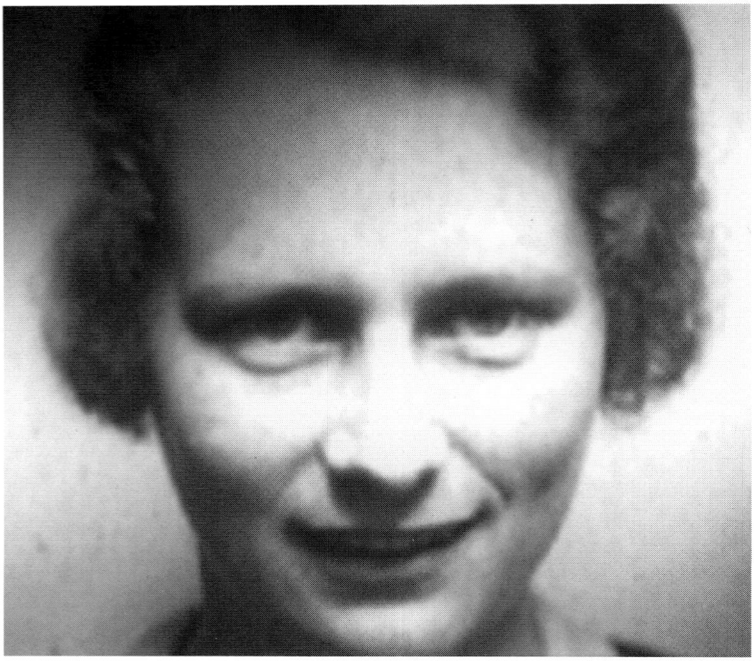

In the autumn of 1935, Hedwig Potthast joined the staff of the newspaper room at Prinz-Albrecht-Strasse 8 in Berlin. Dissatisfied with her duties, she transferred to Himmler's personal office as a secretary, eventually aspiring to the position of principle private secretary. Himmler liked his secretary who was 12 years his junior and the two developed a close relationship which eventually became sexual. Himmler's marriage had become loveless on his part and the young Hedwig filled a void.

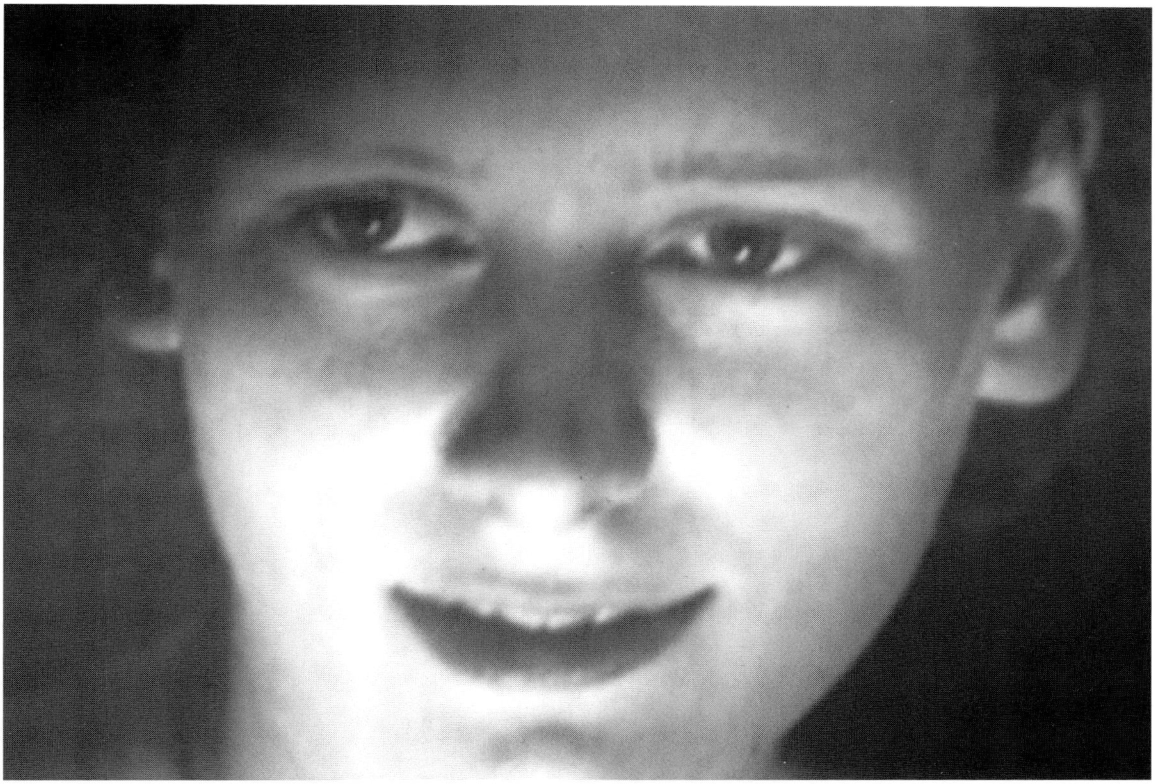

Above: Known photographs of Hedwig are extremely rare. Himmler kept her a guarded secret and he never referred to her in his diaries. There is no doubt that the couple loved each other deeply and she bore him two children, a boy and a girl. Hedwig continued to shun publicity after the war and she died in obscurity in the 1990s.

Right: Hedwig answered to the pet name "Hä'schen" by which she was known in Himmler's immediate close circle.

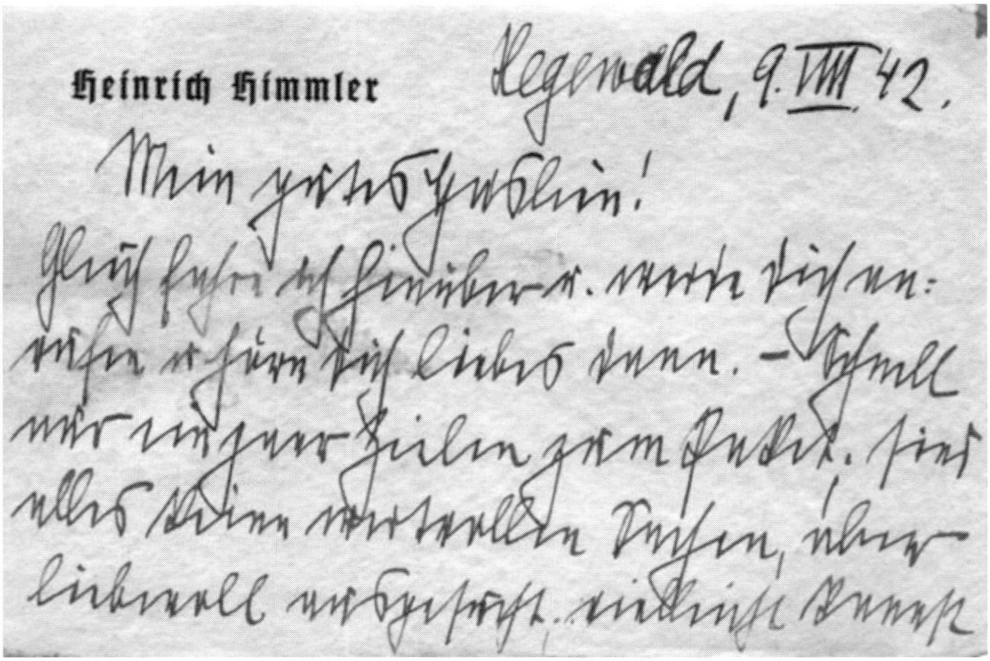

Heinrich Himmler

Hegewald, 9. VIII 42.

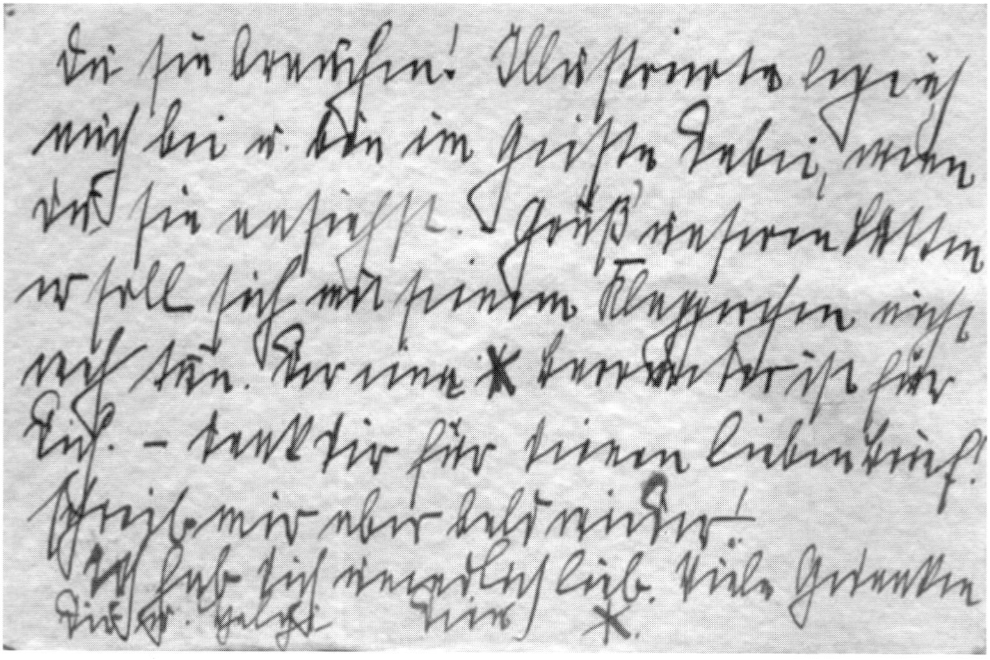

A handwritten correspondence card sent from Himmler at Hegewaldheim to Hedwig on 9th August 1942. Himmler mentions their newborn son, Helge and signs with a runic "h." In full, "Hegewald, 9. VIII 42. My dear little bunny! I'm about to drive over and will call you and hear your dear voice. Quickly just a few lines regarding the parcel, they are all without value but chosen with love; perhaps you can use them! An illustrated magazine is also enclosed and I'll be with you in spirit when you look at it. * Say hello to our sweet one; hope he does not hurt himself with his rattle. The barometer is for you. – Thank you for your dear letter! Write again soon! I love you forever. Many thoughts of you and Walchi. Your *."

Above: Himmler set up a home for his second family at Schönau near Königsee. He obtained the money to pay for it with a loan from the NSDAP arranged by Martin Bormann. The location provided him with ease of access when Hitler was in residence at the nearby Berghof. Unlike Marga, Hedwig was popular with those close to Hitler and she became good friends with Gerda Bormann. (Modern photo of Haus Schneewinkel-Lehen at Schönau.)

Right: Hedwig's Berlin apartment was in this block at Bismarckstrasse.

Above: In 1942, Himmler decided he needed a small country retreat near Berlin. He chose an area called Brückentin in Mecklenburg and concentration camp inmates were tasked with building a secluded love nest for him and Hedwig. It was close to Pohl's residence at Gut Comthurey and Hedwig soon became good friends with Eleonore Pohl. The building still exists with various structural alterations and is today part of a youth summer camp. (Modern photo.)

Left: Himmler had to keep his relationship with Hedwig Potthast discreet and he gave one of his personal staff, Paul Baumert, the role of liaising between him and his mistress. Correspondence between the two passed through Baumert's hands and if Hedwig had any problems she could contact Baumert who was generally always available in Berlin.

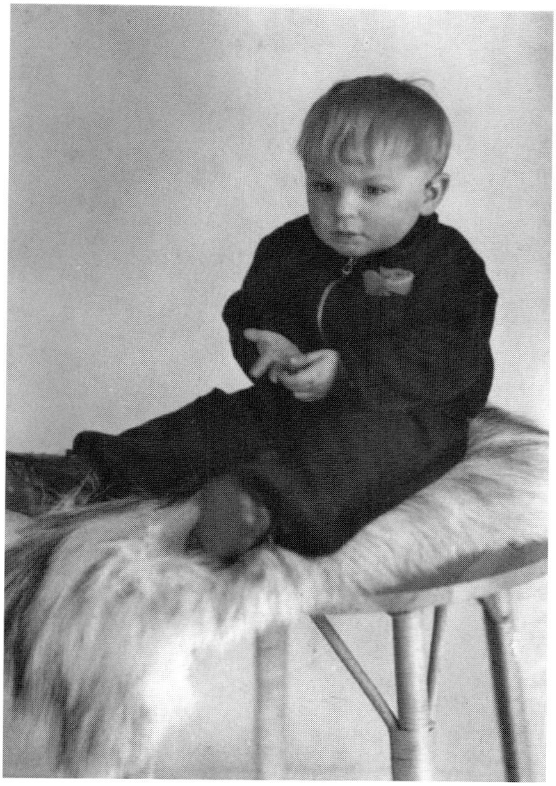

Clockwise from top left:

Helge, Himmler's son by Hedwig Potthast.

Helge Potthast, born 5th February 1942. Both he and his sister, Nanette Dorothea born at Hohenlychen on 3rd June 1944, continued to be protected from publicity by their mother during and after the war. Consequently, photos of Himmler's illegitimate children are very rare. Helge has striking feature similarities to his father as a small child.

A private photo of Himmler in his Berlin office, obtained from and signed on the back by his daughter Gudrun. Note the heavy safe in the background.

The tenth anniversary of Himmler's appointment as Reichsführer-SS occurred on 6th January 1939. The SS marked the occasion with anniversary celebrations, congratulatory messages and articles published in the press. One of the more satirical contributions was produced with authority of the office of the RFSS, but the content carried a political message.

Right: 6th January 1939 at the Berghof. Hitler and Himmler lead a group for a walk to the teahouse. At the top of the steps, in plus-fours, is Dr Karl Brandt.

Below: In this undated photograph, the Reichsführer is in a hurry beside what appears to be an autobahn.

Above: On 12th January 1939, Himmler presented senior members of the SS to Hitler in his study at the new Reich Chancellery in Berlin. Left to right: Heissmeyer, Daluege, Heydrich, Wolff, Pancke, Himmler and Hitler.

Left: On 14th February 1939, Himmler was in Hamburg at the launch ceremony of the battleship Bismarck, the pride of the German navy. Seen here at the launch with Gauleiter Karl Kaufmann.

Clockwise from top left:

One of the new breed of favoured SS men was Gottlob Berger. An SS officer since 1936, Himmler soon recognised his organisational talents and by 1940 he had replaced Heissmeyer as chief of the SS-Hauptamt. Berger can be described as the mastermind behind the multi-national Waffen-SS.

Eric von dem Bach-Zelewski had a reputation for being a ruthless leader. He was delegated with responsibility for anti-partisan warfare. Disliked by many of his SS peers, he attracted outright contempt after giving evidence at Nuremberg.

Heydrich's wife complained that her husband always seemed to be pushing Himmler along in front of him and had to put up with some of Himmler's crank ideas.

An officer who did himself no favours was Udo von Woyrsch. Genuinely liked by Himmler who protected him, von Woyrsch continually antagonised his fellow SS officers by his arrogant behaviour. During the Polish campaign, troops under the command of von Woyrsch attracted complaints from the military high command for their excesses.

The man that Himmler came to rely upon increasingly was his personal advisor, Dr Rudolf Brandt. Often incorrectly referred to as Himmler's secretary, a lawyer by profession, he soon became Himmler's eyes and ears, generally remaining in Berlin and administering his personal correspondence. Usually recognisable by his spectacles, Brandt appears to vainly remove them for posed photograph sittings. As Himmler's responsibilities increased, Brandt became more indispensable, often appending his own signature in reply to letters or on outgoing mail in Himmler's name. It was as a result of this practice that he became implicated in medical experiments in the camps for which he was eventually hanged In Landsberg Prison on 2nd June 1948.

Right: In February 1939, Himmler was a guest of the Polish police in Warsaw. A smiling Reichsführer gives no hint of the impending disaster that awaited his hosts less than seven months away.

Below: On a wet and misty morning, 3rd October 1938, Himmler's entourage waits at the frontier to cross into the Sudetenland. Himmler has alighted and is probably with Hitler off camera. Visible in the vehicle are Heissmeyer, Lorenz, Wolff, von Woyrsch, Heydrich, Daluege and Bastian the driver.

Hitler in the courtyard of Hradcany Castle in Prague. Apparently Himmler was suffering from catarrgh at the time.

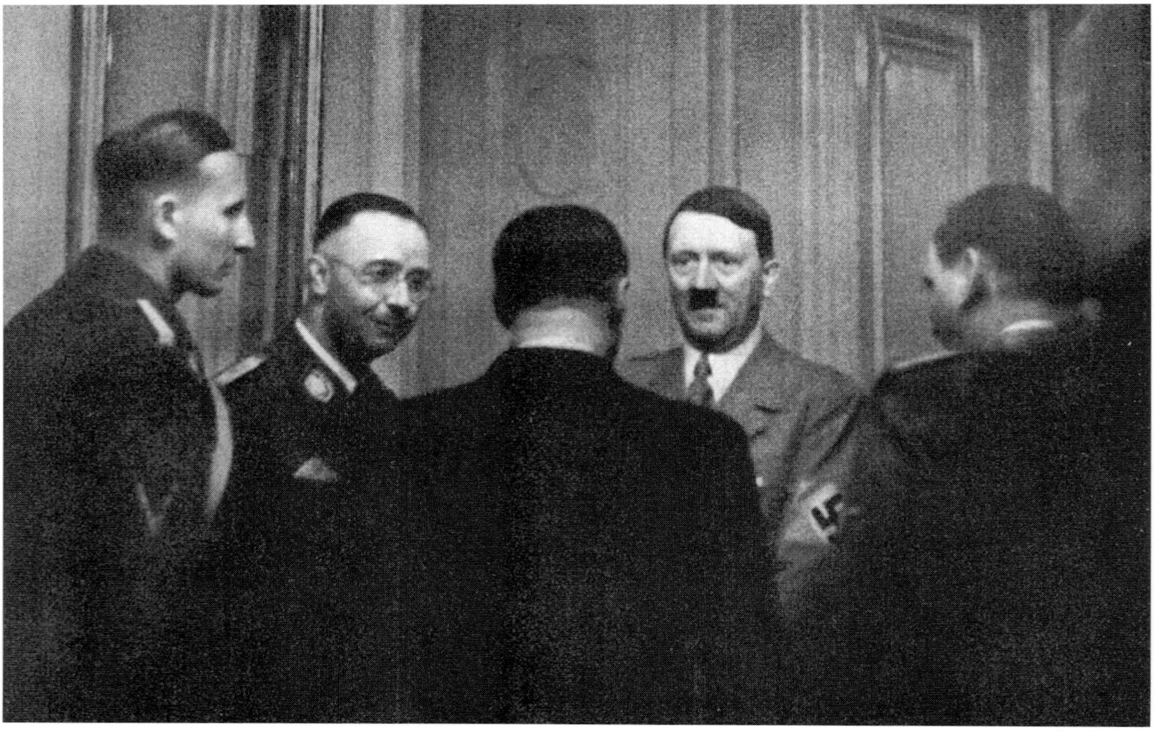

Inside Hradcany Castle, Hitler confers with government officials, Heydrich and Himmler. A photo from the Hoffmann illustrated book "Hitler in Böhmen, Mähren, Memel" published in 1939.

March 1939 aboard Hitler's train. Hitler returned to the Reich by rail after creating the Protectorate of Bohemia-Moravia. In the background are Stuckart, Himmler and Frank.

Hitler soon appointed Constantin Freiherr von Neurath as the first Reichsprotektor for Böhmen-Mähren. A respected diplomat, he held the post of Foreign Minister before von Ribbentrop.

Above: In April 1939, Himmler played host to Wehrmacht officers for a tour of Dachau concentration camp and local SS barracks. The officers, all in civilian attire, included Oberst (later General) Hermann Breith.

Left: On 23rd May 1939, Himmler attended the funeral of Friedrich Graf von der Schulenburg in Potsdam. A retired cavalry General, von der Schulenburg had won the Pour le Merite during WW1. Hitler promoted him posthumously to SS-Obergruppenführer, the only such promotion to that rank.

Above: 1939. Heissmeyer listens intently.

Right: Himmler visited von Ribbentrop several times in August 1939, no doubt discussing the Foreign Minister's upcoming trip to Moscow where he signed the non-aggression pact with Molotov. Once the war had started and then progressed into years, von Ribbentrop's importance to Hitler waned and he never recovered the prestige enjoyed briefly by his masterstroke in Moscow.

Clockwise from top left:

SS-Gruppenführer Wilhelm Freiherr von Holzschuher.

Friedrich Karl Freiherr von Eberstein, the SS power in Munich and Bavaria. One of Hitler's favourite SS Generals, he did not command the same respect from Himmler who considered him as weak and a troublemaker. Himmler seized upon an opportunity to replace him in 1939, but was overruled by Hitler. Himmler finally succeeded in ousting von Eberstein, but not until the final months of the war.

Marga Himmler was a good friend of the wife of Hermann Freiherr von Schade, seen here on the left with Seidel-Dittmarsch and Heydrich. In 1939, Marga suggested that von Schade might be a suitable replacement for von Eberstein and, partly to appease his wife, Himmler informed von Eberstein that he was being transferred. The unfortunate von Schade infuriated Hitler at a parade soon after and the impending transfer did not materialise.

One of the two powerful NSDAP men in Danzig, Senator Arthur Greiser, seen here as Gauleiter of the Wartheland.

A bitter rival of Greiser in Danzig was Albert Forster. A rabid anti-Semite, Forster agitated for the return of Danzig to German rule and preached that Poles would cease to exist on German territory.

Himmler congratulates men from SS-Heimwehr Danzig.

In the weeks leading up to the outbreak of hostilities, intrigue and subterfuge were rife, even stretching to civilian dress codes at secret strategic military meetings. A still from a colour movie, Himmler, Heydrich, Wolff and Hans Hendrik Neumann, Heydrich's adjutant, are filmed on the terrace at the Berghof having attended such a meeting.

Obersalzberg, 21st August 1939. Foreign Minister von Ribbentrop reads aloud a telegram from Stalin for the benefit of Himmler and Hitler. In the background stands Schulze-Kossens.

The man who started the Second World War, Alfred Naujocks, led the team which feigned the attack on the radio station at Gleiwitz.

Left: Heinrich Müller arranged for the "canned goods" delivery at Gleiwitz radio station. (Photo from 1943.)

Below: Prior to the invasion of Poland, Hitler attended a military exercise. Himmler and Steiner examine a map with Hitler. Far right are Schmundt and Keppler.

Right: In the first days of the campaign, Himmler was attached to Army Group North under Generaloberst Fedor von Bock. It was from von Bock's headquarters that Himmler issued the order to execute insurgents without trial. The hitherto secret role of the Einsatzgruppen was now clear to the Army high command.

Below: The Polish campaign, 1939. Far left is von Reichenau listening to a conversation between Himmler and Hitler.

Hitler chose this turbulent period to introduce the 'euthanasia programme' which would be overshadowed by the events on the world stage. Reichsleiter Philipp Bouhler, photographed here in SS-Obergruppenführer uniform, had titular control over the policy. His influence waned as the war progressed until he became a minor character in Hitler's plans. Always a committed Nazi, in May 1945, he killed himself with a phial of potassium cyanide.

Himmler and Heydrich confer at an airfield during the tense period of the Polish campaign, their secret intentions for the Einsatzgruppen now revealed.

Right: Members of an Einsatzkommando consult during the Polish invasion.

Below: The German Army High Command complained about excesses carried out by Einsatzgruppe "von Woyrsch" commanded by Dr Otto Rasch, seen here third from right in this 1936 photo.

Clockwise from top left:

Hitler studies a map with General of Artillery Walther von Reichenau during the invasion of Poland. In the background are Bodenschatz, Dietrich and Himmler.

Hitler examines a captured Polish standard. In SS uniform in the background are Julius Schaub, Otto Dietrich and Himmler.

In this undated photo, Himmler meets some of his SS troops.

Clockwise from top left:

With the outbreak of hostilities, Himmler came under great pressure and his stressful stomach cramps often required treatment from the Swedish masseur, Felix Kersten, upon whom the Reichsführer increasingly began to rely in the war years.

Walter Schellenberg wears the Iron Cross 1sr Class awarded for the kidnapping of the British agents at Venlo.

Himmler in profile, pictured at the victory parade in Warsaw.

The Poles defeated, Hitler created an administrative area of the German conquered territory which became known as the General Government. He installed the Nazi lawyer Dr Hans Frank as Governor General in the Wawel Castle in Krakow from where he ruled an estimated 12,000,000 Poles. The General Government became pivotal in Himmler's racial resettlement programme and he was often at odds with Frank who saw any encroachment in his area of responsibility as an attack on his authority. The two men disliked each other, but tolerated each other's authority through necessity.

Above: Himmler needed a reliable and loyal SS man to administer SS policy in the General Government. He chose Friedrich-Wilhelm Krüger and a prolonged battle of wills between Frank and Krüger began.

Right: Himmler also needed strong SS and Police Leaders in the main Polish cities to execute his policies. For Lublin he appointed Odilo Globocnik, the ex-Gauleiter of Vienna.

Left: In Radom, Himmler installed Fritz Katzmann.

Below: Lublin, October 1939. Globocnik (in white lapels) listens to his Reichsführer. Far left is Krüger, with Fegelein and Wolff behind Globocnik. Hofmann is on Himmler's left. They stand on an open space which could be intended for the site of a new POW camp. Note the wooden structure in the background.

Right: Other important vacancies to fill were the SD and Security Police commanders. For Krakow Himmler chose Bruno Streckenbach (centre) hitherto a reliable SD officer and subsequently the head of the Personnel Office in Heydrich's RSHA.

Below: The powerful men in Krakow. Himmler forcibly makes his point to Frank whilst Seyss-Inquart (right) places his hand on Krüger's back. Left is Otto Wächter, the Governor of Krakow.

Left: Otto Wächter.

Below: Himmler confers with Wächter watched by Jochen Peiper.

Above: Hitler greets his RFSS at the Reich Chancellery. Left is Wilhelm Brückner with Bormann in the background.

Right: An attempt was made on Hitler's life in Munich on 8th November 1939. A bomb exploded in the Bürgerbräukeller, but Hitler had already left and was making his way back to Berlin by train. The Nuremberg Police President, Benno Martin, had the unenviable task of informing Hitler of the assassination attempt during an unscheduled train stop in Nuremberg.

Above: Himmler chaired an investigation commission which met in his office in Berlin. The other supervisory members were Franz Huber, Arthur Nebe, Reinhard Heydrich and Heinrich Müller. Note the painting of Wewelsburg on the wall behind Himmler.

Left: Members of the investigation team on scene at the seriously damaged Bürgerbräukeller.

Opposite above: Remnants of Georg Elser's pipe bomb recovered at the scene placed beside a spare he had manufactured for comparison.

1939. An array of SS Generals gather around Himmler in his office. They include Daluege, Wolff, Pancke, Heissmeyer, Heydrich, Lorenz and Pohl.

Left: Himmler's grand tour of the General Government, Poland, winter 1939/1940. Himmler and Wolff both wear fur collared overcoats over their SS greatcoats against the extreme low temperature.

Below: Near Lublin, winter 1939/1940. Himmler consults with Werner Lorenz at a resettlement centre for ethnic Germans. Krüger in leather greatcoat and Globocnik far left.

Above: Himmler is shown around the resettlement centre near Lublin. Krüger far left and Lorenz next to Himmler.

Below: Johst, Wolff, Himmler and Wächter are entertained by resettled farmers and their families.

Wolff, Krüger, Himmler, Seyss-Inquart and Globocnik at a resettlement centre.

Resettled ethnic German women meet the RFSS.

An ethnic German farmer in traditional dress.

Himmler's group being shown inside a building.

Himmler's party pose for the camera during a visit to a hospital.

German troops help with building materials. Note the cart with personal belongings.

An extremely rare photo of Himmler with his lover, Hedwig Potthast. Himmler gives an after dinner address to his officers. Opposite him are Koppe and von Alvensleben. Possibly taken in Posen, early war.

The same event. Himmler's audience includes Ohlendorf, Conti, von Alvensleben and Koppe.

Ulrich Greifelt looks directly at the camera. Right is Seyss-Inquart.

Faces of the General Government in Krakow. Left to right: Josef Meisinger, Hans Hrank, Friedrich-Wilhelm Krüger, Karl Wolff, Himmler, Karl Brenner and Arthur Seyss-Inquart.

Arthur Greiser takes the wheel with Himmler, Johst and Koppe as his passengers.

Himmler in deep conversation with Artur Nebe. Krüger and Wolff right.

Koppe, Johst, Himmler and Krüger leaving a building.

A street in or near Posen.

Himmler bids farewell to Leonardo Conti, watched by Ulrich Greifelt.

In Krüger's office in Krakow, the Reichsführer studies files.

Himmler talks to a member of Totenkopf. In the background are Schmitt, Heissmeyer and Wolff.

Himmler speaks to a member of his escort. Centre is Wolff.

Inspection, watched by Schmitt and Heissmeyer.

Koppe escorts the group around the town. At the rear is Johst (in civilian attire) and between Koppe and Himmler is Greifelt.

Himmler wears a leather driving hat and is pointing something out to Greifelt. Richard Hildebrandt is left.

Johst, Koppe, Himmler, Wolff and von Gottberg leaving a building.

Above: I'll drive!

Right: On 26th January 1940, Himmler and Werner Lorenz were on the Sanbrücke at Przemysl to meet ethnic Germans who were being resttled. The bridge still stands, but is now only a rail crossing.

The Reichsführer welcomes an ethnic German farmer at Przemysl.

January 1940, Krakow. Himmler visits SS-Totenkopf units. Left is Leo von Jena in front of Krüger, Wolff and Becker.

In this undated winter photograph in Krakow, Hans Frank greets Himmler at a building dedication ceremony.

"Thank you gentlemen; most informative." Himmler at Krakow airfield with Schöngarth and Krüger.

The SS leader in Düsseldorf, Fritz Weitzel, was selected by Himmler to be his SS representative in conquered Norway.

6th March 1940 during an inspectour in the Black Forest region.

Above: A hatless Reichsführer and his chief of staff are passengers in this car.

Right: August Heissmeyer. Himmler found him to be weak and replaced him as head of the SS-Hauptamt. He was placed in charge of national political education.

Schutzstaffel der N.S.D.A.P.

SS-Führer-Ausweis-Nr. 276 15

Partei-Mitglieds-Nr. 2 946 20

Kiermaier, Josef

geboren am 21.12.1897

ist SS- Obersturmführer

im Stab des Reichsführers-SS

(Reichssicherheitsdienst)

Eigenhändige Unterschrift

13364

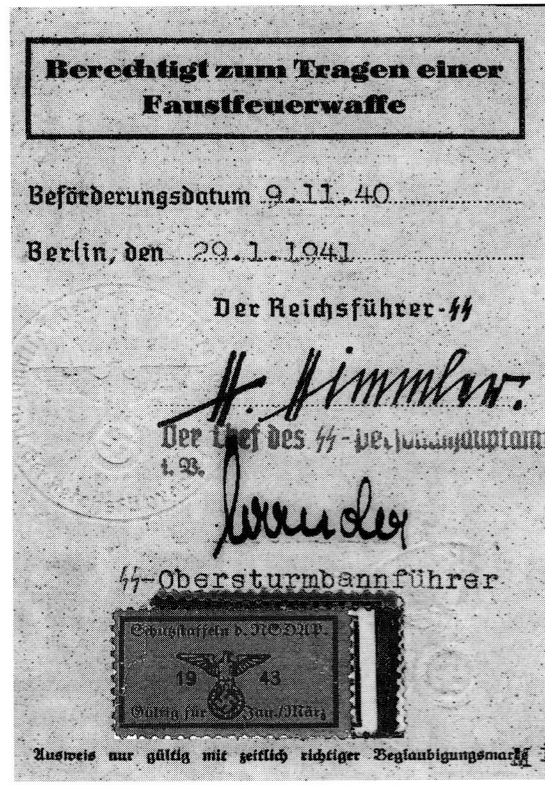

Berechtigt zum Tragen einer Faustfeuerwaffe

Beförderungsdatum 9.11.40

Berlin, den 29.1.1941

Der Reichsführer-SS

Der Chef des SS-Personalhauptamts i.V.

SS-Obersturmbannführer

Schutzstaffeln d. NSDAP. 19 43 Gültig für Jan./März

Ausweis nur gültig mit zeitlich richtiger Beglaubigungsmarke

Clockwise from top left:

All members of the SS were issued with identity cards which bore the holder's name, date of birth, rank, unit, SS number, party number, photo and signature. This example is that of Himmler's bodyguard, Josef Kiermaier.

Close protection officers such as Kiermaier were attached to the Reich Security Service (RSD) commanded by Johannes Rattenhuber. The majority of RSD members were police detectives.

Clockwise from top left:

With the outbreak of war, Marga Himmler reported for nursing duties with the German Red Cross (DRK.) She is seen here in DRK uniform on the left.

When visiting Wewelsburg, Himmler usually flew in and out of Paderborn.

At Paderborn airfield. Burghauptmann Siegfried Taubert in the background.

Above: This photo is believed to have been taken during a break in driving in the vicinity of Wewelsburg. The officer on the left appears to be Siegfried Taubert, with Himmler, Heydrich and Prützmann. Date unknown.

Left: Himmler visiting SS-Totenkopf (probably in 1940) with August Heissmeyer (far right.) Between them are Theodor Eicke and Kurt Brasack.

Opposite above: Himmler visited Lublin on 5th May 1940, staying in the villa of Globocnik. Earlier photo, probably 1939.

Opposite below: Odilo Globocnik's villa in Lublin, where Himmler was an overnight guest on several occasions. The scene of numerous parties and also of discussions and decisions which would have dire consequences on the Jewish populace in the General Government.

Above: Himmler's staff at the Wawel Castle in Krakow. Right is Dr Rudolf Brandt, next to Josef Kiermaier. Of interest is the unidentified man on the left who has only one arm.

Left: A smiling Himmler at Dachau concentration camp.

Above: The western offensive in May 1940 saw Himmler start to use his special train extensively for mobility. Sonderzug "Heinrich" was one of several such trains consisting of luxurious Pullman class train carriages especially manufactured by Wegmann and Company of Kassel.

Right: Inside Himmler's Sonderzug "Heinrich." The power control unit.

Above: Inside Himmler's Sonderzug "Heinrich." The salon car.

Left: Inside Himmler's Sonderzug "Heinrich." Himmler's salon, used for receiving guests and for meetings.

Above: Inside Himmler's Sonderzug "Heinrich." The oblong table used for meetings.

Right: Inside Himmler's Sonderzug "Heinrich." A long view of an internal corridor.

Clockwise from top left:

Inside Himmler's Sonderzug "Heinrich." A relaxation compartment. The seats on the right could be converted into a bed.

Inside Himmler's Sonderzug "Heinrich." The luxurious standard of the seating is obvious.

Himmler's washroom and basin. The doorway on the right leads into the WC and shower room.

Inside Himmler's Sonderzug "Heinrich."
Himmler's shower.

Inside Himmler's Sonderzug "Heinrich."
Shower and toilet.

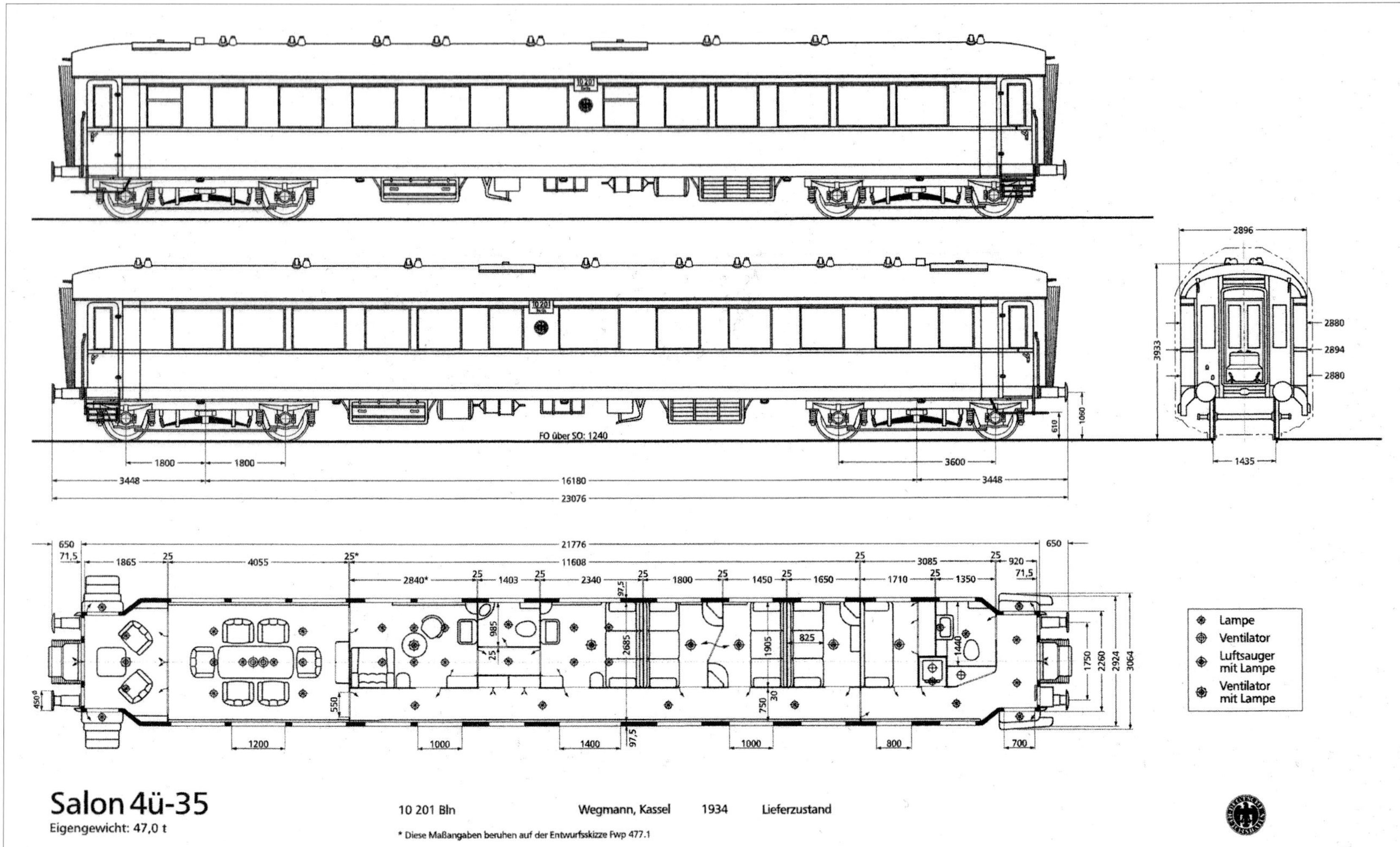

Plans of Himmler's Sonderzug "Heinrich" and Sonderzug "Steiermark" produced by Wegmann and Company.

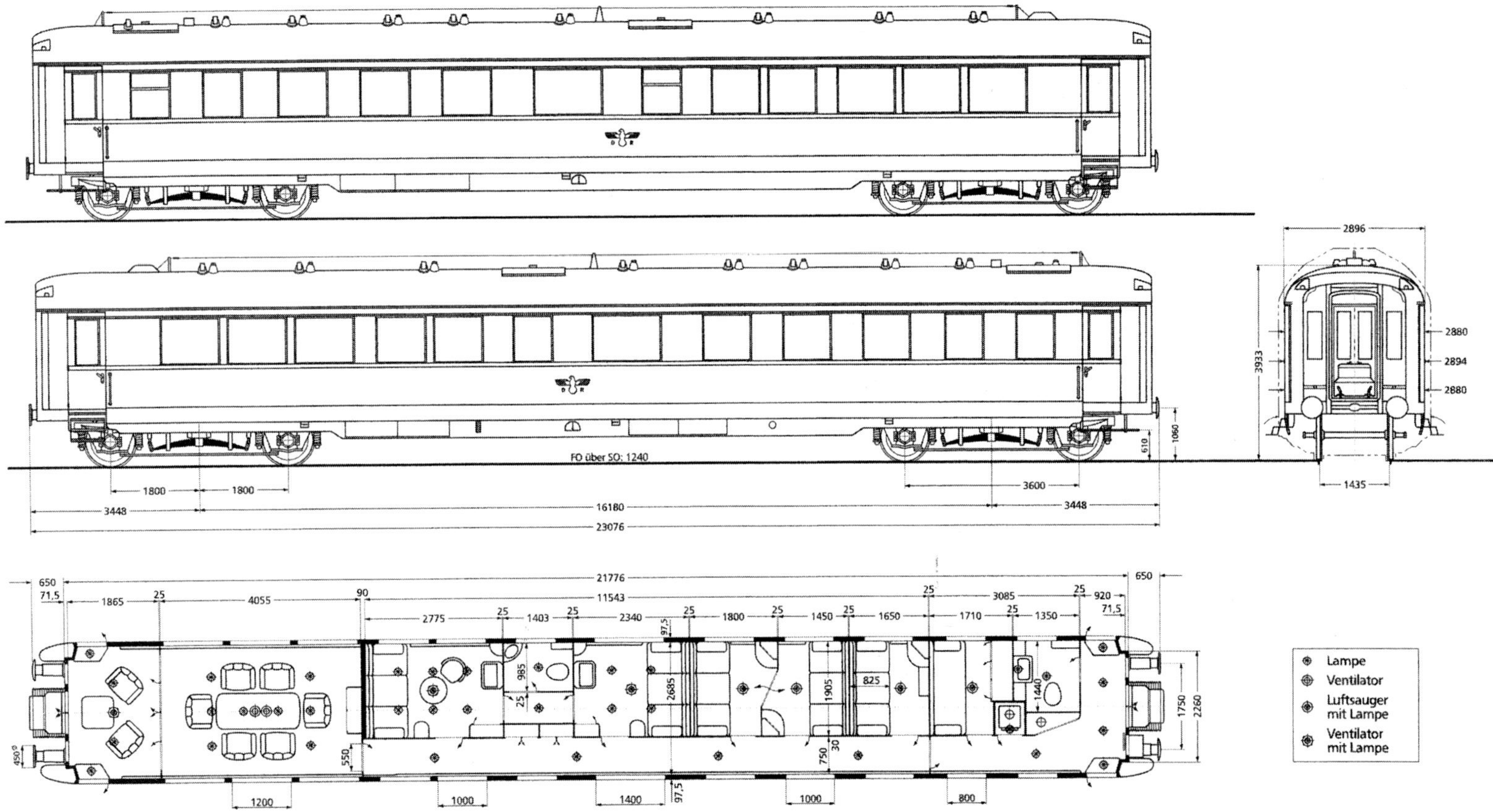

Sal 4ü-35/39

Eigengewicht: 56,0 t

10 201 Bln

Wegmann, Kassel 1934

Zustand nach Umbau 1939
Form der Wagenschürze ist nicht gesichert

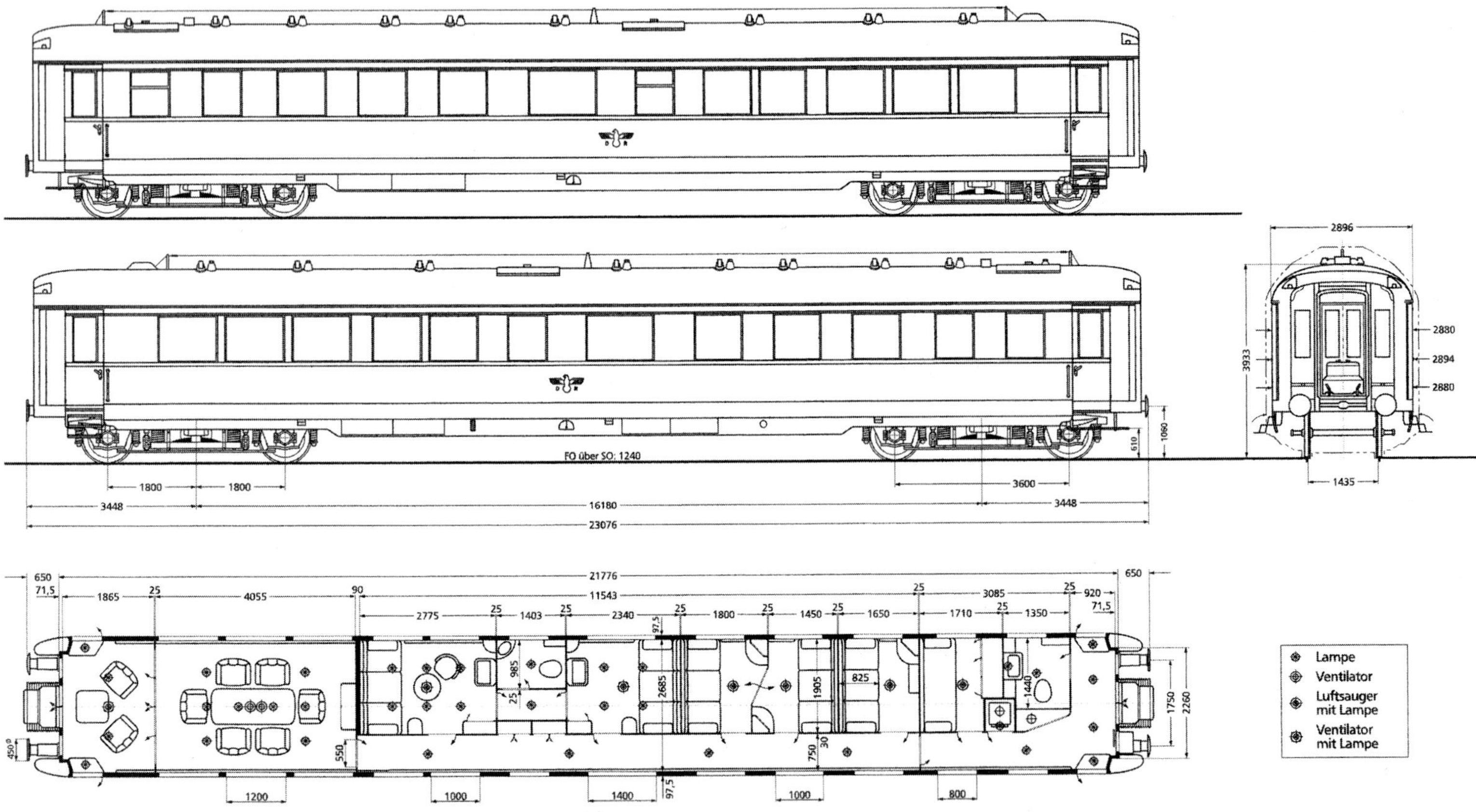

Sdr 4ü-35/39
Eigengewicht: t

10 201 Bln

Wegmann, Kassel 1934

Zustand nach Drehgestelltausch 1943

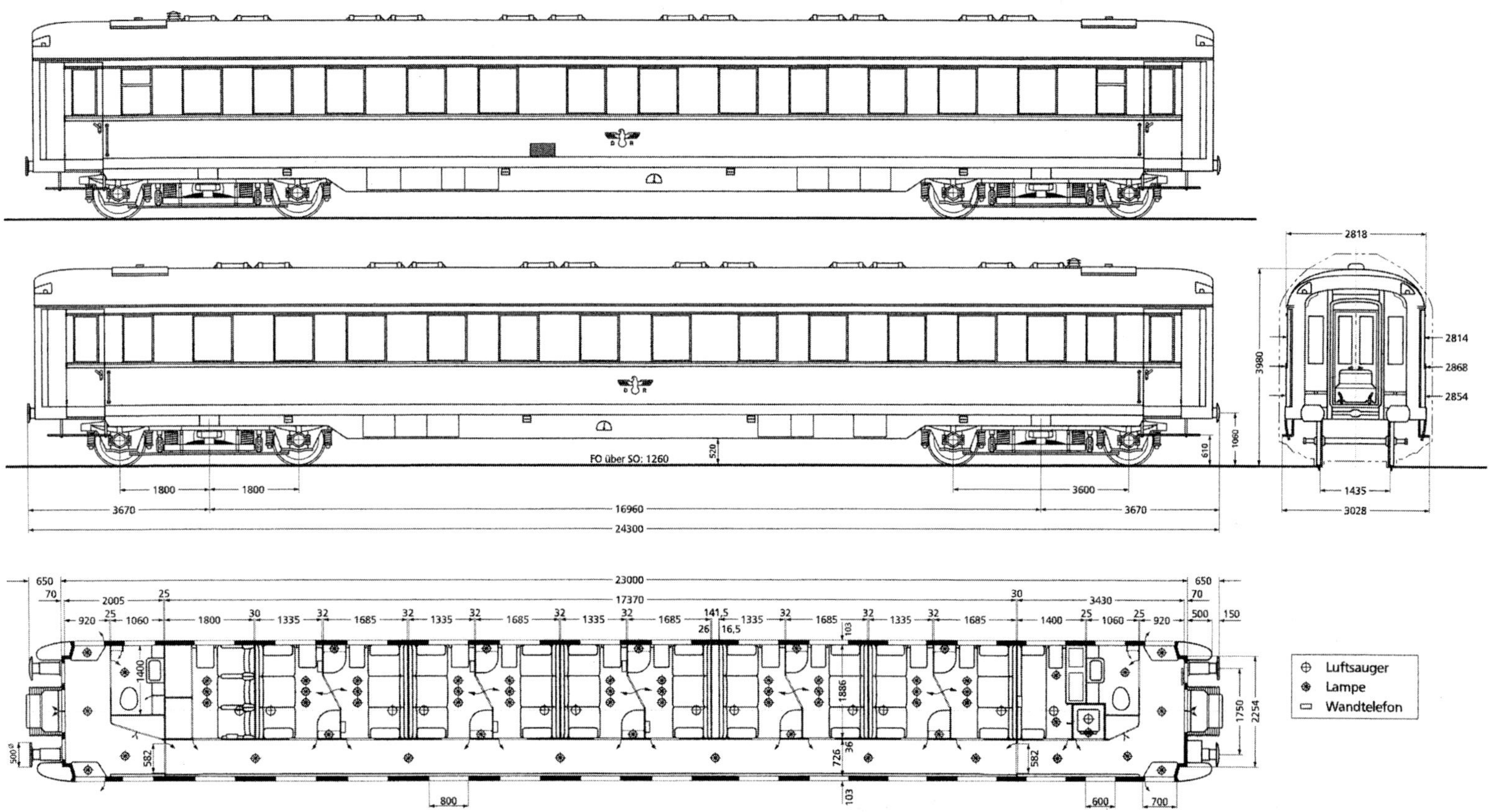

Sal Begl 4ü-37

Eigengewicht: 62,3 t

10 224 Bln - 10 225 Bln Westwaggon, Köln 1942 Lieferung 1942

Above: Sonderzug "Heinrich" was protected from air attack by a Luftwaffe flak unit which travelled with the train wherever it went. Usually one gun carriage, but sometimes two, was inserted behind the engine. Once the train became stationary in a siding, the flak carriage would usually be disconnected and placed beside the main carriages. This particular photo is of Sonderzug "Heinrich" stationary near Bruck an der Mur in Austria between 12th April and 23rd April 1941.

Clockwise from top left:

The flak carriage crew at Bruck an der Mur.

A member of the gun crew.

The SS officer eventually responsible for Himmler's special trains was Ludwig "Lucki" Pemsel, deputy of Josef "Sepp" Tiefenbacher. Here Pemsel works at his typewriter on board Himmler's train.

Opposite below: Sonderzug "Heinrich" at Bruck an der Mur. Note the steel helmets in case of attack and the sentry on foot patrol in the distance beside the train.

Left: Wolff jokes with his boss by portable wooden steps up to Himmler's train.

Below: Hitler visits Himmler's train, date unknown.

Clockwise from top left:

Josef Tiefenbacher (left) the officer responsible for Himmler's Feldkommandostellen (field headquarters) and Josef Kiermaier.

When on the move by road, Himmler had his own Begleitkommando (escort group) named after his special trains. Here men of Begleitkommando "Heinrich" await further movement, probably in Holland.

Once out of his train, he moved around by car and even preferred to take the wheel himself. A smiling Jochen Peiper sits in the rear seat.

Opposite above: Typical of the type of announcement sent by SS men, the Pemsel couple declare their marriage. Note that Pemsel is attached to the Personal Staff RFSS.

Opposite below: A letter sent by Pemsel to his wife from Sonderzug "Steiermark" whilst in the siding at Feldkommandostelle "Hochwald." Note the Feldpost 35360 ink franking.

Left: Himmler with Wolff, apparently having just alighted from a special train. Note the temporary cable laid for either communications or electric current, and both male and female staff in the background.

Below: On 6th May 1940, members of Himmler's personal staff celebrate the marriage of Ludwig Pemsel and Theodora Kleiner. Standing behind the bride are Josef Tiefenbacher and Wolff's deputy, Otto Ullmann.

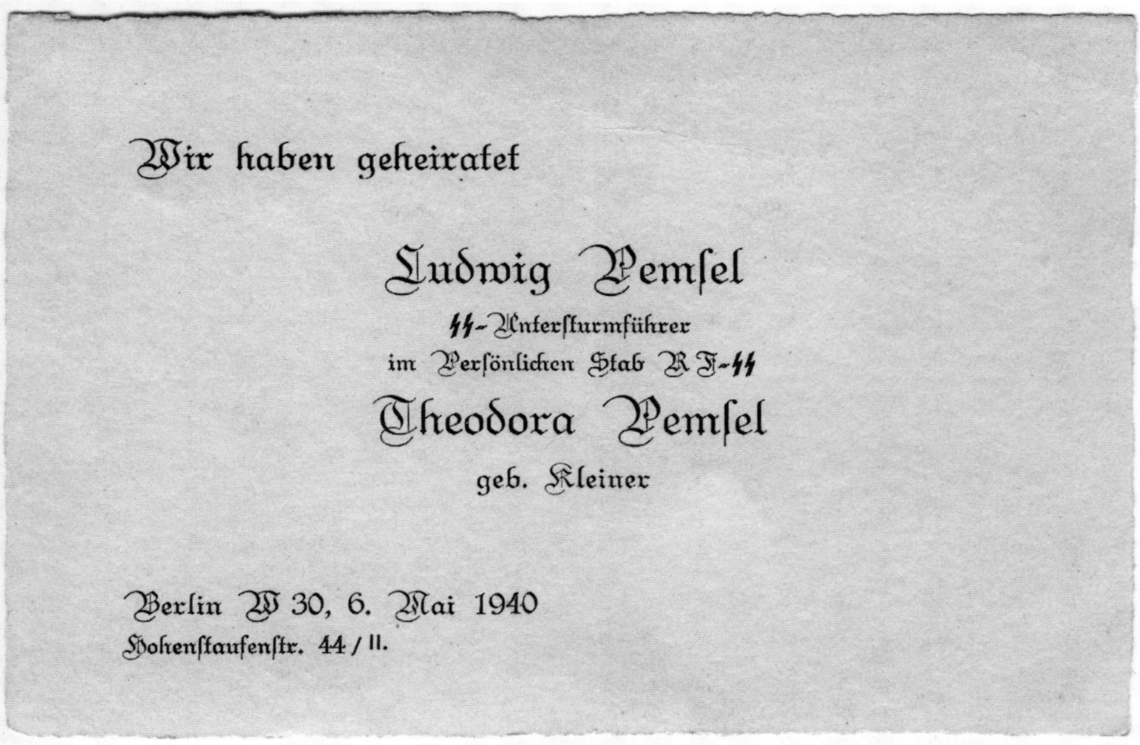

Wir haben geheiratet

Ludwig Pemsel
SS-Untersturmführer
im Persönlichen Stab RF-SS

Theodora Pemsel
geb. Kleiner

Berlin W 30, 6. Mai 1940
Hohenstaufenstr. 44 / II.

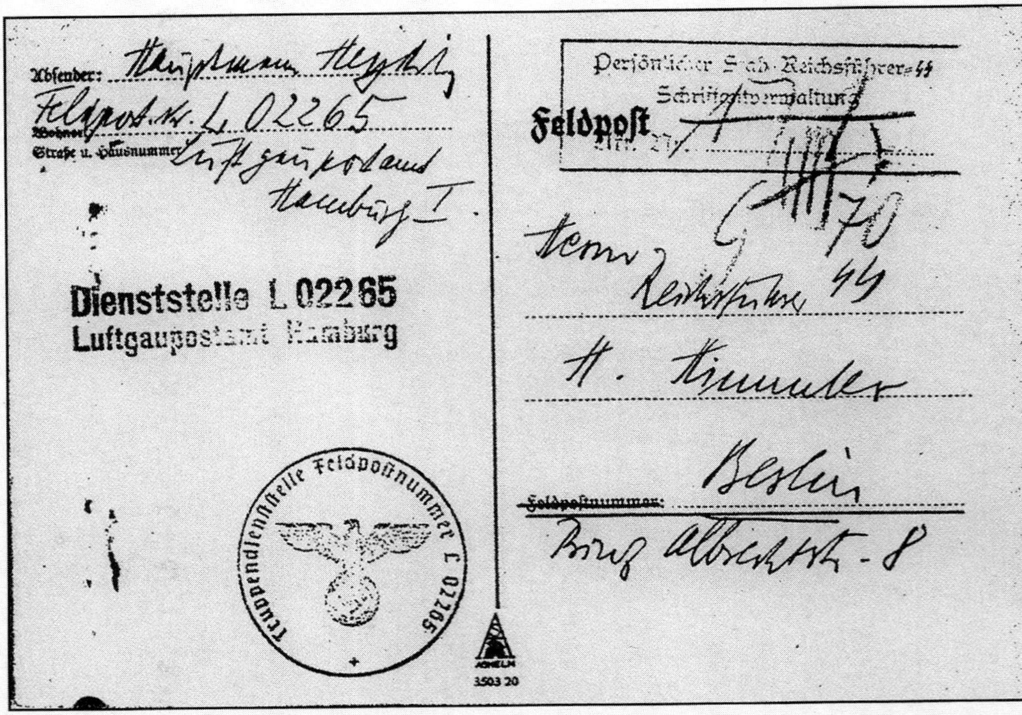

Absender: Hauptmann Heydrich
Feldpost Nr. L 02265
Wohnort
Straße u. Hausnummer Luftgaupostamt Hamburg I

Dienststelle L 02265
Luftgaupostamt Hamburg

Truppendienststelle Feldpostnummer L 02265

Feldpost

Persönlicher Stab Reichsführer-SS
Schriftgutverwaltung

Herrn Reichsführer SS
H. Himmler
Berlin
Feldpostnummer:
Prinz Albrechtstr. 8

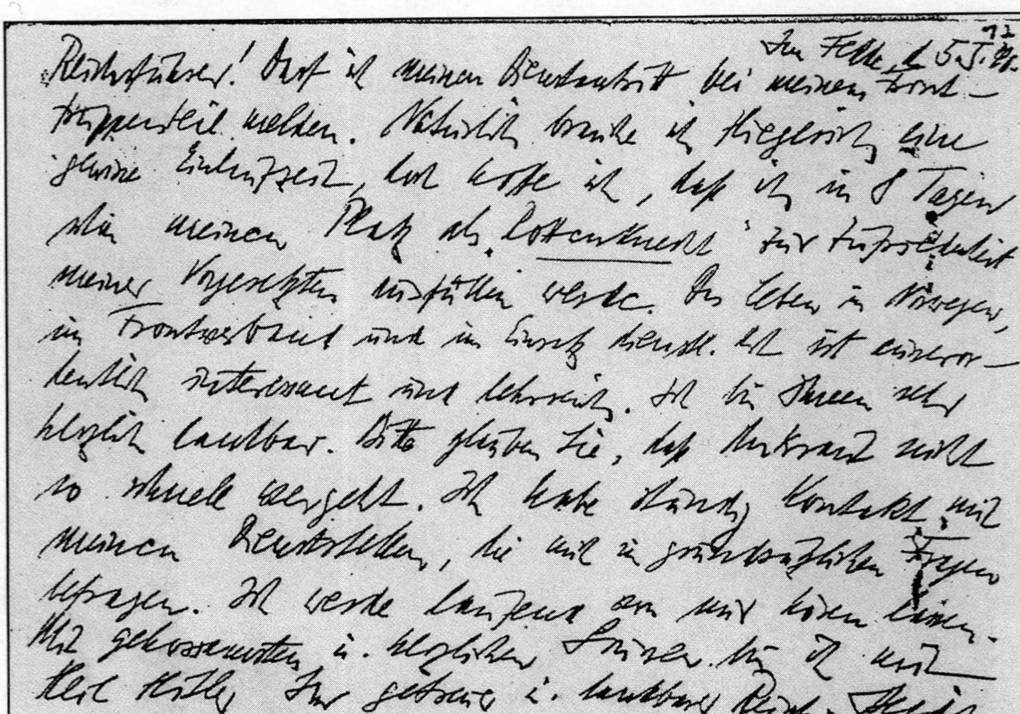

Heydrich writes to the Reichsführer-SS from the front and Himmler replies from Sonderzug "Heinrich." Himmler sends greetings from Wolff, Brandt and Hä'schen, indicating that they were with him at his Feldkommandostelle.

Sonderzug "Heinrich",
15.5.1940.

Mein lieber H e y d r i c h !

Ihre Karte vom 5.5.1940 habe ich erhalten. Inzwischen hat sich ja sehr viel Neues getan. Seit einigen Tagen sind wir hier im Hauptquartier, d.h. das eigentliche Hauptquartier ist dieses Mal an einer anderen Stelle. Den Betrieb kennen Sie ja vom Polenfeldzug her.

Ich denke sehr viel an Sie und hoffe, dass es Ihnen gut geht und wünsche Ihnen erneut viel Glück und alles Gute !

Lassen Sie möglichst täglich von sich hören. Viele herzliche Grüsse von Wölffchen, Rudi Brandt, Häs'chen, besonders aber von mir.

H e i l H i t l e r !

Ihr

Although he had no experience whatsoever in battlefield tactics, Himmler was always keen to issue deployment orders to his men. Seen here with a local commander of SS-Totenkopf, Himmler explains the situation over a map. Left is Jochen Peiper.

Himmler visits men of SS-Standarte "Germania" in the SS-VT on the Western Front. Rarely worn by Himmler, this is one of the few times he is seen in his SS side cap.

Himmler confers with SS-Obersturmbannführer Werner Dörffler-Schuband, CO of 2. Sturmbann / SS-Standarte "Germania."

In conversation with Himmler, Hitler wears his lightweight raincoat, favoured by him in warmer weather in the early war years.

Above: The Reich Governor of Norway, Josef Terboven (left) reported to Hitler at his Felsennest field headquarters with HSSPF Nord, SS-Obergruppenführer Fritz Weitzel (right.) Himmler listens as Bormann speaks.

Right: Himmler and Wolff with Reich SS Physician Prof. Dr Ernst-Robert Grawitz.

Opposite above: Himmler used air travel extensively to cover long distances or numerous locations. Here he alights from his Ju52 aircraft.

Opposite below: Once out of the aircraft, a waiting car would whisk him off to his intended destination.

On 24th May 1940, Himmler appointed Hanns Albin Rauter as his SS representative in Holland.

Himmler's attention is directed towards something.

A rare photograph of Himmler visiting Heydrich at a fighter airfield. Heydrich (back to camera) introduces his fellow pilots. Himmler's pilot, Carl Schnäbele, is 2nd from left.

Himmler relaxes in a car in Reims on 16th June 1940. The General might possibly be Wolfgang Schmidt-Logan, but this is unconfirmed.

Himmler takes time to smoke a cigar during a break in his journey. The man on the right is believed to be Hans Bastian, Himmler's driver, who accidentally shot himself dead when playing around with his MP38. *Inset:* There has always been much discussion over the finger rings that Himmler wore. He does not appear to be wearing a conventional Totenkopfring, but is wearing a plain band with a single Totenkopf on the third finger of his left hand.

With Hitler at a field kitchen. Far right is Wolff, with Lammers next to Himmler and Meissner behind him. The army general is von Kluge.

Hitler's group visits an oil installation, probably in Poland.

Hitler greets Dr Fritz Todt in Poland. Unusually, Himmler wears a Wehrmacht design cap eagle.

Hitler sightseeing with Himmler.

Hitler's group includes Himmler, Keitel and von Witzleben.

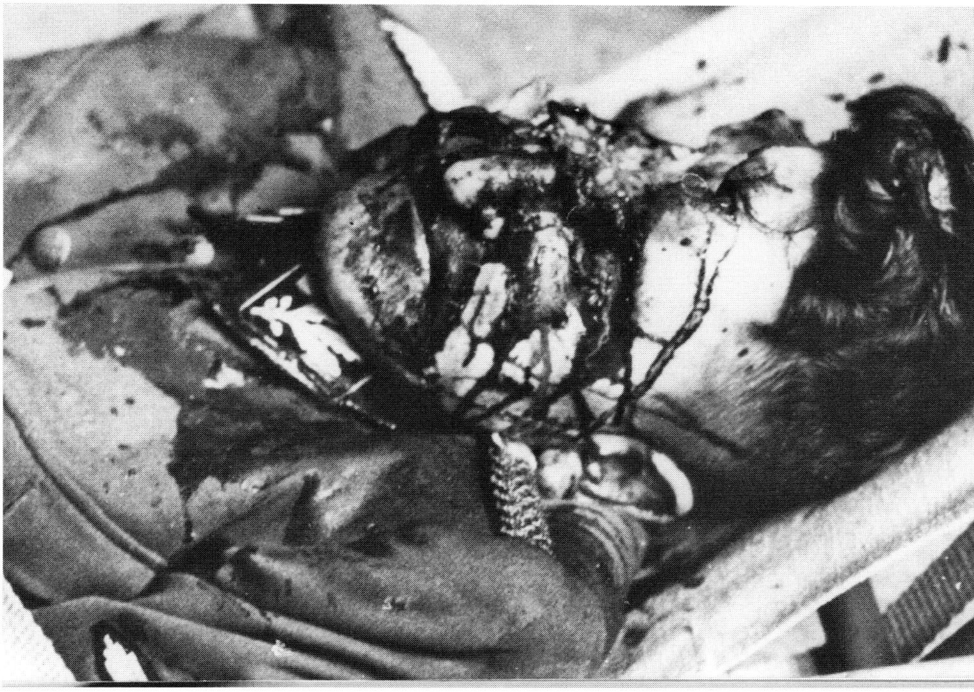

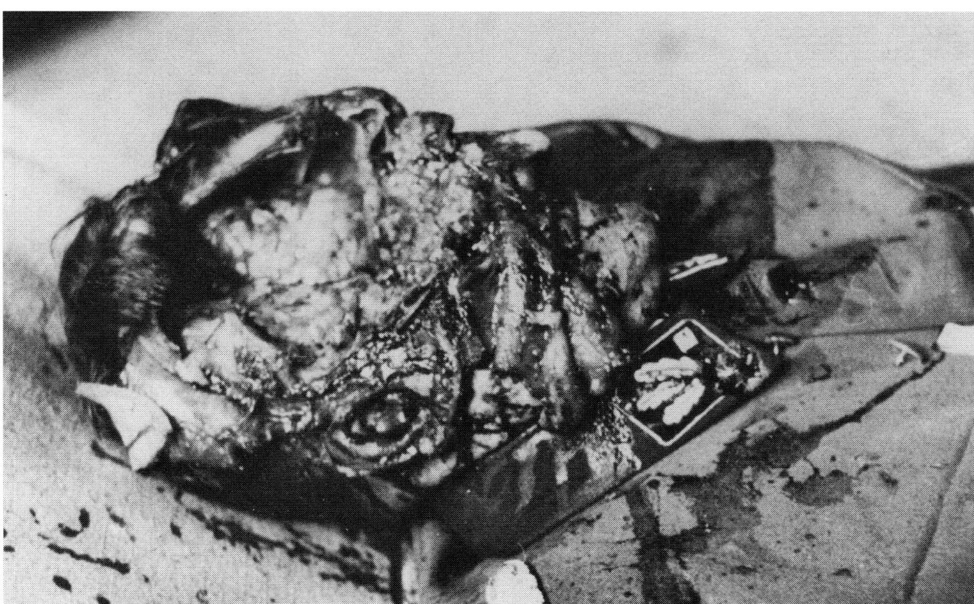

Above and overleaf: SS-Obergruppenführer Fritz Weitzel was transferred from Düsseldorf to Oslo in May 1940. His family remained in Germany. On 19th June 1940, Weitzel was visiting Düsseldorf and was driving alone when the RAF attacked the city during the night. He was stopped by the police and warned to take cover, but ignored the advice. At Martin Luther Platz there was a direct hit and Weitzel's car skidded into a wall in Marienstrasse where it was discovered soon after. Bomb shrapnel had pierced the right side of the windscreen, killing Weitzel instantly at the wheel. His body was found in the car with the right side of his head missing and brain matter exposed. He was in full SS General uniform. He was taken to the mortuary where the corpse was photographed and then re-dressed prior to burial in the city cemetery.

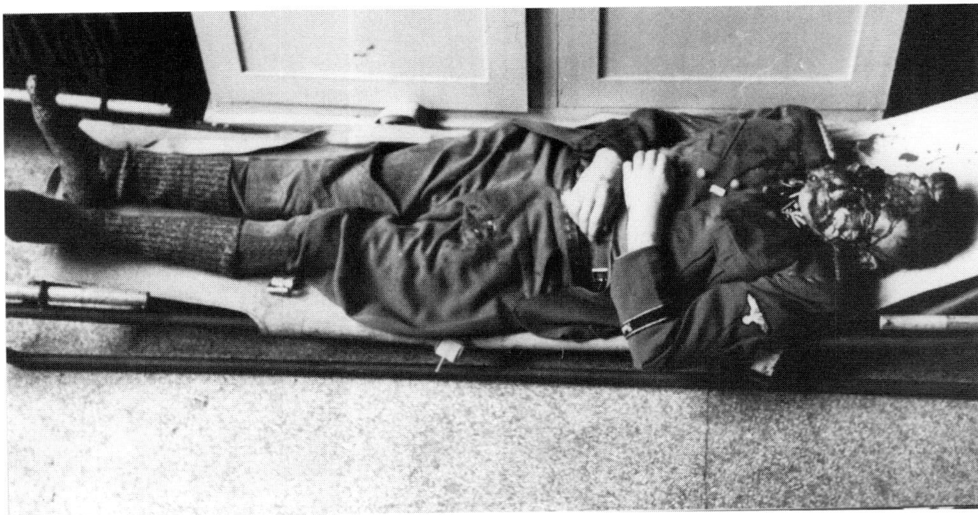

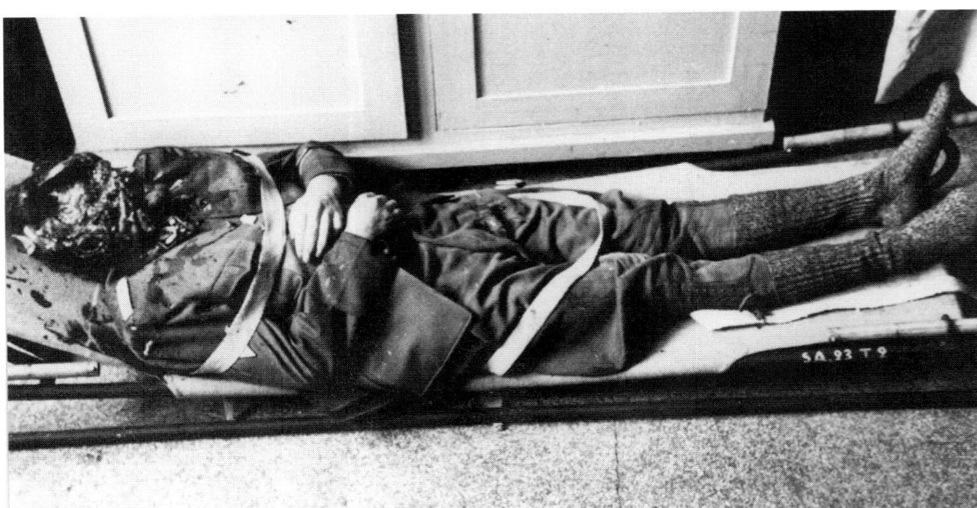

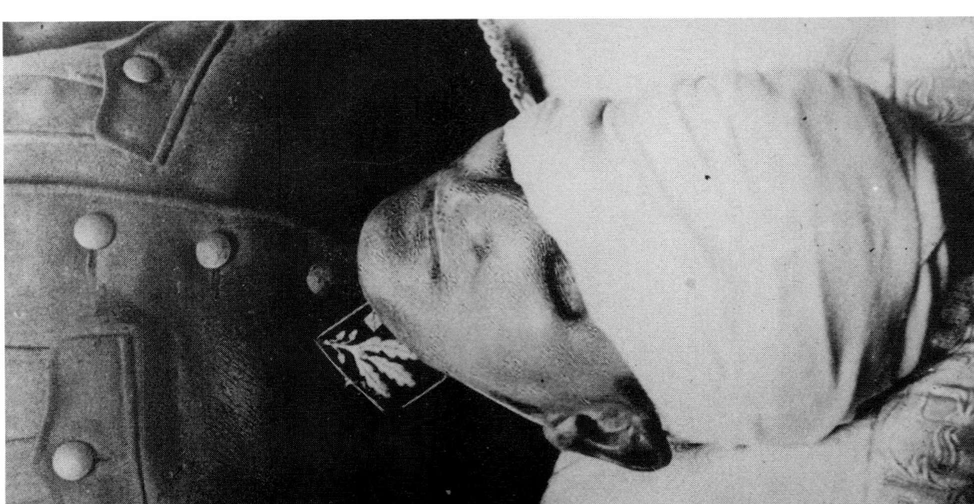

Clockwise from top left:

The original site of Weitzel's grave. Himmler visited on 26th September 1940 and again on 1st September 1942.

The grave was moved from the original site and still exists today in its new location in the large city cemetery.

Wilhelm Rediess was unexpectedly chosen to replace Weitzel in Oslo.

Above: Hitler's field headquarters Wolfsschlucht at Brûly-de-Pesche in Belgium. His concrete bunker and wooden barrack were hidden in the trees. The old school house was used by Keitel and Jodl and the map room was situated there. Hitler also had quarters in the hamlet main house. The small church was used for refreshments and relaxation. Hitler was here at the time the war against the French ended on 25th June 1940.

Above: An extremely rare photo of Himmler taking tea with some ladies on his staff at von Ribbentrop's quarters at Château d'Ardennes. On the reverse is noted: clockwise round the table, von Ribbentrop, Fräulein Rehden, Peiper, Hise (?), RFSS, Edith, Schmidt, Hä'schen. The note also states it was a working tea.

Right: Himmler's adjutant, Jochen Peiper.

Opposite below: Summer 1940 and Hitler is surrounded by his close military and party leaders. Note the large size of Hitler's cap illustrating his abhorrence for tight fitting clothes.

Himmler crosses the frontier on foot.

A stop for lunch somewhere in France.

The Reichsführer's convoy stops in a French town. Standing in the car is Ulrich Greifelt, with Wolff on the right.

Somewhere in France, Himmler checks the map.

France 1940. Next to Himmler is Peiper.

Himmler examines a map.

France, July 1940. Lorenz third from right and Greifelt on Himmler's left.

Himmler and Greifelt inspect part of the Maginot Line, skilfully by-passed by the German Blitzkrieg. Note the tunnel entrance to an underground fort.

A high point to survey the Maginot Line defensive positions.

Belfort, 14th July 1940. Having spent the previous night at the Grand Hotel, Himmler continues his inspection tour.

Above: A happy Himmler leaving the Grand Hotel Belfort.

Right: Belfort, 14th July 1940. Followed by Lorenz and Wolff.

Clockwise from top left:

With Wolff in Belfort.

Himmler takes time to chat in Belfort.

Relaxing with a cigar on the terrace at the Berghof.

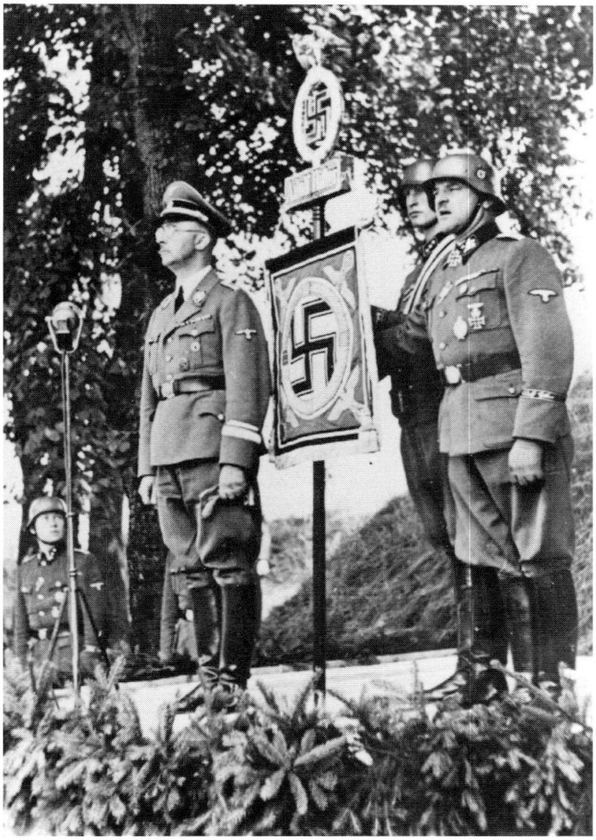

Right: On 6th and 7th September 1940, Himmler was in Metz where he presented the Leibstandarte-SS "Adolf Hitler" with a new unique standard. Dietrich makes his acceptance speech.

Below: September 1940, France. Heissmeyer left and Peiper right.

Above: Theodor Berkelmann and Himmler speak, with Jüttner and Peiper behind.

Left: Sepp Dietrich on the terrace of the Berghof.

Opposite: Heinrich Hoffman's official portrait of Himmler to mark his 40th birthday on 7th October 1940.

Left: The RFSS 1940. Hedwig Potthast complained that Himmler wore his hair too short at the back and sides, so he wore his hair slightly longer to please her.

Below: At the Führer headquarters. Left to right: Schaub, Jodl, Wolff, Himmler and Wegener.

Right: Paul Wegener, served for a while in Norway and ended the war as Gauleiter Weser-Ems. Although attaining the SS rank of Obergruppenführer, Wegener was never a true Himmler supporter and even advised Dönitz to be wary of Himmler during his short lived government in 1945.

Below: A Spanish police delegation visits the barracks of the Leibstandarte-SS "Adolf Hitler" in Berlin-Lichterfelde. The visitors gaze down from the roof. Note the LAH motif on the railings.

Himmler shows the Spanish police chief Don José Finat Conde de Mayalde the fire fighting equipment at the Lichterfelde barracks.

Heydrich and Nebe with the Spanish delegation at the Kripo headquarters.

Departing the Kripo headquarters in Werderscher Markt, Himmler thanks Nebe for hosting his guests.

Left: Reichsführer-SS and Chief of the German Police, Heinrich Himmler.

Right: Himmler confers with a police officer in Königsplatz, Munich, watched by Peiper.

Himmler in Madrid on 20th October 1940. Wolff, Himmler, Franco and Suner, with Peiper between Wolff and the RFSS.

Himmler in Spain, October 1940.

Right: The Reichsführer enjoys a bullfight.

Below: Himmler takes the salute at a parade in Madrid.

Barcelona airport, 24th October 1940, bound for Marseilles. A Spanish press photo.

Krakow, 26th October 1940. Himmler attends the General Government first anniversary parade.

The Soviet Foreign Minister, Vyacheslav Molotov, arrived in Berlin for talks in November 1940.

On 20th November 1940, Arturo Bocchini, the Italian Police Chief, died. A great ally to Himmler, he is pictured here at an earlier visit to Munich with Himmler and von Eberstein.

Above: Himmler, Wolff and Heydrich attend the funeral of Bocchini in Rome.

Left: The Reich SS Physician, Prof. Dr Ernst-Robert Grawitz. During Himmler's visit to Ravensbrück on 14th January 1941, he was angered to discover that Grawitz had not carried out his orders to research a cure for gonorrhoea using camp inmates.

Opposite above: Himmler enters Ravensbrück concentration camp for an inspection on 14th January 1941.

On 20th January 1941, Himmler escorted Anton Mussert around Dachau camp. They were accompanied by Heissmeyer (extreme left,) Pohl and Seyss-Inquart, along with several Dutch National Socialists. Himmler proudly shows off the herb garden laboratory to his guest.

Above: January 1941, Munich. Franz Xaver Schwarz plays host to Himmler's guest in the Verwaltungsbau at Königsplatz.

Left: Himmler examines a monument. On the right is Oswald Pohl.

Right: On 25th January 1941, Himmler relieved his chief adjutant Ludolf von Alvensleben from his post at the latter's request. He is seen here with Hitler's chief adjutant, Brückner, during the Polish campaign.

Below: Werner Grothmann was appointed to Himmler's adjutancy after being seriously injured with SS-Regiment "Deutschland." He eventually held the post of first adjutant.

Matthias Kleinheisterkamp (bottom right) interrogates a prisoner just visible in front of him. The officer on the left is Werner Grothmann.

On 28th January 1941, Himmler flew to Oslo. He has just been greeted at the airport by Terboven (in dark civilian suit) and Rediess (right.)

Part of the reception committee in Oslo.

Another reception in Norway. This time Terboven (left) is in uniform.

Himmler in Norway, leaving his car and approaching a guard of honour.

Himmler's party visit a military cemetery in Norway. The police adjutant next to Kiermaier is believed to be Willy Suchanek, Himmler's police adjutant, but this is unconfirmed.

The more prominent members of the party, left to right: Rediess, Meyszner, Terboven, Himmler, von Falkenhorst and Wolff.

A solemn looking Reichsführer during his visit to the war cemetery.

Above: Himmler is presented to a guard of honour formed by SS-Totenkopf.

Below: Himmler listens to Scandinavian folk music.

Right: Negotiating deep snow and ice in Norway.

Below: Himmler climbs aboard his aircraft prior to departure at Oslo airport in Norway.

Above: Oslo, Norway. The Reichsführer's Ju52 has engines turning and will taxi for take off when the chocks have been removed from the wheels.

Left: Gauleiter Fritz Bracht. Auschwitz concentration camp was situated in the area under his jurisdiction.

Right: On 1st March 1941 Himmler flew to Gleiwitz where he was greeted by Bracht and Eric von dem Bach-Zelewski. They attended a local event before driving to Auschwitz concentration camp where Himmler conducted an inspection in the afternoon.

Below: Himmler receives flowers from two local children. Within hours they were at Auschwitz and Himmler was ordering the commandant to expand the facility to receive large numbers of prisoners.

Above: Himmler visited Auschwitz for the first time on 1st March 1941. During the visit, he ordered Höss to drain an area of marshland north-west of the present camp near the village of Brzezinka to enable the construction of a large prisoner facility. This would eventually operate as the death factory and be known as Auschwitz II or Auschwitz-Birkenau.

Below: Himmler and Auschwitz camp commandant SS-Sturmbannführer Rudolf Höss.

After leaving Auschwitz, Himmler drove with von dem Bach to Breslau where they celebrated von dem Bach's 42nd birthday. He stayed the night at the Hotel Monopol and the next day he addressed a crowd in the Breslau Centennial Hall where he symbolically presented 50 ethnic Germans with documents of German nationality.

20th March 1941, Himmler explains a model to Rudolf Hess at a presentation in Berlin on the planning and construction of settlements in the east.

Above: Left to right: Bormann, Bouhler, Himmler, Hess, Hofmann, Todt, Meyer and Heydrich.

Left: Ernst Heinrich Schmauser. One of the senior SS men entrusted with the news of the impending invasion of the Soviet Union.

Another trusted SS man was Hans Adolf Prützmann.

Jakob Sporrenberg was destined as SS and Police Leader in Minsk.

During a visit to a SS armoured unit. Jochen Peiper far right.

The RFSS visited the Leibstandarte-SS "Adolf Hitler" (LAH) in Greece from 6th to 10th May 1941. Himmler is between Fritz Witt and Jochen Peiper.

Himmler and Dietrich talk with an officer of LAH.

Greece. Fritz Witt (squatting) shows Himmler and Dietrich tactics using objects on the ground. Behind Dietrich are Springer and Peiper.

Himmler was back in Norway on 21st May 1941. Here he is inspecting Norwegian SS volunteers with Jüttner and Quisling.

Terboven speaks.

Above: Now it is the turn of the RFSS.

Right: On 27th May 1941, Professors Carl Clauberg and Ernst Grawitz discussed with Himmler the use of camp inmates for human sterilization experiments. Himmler approved the policy and subsequently part of Block 10 at Auschwitz I was used by Clauberg as a laboratory. Clauberg researched an easy and cheap method and experimented on females with injections of formaldehyde preparations into their uteruses, without anesthetics. All his test subjects were Jewish women who suffered permanent damage, serious infections and in many cases, death.

Left: As Reich SS Physician, Grawitz was heavily implicated in human experiments using camp prisoners. Seen here on the right with Jüttner, he realised when the war was lost that he would be held accountable and he killed himself and his entire family.

Below: April 1941. Himmler arrives at Mauthausen to be greeted by Franz Ziereis, Ernst Kaltenbrunner and Gauleiter August Eigruber (in black uniform.)

Above: April 1941. Inside the protective custody compound Himmler chats with Eigruber, surrounded by Wolff, Kaltenbrunner, Lucas (Himmler's driver) and Ziereis. The police adjutant is Willy Suchanek.

Below: Mauthausen, April 1941. Himmler between Kaltenbrunner and Ziereis.

Mauthausen, April 1941. The curtains and ventilator indicate this building as being for SS personnel and not prisoners.

Mauthausen, April 1941. Both Himmler and camp commandant Ziereis appear pleased with what they see.

Mauthausen, April 1941. A smiling Reichsführer chats with some camp guards.

Mauthausen, April 1941. Inside the quarry, Himmler's party is escorted by Ziereis. Note civilian supervisors in addition to prisoners.

Mauthausen, April 1941. Himmler greets a SS-Scharführer overseer in the quarry.

Mauthausen, April 1941. An interesting photograph taken on the road just outside the camp perimeter. Himmler's group, which includes Pohl, Ziereis, Kaltenbrunner, Wolff and Eigruber, stands in front of the camp boundary wall with the quarry just behind it. Note the civilian cyclists passing within metres of abject human misery. The road sign indicates a rail line which no longer exists.

Mauthausen, April 1941. The inspection over, Himmler prepares to leave by car, much to the relief of commandant Ziereis on the right.

Mauthausen, 31st May 1941. Himmler returned to the camp and showed off the facility to visiting Waffen-SS men from "Das Reich" who were resting near Linz after the Yugoslav campaign. Centre, in waxed greatcoat, is Franz Kutschera and right, in light raincoat is August Eigruber. Just visible over Himmler's left shoulder is Friedrich Rainer.

Mauthausen, 31st May 1941. A prisoner stands at attention and removes his cap as was the rule when encountering any SS officer.

Mauthausen, 31st May 1941. An excellent view of the camp buildings and the exquisitely tended garden area with young trees.

Mauthausen, 31st May 1941. On the left is a smiling Otto Kumm.

Mauthausen, 31st May 1941. Left to right: Ziereis, Wolff, Eigruber, Rainer, Kutschera, Himmler, Kaltenbrunner and Kumm.

Mauthausen, 31st May 1941. The large group, led by Himmler and Pohl, pass a group of prisoners far left.

Mauthausen, 31st May 1941. On this occasion, Eigruber far left, wears NSDAP Gauleiter uniform.

Mauthausen, 31st May 1941. In the quarry, Himmler moves on with Willy Bittrich on his left. Following are Pohl and Kutschera, with Friedrich Rainer, Peter Hansen and Franz Huber in the group behind.

Mauthausen, 31st May 1941. Having seen the quarry up close, the group starts to climb the infamous steps back to the protective custody compound. Left to right in front: Peter Hansen, Franz Kutschera, Himmler and Willy Bittrich. Behind them are Dr Friedrich Dermietzel, Dr Ernst Kaltenbrunner and Oswald Pohl.

Above: Mauthausen, 31st May 1941. Having climbed the quarry steps, the group makes its way back to the prisoner barracks. Left is Fritz Klingenberg. The other side of the barbed wire is the drop to the quarry below and some desperate prisoners killed themselves by jumping over the cliff which became known as "parachutist cliff." Note the watch towers and steps behind Klingenberg.

Above: Lodz ghetto, 6th June 1941. Himmler meets the corrupt Chaim Rumkowski, the Jewish elder.

Right: Himmler with SS-Brigadeführer Felix Steiner.

Opposite below: Mauthausen, 31st May 1941. The visit almost complete, the RFSS chats with Wolff. Many Waffen-SS officers denied knowledge of the camp horrors, but the group in the foregoing images could not have failed to notice the conditions in which prisoners were expected to exist.

Above: In late May 1941 at Schloss Pretzsch on the River Elbe, Heydrich gathered about 120 men and informed them of their forthcoming task behind the front lines in conquered territories. They formed the command structure of the Einsatzgruppen and their task was to liquidate communists, subversives and Jews

Left: Bruno Streckenbach selected the personnel for the Einsatzgruppen. Heydrich himself selected the respective commanders.

Clockwise from top left:

Himmler informed Hans Adolf Prützmann that he would have responsibility in the sphere of Army Group North and Einsatzgruppe A.

Walther Stahlecker was given command of Einsatzgruppe A in the area of Army Group North.

Erich von dem Bach would have responsibility in the sphere of Army Group Centre and Einsatzgruppe B.

Arthur Nebe was the only volunteer when Heydrich informed his senior officers. Nebe soon regretted his eagerness. He was appointed to command Einsatzgruppe B in the area of Army Group Centre.

Friedrich Jeckeln was Himmler's choice for the area of Army Group South which covered Einsatzgruppen C and D.

Otto Rasch would command Einsatzgruppe C in the north, east and west of the region operated by Army Group South.

Otto Ohlendorf commanded Einsatzgruppe D in the south of the region operated by Army Group South.

18th June 1941, near Tegernsee. Himmler finds time to pick wild flowers with his wife and daughter four days before Operation Barbarossa.

Haus "Lindenfycht" 18th June 1941, with Gudrun.

Himmler accepts a posy of flowers from a little girl. Over his shoulder is Gottlob Berger.

Himmler was often attentive to German children.

The day before Hitler attacked the Soviet Union, Himmler sat for the photographer Friedrich Franz Bauer. This is a particularly fine portrait of the RFSS.

A formal portrait.

The day after the beginning of Barbarossa, Himmler played tennis. Here he partners Wolff in a game of doubles.

Hitler first arrived at his new field headquarters Wolfsschanze in East Prussia in the early hours of 24th June 1941. This facility would serve as his main headquarters intermittently over the next three years. Himmler's first visit was the next day. This photo from 1942 gives a good idea of the original single storey buildings.

Inside Hitler's office at the Wolfsschanze. Hitler with his adjutant Julius Schaub and his secretaries Gerda Daranowski (left) and Johanna Wolf.

Wolfsschanze, July 1941. Himmler and Wolff stroll through the field headquarters. Note the Feldpost box on the right.

Above: Hitler, Himmler and Wolff at the Wolfsschanze, July 1941.

Left: Hitler and Himmler in the East Prussian sun.

Lublin airfield, 20th July 1941. Himmler arrives and is greeted by members of Globocnik's staff. Left to right: Hans Maubach, Hermann Höfle, Ernst Lerch and unidentified.

Lublin airfield, 20th July 1941. Himmler and Krüger climb into Himmler's car.

Lublin, 20th July 1941. At the entrance to the Jewish camp, Himmler alights from his car which contains Globocnik, Kiermaier, Krüger and Lucas.

Lublin, 20th July 1941. Himmler discusses his ideas with Dr Hans Kammler. On the left are Krüger and Globocnik whilst Wolff and Peiper are on the right.

Dr Hans Kammler. A construction engineer by profession, Kammler worked for the Air Ministry as a building construction advisor until 31st May 1941. During Himmler's visit to Lublin on 20th July 1941, Himmler ordered Globocnik and Kammler to erect a new POW camp capable of receiving and holding 50,000 Soviet prisoners destined for slave labour in the construction of new settlements in the east. In September 1941, Kammler was also tasked with erecting the buildings at Auschwitz-Birkenau. When Himmler decided to carry out large scale physical extermination at Birkenau, it was Kammler who designed and oversaw the construction of the crematoria. Finally, Hitler entrusted his new secret weapons programme to Kammler who he promoted to SS-Obergruppenführer in March 1945.

Lublin, 20th July 1941. Himmler and Krüger arriving at the villa of Odilo Globocnik.

Lublin, 20th July 1941. Himmler is greeted by Gustav Hanelt at the villa of Odilo Globocnik. Following Globocnik are Josef Nemec, Krüger, Wolff and Fritz Katzmann.

Above: In Globocnik's garden, Himmler and Globocnik discuss policy for the region of Lublin, including the erection of a new camp at Majdanek.

Right: Hermann Fegelein.

Left: Himmler chats with Kurt Knoblauch.

Below: Himmler deep in conversation with SS-Standartenführer Fegelein. On the left is SS-Brigadeführer Kurt Knoblauch.

Above: 5th July 1941 near Lyck. Fegelein on horseback and Knoblauch join Himmler reviewing troops.

Below: Himmler speaks to Knoblauch as he prepares to leave the Totenkopf mounted unit. Kiermaier waits by Himmler's car.

Himmler finished his grand inspection tour of July 1941 by flying to Riga. Here, Prützmann and Daluege are at Riga airfield.

On one of his many inspection visits, Himmler at an airfield hands a boy something, possibly an autograph. Erich von dem Bach is second left with Himmler's pilot Carl Schnäbele at his left shoulder.

Prior to departure, von dem Bach holds the map. Himmler is second left.

On 15th August 1941, Himmler witnessed a mass execution in Minsk conducted by Einsatzkommando 8 under the command of Otto Bradfisch. Following this he inspected a Soviet POW camp.

Opposite above: Minsk, 15th August 1941. Himmler speaks to Soviet POWs.

Opposite below: Minsk, 15th August 1941. Is this Russian boy suitable for Germanization?

Left: Otto Bradfisch, commander of Einsatzkommando 8 of Einsatgruppe B in Minsk.

Below: Minsk, 15th August 1941. Himmler with Otto Bradfisch.

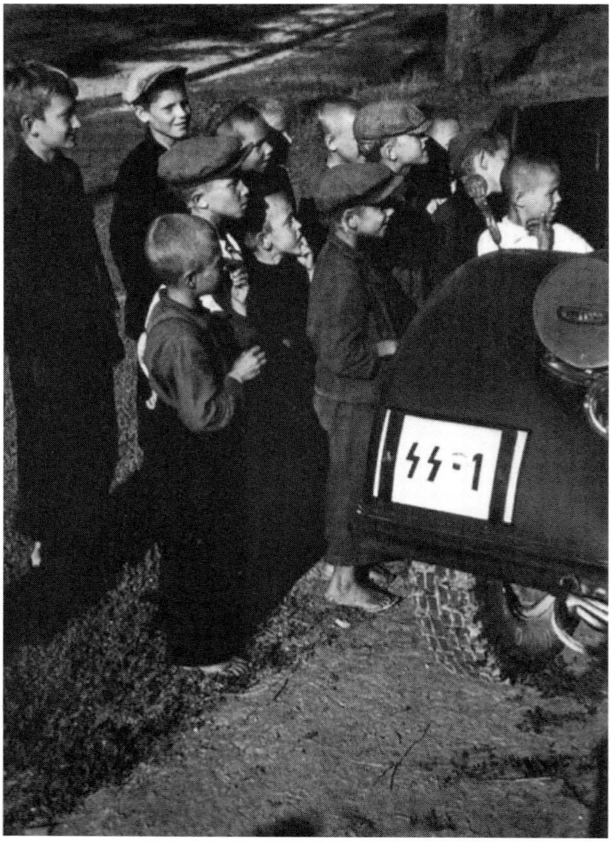

Left: Local children in Minsk gather around the Reichsführer's car, August 1941.

Below: Feldkommandostelle Hegewaldheim, used almost exclusively as a guest house for entertaining, but also for certain conferences. Before the war the building was a holiday guest house, but from 1941 it was requisitioned by the Personal Staff RFSS. The building no longer exists.

Above: Chosen for its elevated position and views over the nearby Zabinker See, it was in this idyllic setting that several important decisions were made, including one fateful conclusion over the destiny of the European Jews.

Right: A rare view of the interior of Hegewaldheim.

Above: Another view of the interior of Hegewaldheim on a postcard from pre-Himmler occupation.

Left: Himmler's housekeepers at Hegewaldheim on the steps below the terrace.

The housekeepers on the pathway between the house and the lake.

Grothmann and Himmler at Hegewaldheim.

Late July/early August 1941, Grossgarten, East Prussia. The area which was designated as Feldkommandostelle Hochwald was initially cordoned off by police who redirected traffic.

Hochwald, July 1941. Outdoor furniture constructed of local materials to enable Himmler and staff to sit away from his train in the summer heat. The barracks had not yet been erected.

Hochwald, 3rd August 1941. The construction of the wooden barracks gets underway using civilian construction workers.

Hochwald, 4th August 1941. The foundation outline of the wooden barrack is laid out on a cleared area in the trees.

Hochwald, 5th August 1941. Sectins of one end of the barrack has been erected while the floor is under construction.

Hochwald, 6th August 1941. Sections of the barrack are awaiting erection. Part of the roof is also up.

Hochwald, 7th August 1941. With one side wall completely erected, this view provides an excellent idea of the scale of the barrack. Himmler's day office was located at one end of the barrack.

Hochwald, 8th August 1941. Discussions on the progress of construction.

Hochwald, 8th August 1941. The carpenters are busy trying to complete the work on the flooring. There are two windows visible at the end of the building. The civilian workers appear to have been replaced.

Hochwald, August 1941. The facility attempted to be self-sufficient with chickens… and pigs.

Gut Gansenstein, East Prussia. Known to Himmler's staff as Friedrichsruh. A contemporary image.

Friedrichsruh today.

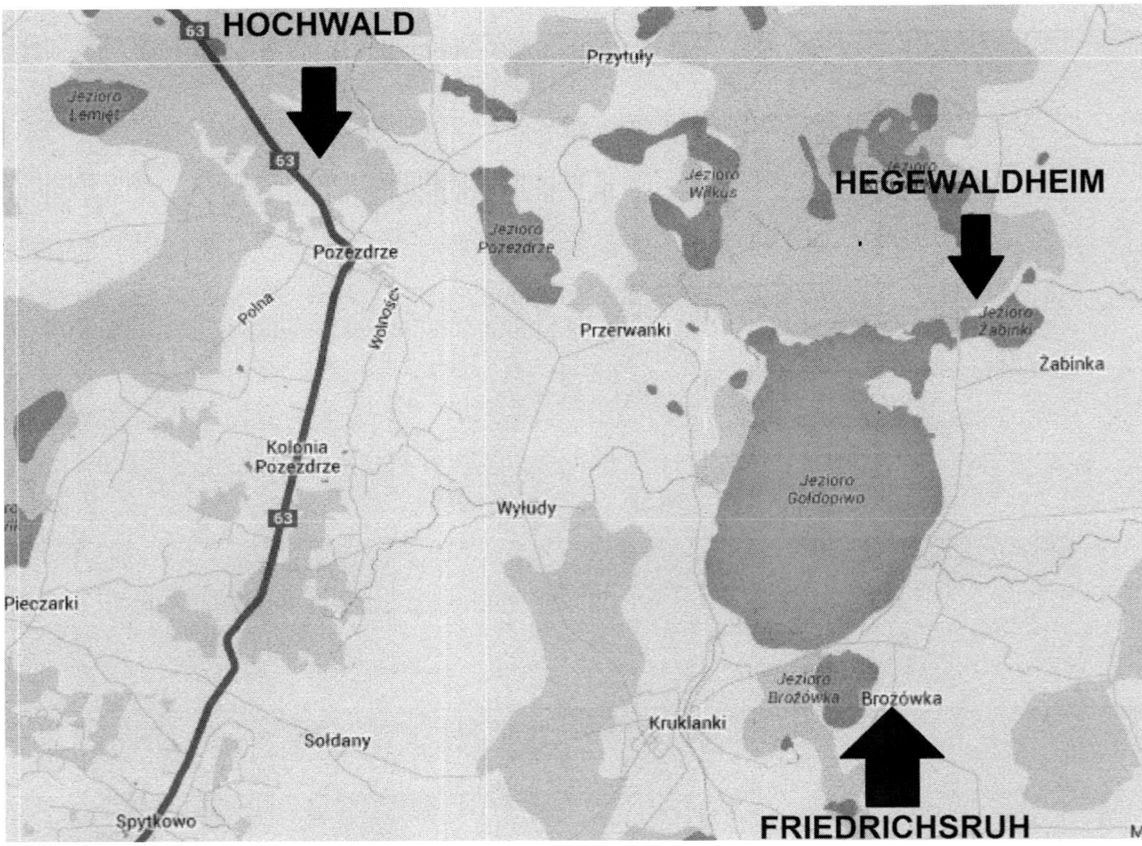
HOCHWALD
HEGEWALDHEIM
FRIEDRICHSRUH
Przytuły
Pozezdrze
Przerwanki
Żabinka
Kolonia Pozezdrze
Wyłudy
Pieczarki
Brozówka
Kruklanki
Sołdany
Spytkowo
Jezioro Gołdopiwo
Jezioro Pozezdrze
Jezioro Brożówka

Opposite above: The sites of Himmler's Feldkommandostellen in East Prussia.

Opposite below: Wolfsschanze, 4th September 1941. Wolff watches as Himmler shakes the hand of Reichsminister Fritz Todt.

On 18th September 1941 Himmler wrote to Greiser to inform him that Hitler wanted the Reich and Protektorat cleared of Jews. Consequently, Himmler would deport many of them to the Lodz ghetto. Within a very short time the ghetto became overcrowded and Greiser directed Wilhelm Koppe to find a solution. Koppe (left centre) stands next to Greiser (right centre.)

Herbert Lange was ordered by Koppe to reduce the excess numbers in the Lodz ghetto. Lange's detachment was centred on an old manor house at Chelmno where Jews were loaded into sealed vans and driven to a clearing in a nearby forest. En route, the van exhaust fumes were fed into the crowded sealed compartment where the unfortunate passengers were overcome by the fatal carbon monoxide gas.

Clockwise from top left

The man credited with the design and development of gas vans was family man Walther Rauff of the SD. Rauff supervised the modification of scores of vans with the assistance of a Berlin chassis builder, to divert exhaust fumes into airtight chambers in the back of vehicles. The trucks could carry between 25 and sixty people at a time.

The Reichsprotektor of Bohemia-Moravia, Constantin Freiherr von Neurath. Considered weak by Karl Hermann Frank and Heydrich, Hitler removed him and replaced him with the firm Heydrich.

The ambitious Karl Hermann Frank.

Clockwise from top left: Hitler promoted Heydrich to SS-Obergruppenführer and installed him in Prague as Deputy Reichsprotektor.

On 4th and 5th October 1941, Himmler visited the staff of Einsatzgruppe D in the Ukraine. Otto Ohlendorf, pictured here in Annanjew in August 1941, had agreed with local army commanders to exclude Jewish farmers from his round-ups. Himmler immediately countermanded this order to include all Jews in the executions.

One of the young intellectuals recruited for the SD by Heydrich, Otto Ohlendorf found himself posted to command an Einsatzgruppe for field experience. He realised from an early stage that the war was lost and was largely protected by Himmler who recognised his economic talents and foresaw a role for him in post-war Germany. His crimes with Einsatzgruppe D proved too great to save him from the scaffold and he was hanged in June 1951 at Landsberg Prison.

Wolfsschanze, 7th October 1941. Hitler congratulates Himmler on his 41st birthday.

On 13th October 1941, Himmler ordered Odilo Globocnik to turn a labour camp at Belzec into a facility for liquidating the Jews of the southern General Government. A newspaper portrait of Globocnik from the time.

Globocnik turned to his construction expert Richard Thomalla who commenced work in early November 1941 using Polish villagers, Trawniki camp prisoners and Jewish slave workers. The installation was finished by early March 1942 and began operating on or about 17th March 1942.

As the first commandant Globocnik chose Christian Wirth who had experience with the T4 euthanasia programme. Wirth proved so successful that he was appointed as inspector of the three Aktion Reinhard death camps at Belzec, Sobibor and Treblinka.

At the end of October 1941, Himmler found time for a three days hunting excursion with Count Ciano. In this undated photo, he is followed by Grothmann, leaving for a shoot.

Himmler arrives at the gates of Hradcany Castle in Prague on 29th October 1941.

Himmler is greeted by Karl Hermann Frank.

Heydrich introduces some of his staff in Prague.

The guard presents arms in Hradcany Castle courtyard.

Himmler enters the residence. Left to right: Frank, Himmler, Wolff, Heydrich and Kluckhohn.

The relationship between Göring and Himmler was one of rivalry.

Every November the "heavyweights" of the NSDAP gathered in Munich to celebrate the anniversary of the Beer Hall Putsch of 1923.

Above: Munich, 9th November 1941. The party faithful listen to Hitler's speech. Easily identifiable in the crowd are Querner, Grawitz, Hildebrandt, Frank, Heydrich, Daluege, Waldeck, Wolff, Schaub, Todt, Schepmann, Hofmann and Schultze.

Opposite below: Himmler speaks in Munich. Keitel, Schwarz, Frick, Fiehler and Lammers behind him.

Right: : Himmler pays an inspection visit to a fire fighters' base.

Below: Kurt Daluege escorts Himmler.

Himmler and Daluege watch a demonstration by fire fighters.

The use of the fire hose is explained.

Above: The fire service came under the control of the Ordnungspolizei.

Right: Himmler shows interest in the fire fighting equipment.

Fire fighters put on a display with water hoses.

In November 1941, Himmler issued a directive to liquidate the ghetto in Riga. He was informed that Hinrich Lohse, the Reichskommissar for the Ostland, had objected to the action to which Himmler retorted "You tell Lohse that is my order, which is also the Führer's wish!" Lohse is pictured here with Hitler at the Wolfsschanze.

On 20th November 1941, Himmler visited Albert Forster in Danzig.

The local SS leader in Danzig was Richard Hildebrandt.

The chief of the SS Race and Settlement Central Office was SS-Gruppenführer Otto Hofmann. During his visit to Danzig, Himmler held talks with Hofmann.

The Chief of the SS Office for the Strengthening of German Nationhood was SS-Gruppenführer Ulrich Greifelt.

Stutthof concentration camp, 23rd November 1941. Himmler arrives for an inspection visit and is received by the camp commandant, Max Pauly.

The officers of Stutthof.

The guard presents arms to Himmler and Hildebrandt.

Inside the protective custody compound, Himmler begins his inspection. Left are Hildebrandt and Wolff.

Angora rabbits were bred at Stutthof for their fur.

Himmler insisted on seeing everything during his inspections. Here he is interested in a drainage outlet pipe.

Himmler's group makes its way back to the Kommandantur where tea was provided in the officers' canteen.

Himmler is entertained by Max Pauly after the camp tour. Partly obscured by flowers is Richard Hildebrandt.

Rudolf Lange, commander of Einsatzkommando 2 of Einsatzgruppe A.

In January 1942, Himmler conducted several visits to the eastern front. Here he is with Theodor Eicke and Heinz Lammerding.

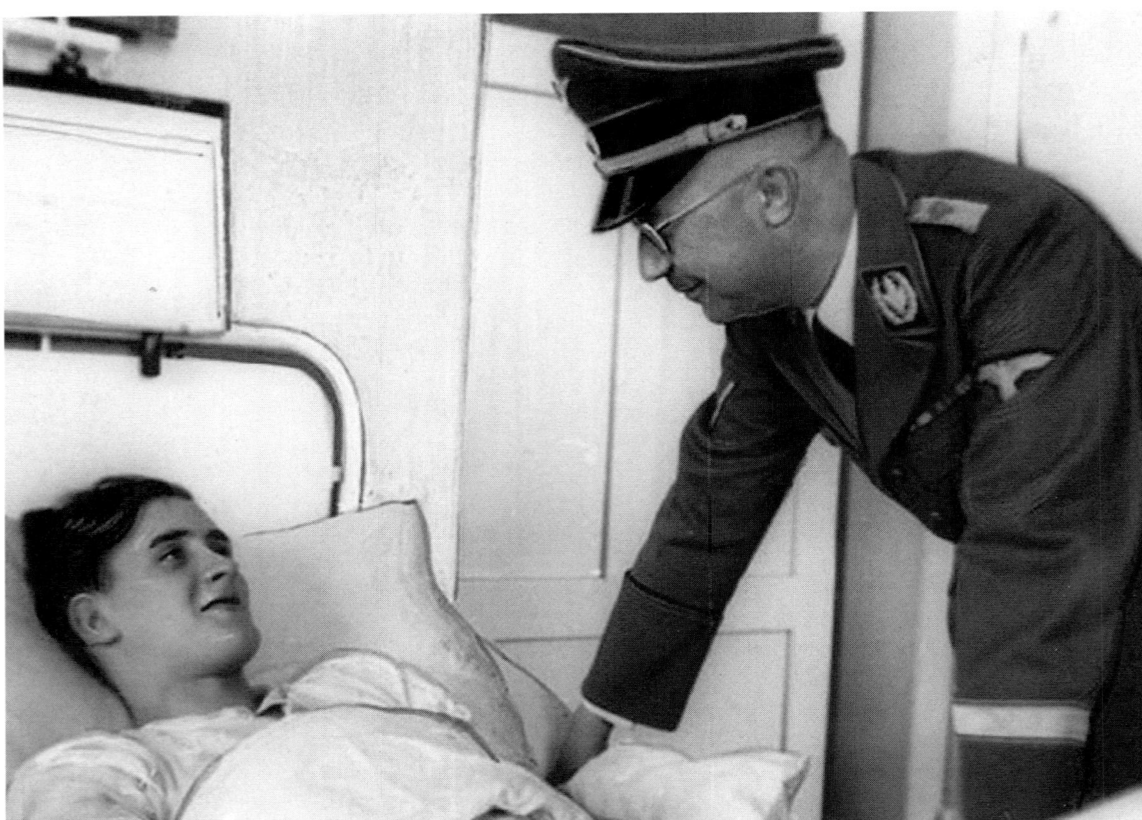

Above: 5th or 6th January 1942, Schloss Krasnogwardiesk, south of Leningrad with a local Wehrmacht officer and Jeckeln.

Right: Schloss Krasnogwardiesk near Leningrad with Jeckeln on 5th or 6th January 1942.

Opposite above: Himmler's entourage has just arrived by air at one of his destinations. Carl Schnäbele, Himmler's pilot (in leather greatcoat and upturned collar) consults his boss for future instructions. Note the cases being unloaded.

Opposite below: Himmler considered morale to be an important cog in the German war machine and consequently took steps to maintain the high spirits of the troops. Here he is visiting the wounded in hospital.

Clockwise from top left:

Himmler departs.

A winter visit from the Reichsführer-SS.

Winter on the eastern front.

Himmler watches manoeuvres through his binoculars on a cold winter day. He has an additional coat over his shoulders for protection against the minus temperatures. Next to him is Karl Wolff and further along is Friedrich Jeckeln (also with binoculars.)

An officer indicates deployment.

Am Grossen Wannsee 56-58, Berlin-Wannsee. On 20th January 1942, Heydrich chaired a meeting which formalised the SS control over the fate of European Jews.

Opposite above: Governor Karl Lasch (second from right) was a close friend of Hans Frank. In January 1942 Lasch was arrested on Himmler's orders for illegal appropriation of Jewish property. Frank's efforts to save his friend came to nought and Lasch was executed at Auschwitz where his death certificate was subsequently discovered post-war.

Opposite below: Hans Frank greets a Slovakian army general. On the left is Karl Lasch, with Eberhard Schöngarth, Josef Bühler and Friedrich-Wilhelm Krüger looking on.

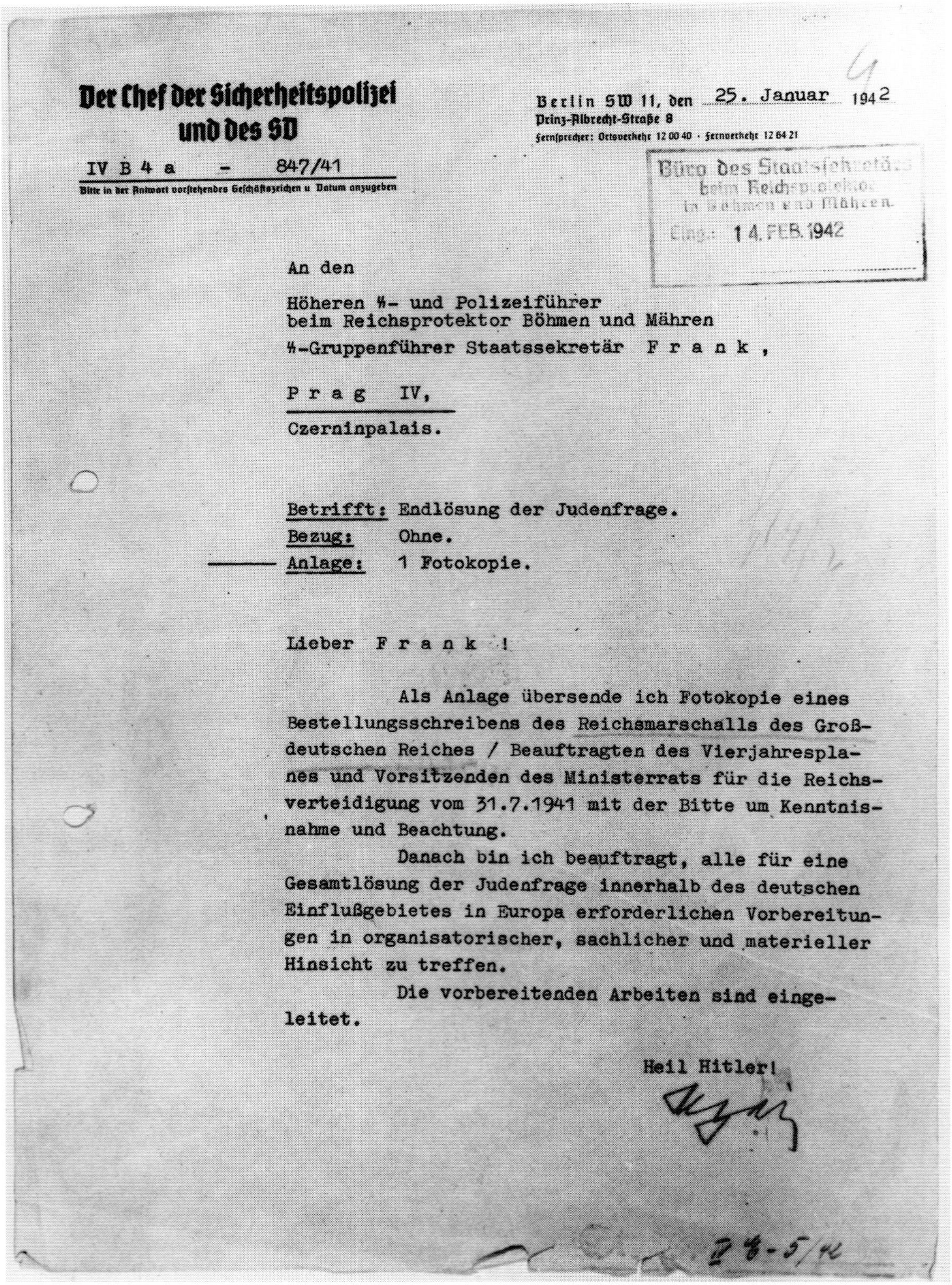

Der Chef der Sicherheitspolizei und des SD

IV B 4 a - 847/41

Bitte in der Antwort vorstehendes Geschäftszeichen u Datum anzugeben

Berlin SW 11, den 25. Januar 1942
Prinz-Albrecht-Straße 8
Fernsprecher: Ortsverkehr 12 00 40 · Fernverkehr 12 64 21

Büro des Staatssekretärs beim Reichsprotektor in Böhmen und Mähren
Eing.: 14. FEB. 1942

An den

Höheren ℌ- und Polizeiführer
beim Reichsprotektor Böhmen und Mähren
ℌ-Gruppenführer Staatssekretär F r a n k ,

P r a g IV,

Czerninpalais.

Betrifft: Endlösung der Judenfrage.
Bezug: Ohne.
Anlage: 1 Fotokopie.

Lieber F r a n k !

Als Anlage übersende ich Fotokopie eines Bestellungsschreibens des Reichsmarschalls des Großdeutschen Reiches / Beauftragten des Vierjahresplanes und Vorsitzenden des Ministerrats für die Reichsverteidigung vom 31.7.1941 mit der Bitte um Kenntnisnahme und Beachtung.

Danach bin ich beauftragt, alle für eine Gesamtlösung der Judenfrage innerhalb des deutschen Einflußgebietes in Europa erforderlichen Vorbereitungen in organisatorischer, sachlicher und materieller Hinsicht zu treffen.

Die vorbereitenden Arbeiten sind eingeleitet.

Heil Hitler!

Following the Wannsee conference, Heydrich informed all SS leaders of his authority from Göring to formulate policy towards finding a final solution to the Jewish problem. Here is Karl Hermann Frank's copy.

Contrary to popular belief, Himmler and his lieutenants had a human side. The vast majority were family men whose private lives bore no resemblance to their service activities. It is difficult to reconcile the two different worlds in which they operated. In this extremely rare private photo of Reinhard Heydrich, the architect of the Holocaust, he relaxes on the beach near his summer retreat on the Baltic island of Fehmarn.

For now, comrades in the world of sabotage, intelligence, intrigue and espionage, but later adversaries. Heinrich Müller (chief of the Gestapo) and Admiral Wilhelm Canaris (head of military intelligence.) Canaris would become involved in the plot to depose Hitler and would be executed at Flossenbürg concentration camp on the orders of Himmler on 9th April 1945.

Above: The winter of 1941/1942 saw heavy snowfall in the east. Himmler's headquarters did not escape the weather. This is the vehicular access track leading to the Hochwald compound after the first snow.

Left: Inside the Hochwald compound with Himmler's barrack on the left.

Above: Sonderzug "Heinrich" on the rail siding at Hochwald, winter 1941/1942.

Right: When stationary on the siding in Hochwald, Sonderzug "Heinrich" was covered with camouflage netting.

Opposite above: Tiefenbacher second from left next to Dr Ludwig Stumpfegger.

Opposite below: Members of Himmler's staff, including a secretary, pose for the camera in the Hochwald snow.

Left: At one end of the barrack, the winter sun begins to thaw the snow.

Below: Members of Himmler's personal staff amuse themselves in the Hochwald snow with a game of curling. Tiefenbacher has just released his curling stone on the ice.

Above: One of Himmler's staff next to Sonderzug "Heinrich." Note the sign forbidding access along the side of the train.

Left: Ludwig Pemsel.

Clockwise from top left:

Walther Wüst of the Leibstandarte-SS "Adolf Hitler," one of numerous members of Himmler's adjutancy over the years.

Fred Conrad.

Dr Helmuth Fitzner.

Clockwise from top left:

Hilmar Gutgesell.

Hans Joachim von Hadeln. A young adjutant on Himmler's staff in the 1930s, he saw active service with SS-Division Wiking and was killed in action on 12th January 1943.

Heinrich Heckenstaller, photographed in the office of the Personal Staff RFSS.

Clockwise from top left:

Franz Lucas, Himmler's personal driver from June 1940. He replaced Hans Bastian after the latter inadvertently killed himself with his own machine pistol.

August Meine transferred from the army to become one of Himmler's adjutants.

Franz Mueller-Darss was Himmler's forest and hunt master on his personal staff. He was also responsible for all dogs used in SS service, including the camps.

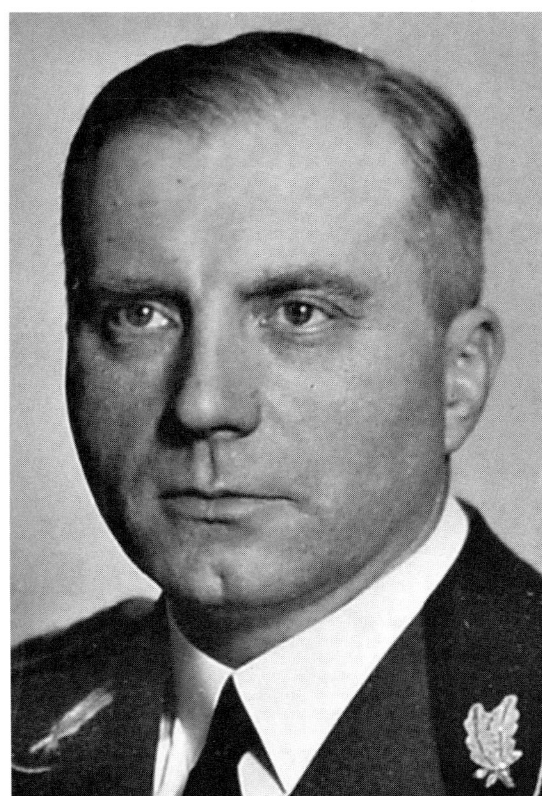

Clockwise from top left:

Dr Ralf Wehser, a legal expert and advisor on Himmler's staff.

Carl Schnäbele, Himmler's personal pilot.

A rare photograph of Carl Schnäbele with his boss.

Clockwise from top left:

Ludolf von Alvensleben was Himmler's chief adjutant from 25th November 1938 until 31st January 1941.

Karl Wolff was Chief of the Personal Staff RFSS.

Himmler extensively used aircraft as a means of transport during the war. Here he is inside his personal Ju52.

The Reichsführer considered himself as the eyes and ears of the nation. As such, his flights provided him with the opportunity to keep abreast of current press reports and magazine articles.

Relaxing in-flight with a book.

Reichsführer-ZZzzz

Although the interior of his Ju52 was adapted to meet his needs, it cannot be described as luxurious.

Above: 1942, with Wilhelm Keitel and Erhard Milch.

Left: From 9th to 10th March 1942, Himmler visited Wilhelm Kube in Minsk. Although Kube was a former SS-Gruppenführer, he had left the SS and was now one of its more vociferous critics.

Right: The Reichsminister for the Occupied Eastern Territories, Alfred Rosenberg (right) and his deputy, Alfred Meyer.

Below: The powerbase in the General Government, left to right: Krüger, Himmler, Frank and Bühler.

Clockwise from top left:

Bitter enemies in Krakow, Frank and Krüger.

Eberhard Schöngarth was the commander of the SD and Security Police in Krakow. Directly responsible for many of the crimes committed in the General Government, they only came to light after his execution by the British for murdering an Allied pilot.

Julian Scherner, the SS and Police Leader in Krakow. He was responsible for clearing the ghetto and deporting the inhabitants to Belzec, Auschwitz and Plaszow.

Himmler is seen here at Lublin airfield with Krüger. It is highly likely that during this visit he ordered Krüger to clear the ghettos at Lemberg and Lublin and deport the inhabitants to Belzec.

To cover short distances rapidly, Himmler had the use of a Fieseler Storch light aircraft.

Above: Late March 1942, over the city of Riga.

Right: On 20th March 1942, Himmler visited SS-Obergruppenführer Friedrich Jeckeln in Krasnoje-Selo.

Opposite above: A photograph taken from Himmler's Fieseler Storch en route to Hitler's Wolfsschanze.

Opposite below: In late March 1942, Himmler conducted a major inspection tour of the northern sector of the Russian front. This photo was taken from his Ju52 en route to Riga.

Above: Kiestinki, Finland, 27th March 1942 with Karl Maria Demelhuber (left.)

Left: Early 1942, leaving a trench bunker in the snow.

Right: On the eastern front. (A magazine photo.)

Below: Himmler's March 1942 grand tour included a visit to SA-Obergruppenführer Karl-Siegmund Litzmann, the Generalkommissar of Estonia. Litzmann (right) is photographed here on a later date with von Eberstein (left.)

Above: Himmler flew to Posen on 16th April 1942 where he held lengthy meetings with Greiser and Koppe and also visited the SS training school at Treskau. The following day Himmler drove to Warsaw where he visited the ghetto. On 20th April, the major resettlement of the Lodz ghetto got underway. In this earlier photo, Himmler is joined by Wolff, Greiser and Koppe leaving a building in Posen.

Opposite below: Himmler was back at the Wolfsschanze on 20th April 1942 to congratulate Hitler on his birthday. Left is Karl Wolff.

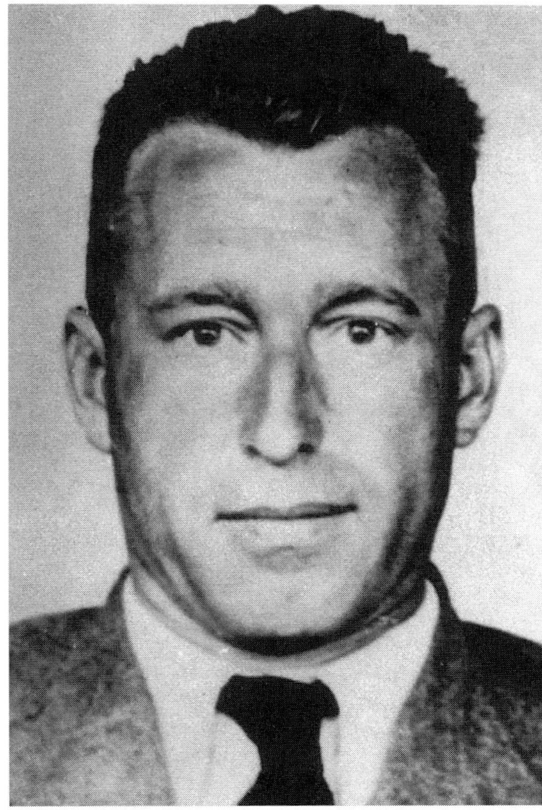

Right: Franz Stangl, the commandant of the new gassing facility at Sobibor.

Below: Odilo Globocnik at the rail station in Sobibor, almost certainly prior to the adjacent camp becoming operational. Ernst Lerch second from left in spectacles.

Hermann Göring and Himmler, with Paul Körner and Kurt Daluege in the background.

Undated photo in Holland. Himmler speaking to Mussert with Rauter and Demelhuber behind.

Himmler reviews Dutch troops in Holland accompanied by Wolff, Berger and Rauter.

The Norwegian volunteers for the SS were commanded by Jonas Lie.

Above: Inside Prinz-Albrecht-Strasse, Himmler receives two Knights Cross winners from the police. Left to right: Bernhard Griese, Himmler, Rudolf Pannier and Daluege.

Left: At 10.32am on 27th May 1942, Czech army parachutists attacked Reinhard Heydrich in his car in Prague. He died from his wounds on 4th June 1942. One of the police photos of his car in situ at the scene, taken from inside a tram.

Himmler ordered Gebhardt to Prague to supervise Heydrich's medical care.

Prof. Dr Ferdinand Sauerbruch, a personal friend of Heydrich, was also despatched to the Czech capital.

Left: Karl Hermann Frank hoped to succeed Heydrich, but his hopes were dashed when Himmler persuaded Hitler to replace Heydrich in Prague with Kurt Daluege.

Below: Daluege happened to be already in Prague on 27th May 1942 and immediately instigated harsh reprisals. He is seen here with Viktor Lütze (right) and Franz May (centre.)

Heydrich's coffin stands before the Matthias Gate, Hradcany Castle, 7th June 1942.

Prague, 7th June 1942. The two Heydrich boys with their Godfather. Left is Bruno Streckenbach.

Hradcany Castle, 7th June 1942. Left to right, front row: Jürgen von Osten, Maria Heydrich, Elisabeth Heydrich, Heinz Heydrich, Heider and Klaus Heydrich, Himmler.

Himmler stands between the two Heydrich boys as their father's casket is loaded onto a gun carriage. Far left is Kiermaier, then Daluege (obscured) Wolff, Maria Heydrich, Elisabeth Heydrich, Heinz Heydrich, KH Frank, von Osten and Gebhardt.

The gun carriage is about to move off.

Berlin, Anhalter station, 8th June 1942. Heydrich coffin has been removed from the train and is followed along the platform by Himmler.

Opposite above: Listening to the speech of the RFSS.

Opposite below: Himmler at the rostrum. The bronze eagle and swastika above the doorway is today on display at the Imperial War Museum in London.

Left: The Mosaic Hall at the Berlin Reich Chancellery, 9th June 1942. Standing for the arrival of Hitler.

Below: Berlin, 9th June 1942. Himmler hands Hitler a note from the widowed Lina Heydrich who was heavily pregnant and unable to attend her husband's funeral.

Opposite above: Himmler leads the funeral cortege towards the Invaliden cemetery.

Opposite below: Invaliden cemetery, Berlin, 9th June 1942. Himmler salutes the grave of Heydrich.

Farewell.

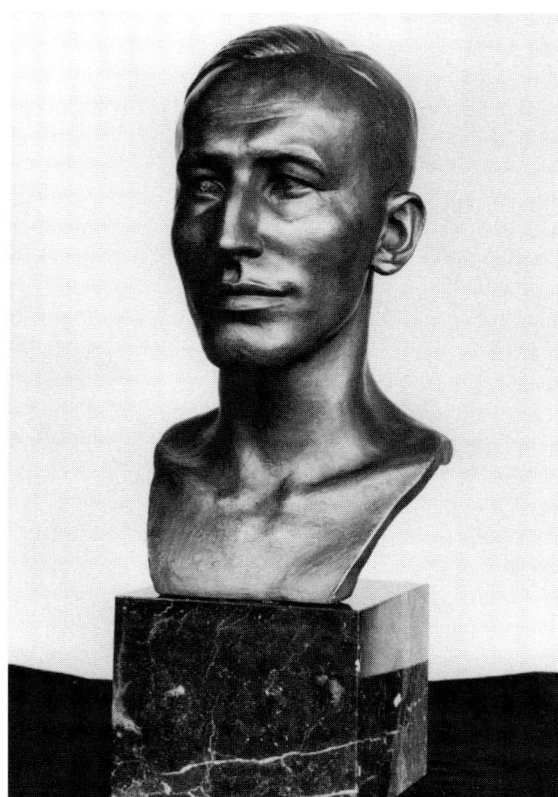

Franz Rotter produced a bronze bust from a casting taken on Heydrich's deathbed. Himmler ordered two examples.

At Heydrich's funeral: Bruno Streckenbach (left in front of Müller and Nebe) was the most obvious candidate to replace Heydrich as head of the SD and Security Police. Next to him are Wewelsburg Burghauptmann Taubert and Grawitz.

Himmler attended the funeral of Adolf Hühnlein on 21st June 1942.

An undated photo taken at the Berlin Sportspalast. Left to right: Schmundt, Schaub, Hitler, Keitel, Milch and Himmler.

At the same event, Keitel, Milch and Himmler listen to their Führer speak.

Hochwald, 7th July 1942. Hans Heinrich Lammers visits Himmler's headquarters. On the left are Tiefenbacher and Berger. Note Lammers is still wearing the old style rank insignia on his white summer tunic.

Hochwald, 7th July 1942. Reichsminister Alfred Rosenberg visited Himmler at his headquarters. He is seen here on the left with Himmler and Lammers beside Sonderzug "Heinrich."

The anti-British Indian leader Subhas Chandra Bose (left) was the guest of Himmler at Hegewaldheim on 15th July 1942.

Left to right: Werner Grothmann, Subhas Chandra Bose, Himmler and Walther Wüst.

Prof. Wüst (far left) with Chandra Bose and Himmler on the terrace at Hegewaldheim.

Himmler speaks into a microphone as he meets wounded SS troops back from the front.

An undated image of Hitler reviewing the Berlin Standort guard. He is followed by Bormann, Schaub, von Jena, Wolff, Schulze-Kossens and Himmler.

Auschwitz, 17th - 18th July 1942. Himmler's second visit to the camp. He meets Max Faust of I.G. Farben Industries at Monowitz.

Auschwitz-Monowitz, 17th – 18th July 1942. Schmauser shakes hands with Faust as Himmler and Höss start to walk away on the inspection tour.

The group inside the Buna rubber plant complex.

A representative of I.G. Farben explains the plans of the plant. Max Faust in hat with Höss and Schmauser on the left.

Himmler wipes the sweat from his brow.

Himmler tours the main camp at Auschwitz, 17th – 18th July 1942. The group are outside the Kommandantur. Hans Kammler second from right.

DAS KONZENTRATIONSLAGER AUSCHWITZ I ("STAMMLAGER")

AUSBAUSTAND AUGUST 1944

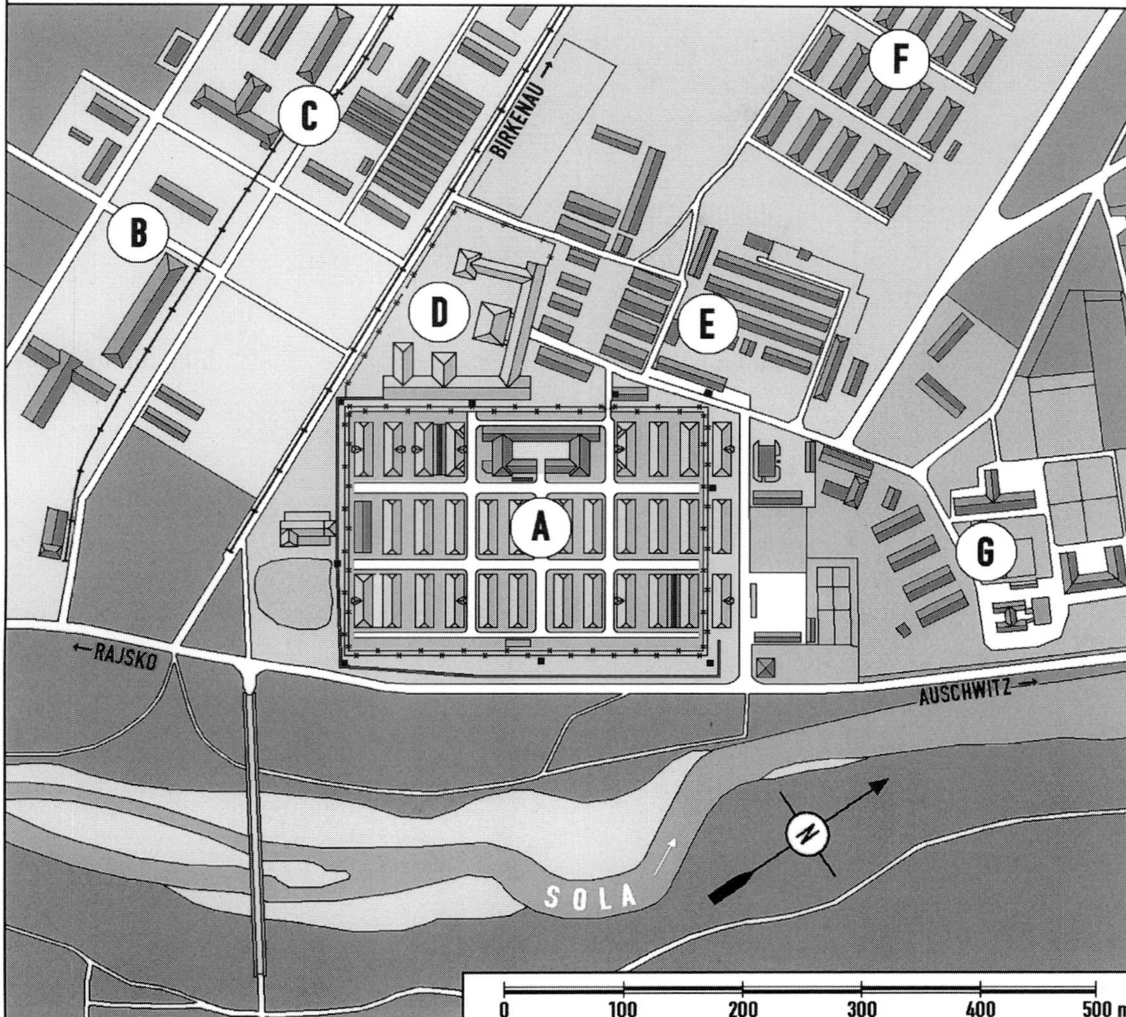

A - Häftlings-Lagerbereich
siehe Plan "Häftlings-Lagerbereich"

B - Gebäude der ehemaligen polnischen Tabak-Monopol-Gesellschaft, hier waren 1940 die ersten KL-Häftlinge untergebracht

C - Industriebetriebe, in den KL-Häftlinge und Zwangsarbeiter "beschäftigt" waren

D - Aufnahme/Registraturgebäude für neue KL-Häftlinge

E - SS-Werkstätten und Lager

F - "DAW" (Deutsche Ausrüstungswerke)
eine SS-eigene Firma, in der KL-Häftlinge arbeiten mußten

G - SS- Unterkünfte und Wirtschaftsgebäude

Auschwitz I, August 1944.

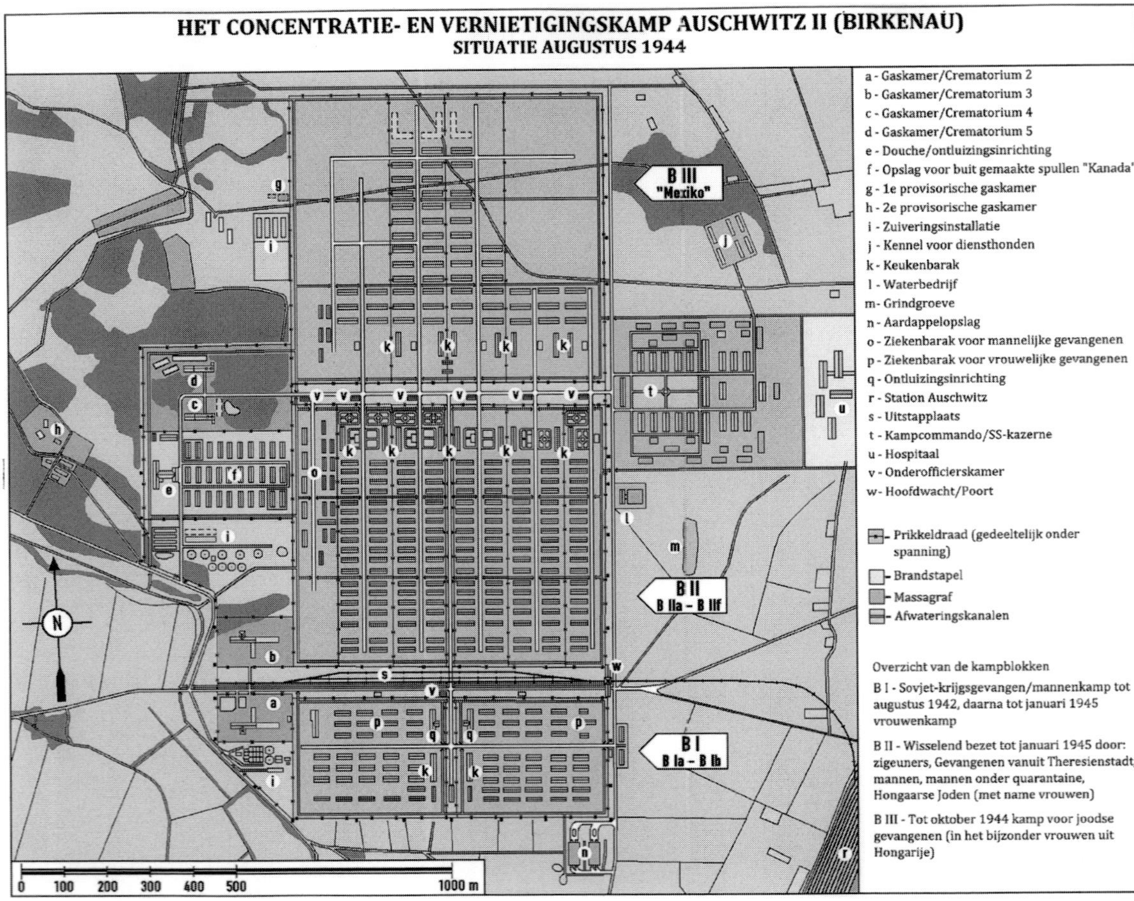

Auschwitz-Birkenau, August 1944.

Aerial photo of Auschwitz-Birkenau, 25th August 1944. A transport has just been unloaded and the selection completed. Only crematoria II and III are visible in this image at lower right.

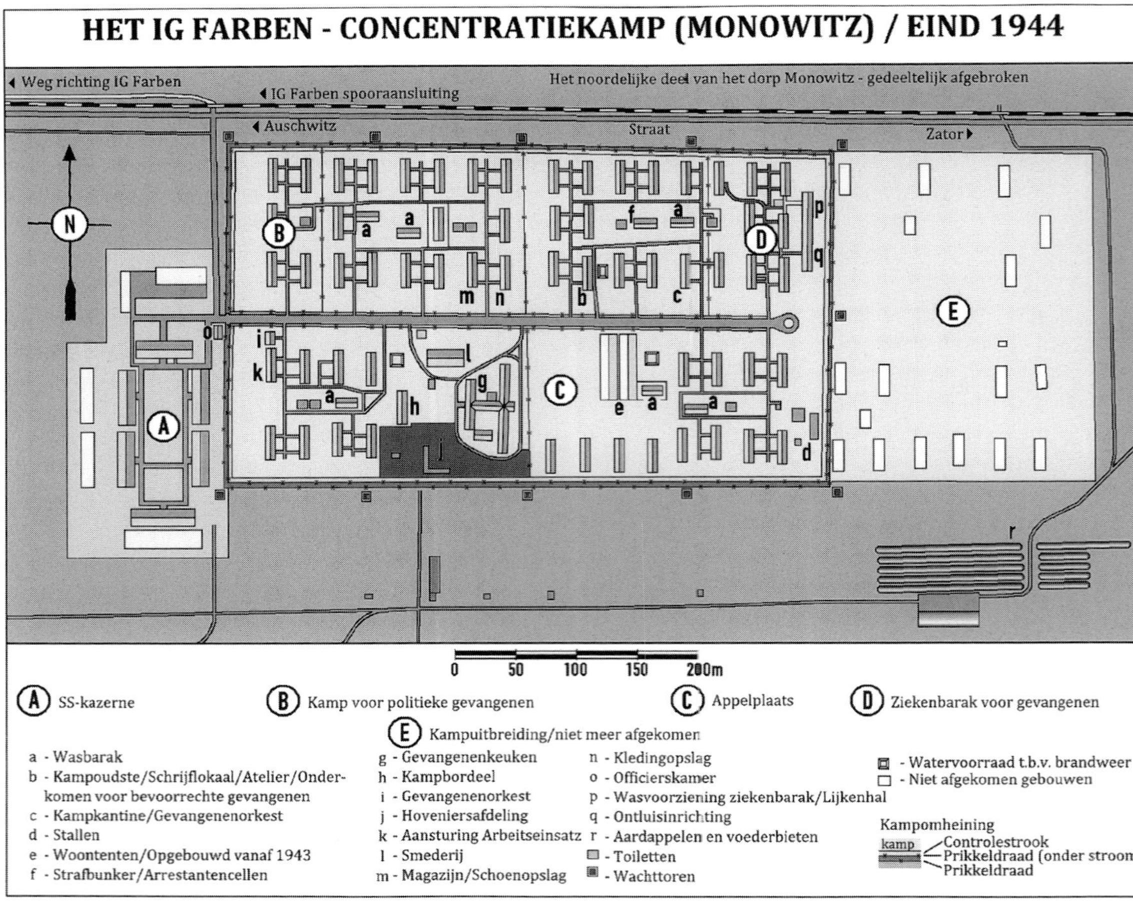

Auschwitz III, 1944.

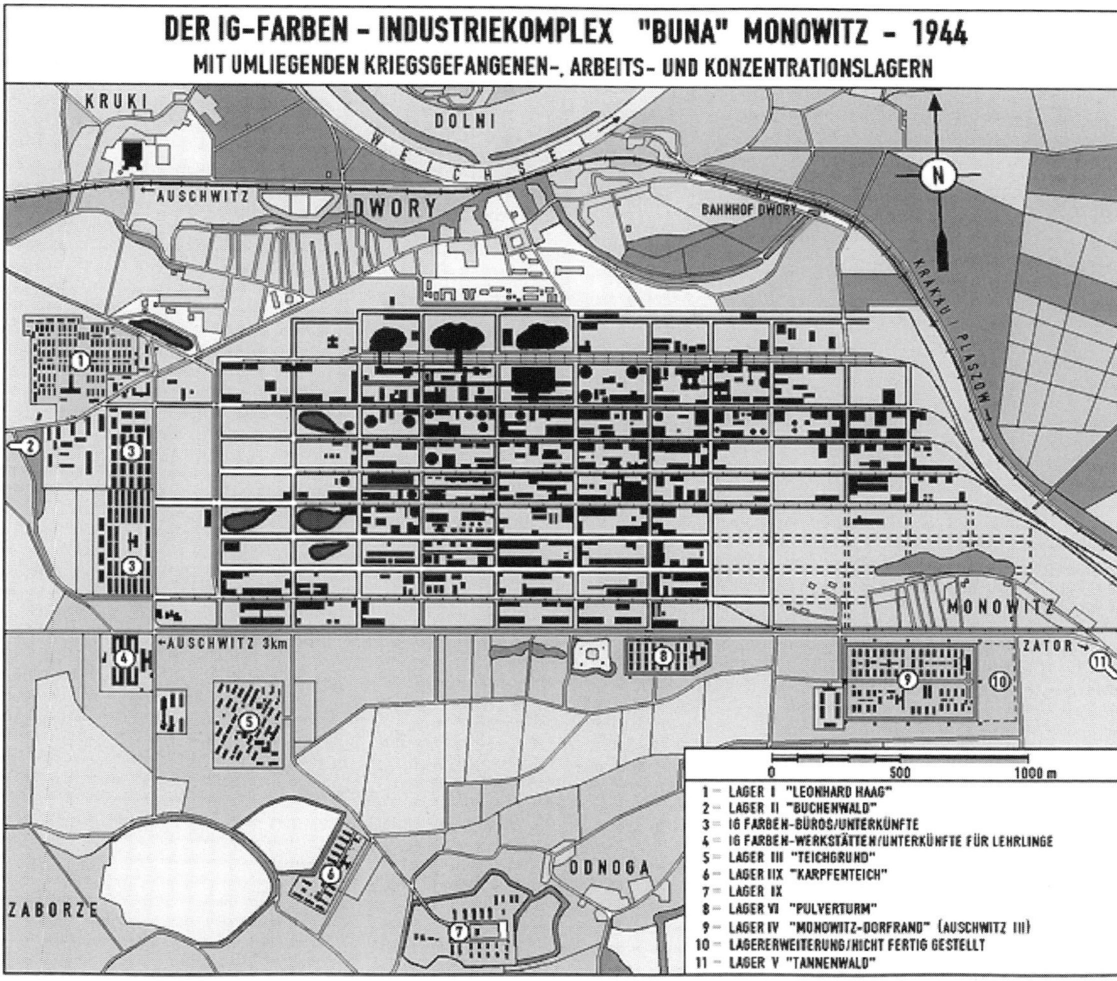

The I.G. Farben Industries complex at Auschwitz-Monowitz, 1944.

Clockwise from top left:

The first camp commandant at Auschwitz, Rudolf Höss.

The second camp commandant, Arthur Liebehenschel.

The third camp commandant at Auschwitz, Richard Baer.

Opposite above: Female SS auxiliaries were used as camp guards to look after female prisoners. Many were as brutal as their male counterparts and some were executed for their crimes after the war.

Himmler had experienced at first hand the "difficult work" his Einsatzkommandos had to endure. He was keen to find a more clinical method of killing and Auschwitz officer Karl Fritzsch suggested using Zyklon B crystals in a sealed compartment. The blue pellets were already effectively used to exterminate fleas and lice on prisoners' clothing and Fritzsch experimented successfully on Soviet POWs in a sealed basement in Auschwitz I.

An alternative method of execution widely used by Einsatzkommandos and various Wehrmacht units was hanging. Although hanging was used in the camp system, large scale executions could not be achieved. Hanging remained the favoured method to execute partisans and hostages as it was highly visible and carried a definite message.

Rudolf Höss settled upon Zyklon B as his preferred method of mass killing as it was more efficient than the unreliable carbon monoxide where machinery would often break down. Ethnic groups targeted by Himmler for deportation to Auschwitz included the Roma or gypsies. As with the Jews, their numbers were decimated and young Sinti children such as those pictured here from Rumania, stood little or no chance of surviving Auschwitz-Birkenau.

To carry out mass killing on an industrial scale, Himmler needed to erect purpose built facilities at Auschwitz. He consulted Dr Hans Kammler, seen here in conversation with Walter Krüger.

A high level conference of senior SS officers. Visible are Leo von Jena, Walter Krüger, Max von Herff, Ernst-Robert Grawitz, Walter Schmitt and on the right, in the second row, Hans Kammler.

On 11th July 1942, Dr Irmfried Eberl was appointed as commandant of the new Treblinka extermination facility. Unable to manage and process the number of transports sent to the camp, he was replaced just over a month later by Franz Stangl.

Himmler poses in his new field headquarters Hegewald south of Zhitomir which he used from 24th July 1942.

Himmler and Daluege in conversation at Feldkommandostelle Hegewald.

The conference table in Himmler's office at Feldkommandostelle Hegewald.

Himmler speaking to an unidentified SS man at Hegewald. Tiefenbacher in the background.

Himmler and Tiefenbacher in Himmler's office at Hegewald. Note the Allach candlestick on his desk.

Himmler makes a point to Daluege at the conference table in Himmler's office at Hegewald. Note the simple furniture.

Himmler's Feldkommandostelle Hegewald near Zhitomir. This photograph was taken prior to Himmler's occupation when it was used by a Luftwaffe communications unit. Previously a Russian army building, it was completely destroyed at the end of the war. (*Photo courtesy Martin Bogaert*)

Opposite above: Rovaniemi, Finland, 31st July 1942. Himmler visits General Dietl (left.)

Opposite below: Himmler during his visit to General Dietl.

Left: Max von Herff was another participant in the meeting at Hegewald on 26th July 1942. This photo of him was taken at Hochwald on a later date.

Below: Mikkeli, Finland, 30th July 1942. Himmler dined in the officers' mess at 7pm with Field Marshal Carl Mannerheim and General Waldemar Erfurth.

Himmler accompanies Dietl to a Finnish military installation.

Finland, 1st August 1942. Himmler takes his leave of General Dietl.

Finland, August 1942. Himmler meets some of his junior SS officers serving on the north-eastern front.

Finland, 2nd August 1942. The RFSS with SS-Brigadeführer Kleinheisterkamp opening what appears to be a box of books for distribution to his men. Grothmann (left) is behind Himmler.

Above: Kananeinen, Finland, 2nd August 1942 with Kleinheisterkamp (left) and General Franz Böhme.

Below: Himmler reviews troops with Kleinheisterkamp.

Right: July 1942, Finland. Relaxing by a lake with bodyguard Kiermaier.

Below: Both Himmler and Kersten appear uneasy as passengers in a boat in Finland, July 1942.

Clockwise from top left:

Adolf Eichmann, who met with Himmler and Müller at Hegewald on 11th August 1942 to discuss the progress of the final solution of the Jewish question.

Heinrich Müller, who as chief of Amt IV in the RSHA was Eichmann's boss and ultimate responsibility for the Jewish problem. Photographed here at Himmler's Hegewald Feldkommandostelle near Zhitomir.

Hanns Johst (left) was a close friend of the Reichsführer and was constantly at his side in late 1942 and into 1943. Fritz Klingenberg on the right.

In August 1942, Hitler gave Himmler full responsibility for anti-partisan warfare. Erich von dem Bach was delegated as anti-partisan supremo. In this late war image, von dem Bach wears his anti-partisan badge in silver which he was awarded in November 1944.

August 1942. Erich von dem Bach pays a visit to Himmler's field headquarters. On the right is Sepp Tiefenbacher.

Abcve: At his various Felckommandostellen Himmler maintained his prowess with a handgun by practising often, as here on the range with Kiermaier.

Left: Paul Scharfe was chief of the SS Legal Office and chief SS judge. He died on 29th July 1942.

Right: Werwolf, Ukraine, 26th August 1942. Alfred Jodl and Himmler study a map.

Below: Werwolf, Ukraine, 26th August 1942. Left to right: Grothmann, Albert Bormann, Hitler and Himmler.

Werwolf, Ukraine, 26th August 1942. Himmler takes his leave from the Führer with Albert Bormann on the right.

Right: Himmler visited Scharfe's grave at the end of August 1942. The grave still exists.

Below: Wiesbaden airport, 31st August 1942. Himmler starts his inspection tour of the Rhine cities. On the left is SS-Obergruppenführer Theodor Berkelmann.

Opposite above: Düsseldorf, 1st September 1942. Himmler is shown bomb damage from Allied air attacks. Right is Gauleiter Karl Florian.

Opposite below: Düsseldorf city cemetery, 1st September 1942. Himmler visits the grave of the late Fritz Weitzel.

Left: Wiesbaden, 31st August 1942. Himmler in conversation with Gauleiter Sprenger. Left is Berkelmann with Wolff.

Below: Mainz, 31st August 1942, with local police chiefs.

Above: At the Weitzel grave with Wolff, Florian, unidentified, Gutenberger, Lankenau and Korreng.

Left: Düsseldorf, 1st September 1942. Himmler is shown defused ordnance. Left to right: Wolff, Lankenau, Himmler, Gutenberger and Grothmann.

More unexploded ordnance. Left to right: Korreng, Lankenau, unidentified, Himmler, Grothmann (obscured) unidentified Luftwaffe officer, Gutenberger and Florian.

Florian and Himmler are shown unexploded aerial bombs.

Above: Himmler's entourage at one of the airfields during Himmler's tour of the Rhine cities from 31st August to 2nd September 1942.

Left: On 3rd September 1942, SS-Gruppenführer Rudolf Querner showed Himmler the bomb damage to the city of Lübeck. Three days later Himmler issued orders that concentration camp prisoners were to clear the bombed cities.

Right: Himmler and Count Ciano.

Below: On 17th October 1942, Himmler carried out an inspection of SS-Gebirgsdivision Prinz Eugen in Kraljewo. He is greeted by Artur Phleps at the airfield.

Kraljewo Serbia. Himmler and Phleps confer. Kiermaier far right.

17th October, 1942, Kraljewo Serbia. Himmler speaks to a member of Prinz Eugen. Far left is Kiermaier and behind Himmler are Meyszner and Phleps. Fourth from right (in light coloured greatcoat) is Viktor Brack from the Führer Chancellery in Berlin and former administrative head of the euthanasia programme, who was on an active service attachment with Prinz Eugen at the time.

The Prinz Eugen inspection. Included are (left to right) Kiermaier, Wolff, Konradt, Himmler, Johst, Müller, Phleps, Schäfer and Meyszner.

The HSSPF Serbia, August Meyszner (left,) accompanied Himmler and Wolff on the visit to Prinz Eugen.

Left: Himmler stands in his vehicle to address the men of Prinz Eugen. Note the automatic weapon by his side.

Below: An original newspaper photo of the funeral of Himmler's personal pilot, Carl Schnäbele, at the Hegewald cemetery.

Abschied von einem Getreuen

Auf einem Heldenfriedhof im Osten nahm der Reichsführer SS Heinrich Himmler Abschied von seinem getreuen, langjährigen Flugkapitän, SS-Obersturmbannführer Schnäbele. Obersturmbannführer Schnäbele, bewährt und ausgezeichnet in zwei Kriegen, fand mit seinem Kameraden, SS-Untersturmführer Maurus, bei einem feigen bolschewistischen Bandenüberfall den Soldatentod. Als SS-Mann ohne Furcht und Tadel bleibt er lebendig unter uns

Aufn.: SS-PK.-Archiv

Above: The Crimea, 27th October 1942. Himmler arrived at Sarabus at 4.30pm and was met by Ludolf von Alvensleben (left) and Gunter d'Alquen. A smiling Prützmann is just visible extreme left.

Right: Himmler and d'Alquen admire some local wild flowers in the Crimea.

Left: Himmler about to climb into his car at Yalta in the Crimea.

Below: On 31st October 1942 Himmler visited the hospital at Halbstadt (today Molotschna, Ukraine.) He is in conversation with Dr Klassen.

Prützmann confers with his boss at an airfield during Himmler's inspection tour of the Crimea and southern Ukraine.

Himmler returned to Hochwald at Grossgarten in East Prussia on 2nd November 1942. While he had been using Hegewald at Zhitomir in the Ukraine, concrete bomb proof bunkers had been erected at Hochwald. Himmler's bunker ruin still exists, providing testament to its solid construction.

Above: The Hochwald site today at Pozezdrze.

Left: On 13th November 1942, Himmler visited Dachau concentration camp again. Since his previous visit, the camp commandant had changed and now Martin Gottfried Weiss was in command. One of the more efficient, but brutal commandants in the camp system, Weiss had commanded Neuengamme and would also command Majdanek. Found guilty at the Dachau trial, he was hanged in 1946.

Opposite above: Himmler was always interested in nutrition. At one of his Feldkommandostellen, he examines food samples as part of a nutrition presentation with Georg Lörner (left) and Dr Ernst Schenck.

The Reichsführer-SS discusses aspects of nutrition with Georg Lörner. Behind Lörner (left to right) are Pemsel, Grothmann, Brandt and Schenck.

Himmler makes his point. Left to right are Pemsel, Schenck, Pohl, unidentified, Lörner and Brandt.

For ease of access when Hitler was in residence at the Berghof on the Obersalzberg, Himmler requisitioned the former von Trapp family mansion near Salzburg. This became Feldkommandostelle Bergwald.

Himmler still extensively used his special train as a mobile field headquarters and every time he stayed for any length of time, a suitable location or rail siding had to be found for the train to stand. Josef Tiefenbacher and Ludwig Pemsel are seen here searching for such a site. The civilian is a railway official.

Tiefenbacher is about to alight to discuss the site with railway officials. Pemsel is beside him.

Tiefenbacher explains his requirements to the railway officials.

Pemsel (left) and Tiefenbacher. Tiefenbacher had overall responsibility for all Himmler's Feldkommandostellen while Pemsel was the train commander.

Bomber pilot Werner Baumbach and Sepp Tiefenbacher in the dining car aboard Sonderzug "Heinrich" in 1942. That year, Baumbach was withdrawn from active service and tasked with designing new secret aircraft.

Baumbach enjoys a joke by Tiefenbacher.

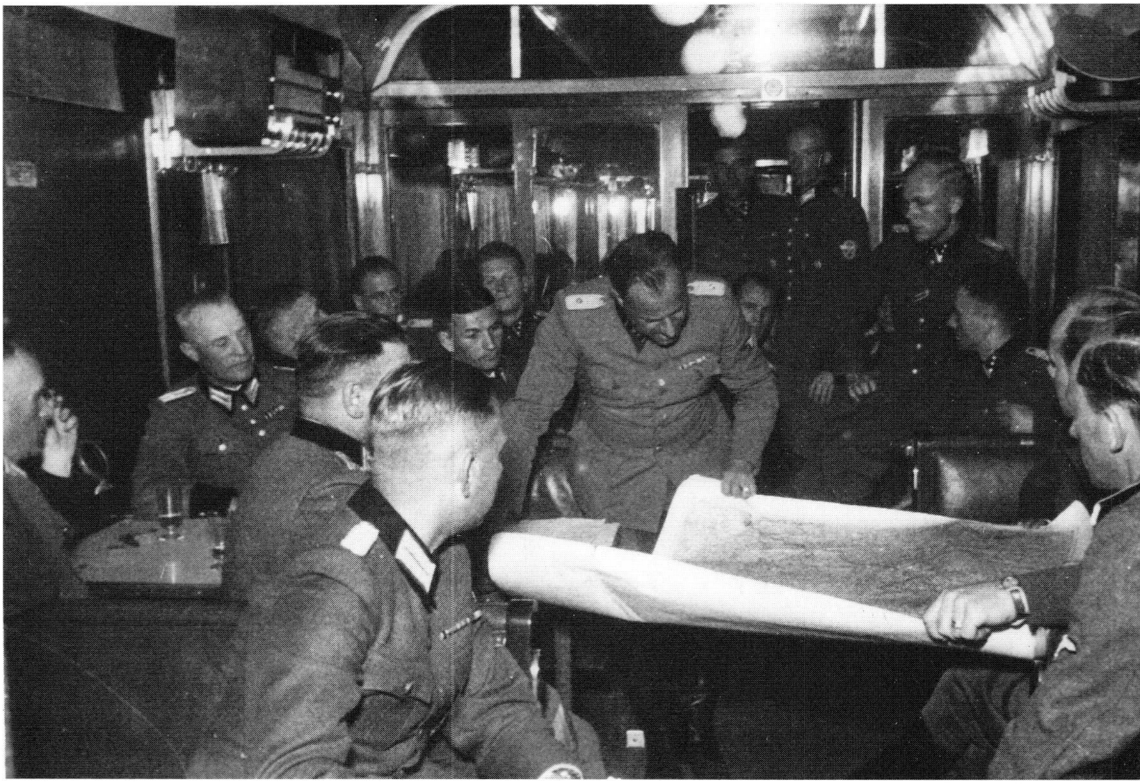

Above: In this 1942 photograph aboard Sonderzug "Heinrich" Sepp Tiefenbacher discusses movements over a map at a meeting with Himmler's mobile staff. Ludwig Pemsel is third from right.

Left: On 30th December 1942, Ulrich Greifelt suffered a heart attack, the cause of which Greifelt cited as a major disagreement with Himmler. His health would never fully recover.

Right: Albert Ganzenmüller, Secretary of State in the Reich Ministry of Transport with special responsibility for railways. Without his co-operation Himmler would have been unable to use the rail network for deportations and the industrial scale gassing operations at the death camps could not have been achieved.

Below: On 11th December 1942, Himmler conducted a comprehensive tour of the secret weapons facility at Peenemünde on the Baltic coast. This photograph, usually incorrectly captioned as June 1943, shows him during this December visit, confirmed by the greatcoats and scarf being worn.

Above: Himmler about to leave an unidentified SS facility.

Left: Himmler entertained Oberst Helmuth von Pannwitz at his Feldkommandostelle on 19th January 1943. Four days earlier, whilst receiving the award of the Oakleaves to his Knights Cross of the Iron Cross from Hitler, von Pannwitz had courageously voiced his opinion that the German policy towards the Slavic races was fundamentally flawed.

Himmler still relied heavily upon the advice of Wolfram Sievers of Ahnenerbe, by now promoted to SS-Standartenführer. Sievers was convicted at the Nuremberg Doctors' Trial and was hanged on 2nd June 1948.

Himmler held a meeting on 25th January 1943 with Reichsminister for the Eastern Territories, Alfred Rosenberg.

Above: On 5th February 1943, Himmler discussed the recruitment of Hitler Youth members for the Waffen-SS. He is seen here with youth leader Artur Axmann and Gerhard Hein far right.

Left: SS-Obergruppenführer Theodor Berkelmann was a favourite of Himmler and was an old style SS leader. In early 1943 Berkelmann held the dual appointment of HSSPF in both Rhine and Westmark. On 21st May 1943, Himmler decided to combine the posts and Berkelmann was placed in charge. Himmler decided on Berkelmann to succeed Koppe in Posen as he was being moved to Krakow. Berkelmann had hardly arrived when he was taken ill and finally succumbed to a brain tumour on 27th December 1943.

Right: Eventually Himmler decided upon a suitable replacement for the deceased Heydrich. He chose Dr Ernst Kaltenbrunner to head up the important SD and Security Police Central Office, effective from 30th January 1943.

Below: On 26th February 1943, Himmler carried out an inspection of Buchenwald concentration camp. The commandant, Hermann Pister (2nd right, back row) is photographed with several of his camp guards outside a SS building at the camp.

SS-Obergruppenführer Theodor Eicke was killed in action on 26th February 1943.

The first grave of Eicke. Himmler ordered that the remains of the Totenkopf commander be removed to the Hegewald cemetery near Zhitomir. Eicke's grave was eventually abandoned in the spring of 1944 following the Soviet advance and his remains are today anonymously interred in a communal grave.

On 13th March 1943, the Reichsführer flew into Riga where he was met by Friedrich Jeckeln (centre) and Alfred Wünnenberg (left.)

Also at Riga airfield on 13th March 1943 was SS-Brigadeführer Fritz von der Scholz (right.)

A photograph taken inside Jeckeln's office with Himmler and von der Scholz.

Himmler arrives by aircraft for one of his numerous inspection visits. He often used his aircraft to 'hop' from one location to another, covering a large area in a very short space of time.

There was always a reception committee awaiting the arrival of the Reichsführer.

More greetings and salutes.

Himmler was not always impressed with what he found and his visits were a tense time for the local SS commanders.

Good news or bad?

Himmler passes something to an orderly. This photo is possibly taken at Hegewald near Zhitomir, but is unconfirmed.

Hitler attends the trials of some new armoured vehicles. A panzer officer explains something to Hitler with Himmler listening in. Far left is Sepp Dietrich.

Above: Otto Baum, Josef Kiermaier and Himmler during a visit to the SS-Totenkopf Division.

Left: April 1943, as an observer at an exercise of the SS-Totenkopf Division, with Hermann Priess (left) and Otto Baum (right.)

Right: Himmler held a meeting in Paris on 3rd April 1943 with Carl Albrecht Oberg and René Bousquet, the Vichy police general secretary. Oberg is pictured here in 1944 with Joseph Darnand, the leader of the Vichy Milice.

Below: On 20th April 1943, two men attempted to assassinate Friedrich-Wilhelm Krüger in Krakow. They were subsequently arrested after an investigation and were executed. These are the two would-be Polish assassins in captivity prior to execution.

Left: The Jewish uprising in the Warsaw ghetto resulted in Himmler appointing Jürgen Stroop as SS and Police Leader in Warsaw. The efficient Stroop deployed his forces to kill the insurgents and destroy the ghetto.

Below: Stroop (with goggles) during the battle for the Warsaw ghetto. Note the buildings ablaze behind him.

Himmler, Hausser and von Alvensleben.

Between 23rd and 27th April 1943, Himmler was in the Kharkov area for a major inspection of Waffen-SS armoured units. He is seen here with SS-Gruppenführer Felix Steiner.

Above: Near Kharkov, April 1943. Steiner (right) receives Himmler and Prützmann with the ever watchful Kiermaier far left.

Left: Steiner in deep conversation with his Reichsführer.

Above: On 26th and 27th April 1943, Himmler visited SS-Panzer Division Das Reich in the Kharkov area. He is between Walter Krüger (left) and Paul Hausser (right.)

Right: Himmler discusses something with Paul Hausser while Walter Krüger listens in. Far left is Vinzenz Kaiser.

Above: Himmler makes his way across the exercise terrain with his large entourage in pursuit. Those following include Prützmann, Hausser, Gebhardt and Johst.

Left: Using periscope binoculars.

Right: Himmler photographed in the turret of a Tiger tank of SS-Panzer Division Das Reich.

Below: A tank commander explains equipment to Himmler.

Left: Himmler's column of vehicles in the background as a Das Reich man greets the Reichsführer-SS.

Below: Himmler's group halts for a refreshment break. Prützmann and Gebhardt on Himmler's right.

An official newspaper portrait of the Reichsführer-SS.

Another newspaper portrait in which Himmler looks thin in the face, giving him a more youthful appearance.

Above: With Himmler are Admiral Hans-Erich Voss and Josef Kiermaier. In the background is Hanns Johst.

Left: A photo of Himmler believed taken in Austria 1943.

Above: Hmmler, Wolff and staff with local girls in Austria. Far right is Tiefenbacher.

Right: Himmler, Wolff and Tiefenbacher in Austria.

Above: Himmler with Flemish volunteers at Meseritz on 24th May 1943. Gottlob Berger is on Himmler's left.

Below: Himmler is chatting with Flemish officer volunteers at Meseritz on 24th May 1943.

Right: Meeting some of the Flemish volunteer troops at Meseritz.

Below: Meseritz, 24th May 1943. With Flemish volunteers. The Belgian Rexist leader, Leon Degrelle, is second from left.

Opposite above: Himmler at the SS-Ausbildungslager Sennheim with the unit commander SS-Standartenführer Ernst Fick and the local SS commander SS-Oberführer Rudolf Lohse.

Opposite below: Two members of Himmler's staff take a relaxing smoke break in a compartment on board Sonderzug "Steiermark." The man laying on the right resembles Josef Tiefenbacher.

Left: SS-Obergruppenführer Josias Erbprinz zu Waldeck und Pyrmont is standing on the platform siding at Hochwald in East Prussia.

Below: At the beginning of June 1943, Himmler was in Alsace. Although not recorded in his diary, it is most likely he visited the SS-Ausbildungslager Sennheim as it is known he was there in 1943. He is seen here at an earlier visit with Ernst Fick (2nd right) and Rudolf Lohse (right.)

A member of Leibstandarte-SS "Adolf Hitler" attached to Himmler's staff poses for the photographer on Sonderzug "Steiermark."

A member of Himmler's staff in the dining compartment on Sonderzug "Steiermark."

With the Reichsführer engaged elsewhere, the staff on board his special train could relax whilst awaiting his return. Some found time to do tasks such as getting a haircut.

In early June 1943, Himmler visited the Berghof several times. He is pictured relaxing on the terrace with Walter Hewel and Martin Bormann. In the background is Hitler's dentist, Prof. Dr Hugo Blaschke.

Left: Berchtesgaden railway station 1943. The powerhouse of Germany: left to right, Keitel (army) Göring (Luftwaffe) Dönitz (navy) Himmler (SS and police) and Bormann (party.)

Below: Himmler revisited the secret rocket establishment at Peenemünde on 28th June 1943. He is pictured during that visit with Oberstleutnant Gerhard Stegmaier (extreme left) and General Dornberger (centre.) The SS officer in black uniform behind Himmler is believed to be Wernher von Braun.

Gebhard Himmler speaking at the Automobile Association in Prague.

Hegewaldheim East Prussia, 4th July 1943. Himmler greets Haj Amin al-Husseini, the Grand Mufti of Jerusalem.

The Reich Women's Leader and wife of SS-Obergruppenführer August Heissmeyer, Gertrud Scholz-Klink, visited Himmler at Hochwald on 3rd August 1943.

Beside Sonderzug "Steiermark," Himmler greets his senior SS officers before a meeting. He is about to shake the hand of Otto Hofmann. Among those also present are Erwin Rösener, Georg-Henning Bassewitz-Behr, Wilhelm Stuckart, Udo von Woyrsch, Günther Pancke and Hanns Johst.

High ranking officers attend the meeting aboard Himmler's train. During a break, they gather beside the train. Some of those present are Pancke, Steiner, Stuckart, Schimana, Meyszner and Kammerhofer.

Left to right: Steiner, Pancke, Stuckart, Meyszner and (with back to camera) Kammerhofer.

Inside Hochwald aboard Sonderzug "Steiermark" Hinrich Schuldt speaks on the telephone.

In the saloon car of Sonderzug "Steiermark" SS-Obergruppenführer Josias Erbprinz zu Waldeck und Pyrmont chats with a police officer, possibly Willy Suchanek (unconfirmed.)

Waldeck enjoys a smoke with Johst in one of the train compartments.

The Reichsführer was a frequent visitor at the Wolfsschanze. He is greeted on the rail siding by Wilhelm Keitel as Hitler looks on and Rudolf Schmundt salutes.

Above: Himmler arrives by car at an unconfirmed location to be greeted by an unidentified General and Hermann Fegelein (front left.) Possibly taken at Hitler's field headquarters (note the camouflage netting.)

Left: Himmler in conversation with Karl Bodenschatz and Göring at the Wolfsschanze. Close by are Dr Karl Brandt and Karl Wolff.

Opposite above: Himmler's presence at all the Führer headquarters was not unusual. He is photographed here at Werwolf between Richard Schulze-Kossens and Karl Wolff.

Opposite below: Hitler and Göring lead the group at the Führerhauptquartier. Behind them are Schulze-Kossens, Bormann, Ley, Wolff, Dietrich, Milch, Himmler, Bodenschatz and Hoffmann.

Above: Göring and Himmler lead the group on this occasion. Behind them are Milch and Speer, with von Below far right.

Left: Himmler walking with Albert Speer at the Führerhauptquartier.

Opposite above: Himmler shakes hands with Hitler's favoured photographer. Heinrich Hoffmann was an alcoholic and a heavy smoker and Hitler retained him more out of loyalty than for his professional ability.

Opposite below: Werwolf field headquarters in the Ukraine. Himmler chats with Rudolf Schmundt and Karl Wolff.

Above: Himmler makes an impromptu entry in what appears to be a diary. Right is Friedrich Rainer.

Right: Gauleiter Friedrich Rainer and Himmler at the FHQ.

Opposite above: At Werwolf in 1942, Himmler turns the pages of the presentation portfolio of the Great German Art Exhibition of 1941. Schulze-Kossens, Hoffmann and Wolff show interest.

Opposite below: Martin Bormann and Joachim von Ribbentrop join Hitler in studying reports at his field headquarters. Hitler wears his unique SS tunic presented to him by the Leibstandarte on the outbreak of war and which he vowed to wear until the day of victory.

Gauleiter Wilhelm Murr and Himmler.

Wilhelm Kment, Himmler's decorations officer at Hitler's field headquarters. He arranged and administered all presentations of awards by Hitler.

In July 1943, SS-Oberst-Gruppenführer Kurt Daluege suffered a heart attack. The following month, on Himmler's advice, Hitler replaced Daluege in Prague with a permanent Reichsprotector. Wilhelm Frick was despatched to Prague. Daluege survived, but his health never fully recovered.

Wilhelm Frick and Kurt Daluege.

Left: With the sideways move of Frick, a vacancy opened up for Reichsminister of the Interior. Himmler was appointed as Frick's replacement on 25th August 1943, elevating him to the pinnacle of his power. The following day, Dr Wilhelm Stuckart (right) introduced the new Reichsminister to his staff.

Below: The Reich Ministry of the Interior, 26th August 1943. Wilhelm Stuckart introduces senior civil servants.

Right: On 23rd September 1943, Himmler flew into Riga. Friedrich Jeckeln and General Walter Braemer await the arrival of the Reichsführer at the airfield.

Below: Riga aifield, 23rd September 1943. Left to right: General Walter Braemer, SS-Obergruppenführer Friedrich Jeckeln, SS-Brigadeführer Carl-Friedrich Graf Pückler-Burghaus and Reichsführer-SS Himmler.

On 28th September 1943, Himmler was the guest of Franz Augsberger, the commanding officer of the 3rd Estonian SS-Volunteer Brigade. Augsberger, seen here on the left with Fritz Klingenberg, spent most of his active service commands in charge of foreign volunteers. A highly decorated and efficient Waffen-SS commander, he was killed in action on 19th March 1945.

Himmler in Posen. On the left is SS-Obergruppenführer Wilhelm Koppe.

Above: 7th October 1943, Wolfsschanze. Hitler congratulates Himmler on his 43rd birthday.

Right: Hitler and Himmler stroll in the Wolfsschanze on Himmler's 43rd birthday.

Left: Wolfsschanze, 7th October 1943. Hitler held a conference for Reichsleiter and Gauleiter at his field headquarters.

Below: A smiling Himmler looks up to his beloved Führer at the 1943 anniversary meeting of the November Putsch, held in the Löwenbräukeller in Munich.

Right: By November 1943, the ongoing dispute between Friedrich-Wilhelm Krüger and Dr Hans Frank in Krakow reached a climax. Himmler decided to replace Krüger and despatched him to the front in command of a Waffen-SS unit. He proved himself to be an able active service commander and was awarded the Knights Cross.

Below: Krüger's replacement in Krakow was Wilhelm Koppe, seen here in leather greatcoat deep in conversation with State Secretary Josef Bühler. Far left in white lapels is Walther Bierkamp, the Sipo and SD chief in Krakow.

Holland. Left to right: Berger, Himmler, Seyss-Inquart and Mussert.

Himmler as guest of honour at a banquet in Holland. On his left are Friedrich Christiansen and Anton Mussert.

The Netherlands. Berger, Himmler, Seyss-Inquart, Mussert, Rauter and Wimmer.

Avegoor Holland, 1st February 1944. Himmler attends the presentation of the new SS-Proficiency Badges. With him are Seyss-Inquart, Mussert and Rauter.

Above: Himmler during an earlier visit to Holland. Also present are Rauter, Berger and Wolff.

Left: Unlike Reinhard Heydrich, Himmler was a confident speaker. He delivers a speech to a Dutch audience.

The Reichsführer-SS speaks.

Franz Kutschera, the SS and Police Leader in Warsaw, had Himmler's confidence. His ruthless methods resulted in him becoming a target for Polish assassins who carried out a successful attack on 1st February 1944 outside the Warsaw SS headquarters. Kutschera was killed at the scene.

Above: 20th February 1944. Himmler and Fegelein bear witness to the award of the Swords to the Knights Cross of the Iron Cross for Herbert Gille and the Knights Cross for Leon Degrelle.

Left: Himmler joins Hitler on a snowy spring afternoon walk on the Obersalzberg.

Right: A walk in the snow. Following (in leather greatcoat with walking stick) is Hermann Fegelein.

Below: Himmler's train at Neuhammer for a visit to the Croatian SS-Volunteer Division. Himmler visited the division twice, once in November 1943 and again in January 1944. He is seen here with Tiefenbacher (left) Gebhardt and Sauberzweig on Himmler's left (with eye patch.)

Above: Himmler watches as horses are put through their paces. On his left are Gebhardt, Sauberzweig and Hanke. Fegelein is in front.

Left: Himmler collecting for Wintershilfswerk in Breslau. Left is Gauleiter Karl Hank and right is adjutant Werner Grothmann.

Right: Himmler at the podium inside the SS officer training school at Braunschweig.

Below: A meeting of senior SS officers at the Junkerschule Braunschweig. Hans Jüttner is on his feet. On his left is Kurt Knoblauch and on his right are Himmler, Schmauser, Hanke and Keppler.

Opposite above: Hans Jüttner presents SS officers to the Reichsführer-SS. Left is Georg Keppler.

Opposite below: An undated photo of Himmler with two unidentified SS officers. The background suggests the location to be the SS officer training school Braunschweig, but this is unconfirmed.

Right: An undated photo, probably from 1944. Teddy Wisch (centre) and Himmler (right.)

Below: France 1944. Vehicles are put through their paces for the Reichsführer-SS. In black panzer uniform is Sepp Dietrich.

France 1944. Himmler is greeted at an airfield. Behind him are adjutants Grothmann (at his right shoulder) and Conrad (2nd from right.)

Himmler and Dietrich in discussion with another officer.

Dietrich and Oberg behind Himmler in France.

With the Reichsführer's column of cars behind on the road, Himmler, Dietrich and Oberg take a break.

A rare photograph taken inside the former von Trapp mansion used as Feldkommandostelle Bergwald by Himmler. Here he entertains Sepp Dietrich in 1944.

Sepp Dietrich about to leave Feldkommandostelle Bergwald. Behind him are Grothmann, Kiermaier, Wünsche and Gesche, with Erwin Rösener in the right foreground.

Bergwald Feldkommandostelle, 8th March 1944. Another rare photo taken inside Bergwald. Himmler examines a high powered telescope. In the background is Dr Sigmund Rascher who would soon after be arrested for falsifying the parentage of his children.

At the state funeral of Generaloberst Hans Hube in the Mosaic Hall of the Berlin Reich Chancellery, with von Kluge, Dönitz and Keitel on 26th April 1944.

In May 1944, the deportations of Hungarian Jews began in earnest. Here Jews from Koszez await their train for transportation to Auschwitz-Birkenau.

The destination of the Hungarian Jews....the newly constructed ramp inside the camp at Auschwitz-Birkenau. Men, women and children are separated amid chaotic scenes. Note the man segregated on the right for the way he is dressed. Children, women with children, older women and those deemed unfit for work are sent to the left. The women and children are about to begin their walk to the gas chamber and within a short period they will all be dead.

This group is classified as non-essential and consequently they are all destined for the crematoria. All children, older men and women, women with children and those unfit for work are deemed as suitable for "special handling," a pseudonym for extermination.

The deportaion of Danish Jews had been an entirely different story. Himmler's two senior SS officers in Copenhagen were Werner Best (left) and Günther Pancke (right.) Best continually created obstacles to mass deportation and as a result Danish Jewry was less decimated than any other occupied country.

Left to right: Fritz Freitag, Himmler and Otto Wächter; taken in Neuhammer on 17th May 1944 during a visit to the Galician Division.

Wächter, Himmler and Freitag on 17th May 1944 at Neuhammer.

Salzburg city hall, 3rd June 1944. Himmler officiated at the civil marriage of Hermann Fegelein and Gretl Braun, the sister of Eva Braun. Bormann was a witness.

Himmler toasts the happy couple. Left is Bormann. Note the silver beakers used by Fegelein and his bride.

Berghof, 3rd June 1944. Of special note in the line-up are: front row L to R, Fritz Braun, Fegelein, Gretl Braun, Hitler, Eva Braun, Franziska Braun, Heinrich Hoffmann. Back row L to R, Waldemar Fegelein, Himmler, Dr Karl Brandt (centre,) Dr Theo Morell and Otto Dietrich.

A 1944 official portrait of Reichsminister of the Interior Reichsführer-SS and Chief of the German Police Heinrich Himmler.

A portrait of Himmler taken by Walter Frentz at the Wolfsschanze.

A profile portrait without his trademark spectacles. This image clearly shows the slight Roman bridge of his nose.

Wolfsschanze, 20th July 1944. Bormann and Schaub show Göring the destruction caused by von Stauffenberg's bomb which had detonated under the map table, the remains of which are visible in the middle of the room.

A photograph taken in the aftermath of the assassination attempt. A clearly injured Hitler walks with Keitel, Göring and Bormann. Following is Otto Guensche.

Wolfsschanze, 20th July 1944. Hitler has recovered sufficiently to receive guests. Several of his Nazi lieutenants rushed to his side to profess their loyalty.

On the afternoon of the assassination attempt, Mussolini arrived at the Wolfsschanze. He is chatting with Göring behind a visibly shaken Hitler, Himmler, Schaub and Loerzer.

Hitler was unable to use his right arm properly for several weeks after the bomb explosion. Here he is using his left hand to greet Hermann Fegelein at the Wolfsschanze.

Many of the Nazi hierarchy rushed to the Wolfsschanze to affirm their loyalty to Hitler who had injured his right elbow in the blast. He uses his left hand to greet Dr Robert Ley, between Himmler and Goebbels.

Still showing signs of discomfort with his right arm, Hitler greets Hans Jüttner with his left hand. This photo almost certainly taken on 10th August 1944.

In August 1944, as the Red Army pushed the Wehrmacht back across eastern Europe, the Polish Home Army staged an uprising in Warsaw. Erich von dem Bach was placed in command of the German forces and eventually received the Polish surrender from General Bor-Komorowski on 3rd October 1944.

A front cover image from the illustrated magazine "Volk und Wehr" showing a close-up of Himmler addressing troops.

Walter Schellenberg had the ear of the Reichsführer-SS who began to rely upon his judgement as the war turned against Germany. At Schellenberg's instigation, Himmler made it clear that he was prepared to negotiate over the position of the Jews. Schellenberg is pictured here second from right at an earlier time with SD colleagues in Berlin. On his right is Hermann Kluckhohn, the adjutant of Heydrich.

Left: The Swiss politician Jean-Marie Musy, with whom Himmler held secret negotiations in late October 1944 over the exchange of Jews for raw materials.

Opposite above: On 10th October 1944, Himmler gave a rousing speech to Volkssturm units in Königsberg. On the left is Generaloberst Heinz Guderian next to Hans Lammers.

Königsberg, 10th October 1944. Next to Himmler are Keitel and Gauleiter Koch.

The site of crematorium IV in 1990. On 7th October 1944, the building was badly damaged during the revolt of the Sonderkommando and ceased to operate.

Opposite above:On 26th November 1944, Himmler ordered the physical destruction of the crematoria at Auschwitz-Birkenau. The dismantling of crematoriums II and III began in early December 1944. This is the collapsed ceiling of the gas chamber of crematorium II in 1990.

Opposite below: The original gateway and ruin of crematorium III in 1990. Through these gates, thousands of victims passed on their way to the gas chamber.

Opposite above: Himmler's chief of telecommunications was SS-Brigadeführer Wilhelm Keilhaus, pictured here as a POW of the British.

Left: Himmler's first combat command began on 10th December 1944 when he was appointed as c-in-c of Army Group Oberrhein. Totally lacking in experience, he relied heavily upon his military adviser, the aged First World War General, Dr Heinrich von Maur. The posting was a disaster.

Below: Heinrich von Maur in SS uniform (right.)

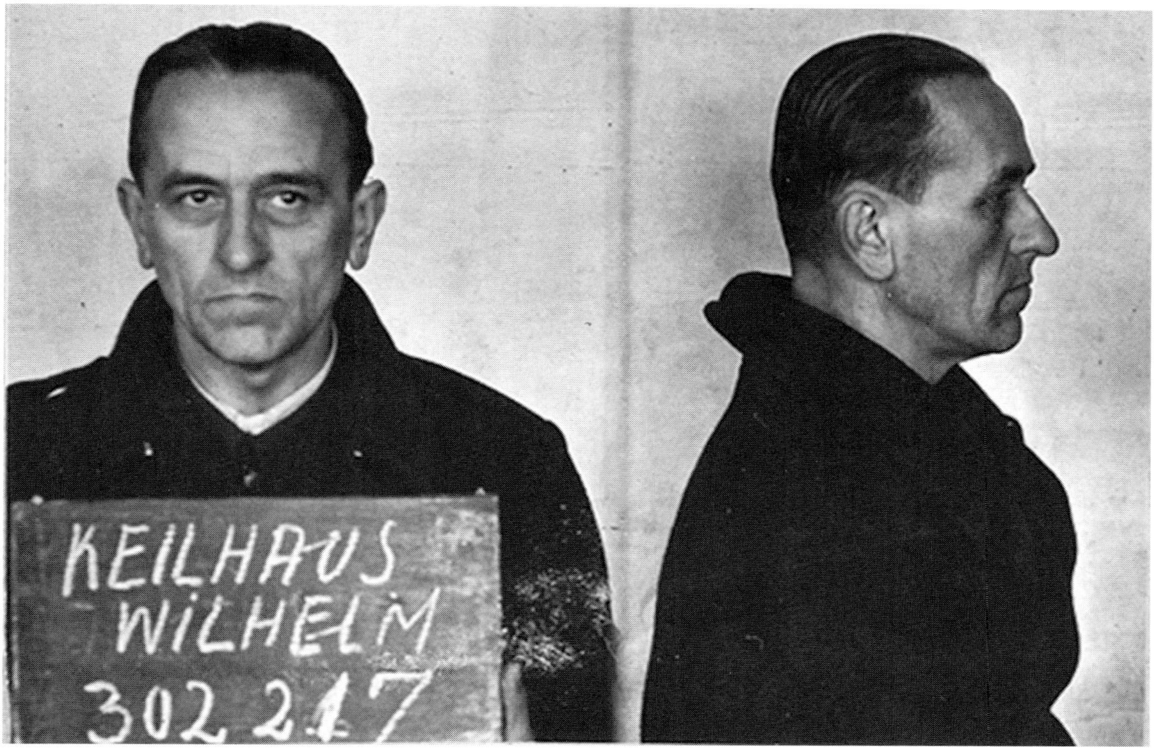

Below: Himmler receives men from the army in the saloon car of Sonderzug "Steiermark" for presentation of awards. The caption for this image dates it as October 1944, but it is more likely to be December 1944. Himmler wears a Letewka style SS tunic, the only known photo of him wearing such a jacket.

Above: Himmler presenting what appears to be Close Combat Badges. Behind him stands Fred Conrad.

Below: Himmler at Illmensee.

Above: In his capacity as an army group commander, Himmler presents Oakleaves to the Knights Cross of the Iron Cross. This photo is dated 5th January 1945, but may have been taken a day or so earlier.

Right: A pre-war photo of the Fritz Kiehn family. Himmler visited them on 6th January 1945 for afternoon tea and met up with Karl Hermann Frank and Lina Heydrich who were also visiting the Kiehns.

A newspaper photo of Himmler receiving army snipers aboard Sonderzug "Steiermark" prior to presenting them with Sniper Badges. Possibly dated January 1945.

Himmler flicks through an illustrated magazine with some Wehrmacht Knights Cross winners.

Himmler arrived at the Luftwaffe barracks at Schneidemühl on 21st January 1945 where he sent a teleprinter message stating that he had been appointed to the command of Army Group Vistula. His first order in that capacity, the same day, was to direct the local commander in Posen to defend the city "....to the last breath."

Signature and portrait of SS-Standartenführer Karl-Otto von Salisch; shot on the direct order of Himmler, as an example, on 31st January 1945 in the courtyard of the Gestapo building in Danzig. He had ordered a retreat before being overwhelmed by the Red Army and paid the ultimate price.

Himmler's personal building, the "R hut" at Birkenwald Feldkommandostelle, Birkenhain. When first constructed, it cost 930,000 Reichsmarks and boasted central heating and several bathrooms. Post-war it was used as an education establishment, a summer camp and a hospital recuperation facility. Today, it is listed as a historical monument. (Recent photograph.)

Opposite: The layout of Birkenwald.

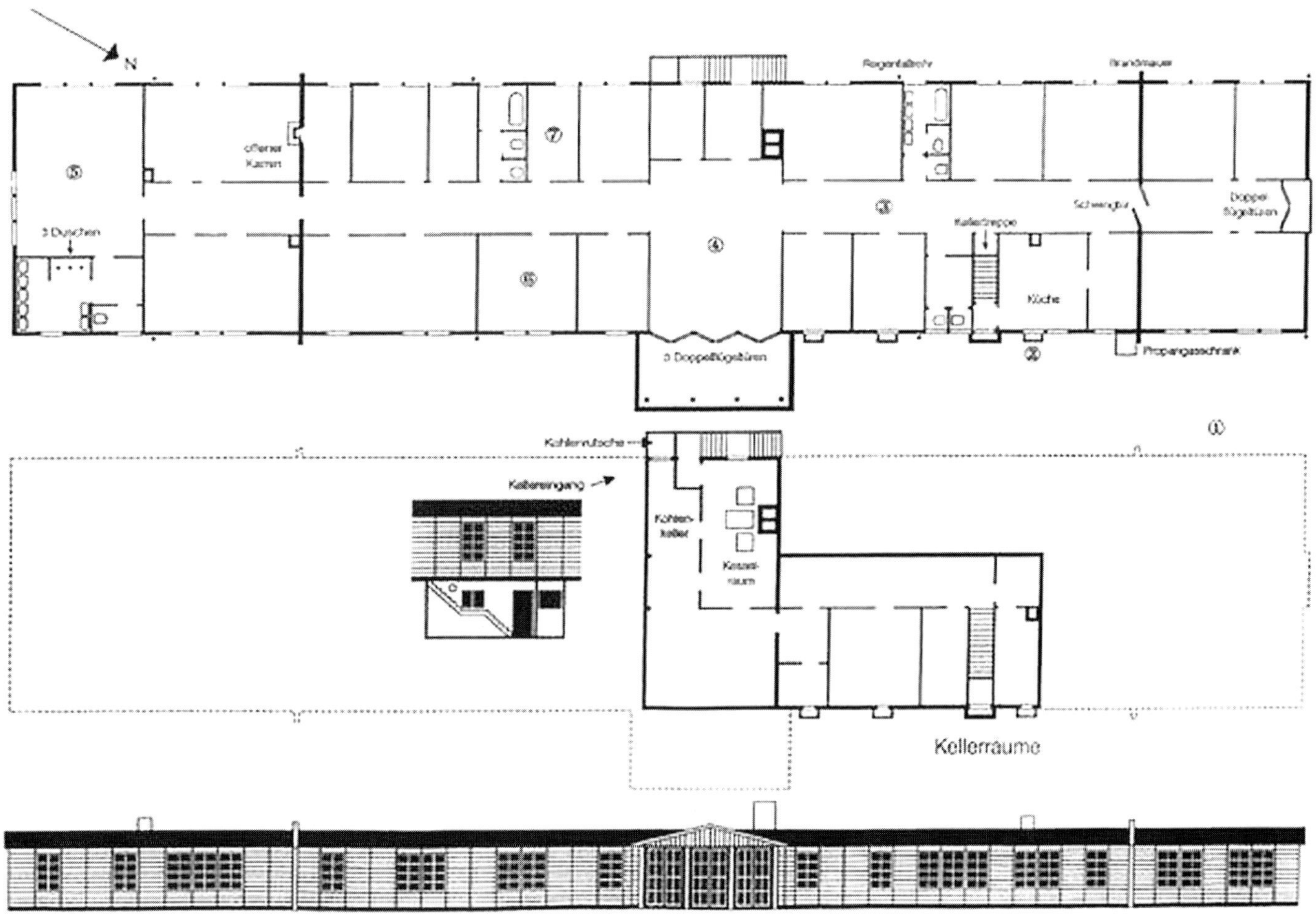

Grundriss der Baracke Birkenhain

Größe: 66 m x 13 m
Baujahr: 1944

Legende

1 Informationstafel
2 Eingang zur Ausstellung
3 Flur
4 Ausstellungsraum (ehem. Eingangsbereich, 60 m²)
5 ehem. Kartenraum (52 m²)
6 typischer Wohnraum 1 (23 m²)
7 typischer Wohn- und Wirtschaftsraum 2 (12 m²)

Plan nach Reimann, 1982
Maßstab 1 : 250

Above: An immediate post-war photo of Birkenwald providing an idea of the appearance of the facility as used by Himmler as his Feldkommandostelle.

Left: The Swedish diplomat, Count Folk Bernadotte.

Promoted beyond his capabilities, Dr Ernst Kaltenbrunner subsequently gained the trust and the ear of Hitler and proved to be a dangerous adversary for Himmler during negotiations over the trade of Jews in the last months of the war.

Dr Hans Kammler was Himmler's construction expert. Having planned and built the crematoria at Birkenau, Himmler delegated responsibility for rocket research and manufacture to Kammler. He was the last man promoted to SS-Obergruppenführer when Hitler promoted him in March 1945. He committed suicide, probably using cyanide, on or about 9th May 1945.

Above: On 2nd March 1945, Himmler moved his field headquarters to the now abandoned SS clinic at Hohenlychen. For the short duration he used this location, it became known as Feldkommandostelle "Steiermark Hohenlychen." The former hospital buildings consisted of a large complex which was first used as a hospital by the Soviets and was then purchased for renovation into a residential estate. The building work stalled and the large site is now in a dilapidated condition.

Left: One of the entrances to the admin wing of the clinic at Hohenlychen. Russian writing is visible above the door. The room where Himmler held negotiations with Count Bernadotte cannot be confirmed.

Schloss Ziethen at Wustrau. Also known as Schloss Wustrau, it had been the seat of the aristocratic Zieten family.

On 30th March 1945 at Prenzlau (probably Birkenwald) Himmler ordered Heinz Macher to proceed immediately to Wewelsburg and blow up the castle. Macher is seen here in an earlier photograph (front left) with Magda Goebbels (centre) the Goebbels children, Max Wünsche (on Magda's left) and Werner Naumann (seated on the arm next to Wünsche.)

Left:SS-Standartenführer Kurt Becher. Himmler appointed Becher as Reich Special Plenipotentiary for the Affairs of Jewish and Political Prisoners.

Right: SS-Gruppenführer Prof. Dr Karl Brandt, Hitler's private escort physician and a member of his inner circle. Often confused with Himmler's personal adviser, Dr Rudolf Brandt, the popular Karl Brandt was arrested for defeatism, but escaped Nazi justice by the intervention of Himmler. His luck ran out when he was convicted by the Allies for crimes against humanity and he was hanged at Landsberg Prison on 2nd June 1948.

Karl Wolff was attempting his own negotiations with the western Allies. An important member of his staff was Otto Jungkunz, seen here on the left at an earlier date.

An enraged Hitler discovered that Himmler had made secret overtures to the Western Allies and formerly dismissed him from all his posts on 29th April 1945. Hitler appointed Gauleiter Karl Hanke as the new Reichsführer-SS with immediate effect.

Left: Hitler nominated Grossadmiral Karl Dönitz as his successor as head of state.

Below: Schloss Kalkhorst, east of Travemünde. Himmler moved here on 30th April 1945 and it was during his stay in this building that Himmler was informed of Hitler's death.

Dönitz set up his government offices in the sports wing at the Marineschule Mürwick, Flensburg.

Grossadmiral Dönitz leaving his headquarters at the Marineschule Mürwick. His government lasted 23 days.

Left: On 4th May 1945, Himmler held a meeting with Gauleiter Ernst Bohle when he confirmed that he wished to retain his posts as Reichsführer-SS and Chief of the German Police in order to maintain law and order. The two men are pictured here at an earlier meeting.

Below: An aerial view of the fire fighters' training facility at Harrisleefeld Flensburg in the 1940s. The site was used by SS-Obergruppenführer Alfred Wünnenberg as his field headquarters.

Above: The school building of the fire fighters' training facility at Harrisleefeld Flensburg in 1936. Himmler held his last conference with his senior SS cadre and issued his final orders in this building on 5th May 1945.

Right: Gebhard Himmler turned up at Harrisleefeld looking for his brother, but the Reichsführer had already left.

Left: Rudolf Höss, the ex-commandant of Auschwitz, asserted that he received false papers and a new identity at Harrisleefeld on 5th May 1945 along with other members of the camp inspectorate from Oranienburg. He evaded capture until 11th March 1946 when he was arrested as farm worker Franz Lang. He bears the marks of a severe beating from his British captors in this photograph.

Below: An entrance of the now disused Marine School Hospital at Mürwick Flensburg. Richard Glücks committed suicide in this building on 10th May 1945.

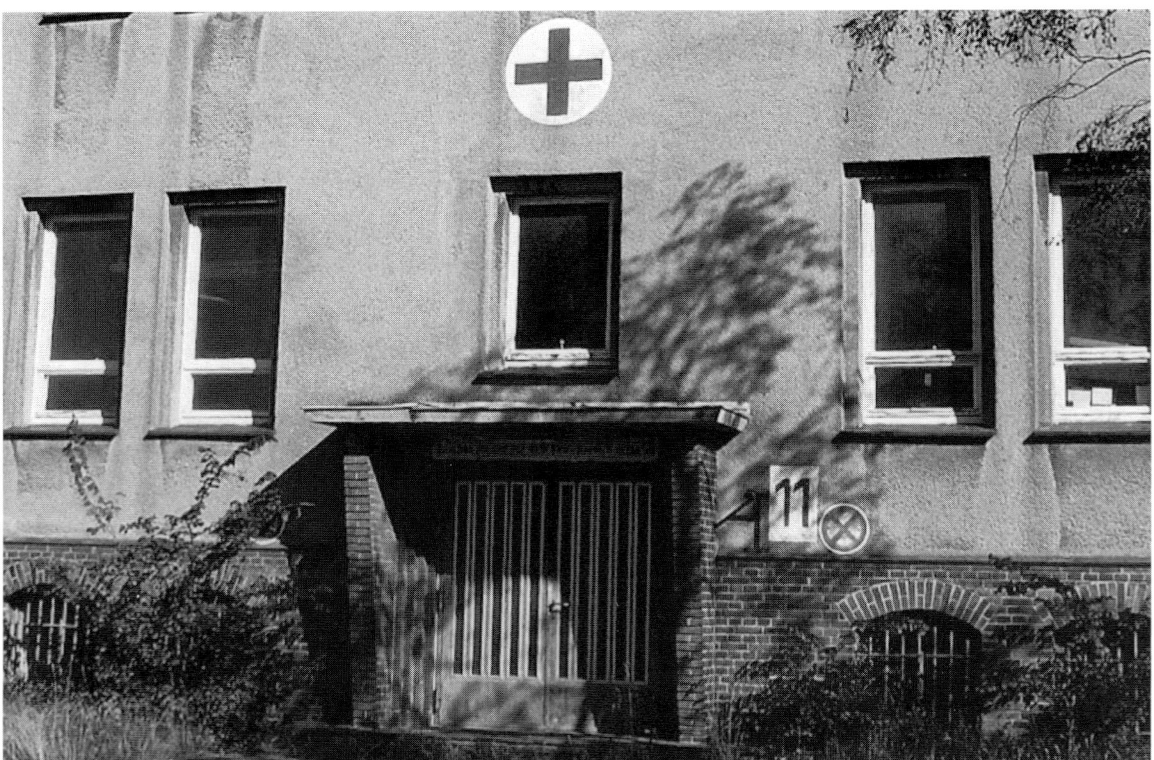

Above: The former home of Hinrich Dankers at Waldstrasse 165, Bremervörde, where Himmler and his party stayed for a few nights before attempting to cross the River Oste. (Modern photo.)

Below: Some sources state that Karl Gebhardt was with Himmler's party when it left Flensburg and that he too was arrested in Bremervörde. This cannot be confirmed and Gebhardt is not mentioned in official records concerning Himmler's capture.

Above: On 22nd May 1945, Himmler was taken to the mill of Wilhelm Lohse in Bremervörde where his arrest report was typed and where he spent the last full night of his life. The buildings in the photo have all since been demolished. The mill is the dark building on the far left and the site of the buildings to the right is now occupied by the new Oste Hotel.

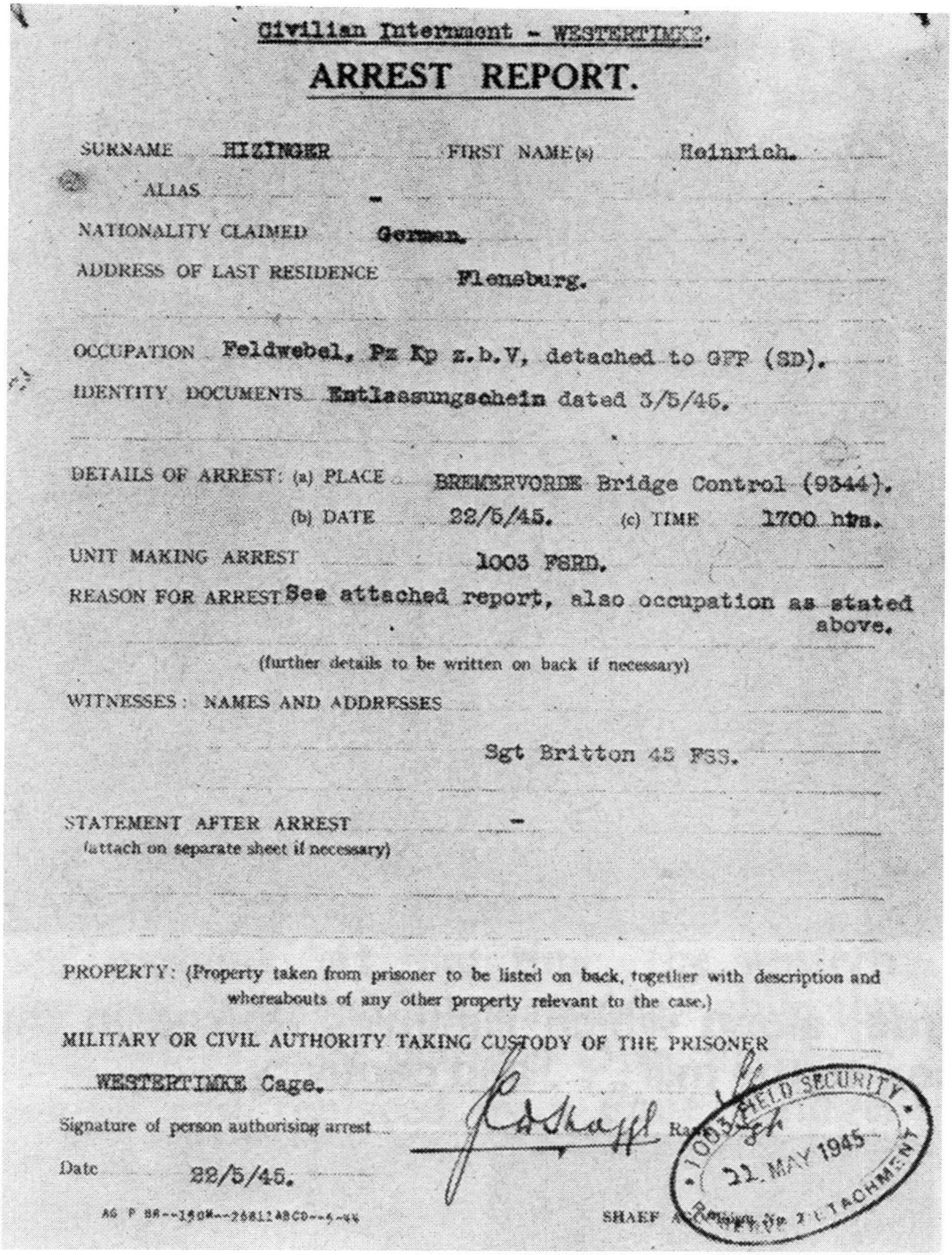

Civilian Internment - WESTERTIMKE.

ARREST REPORT.

SURNAME HIZINGER FIRST NAME(s) Heinrich.

ALIAS -

NATIONALITY CLAIMED German.

ADDRESS OF LAST RESIDENCE Flensburg.

OCCUPATION Feldwebel, Pz Kp z.b.V, detached to GFP (SD).

IDENTITY DOCUMENTS Entlassungschein dated 3/5/45.

DETAILS OF ARREST: (a) PLACE BREMERVORDE Bridge Control (9344).

(b) DATE 22/5/45. (c) TIME 1700 hrs.

UNIT MAKING ARREST 1003 FSRD.

REASON FOR ARREST See attached report, also occupation as stated above.

(further details to be written on back if necessary)

WITNESSES: NAMES AND ADDRESSES

Sgt Britton 45 FSS.

STATEMENT AFTER ARREST -

(attach on separate sheet if necessary)

PROPERTY: (Property taken from prisoner to be listed on back, together with description and whereabouts of any other property relevant to the case.)

MILITARY OR CIVIL AUTHORITY TAKING CUSTODY OF THE PRISONER

WESTERTIMKE Cage.

Signature of person authorising arrest

Date 22/5/45.

AG P 88--150M--26812ABCD--5-44

SHAEF

Heinrich Himmler's arrest report, typed and signed by Staff Sergeant John Hogg who was unaware of the true identity of Heinrich Hizinger [sic, correct Hitzinger] and who was claiming to be a former Feldwebel with a panzer company, attached to the GFP for special duties. This in itself was grounds for immediate arrest as the GFP was recognised as an arm of the SD. [Efforts to trace the whereabouts of the original report have proved fruitless and it is therefore with gratitude that this copy has been provided by After the Battle magazine, number 14 of 1976.]

Opposite below: The location today of Himmler's overnight stay on 22nd May 1945 in Wilhelm Lohse's mill, now demolished. The mill stood on an island at the far end of the Oste Hotel which is on the right of the picture. Himmler, Grothmann and Macher spent an uncomfortable night in a grain store on the upstairs first floor.

Appendix "C" to Main HQ 30 Corps.
111/21/GSI(b) dated 26 May 45.

The Arrest of Heinrich HIMMLER.

During the morning of 20 May 45 a group of five German officers and seven other ranks were detained at the bridge control at BREMERVÖRDE 9444 and referred to the NCOs of 45 FS Section and 1003 FSRD for checking. At first the Germans denied being all in the same party, and one of them, a doctor, claimed that the ORs were in his care as walking patients.

All the members of the party carried discharge papers issued since 1 May 45, and some of these papers were stamped G.F.P. Under interrogation one of the ORs admitted that they were all in the same party, and were all in fact G.F.P.

The party stated that they were policemen from MUNICH, and had received orders from the unit to report to the Polizei Präsidium there.

The party expressed concern about two other comrades, whom they had been forced to leave behind at a farm, since they were sick. The FS NCOs offered to go to collectthe missing members, and one of the German officers was taken along as a guide. They drove to the supposed resting place of the other two, but found no one.

The German expressed his apologies and said the other two must have gone.

That evening the twelve G.F.P. men were despatched to WESTERTIMKE and a general warning was issued that two further members of the party might turn up in the area.

At 1700 hrs 22 May a party of three German civilians were detained at the same bridge control at BREMERVÖRDE. Their papers indicated that they were recently discharged from the German Army, and the tell-tale G.F.P.(SD) stamp was again present. They were put under arrest by Sjt. BRITTON of 45 FS Section.

In interrogation it became clear that they were the rearguard of the G.F.P. and stated that they were en route for MUNICH.

One of the second party was Sjt. Heinrich HIZINGER, an unimpressive figure with several days growth of beard, long hair, no glasses and a patch over one eye. He was dressed in an odd collection of civilian garments, with a blue raincoat on top.

They were despatched to WESTERTIMKE and thence to O31, and Heinrich HIZINGER's arrest report was duly submitted.

Capt

Opposite: Supplementary report of the arrest of Himmler.

The GFP (Secret Field Police) was affiliated to the SD and its members were therefore subject to immediate arrest. Run by Willi Krichbaum, the GFP was a common source for false identity papers.

Having revealed his true identity, Himmler was driven to 31a Uelzener Strasse in Lüneburg. He was hurried up the steps on the left and in through the main entrance. Once inside, he was taken into the octagonal shaped room on the ground floor. During a medical examination on his mouth, Himmler clamped his teeth on a glass capsule of lethal hydrocyanic acid and breathed his last on the floor of this room at 11.14pm on 23rd May 1945.

No photographs of Himmler alive at 31a Uelzener Strasse exist. This sketch is credited with being the last known living picture of Himmler, which was drawn by artist Captain Bryan de Grineau of the Illustrated London News.

Opposite above: During an initial search, this brass holder and glass ampoule were discovered on Himmler. There was also another empty brass holder which alerted his captors to the probable presence of another glass ampoule secreted upon his person.

Himmler, wearing no trousers, lies dead on the floor, his boots beside him. Sketch by Captain Bryan de Grineau.

Left: The lifeless body of Heinrich Himmler.

Below: Himmler's body, covered by two blankets, with other evidence of the futile and unsuccessful attempts to save his life.

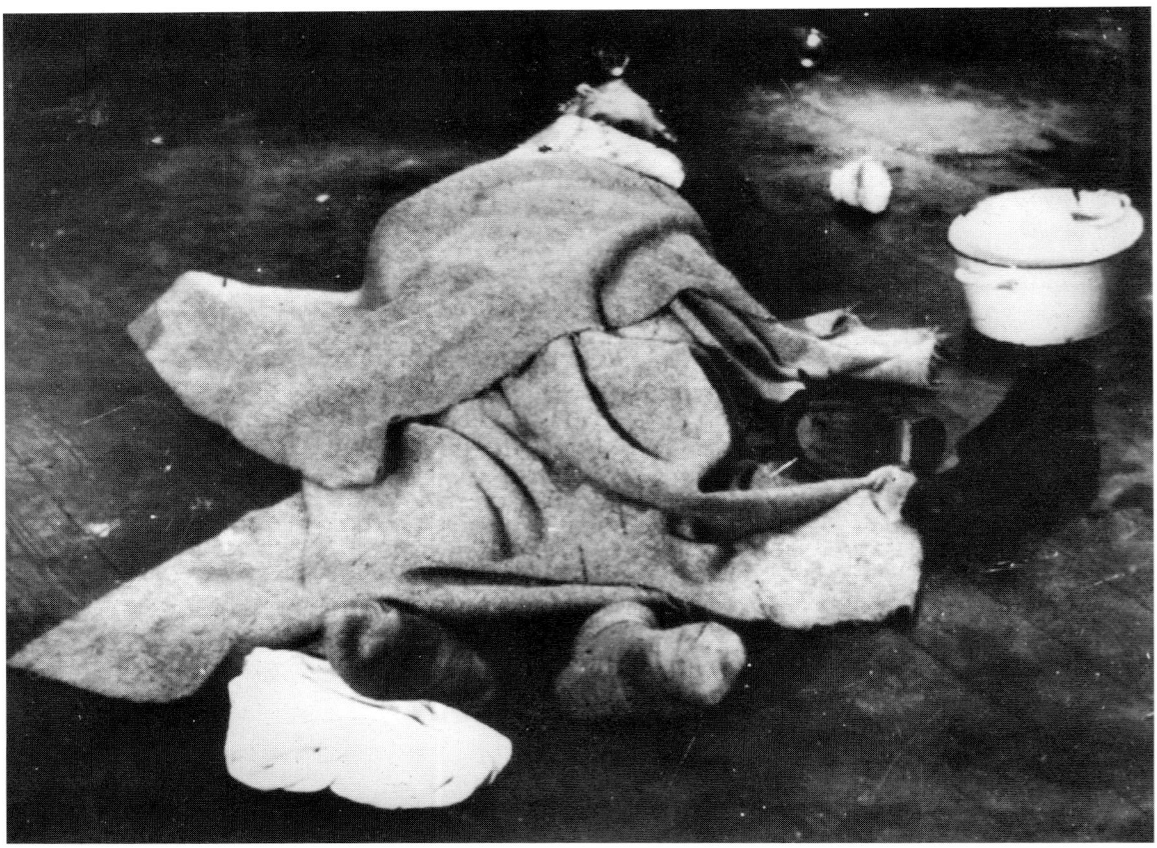

Above: Himmler's body was propped up for the benefit of the press and newsreel cameras.

Right: A delegation of Russian officers viewed the body to confirm Himmler's death for Stalin and Marshal Zhukov. Sketch by Captain Bryan de Grineau.

Dr Ludwig Stumpfegger almost certainly supplied Himmler and his staff with ampoules of potassium cyanide, including the one that killed the Reichsführer. Stumpfegger also supplied Hitler and Eva Braun with the phials of the lethal poison which they successfully used in the Berlin bunker. Stumpfegger was killed attempting a breakout from the bunker with Martin Bormann.

The Himmler gravediggers. Left, Ray Weston and right, William Ottery. Himmler's corpse was wrapped in camouflage netting and buried at a secret location on Lüneburg Heath, not far from the scene of death.

Werner Grothmann and Heinz Macher pose for the press outside the intake hut at Kolkhagen on 24th May 1945, unaware that Himmler had taken his own life the night before.

Marga and Gudrun Himmler in Allied hands.

Allied prisoner of war, SS-Obergruppenführer Karl Wolff, pictured soon after his surrender.

Former SS-Standartenführer Dr Rudolf Brandt at Nuremberg. Found guilty at the Doctors' Trial, he was hanged at Landsberg Prison on 2nd June 1948.

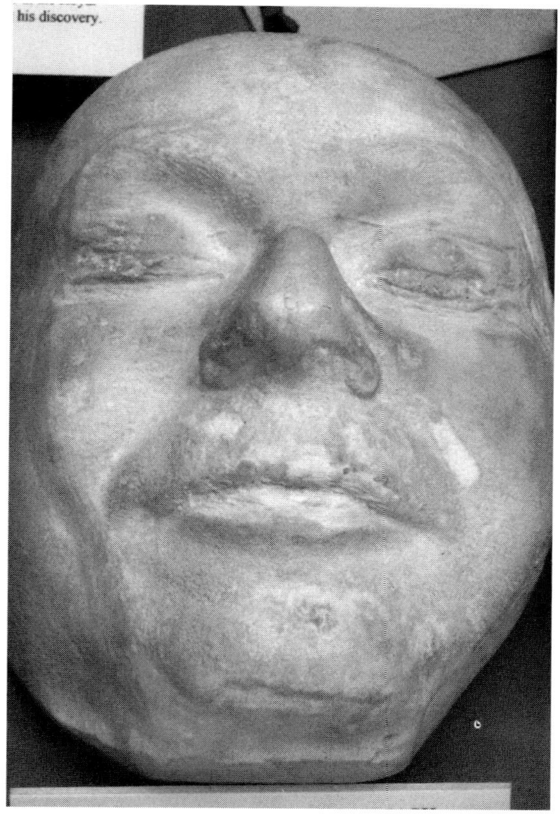

The British made plaster casts of Himmler's features post-mortem. One is in the Military Dental Museum in Aldershot and the other resides in the Black Museum at Scotland Yard.

This photograph was discovered among the files of a now deceased Himmler researcher and was captioned "Frau Himmler and daughter." Although clearly not Marga Himmler, it is possibly an unconfirmed post-war image of Hedwig Potthast with Himmler's daughter Nanette-Dorothea.

Clockwise from left:

Walter Schellenberg giving evidence at Nuremberg. He was sentenced to six years imprisonment, but was released early in 1951 due to ill health. He died of cancer in Turin on 31st March 1952.

Dr Rudolf Brandt stands upon the gallows at Landsberg Prison on 2nd June 1948.

Professor Dr Karl Gebhardt was convicted at the Doctors' Trial in Nuremberg and hanged at Landsberg Prison on 2nd June 1948.